THE HOLOCAUST
&
THE EXILE OF YIDDISH

THE
HOLOCAUST
&
THE EXILE OF YIDDISH

A History of the *Algemeyne Entsiklopedye*

BARRY TRACHTENBERG

RUTGERS UNIVERSITY PRESS

New Brunswick, Camden, and Newark, New Jersey, and London

Library of Congress Cataloging-in-Publication Data

Names: Trachtenberg, Barry, author.

Title: The Holocaust and the exile of Yiddish: a history of the Algemeyne Entsiklopedye / Barry Trachtenberg.

Other titles: History of the Algemeyne Entsiklopedye

Description: New Brunswick: Rutgers University Press, [2022] | Includes bibliographical references and index.

Identifiers: LCCN 2021028272 | ISBN 9781978825451 (cloth) | ISBN 9781978825475 (epub) | ISBN 9781978825499 (pdf)

Subjects: LCSH: Encyclopedias and dictionaries, Yiddish—History and criticism. | Jews—Encyclopedias—History—20th century. | Yiddish literature—Bibliography. | Holocaust, Jewish (1939–1945)—Influence. | Central Yiddish Culture Organization—History—20th century.

Classification: LCC DS102.8 .T73 2022 | DDC 940.53/18—dc23

LC record available at https://lccn.loc.gov/2021028272

A British Cataloging-in-Publication record for this book is available from the British Library.

www.rutgersuniversitypress.org

Manufactured in the United States of America

FOR MY PARENTS,

Eleanor P. Trachtenberg and Harvey Trachtenberg, ז"ל,

with love.

CONTENTS

THE HOLOCAUST
&
THE EXILE OF YIDDISH

FIGURE I.1 Original volumes of the *Algemeyne entsiklopedye* and *The Jewish People: Past and Present*. Photo by Dan Routh.

INTRODUCTION

There is no insight into a nation's way of thought
like a copy of its chief work of reference.

—MARK KHINOY,
"What Happened to Abramovich?: Leafing through
Volume 'A' of the New Soviet Encyclopedia"

Jewish books have often shared the
persecutions inflicted upon the Jews....

—PHILIP FRIEDMAN,
"The Fate of the Jewish Book"

ABOVE ALL, AN encyclopedia set conveys to its readers a sense of authority. Its sheer size and uniform format announce that all relevant information has been cataloged and contained within its many volumes (at least until the next edition is released). Representing the best encapsulation of knowledge at the moment when it is published, encyclopedias are meant to sit on our shelves and wait patiently for us to turn to them in order to answer a question, settle a dispute, or clear up confusion.

Although few people today ever think to consult a physical encyclopedia, let alone purchase an actual set, and while our notion of what an encyclopedia comprises is in complete flux ("Welcome to Wikipedia, the free encyclopedia anyone can edit"), there remains much to be learned by investigating the encyclopedias of the past. As transformative as Wikipedia, Google, and the Internet as a whole have been for our ability to retrieve information and access knowledge, the bound multivolume encyclopedias that are now often

1

relegated to attics and basements can serve as illuminating points of entry into the times in which they were produced. Perhaps unsurprisingly, the calm, quiet exteriors of most encyclopedias mask what was often a turbulent process in the reference works' production. Scholarly studies of the ways that information was managed prior to the digital age have demonstrated that the classification, curation, dissemination, and storage of knowledge were typically defined by messiness, conflicts, and uncertainty, rather than by the calm and order that the completed volumes were intended to project.[1] The challenges of publishing an encyclopedia—raising vast sums of money; settling what are often fierce disputes over content, ideological perspectives, scholarly interpretations, entry lengths, and spelling systems; and just simply selling the volumes—are, by the end, smoothed over by the polished appearance of a completed set, whose credibility rests upon its premise of scholarly objectivity and the consistency of presentation and information.

As figure I.1 of this book indicates, there is at least one encyclopedia that displays its interior messiness and turbulent history prominently on its exterior. The photograph is of a set of original volumes (not including reprints or reissues) of the Yiddish-language *Algemeyne entsiklopedye* (General encyclopedia), which was the first sustained attempt to produce a comprehensive encyclopedia in the Yiddish language. The thin sample volume (known in Yiddish as a *probeheft*) on the far right was published in Berlin, Germany in 1932. The now-tattered covers of the earliest volumes were published in interwar Paris during a time of material dispossession, economic distress, and the menacing threat of Nazism. They stand in stark contrast to the unblemished— and generally unread—final Yiddish volumes that were published in New York City in the mid-1960s at a moment when American Jews, now rarely speaking Yiddish, were enjoying unparalleled success and acceptance.

Notwithstanding the physical damage caused to the earliest volumes that journeyed from prewar Europe to the United States, the variation in volume size and color of the full set points to the many different publishing houses that were engaged to print the volumes as well as to the ever-changing materials that were available in the decades in which the encyclopedia was printed. The original slipcase for the *Yidn beys*/ב יידן volume still protects what is one of the very few surviving copies in the world; the majority were lost at sea on the eve of Germany's invasion of Western Europe. The dual classification systems—numerical for the first five volumes, then shifting to alphabetical from *alef*/א to *zayen*/ז—reflect a persistent tension among the project's editors over what sort of knowledge should the *Entsiklopedye* provide to its readers: that of the larger world or that of the Jewish people on whose behalf it was being published. The four English-language volumes that stand on the left and bear the name *The Jewish People: Past and Present* speak to the post-Holocaust attempt by the surviving encyclopedists to translate the millennia-old history of European Jews' triumphs and tragedies for their American Jewish counterparts. The only exterior indications of coherency among the entire sixteen (excluding the *probeheft*) volumes are the twin sets of gold double bars that mark the top and bottom of their spines.[2]

The Holocaust & the Exile of Yiddish is a history of the *Algemeyne entsiklopedye*. It reveals how the *Entsiklopedye*—a project of Yiddish-speaking Jews who had migrated from Eastern Europe to Berlin and subsequently fled to Paris and then to New York City—both shared in and came to symbolize the plight of the Yiddish language and culture during the middle decades of the twentieth century.[3] The *Entsiklopedye* began in the midst of the Great Depression and at a time of great political uncertainty, yet was fueled by the excitement and dynamism of Germany's Weimar era and a golden age for Yiddish culture internationally. When its publication was proposed in 1930, the *Entsiklopedye* was widely embraced as a landmark in the development of the language and the culture of its speakers, who at the time numbered nine to ten million around the world but who were rooted in Eastern Europe. An encyclopedia in Yiddish was to have marked a new stage for Yiddish culture, and the fact that it was to have been a *general* encyclopedia—in contrast to a specifically *Jewish* one—was hailed by many as a sign that Eastern European Jews were ready to join the nations of the world on equal terms. Over the next three dozen years, however, the fortunes of European Jewry declined at a dizzying pace, turning from precarious to murderous to catastrophic. The surviving editors of the *Entsiklopedye*, fleeing for their lives, would be displaced ever further from the centers of Yiddish culture in Europe and they nearly ceased publishing the *Entsiklopedye* altogether. Instead, after finding refuge first in France and then in the United States, the editors repeatedly altered the *Entsiklopedye*'s central mission by responding to the radically shifting needs of its declining number of readers and desperately attempting to preserve the Yiddish language and its culture.

The disarray of the *Entsiklopedye*, with its sudden stops and starts, redirections, and multiple displacements, reflects not only the challenges of sustaining such a complex and monumentally expensive publishing venture in the absence of any state structure or wealthy financial backers but also the deep commitment of its editors to employ the *Entsiklopedye* as a mechanism for meeting the ever-shifting needs of Yiddish-speaking Jewry during what were unquestionably some of the most traumatic and transformative decades in the last two millennia of Jewish history. As one of the very few Jewish publishing ventures—or collaborative intellectual projects of any sort—to begin in interwar Europe and successfully transition to North America, the *Entsiklopedye* serves as one of the rare chains of continuity whose links stretch across the profound abyss of the Holocaust.[4]

This book's chapters trace the *Entsiklopedye* through its three phases: its inception as an encyclopedia of general information in Berlin in the waning days of the Weimar Republic (chapter 1), its exile in interwar Paris and the publication of its first six volumes (chapter 2), and its final quarter century in New York, where its surviving members utilized the encyclopedia as a means to contend with the aftermath of the Holocaust (chapter 3). Over the thirty-six years from the *Entsiklopedye*'s beginning in 1930 to the release of its final volume in 1966, the original universalist goal of providing the masses of Yiddish readers with the latest in knowledge from the worlds of science, culture, economics, and politics gave way to the decidedly particularistic tasks of documenting the destruction of European Jewry, memorializing those Jews who had been destroyed, preserving a record of European Jewish civilization, and shaping the Jewish (and potentially Yiddish) future in the Americas.

When it was first envisioned by its founders, the planned ten-volume encyclopedia of general knowledge was also to include a supplemental eleventh volume containing specifically Jewish subject matter, which would serve both as a promotional incentive for subscribers and as a way to satisfy the demands of critics who argued in favor of the inclusion of more Jewish content. However, in response to the worsening condition of European Jews in the second half of the 1930s, the supplement grew from one volume to two, and soon, volumes on Jews began to overtake the project entirely as the informational needs of Yiddish readers radically changed. By the end of the war, having reached only partway through the second letter of the alphabet, the volumes on general knowledge ceased altogether and were overtaken entirely by Jewish ones.

To a large degree, the continual westward movement of the Yiddish encyclopedists from their homes in the lands of the Russian empire to Germany, France, and the United States was possible because of the fact that by the 1930s a transnational community of Yiddish speakers and cultural activists had already established itself far beyond the language's centers in Eastern Europe. Historian Tony Michels has shown that this expansion of Yiddish culture began at least as early as the 1890s, when Yiddish-speaking socialist Jewish émigrés from Russia who were living in New York began shipping large quantities of "Yiddish fiction, plays, and popular science, in addition to socialist propaganda" to Jews in Russia, who had neither the legal authority nor the financial means to publish this material themselves.[5] With the mass emigration from Russia of some

2.5 million Jews—nearly all of whom spoke Yiddish as their first language—in the last decades of the nineteenth century and the first decades of the twentieth, many cities outside of Eastern Europe became important sites of Yiddish cultural production. By the interwar period, these included not only Berlin, Paris, and New York, but also London, Montreal, Buenos Aires, and Cape Town. As the possibility of maintaining an independent Yiddish life in Eastern Europe began to diminish with the threats to Jewish culture that arose from Bolshevism and Nazism, these new locations provided the means by which to continue with the work of the *Entsiklopedye*. However, as the history of the *Entsiklopedye* demonstrates, once the Eastern European center of Yiddish was destroyed, the growth and development of Yiddish culture that had previously been enabled by its transnational connections waned—but most markedly did not disappear—as its ancillary sites found it extraordinarily difficult to sustain the cultural and intellectual vibrancy that had existed prior to the war.

Over the course of two *probeheftn*, twelve Yiddish volumes, and four English volumes, the *Entsiklopedye* became a singularly rare meeting place not only for Yiddishists and adherents of those movements associated with modern Yiddish culture, such as Bundists, left Labor Zionists, Territorialists, and Folkists, but also for Mensheviks in exile from the Soviet Union, anarchists, Zionists, and Hebraists, as well as religious Jews, secular Jews, and those Jews who remained generally unaffiliated with both religious and secular Jewish communal life. The *Entsiklopedye* began as an initiative by figures who, from their base in Berlin, were themselves already at a remove from the masses of Yiddish speakers in Eastern Europe. Representing a relatively narrow yet influential sector of the Jewish ideological spectrum, its first editors were primarily members of the secular Yiddish intelligentsia who advocated for fostering Jewish national life in the Diaspora, and who often stood in opposition to Zionists who sought to establish a Jewish state, to assimilationists who encouraged Jewish loyalty to the countries in which they resided, and to communists who insisted that Jews bind their fate to the Soviet Union. By the time of the *Entsiklopedye*'s final volume, however, the project had assumed such a prominent stature in the Jewish world that it involved dozens of influential Jewish intellectuals who represented a much wider range of ideological perspectives, including many who earlier would never have considered submitting to its initial volumes.

The *Entsiklopedye* included contributions from some of the best-known figures from the world of Jewish scholarship, such as Max Weinreich, the head of the Yiddish Scientific Institute (YIVO); the demographer Jacob Lestschinsky; the Hebraist Simon Rawidowicz; and the historians Simon Dubnow (in whose honor the project first began), Elias Tcherikower, Salo W. Baron, and

Gershom Scholem, as well as several of the first historians of the Holocaust, including Philip Friedman and Raul Hilberg. Among its editors and contributors were the Menshevik leader Raphael Abramovitch, the Social Democratic leader and Marxist theorist Eduard Bernstein, and Sholem Schwartzbard, who was famous for assassinating the Ukrainian leader Symon Petliura for his role in leading anti-Jewish pogroms during the Russian Civil War. Many luminaries from the world of Jewish arts and letters also contributed, including the literary critic Shmuel Charney,[6] the art historian Rachel Wischnitzer, the art critic Chil Aronson, and the theater critic Alexander Mukdoni. Albert Einstein, Sigmund Freud, Claude Lévi-Strauss, and Milton Himmelfarb also lent either their names or expertise to the initiative.

Universal Encyclopedias and National Self-Definition

Histories of encyclopedias often begin with a reference to Denis Diderot's revolutionary efforts on behalf of the French-language *Encyclopédie, ou dictionnaire raisonné des sciences, des arts et des métiers* (Encyclopedia, or a Systematic Dictionary of the Sciences, Arts and Crafts), published between 1751 and 1772, but the term *encyclopedia* (or its variants) came into regular use in the seventeenth century, and the ordering of knowledge is an undertaking that dates back to ancient Greece and China.[7] Kathleen Hardesty Doig summarizes the trajectory from the pre-Enlightenment encyclopedia's systematic or thematic arrangement to the modern encyclopedia's alphabetical format:

> Medieval encyclopedias saw themselves as timeless reflections of the
> unchanging divine mind, while Renaissance works were conceived as
> summaries of essential subjects. . . . The tradition of dictionaries of arts
> and sciences, of history, and of "hard words" evolved gradually into the
> Enlightenment model of a small number of volumes giving comprehensive
> coverage of both old and new knowledge, organized according to a
> unifying scheme and edited by a single polymath. But by the end of the
> [eighteenth] century, the typical encyclopedia was a multi-volume work
> composed of text furnished by specialist contributors; the only organizing
> principle was the non-hierarchizing alphabet.[8]

What distinguished Diderot's project from earlier efforts was its claim to represent the sum of human knowledge, its polemical valorization of innovation and free thought, and the scandal that its publication initially caused.[9] It was intended (and generally received) as a text that threatened to revolutionize knowledge and move readers away from knowledge based in theology and revelation and toward a rational, scientific understanding of the world. Diderot himself explained: "In truth, the aim of an *Encyclopédie* is to collect all the knowledge scattered over the face of the earth, to present its general outlines and structure to the men with whom we live, and to transmit this to those who will come after us, so that the work of past centuries may be useful to the following centuries, that our children, by becoming more educated, may at the same time become more virtuous and happier, and that we may not die without having deserved well of the human race."[10]

The first complete edition comprises twenty-eight volumes, which contain a total of 71,818 articles and 3,129 illustrations. Divided into three general areas of the sciences, arts, and trades, the *Encyclopédie* sought to unite previously disparate realms of knowledge into a complete and organic system. John H. Lienhard has suggested that "the *Dictionnaire*, as it was called, laid bare the workings of the known world in a way no one had ever tried to do. It boldly told the average man that he could know what only kings, emperors, and their lieutenants were supposed to know. It suggested that anyone should have access to rational truth. In that sense it was a profoundly revolutionary document."[11] According to Richard Yeo, the *Encyclopédie* "became almost synonymous with Enlightenment" itself.[12]

The *Encyclopédie* soon inspired others, and Madeleine Herren has demonstrated that encyclopedias quickly became a "global phenomenon."[13] Indeed, a sort of an encyclopedic "arms race" developed in its wake among the major powers of Europe. The English-language *Encyclopædia Britannica* was first published between 1768 and 1771. The German-language *Allgemeine Encyclopädie der Wissenschaften und Künste* was published by Ersch and Gruber between 1818 and 1889, at which point it was terminated after 167 volumes (out of a projected 295). Encyclopedias for popular audiences likewise quickly appeared, such as the eight-volume German *Brockhaus Enzyklopädie* (1796–1808), which was translated into many languages and greatly expanded over the nineteenth century.[14] In time, the French, English, and German encyclopedias became models for the speakers of other languages, who embraced the encyclopedic form as central to the task of nation-building. By the final quarter of the nineteenth century, for example, local versions of the *Brockhaus* were published in Danish, Swedish, Dutch, Hungarian, Russian, Polish, Czech, Italian, Spanish, English (in the United States), Portuguese, and Bengali. Each promised to provide a complete portrait of human knowledge, yet each was also particular to its own language and national community.

Encyclopedias served as "civil societies' reference manuals" by delimiting the particular histories, borders, and contents of nations.[15] In service to this task, encyclopedias helped define a nation's literary and historical canon by describing its origins, territories, and boundaries and standardizing its language—thereby uniting otherwise disparate peoples, excluding others, and determining what would be remembered and forgotten by future generations. By the mid-nineteenth century, encyclopedias were assuming a more popular and condensed format, and often served as guides for salon-style "conversations" for a growing bourgeoisie and as a tool to help immigrants assimilate into new societies. In the early twentieth century, cheap mass-produced "encyclopedic handbooks" appeared for broad reading publics, and specialized volumes were published for specific subject areas in the sciences, arts, and trades.[16]

While great world powers produced encyclopedias as a means to assert their imperial reach, encyclopedias also became a part of "strateg[ies] of national resistance" by colonized peoples and national minorities, a phenomenon that shows no sign of abating.[17] In service of emancipatory or liberationist goals, these encyclopedias push back against imperial regimes by asserting their nation's political, historical, and cultural independence via the same "scientific" means that were employed to deny their existence. This includes, for example, the mid-nineteenth-century Polish *Encyklopedia Powszechna* (Universal Encyclopedia), W. E. B. Du Bois's unfinished "Encyclopedia Africana" project in the twentieth-century United States, and the twenty-first-century *Encyclopedia of the Palestinians*.[18]

The Jewish Turn to Encyclopedias

Although there had long been a practice among Jewish scholars to collect Jewish sources of wisdom—notably, the Mishnah, the written compilation of oral Jewish law that forms the first section of the Talmud, dates to the third century—some of the earliest encyclopedic works in the Hebrew language are not concerned with particularly Jewish knowledge. Rather, such works, which date to the twelfth century, are adapted from Arabic compendiums "of the sciences in the medieval Aristotelian scheme" and cover topics in "mathematics, geometry, astronomy, optics, and music."[19] When interest in science among Jews waned during the fifteenth to the eighteenth centuries, the publication of encyclopedic volumes similarly declined. However, the encyclopedic form itself remained useful, as Nathanael Riemer and Sigrid Senkbeil have shown, and volumes continued to be published during these centuries. For example, they note the seventeenth-century Yiddish-language Kabbalistic encyclopedia by the Rabbi of Prague, Beer Shmuel Issachar Perlhefter, and his wife, Bella Perlhefter, entitled *Be'er Sheva* (Seven wells).[20] The text's seven sections—each dedicated to one of their deceased children—"provide both a universal worldview and a history of the salvation of the Jewish people" and consider topics such as the creation of the world, the arrangement of the cosmos, a biblical history of humankind in general and the Israelites in particular, and matters of eschatology and penance.[21]

Interest in encyclopedias among Jews was renewed with the emergence of the Haskalah (Hebrew, "wisdom" or "intellect"), a Jewish Enlightenment movement that began in the late eighteenth century and was dedicated to the preservation of Jewish continuity through an embrace of the principles of scientific discovery and reason. The many Hebrew-language encyclopedias that were planned (and only very occasionally came to fruition) were a part of the larger European phenomenon of encyclopedic publishing and served a multitude of agendas. Some Jewish encyclopedias sought to reconcile Jewish and general knowledge, following a tradition that dates back to antiquity. Others highlighted Jews' compatibility with their host societies, while still others asserted Jewish distinctiveness.[22]

One of the first proposals for a modern Jewish encyclopedia was put forth in 1843 by David Cassel and Moritz Steinschneider, German Jewish scholars of *Wissenschaft des Judentums* (literally, "science of Judaism," a progenitor of modern Jewish studies) who aimed to compile the achievements of their scholarly discipline, which had begun twenty-five years earlier.[23] Their encyclopedia, Arndt Engelhardt has shown, was intended to provide "the interested lay public with concise summaries of the results of this research, and function as a stimulus for further scholarly inquiry."[24] Following the model of extant encyclopedias, Cassel and Steinschneider planned to present the most up-to-date research on topics within Jewish studies, all arranged in an alphabetical manner. As a German-language work, it would be available both to a Jewish and to a non-Jewish readership and was intended, in part, to correct the inaccurate and at times disparaging depictions of Jews and Judaism that appeared in existing encyclopedias. As Kirsten Belgum demonstrates, mid-century German-language encyclopedias tended to reinforce negative attitudes about Jews (often questioning whether they were suitable candidates for assimilation) at a time when German Jews were strongly invested in participating fully in the larger society.[25] Cassel and Steinschneider also hoped to define *Wissenschaft des Judentums* for future generations by establishing its research agenda.[26] They envisioned *Wissenschaft des Judentums* as encyclopedic in scope, engaging "the history of Judaism in the broadest sense, up to the present," with special attention paid to the relationship between Jewish nationality and the Jewish state.[27]

Their proposal for an encyclopedia was significant enough to garner both support and criticism. Foreshadowing debates that would occur nearly a century later around the *Algemeyne entsiklopedye,* some objected to the very idea of an encyclopedia that was dedicated to Jewish subjects, as opposed to one on general subject matters, arguing that it was an unwelcome assertion of Jewish particularism at a moment when Jews in large numbers were embarked upon a process of Germanization in the name of attaining equal civic rights. Supporters countered that the encyclopedia was not about Jews per se but rather about Judaism as a religion and its place within "the continuous chain of world history."[28] In any event, the *Real-Encyclopädie des Judenthums* did not go beyond the planning stages, as the project was soon halted largely for financial reasons. Although it would be another two generations before a full German-language Jewish encyclopedia would appear, Engelhardt demonstrates that much of the preparatory work performed by Steinschneider and Cassel made its way into comprehensive general encyclopedias, such as Ersch and Gruber's *Allgemeine Encyclopädie,* while other work that had been initially composed for the Jewish encyclopedia appeared as separate books or articles.

At the end of the nineteenth century, the cultural Zionist leader Ahad Ha'am (pen name of Asher Zvi Ginzburg) proposed an encyclopedia comprising "the national possessions" of the Jewish people.[29] In both language and focus, this project marked a significant shift from Cassel and Steinschneider's vision. Rather than an encyclopedia highlighting the accomplishments of Jewish scholarship for Jewish and non-Jewish readers of German alike, Ahad Ha'am's *Otsar hayahadut belashon 'ivrit* (Treasury of Judaism in the Hebrew language) was to be a secular work that would reconnect disaffected and assimilated Jews to the sources of Jewish tradition and creativity. Ahad Ha'am's plan stemmed from his concern that the modernizing changes of the late nineteenth century increasingly left Jews severed both from their national cultural heritage and from one another as they assimilated linguistically and culturally into their host countries. Adam Rubin has shown that Ahad Ha'am was seeking to shape the direction of a growing Jewish national revival movement by proposing that his encyclopedia appear in the Hebrew language, which was spoken only by a very small percentage of Jews at the time but had significant symbolic value as the ancient language of the Jewish people. Rubin states: "Ahad Ha'am hoped that a Hebrew encyclopedia would bring young Jews who knew little about their heritage 'to an enlightened, penetrating knowledge of Judaism, so that they will love, honor, and devote themselves to it.'"[30] Like Cassel and Steinschneider's, Ahad Ha'am's plan for a twelve-to-fifteen-volume encyclopedia stretching over seven or eight years never came to fruition. Rubin offers several possible reasons, including "tepid support from his allies and surprisingly fierce opposition from his critics," many of whom saw his plan as a radically secular departure from traditional religious studies.[31] The small number of Hebrew readers was also a significant hindrance to producing and publishing such an extensive set of volumes. Ahad Ha'am's unrealized plan also had its own afterlife. It influenced Yosef Klausner's six-volume Hebrew-language encyclopedia in the 1930s, and Chaim Nachman Bialik's project to disseminate classic works of Hebrew literature and folklore.

Rubin demonstrates that "Ahad Ha'am's *Otsar hayahadut* represents the first true articulation of what might be called 'the encyclopaedic impulse' of modern Jewish nationalism."[32] The late-nineteenth-century turn toward Jewish nationalism was in part a reaction to the seeming failure of the Haskalah to bring about the civic emancipation of most of Europe's Jews and to the sharp spike in antisemitic violence across the continent. Drawing from the models of other European national minority groups, Jewish nationalism was manifested in a wide variety of expressions. Some thinkers, like Ahad Ha'am, advocated for a cultural Zionism, a Jewish cultural and spiritual national revival. Others strove to attain collective political rights for Jews in the lands in which they resided, and still others endeavored to establish a Jewish national homeland in Palestine or other locations around the globe. Nearly all of these movements—which often overlapped and clashed with one another—advocated the modernization of Jewish languages and literatures, the increased productivization of European Jewry in order to strengthen the nation both physically and spiritually, and a return to Jewish tradition and practices in a secularized form. Compendiums of Jewish history and culture were to help Jews access their long-forgotten heritage and reimagine themselves as a discrete nation. As this didactic impulse gained momentum over the next several decades, the near frenzy to collect and preserve Jewish cultural treasures resulted in a seemingly endless stream of anthropological expeditions, historical investigations, literary anthologies, linguistic compilations, and sweeping historical surveys, which together would form much of the foundation of the modern scholarly discipline of Jewish studies.[33]

The many efforts to produce encyclopedias in Hebrew and Yiddish failed in this period, however, in large measure on account of the perception that these languages were limited in what they were able to express. Although Hebrew was increasingly championed—especially among younger adherents of Zionism—as a language of day-to-day communication and as a literary tongue that could link an imagined Jewish national past to a hoped-for independent Jewish future, it had been millennia since either spoken or written Hebrew enjoyed wide use beyond religious and ceremonial functions.[34] And while Yiddish *had* been a language of day-to-day communication for many Jews for perhaps as long as a millennium, its capacity to express sophisticated and esoteric thoughts was only just beginning to be recognized in the late nineteenth century as it was embraced as the language of a revitalized diasporic Jewish nation.[35] In the first years of the twentieth century, therefore, neither language movement had the necessary publishing houses, academies, or financial backers to sustain a significant undertaking like an encyclopedia. Nor did either language have a sufficiently large reading audience eager to or capable of purchasing such a work.

In spite of the dramatic growth of literature in both Hebrew and Yiddish, the first successful Jewish encyclopedias to be in the early twentieth century were in non-Jewish languages. The first of these was the twelve-volume English-language *Jewish Encyclopedia* (New York, 1901–1906), which was an effort begun by Isidore Singer, an editor and initiator of several overly ambitious schemes on behalf of Jewish communal prosperity and advancement.[36] In the early 1890s, while based in Europe, Singer floated the idea for a Jewish encyclopedia in German. When it received little support, he proposed it be written in French, an idea that was also met with ambivalence. It was only upon his arrival in the United States, in 1894, that Singer found scholars willing to support his project and publishers (the progressive Lutherans Isaac Kaufmann Funk and Adam Willis Wagnalls) able to finance it. The German Jewish community that had been in America for the previous half century was moving into new positions of prominence and economic security and seeking to manage the arrival of vast numbers of Russian Jewish migrants to the United States. At the same time, new racialized forms of antisemitism were making their way into the United States from Europe and starting to inform perceptions of all Jews, new immigrants or not. Yaakov Ariel has shown that in response, Jewish leaders launched a number of initiatives designed to correct negative stereotypes of Jews, such as the 1888 Jewish Publication Society, the 1892 American Jewish Historical Society, and the *Jewish Encyclopedia*.[37]

The planning and execution of the *Jewish Encyclopedia* was marred by ideological disputes among editors and contributors, concerns about Singer's competency, editorial inefficiencies, and cost overruns. Nevertheless, the first volume appeared in 1901, after only two years of active planning, and eleven subsequent volumes appeared over the next five years. The inaugural editorial committee included prominent scholars and theologians such as Cyrus Adler, Louis Ginzberg, Morris Jastrow, and Kaufmann Kohler. Simon Dubnow is among those listed as serving on the Foreign Board of Consulting Editors, as are the philanthropist Baron David Günzburg, the linguist Alexander

Harkavy, and the theologian Solomon Schechter. Topics that the encyclopedia covered included Jewish history, biography, sociology, literature, theology, and philosophy. A large percentage of the editors were trained in German Jewish seminaries. Rather than seeking to impart a unified definition of Judaism, the *Jewish Encyclopedia* assumed a pluralistic approach, and it became a forum for debates between Reform-minded Jewish theologians and their traditionalist counterparts over how best to present Judaism to an American audience.[38]

Although it was largely contemporaneous with Ahad Ha'am's mission of Jewish cultural renewal, the *Jewish Encyclopedia* reflected a vision entirely contrary to the *Otsar hayahadut*. Whereas Ahad Ha'am's project had been motivated by a nationalist concern to unite assimilated Jews across the globe with a text that would gather and transmit their national heritage, the *Jewish Encyclopedia*'s editors and supporters aimed to combat the growing influence of antisemitism by asserting Judaism's (and by extension Jews') place squarely within the Western democratic tradition of tolerance and pluralism. Singer's encyclopedia differed from Ahad Ha'am's to such an extent that its intended primary audience was not Jewish, but rather Christian, readers.[39]

The *Jewish Encyclopedia* saw only modest financial returns. Only nine thousand copies were sold in its early years, and many of those were subsidized by wealthy patrons who were committed to its distribution. At $60 a set (the equivalent of approximately $2,000 in 2021), it was far out of reach for most American Jews, and there was not a broad enough base of Christian readers interested in buying it. Nevertheless, its impact on subsequent attempts was great, for it not only demonstrated that the task itself could be completed but also set the terms against which future projects had to differentiate themselves when employing the encyclopedic form to advance competing definitions of Judaism and the Jewish people.

Following the relative success of the *Jewish Encyclopedia*, a group of Russian Jewish intellectuals embarked upon a project to publish a Russian-language version. The historian Jeffrey Veidlinger has shown that that although the organizers of the sixteen-volume *Evreiskaia entsiklopediia* (Jewish encyclopedia, 1906–1913) initially intended for their project to be a relatively straightforward translation of the *Jewish Encyclopedia*, their focus quickly shifted once the work began. Rather than follow Singer's model of an encyclopedia that would introduce Jews and Judaism to non-Jewish readers and demonstrate the compatibility of Jews with the states in which they resided, the *Evreiskaia entsiklopediia* "developed first into an expression of pride in the Russian Jewish experience and second into an assertion of the Jewish people as a national entity."[40] It was published for a learned Jewish reading audience and was part of a much broader effort to create institutions of Jewish high culture in Russia, including the establishment of historical societies, libraries, publishing houses, theater companies, and literary societies.[41]

The *Evreiskaia entsiklopediia* covered topics such as Jewish history, major Jewish figures from the biblical period through the early twentieth century, Talmud, philosophy, and Jewish texts, holidays, and customs. The editors also sought to use the encyclopedia to combat antisemitic violence, which had reached new heights following the failed 1905 Russian Revolution, in which exceptionally large numbers of Jews had participated. Veidlinger demonstrates that the editors of the *Evreiskaia entsiklopediia* expanded many individual entries (the one on antisemitism increased from 18 pages in the English to 125 pages in the Russian) and also raised the level of erudition significantly. Unlike Singer's project, which chiefly drew upon seminarians and rabbinical figures to compose many of its entries, the *Evreiskaia entsiklopediia* engaged mostly scholarly experts, including some of the most prominent Russian Jewish intellectuals of the day. Moreover, whereas the *Jewish Encyclopedia* was the initiative of one visionary who lacked experience in large publishing ventures, the *Evreiskaia entsiklopediia* was headed by Il'ia Abramovich Efron, who had founded the Brockhaus-Efron publishing firm in 1890 and had published several Russian-language encyclopedias. Simon Dubnow was an editor for a short period but soon left to pursue his own scholarship. Dubnow had praised the work as "a national monument to Judaism" but lamented that it was written "in a foreign [meaning non-Jewish] language."[42]

After World War I, a third modern Jewish encyclopedia was published, this time in Berlin. An initiative of the philosopher Jakob Klatzkin and the Zionist publisher Nahum Goldmann (who would later become the president of the World Jewish Congress), the German-language *Encyclopaedia Judaica* was published at a time when many German Jews were reconsidering their identity as Jews and their place within the larger German national community.[43] The sharply rising incidents of antisemitism that occurred around the country after its loss in the war led to German Jews' growing disillusionment about the many concessions that they had made over the long nineteenth century in order to be accepted as Germans. Increasing numbers of Jews were turning toward Zionism, Jewish traditions and texts, and Eastern European Jewish culture as a way of asserting a seemingly more authentic form of Judaism. This "renaissance" of Jewish culture among German Jews, as the historian Michael Brenner has called it, expressed itself in many religious and cultural forms, including increased synagogue attendance, membership in Jewish cultural,

sporting, and Zionist organizations, and enrollment in new educational programs.[44] The Weimar period also saw a burst in new publishing ventures such
as Martin Buber and Franz Rosenzweig's translation of the Hebrew Bible into
German and the launching of the Schocken publishing firm, as well as many
major reference works and scholarly volumes.

Klatzkin and Goldmann's vision for the *Encyclopaedia Judaica* was that it
would help turn the tide on Jewish assimilation and provide a means by which
German Jews could reacquaint themselves with the sources of their tradition
while staying fully within the modern world. Engelhardt argues that the encyclopedia was to be a tool "to preserve a common canon of knowledge in the
context of Jewish communities in transformation under the impact of modernity, and to translate that canon for subsequent generations, making it
accessible." He continues, "In this way, it sought to invent a modern form of
Judaism grounded in a mixture of tradition and memory."[45] In doing so, the
Encyclopaedia Judaica built upon the successes of the *Jewish Encyclopedia* and
the *Evreiskaia entsiklopediia*, and its format, goals, and organization were influenced as well by the aims of Cassel and Steinschneider's *Real-Encyclopädie*
and Ahad Ha'am's *Otsar hayahadut*. Among the *Encyclopaedia Judaica*'s contributors were some of the most illustrious German Jewish scholars, such as
Ismar Elbogen, Joseph Klausner, Fritz Baer, and Walter Benjamin, as well as
several scholars from Eastern Europe who were residing in Germany, including the historians Simon Dubnow, Elias Tcherikower, and Mark Wischnitzer
(who would all go on to play significant roles in the *Algemeyne entsiklopedye*).
Between 1928 and 1932, nine volumes appeared, covering *A* through *L*. A tenth
volume, covering *M* through *N*, was delayed by the Nazi takeover of power but
eventually released in 1934. No other German-language volumes were completed. Another two volumes were published in Hebrew, and three others in
preparation never made it to press.

The success of the Jewish encyclopedias in the English, Russian, and German
languages helped pave the way for the *Algemeyne entsiklopedye*, as did the
tremendous expansion of encyclopedia publishing in the early twentieth
century. In practical terms, not only did the three encyclopedias provide models for the new venture in Yiddish, but several of their contributors became intimately involved with the *Algemeyne entsiklopedye*. More broadly speaking,
the *Jewish Encyclopedia*, *Evreiskaia entsiklopediia*, and *Encyclopaedia Judaica*
served to acquaint many Yiddish readers—many of whom were multilingual—
with the encyclopedic form and to cultivate reading and subscribing audiences,
as well as to make it possible to imagine such a work in their own mother
tongue.

Laying the Groundwork for a Yiddish Encyclopedia

Concurrent with these early-twentieth-century Jewish encyclopedic projects was an intensive effort on behalf of Yiddish language development. A burst of Yiddish scholarly activity that occurred in the wake of the 1905 Revolution aimed to modernize Yiddish by standardizing the spelling of Yiddish words, identifying its underlying grammar, establishing a corpus of words, charting its history, canonizing its major writers, and expanding the possibilities of what could be conveyed in it. These projects were often linked directly to or led by activists within the various political and labor movements that were fighting for the national minority rights of Jews in the lands of the Russian Empire and the rights of working-class Yiddish-speaking Jews more globally. As the editors of the new modernist Yiddish literary journal *Literarishe monatsshriftn* (Literary monthly) explained in 1908, "the conviction is growing that the Jewish *folk* has the same rights as all other people to create their own culture, to express its national self in original forms, and to bind its own unique page into the great book of the world."[46] In the years after World War I, following the collapse of the Russian Empire and the establishment of independent nation-states in East Central Europe, these processes accelerated and Yiddish print culture fully came into its own. In the 1920s, there were thousands of newspapers, journals, magazines, chapbooks, and books of nearly every imaginable genre being composed in and translated into Yiddish. By the end of the decade, in addition to large networks of Yiddish secular schools in many parts of Europe and the United States, there were three scholarly institutes dedicated to the study and advancement of the Yiddish language and Eastern European Jewish culture: the Soviet Union's Jewish Department at the Institute for Belarusian Culture, in Minsk; the Institute for Jewish Proletarian Culture at the Ukrainian Academy of Sciences, in Kiev; and the Yiddish Scientific Institute, known as YIVO, in Vilna, Poland.[47] What was missing among the many Yiddish-language works of reference produced in this period was an encyclopedia.

It for was not for lack of trying, however. There had been several attempts to publish a comprehensive Yiddish-language encyclopedia in the early decades of the twentieth century, but all of them stalled either in the planning stages or after only a few volumes were published. They tended to fail for a variety of reasons, including the difficulty of acquiring the necessary funds, the lack of expertise among the editors, and the absence of organizational structures with the means to sustain such an undertaking. Perhaps above all, these projects failed due to the widely held perception, even among Yiddish speakers, that Yiddish was mere "jargon" that did not have the stature or expressive range of more established languages such as German, Russian, or English. Reflecting on the failed 1904 effort by writers connected to the St. Petersburg Yiddish daily newspaper *Der fraynd* (The friend), the bibliographer Shimeon Brisman wrote, "The publication of this first Yiddish encyclopedia was premature. Neither the publisher nor the editors or readers were ready for such a work."[48]

The repeated efforts to publish a Yiddish-language encyclopedia despite the many obstacles evince the commitment to the encyclopedic genre as a necessary step toward the establishment of a Yiddish cultural nation. Emerging from the same impulse as that of other European minority groups who were asserting their place among the nations of the world, an encyclopedia in their own language would announce to the world that the Yiddish nation had *arrived*. When the decision to publish the *Algemeyne entsiklopedye* was first publicly announced in 1931, it was celebrated in the Yiddish press. When a *probeheft* was produced to solicit subscriptions and donations in 1932, it garnered its own reviews in literary journals. When volume 1 appeared in late 1934, it was widely hailed as an important milestone in the development of the Yiddish language and the community of Jews who spoke it.

As the subsequent chapters discuss, the *Algemeyne entsiklopedye* was not without its detractors. Early skeptics expressed doubts over the ideological and partisan character of the *Entsiklopedye* and its editors. They were concerned that it would not be sufficiently objective and would therefore not meet the needs of the ideologically diverse Yiddish reading public. More broadly, the project faced the longstanding question of what sort of an encyclopedia was actually needed by Yiddish-speaking Jews of the period. The *Entsiklopedye* differed from its English, Russian, and German precursors not only because it was written in a Jewish language, and therefore inaccessible to most non-Jews, but also because it was to be a general encyclopedia—not a specifically Jewish one. Its primary goal was to serve as a bridge to the modern world and help Yiddish-speaking Jews navigate their way within it. The *Entsiklopedye*'s initial critics (many of whom ultimately became involved with its planning, editorial work, and contributions) were concerned that such a work threatened to accelerate the linguistic and cultural assimilation of Jews and ultimately weaken the Jewish nation. This tension between general and Jewish knowledge would persist throughout the first two decades of the project and—along with its desperate financial constraints and the tenacity of its editors—would be one of its most defining characteristics.

In recent years, scholars have brought to light many of the courageous (and sometimes ethically fraught) efforts by mid-century Jewish scholars and cultural

activists to compose, protect, and recover Jewish literary treasures during and
after the Holocaust. These deeply compelling studies have demonstrated that
even in the midst of the worst imaginable violence, Jews went to heroic lengths
to record their experiences under Nazi rule and to protect the cultural artifacts
of European Jewish civilization. Their efforts included maintaining secret archives of Jewish communal organization and resistance in the Warsaw ghetto,
secreting precious documents and volumes away from Nazi hands, and keeping
diaries and chronicles while in hiding, in ghettos, and in camps.[49] In the immediate aftermath of the Holocaust, teams of Jews, including many Holocaust
survivors, dedicated themselves to recording the testimony of those who had
experienced the genocide. Others committed themselves to the rescue of millions of Jewish books, community records, and sacred objects that otherwise
might not have been preserved in the aftermath of the war.[50] Many of these
early eyewitness accounts and rescued treasures were utilized as sources in the
first histories of the Holocaust and as evidence to fight for justice for victims.[51]

They were also used as some of the building blocks for the postwar reconstruction of Jewish culture. The late-nineteenth-century imperative to preserve the shared heritage of Jewish life in Europe took on a new sense of
urgency after the Holocaust in order to make it available to American Jewry.
This often required relinquishing many of the political aims of pro-Diaspora
Jewish nationalists and simultaneously asserting the cultural aims and accomplishments of Eastern European Jews. The result was a burst in Yiddish-
language activism in the two decades after the war that arose in the name of
maintaining a community of Yiddish speakers that was sufficiently strong to
ensure the perpetuation of the language, as well as in a desperate race against
the clock to collect and record the cultural, scholarly, and literary record before the last surviving members of the "old world" perished. This included the
launching of new Yiddish-language publishing ventures, reference works, language schools, and cultural programs. It also involved many initiatives to
translate this legacy both literally into English and metaphorically into terms
American Jews might accept.[52] In terms of the *Algemeyne entsiklopedye*, this
led to the publication of Yiddish-language volumes on Eastern European
Jewish history, Jewish life in the Americas, and the Holocaust. It also motivated the publication of the four-volume English-language set *The Jewish
People: Past and Present*, which translated and expanded upon subject matter
from the Yiddish volumes.

As *The Holocaust & the Exile of Yiddish* demonstrates, the *Algemeyne entsiklopedye* allows us to view these various efforts to document, salvage, recover,
and reassert modern Yiddish culture as interrelated projects that when joined

together form a united history that spans the middle decades of the twentieth century. For entirely understandable reasons, histories of Jewish life in the twentieth century—as well as many popular conceptions—often treat the years 1939–1945 as a period of near-complete rupture and tend to either begin or end their examination with the Holocaust itself. Consequently, Jewish history is often represented as containing an interregnum that brackets off this period as if it existed outside of normal historical development.[53] Given that it is nearly impossible to represent this period without the language of rupture and annihilation, it is worthwhile to note the very rare and frayed threads of continuity—such as the *Algemeyne entsiklopedye*—that bind the pre- and post-Holocaust eras together. This book argues for the importance of examining those few cultural projects that began in Europe in the optimistic years following World War I, endured through World War II and the Holocaust, and continued afterward in the United States.

Notwithstanding the hundreds of Jewish scholars and cultural activists who ultimately collaborated in the making of the *Algemeyne entsiklopedye* and the dramatic and compelling history of its production, it has been almost entirely overlooked by scholars since its final volume was published in 1966.[54] It is not hard to understand why. This treasure of Jewish civilization is written primarily in a language that few readers today can understand; its archival materials are scattered in more than two dozen collections located on several continents; and complete sets are extraordinarily difficult to obtain. But in spite of, and perhaps because of, the disarray that marks the *Entsiklopedye*, there is much to be learned about the fate of Yiddish culture from examining its history. Among the goals of this book is to reintroduce the *Algemeyne entsiklopedye* to contemporary readers and make the case not only that its volumes can serve as a valuable source of information from which to draw, but that they show how the fate of modern Yiddish culture and its speakers were deeply intertwined with the much larger historical forces of geopolitical realignment, the rise of communism and fascism, world war, displacement, and genocide. If Diderot's *Encyclopédie* symbolizes the Enlightenment's triumph of reason over superstition and order over chaos, the *Algemeyne entsiklopedye* embodies the disorder and irrationality of the Enlightenment's demise in the Nazi Holocaust. Moreover, the *Algemeyne entsiklopedye* symbolizes the tenacity of that disorder's victims and their resolve to continue advocating on behalf of their language and culture.

1

A BIBLE FOR THE NEW AGE

Berlin, 1930–1933

A People's Book

IN FEBRUARY 1931, in Berlin, Germany, the celebrated Russian Jewish historian Simon Dubnow opened a gathering of leaders from the Yiddish intellectual and cultural world. They had convened to embark upon a project that, as they believed at the time, would be instrumental in transforming the lives of Yiddish-speaking Jews around the world. Their goal was to create a popular and comprehensive encyclopedia of general knowledge in the Yiddish language, which they envisioned would serve as a bridge that would lead Yiddish speakers to the larger world and as an instrument with which to make their own mark upon it. In his opening address, "How we went from a Jewish Encyclopedia to an Encyclopedia in Yiddish," Dubnow reflected upon his participation in several earlier attempts to create Jewish encyclopedias over the previous forty years.[1] From 1897 until 1901, he recalled, he had served as a consulting editor for the twelve-volume English-language *Jewish Encyclopedia*, whose success inspired the Russian-language *Evreiskaia entsiklopediia*, for which he likewise served as an editor. Dubnow made mention of several failed efforts to publish encyclopedias in specifically Jewish languages, including the prewar effort by the cultural Zionist leader Ahad Ha'am to launch the Hebrew-language *Otsar hayahadut*. He also lamented that the tumult of the years after the Russian czar's overthrow, in 1917, when "we suffered from hunger and terror," prevented the completion of an encyclopedia for the Yiddish-reading masses.

This meeting, which included heads of communal organizations, journalists, political leaders, Yiddish writers, artists, and Yiddish scholars, nearly all of whom looked to Dubnow as a mentor and guide, was convened to formalize plans for the encyclopedia, a project that many Yiddish-language activists had dreamed of for decades. Dubnow, whose recent seventieth birthday was the occasion for the initiative, hoped that this effort would succeed where the others had failed and, moreover, that it would mark the beginning of a new era for Yiddish-speaking Jews. Although those assembled before him held a range of often-competing ideological and political positions on the best path forward for the Jewish people, they had come together in support of this project. Dubnow concluded his speech by pointing to the intellectual strength and commitment of the assembled as proof of the viability of the proposed encyclopedia:

> This is the best evidence of how important it was then and how necessary it is now to have an encyclopedia in Yiddish. Although times are difficult, we must not now cease as we did then in 1917. An encyclopedia is a people's book, one that each nation must possess. A people, ten million of whom speak Yiddish, must have an encyclopedia in their own language. Moses Mendelssohn gave us the bible in German. We must provide an encyclopedia, which will be a bible for the new age, in Yiddish. I hope that those who believe in the people will understand the level of enthusiasm that the idea of an encyclopedia will generate among them. Let us all join together to help realize the plan of the encyclopedia in Yiddish.[2]

As Dubnow described, the early 1930s were difficult times for European Jewry, especially for those who spoke Yiddish. Not only were Jews suffering along with other Europeans from the effects of the economic collapse of the Great Depression (where one in five persons in central Europe was unemployed), but the millions of Eastern European Jews found themselves suddenly fractured geographically and wrestling with the post–World War I realignment of Europe. Prior to the war, Eastern European Jews—most of whom were Yiddish speakers—had lived within the Russian and Austro-Hungarian empires and could imagine themselves simultaneously as belonging to a larger international Jewish community as well as holding more particular regional (or religious and political) identifications. Following the war, these Jews now resided within the Soviet Union or lived as national and religious minorities in one of many new nation-states established after the war. In the decades between the world wars, the more than two million Jews in the USSR gradually became cut off from the rest of Eastern European Jewry and experienced forced Sovietization, which included the resettlement of many Jews to agricultural areas, the dismantling of their religious and communal institutions, and attacks on traditional ways of life. Jews to the west of the Soviet border were a part of the newly independent states of Poland, Hungary, Romania, Lithuania, Latvia, Estonia, and Ukraine (which was sovereign for a brief period after World War I). Although Jews were supposed to be given full legal protections within these countries to build their own national culture in their own language, such minority rights were never entirely permitted by the new states, as Jews were widely viewed by government leaders as an obstacle to national consolidation.[3]

The expectation of these rights and the fact that they never came to pass gave new energy to cultural and political movements that had been founded in the previous decades in response to the ever-pressing crises and questions facing Jews in modern Europe, including where should Jews—who were scattered across the continent—permanently reside? Should they seek to forge a place for themselves within the new and ever-more hostile European order or establish an independent homeland outside of it? Should they join the large communities of Eastern European Jews who had emigrated to the Americas? In what language should they speak and publish, that of their country or a Jewish language such as Yiddish or Hebrew? Should they consider themselves members of the nations in the countries in which they lived, or as members of a distinct Jewish nation that eclipsed state boundaries? Should they join the international labor movement and work toward revolution to remedy their dire economic straits since they, like most other Europeans, suffered from the injustices of capitalism? Should they instead try to make their way up the economic ladder by embracing capitalism and liberal democracy? How should they respond to an ever-growing antisemitism that was emanating from increasingly strident European nationalist movements, which often portrayed Jews alternately (or at times, simultaneously) as interlopers, usurpers, revolutionary provocateurs, and as agents of hedonistic capitalism and cosmopolitanism?

Perhaps nowhere were these questions debated more vigorously in the years after World War I than in Poland. Prior to the war, most Polish lands and people had been under Russian imperial rule, with the Austro-Hungarian empire and Prussia also controlling smaller parts of the onetime Kingdom of Poland. At the war's end, Poland was reconstituted as an independent state, fulfilling a 125-year-old dream of Polish nationalists for a return to sovereignty. Yet the country that emerged was hardly homogenous, either ethnically or nationally. The historian Ezra Mendelsohn has noted that one out of every three persons in the new Polish state was a non-Pole. There were millions of others, including Ukrainians, Belarusians, Lithuanians, and Germans. One in every ten new citizens was Jewish. This led to resentment among many Polish nationals, whose dreams of a restored country were now complicated by the presence of so many non-Poles, each of whom had their own national identity, and many of whom spoke a language other than Polish and had their own ambitions toward national self-determination. As Mendelsohn writes, "In short, for many Poles the national-minorities problem constituted a serious challenge to the integrity of the state, and the question of how to deal with it became a major issue in interwar Polish politics."[4]

While ethnic Ukrainians, Belarusians, Lithuanians, and Germans who resided in Poland often expressed their nationalism by seeking to reunite or strengthen ties with the Ukrainian, Belarusian, Lithuanian, and German lands that lay across Poland's borders, Jews had no such adjacent territory that they could consider their homeland. They were not clustered in one region of the country but instead lived throughout it. In fact, in many of Poland's cities, such as Chełmno, Grodno, and Tarnow, Jews were one of the largest population groups. In others, such as Brest-Litovsk, Rovno, and Pinsk, they were an outright majority. The capital city, Warsaw, was home to more than 350,000 Jews, about 30% of the city's total.[5] When Jewish political and cultural activists sought to take advantage of the legal right to preserve their distinct national culture that was afforded to them in the Minorities Treaty that had been signed by Poland and the League of Nations in 1919, they found themselves repeatedly thwarted.[6] The promised financial aid for their national development, which included funds for Jewish schools and social and communal services, never materialized. The initial wave of enthusiasm among Jews over the promises of the Minorities Treaty and the subsequent failure to realize them produced what Mendelsohn elsewhere has described as a "cycle of exaggerated hope and deep depression," which he identifies as "an integral part of Jewish political culture" in Poland.[7]

At over 3 million in the 1920s, Jews in Poland made up the second largest Jewish community in the world after the United States. It was also highly diverse. Although most Jews resided in cities and larger towns, many still lived in traditional *shtetl* communities. Some Jews remained committed to a religiously orthodox way of life (which was itself exceedingly diverse) while others were highly secularized. Given the expectations among many Jews that the time had at last come for the realization of their own national and civic aspirations—indeed, it was only with the fall of the Russian empire that most Polish Jews experienced any sort of civil emancipation—the years between the world wars were extraordinarily active ones. Many political parties and cultural movements (often overlapping with one another) emerged to solve the problems faced by Polish Jewry.

There is no easy way to categorize accurately the myriad Jewish parties, movements, and groups that formed in this period. However, there were some important dividing lines along matters of territory, economics, and language. There were those who advocated territorial solutions to the Jewish Question, such as the many Zionist groups (ranging from the far left to the far right, as well as religious Zionist groups), which tended to promote the Hebrew language and culture and the vision of a future Jewish homeland in British Mandate Palestine. By contrast, other parties advocated Diaspora Nationalism, an ideology that insisted on Jews' right to make a place for themselves within the countries in which they lived. These parties, such as the Jewish Labor Bund, focused simultaneously on the need to remedy working-class Jews' often dire economic status via a commitment to socialism and to strengthen Jewish cultural ties through a commitment to Yiddish. To confuse matters further, some parties, such as the highly visible left-wing *Poyle-Tsien* (Workers of Zion), were committed both to Jewish existence both in the Diaspora and in Palestine, as well as to Yiddish. A result of this dynamic political activism was that Poland became the epicenter of Eastern European Jews' efforts to solve the Jewish Question for themselves.

This vibrancy was also expressed culturally, and the 1920s and 1930s are often looked upon as a golden age for Jewish culture, especially in Yiddish. Although it had been the mother tongue of most European Jews for many centuries, Yiddish was only widely recognized—even by its speakers—as an actual language in the late nineteenth and early twentieth centuries. Prior to that, it was considered a substandard jargon that lacked a consistent grammar, orthography, and vocabulary. Because of factors internal to Eastern European Jews, such as growing national identification and the committed efforts of Yiddish cultural scholars and activists, as well as external factors external such as rising antisemitism, the growth of national minority movements in the Russian empire, and the increased ease and availability of print culture, Yiddish began to emerge as a language in its own right and the basis of a reinvigorated national culture.[8] Yiddish quickly became the dominant language (with Polish and Hebrew in distant second and third places) of the Jewish press as well as the language of theater, schools, radio, film, choirs, literature, and the fine arts.

By the early 1930s, however, many Yiddish activists found themselves in a paradoxical situation: the very conditions that allowed for Yiddish culture to reach new heights of sophistication and influence were also hastening the linguistic assimilation of many its speakers. The modernizing factors that had facilitated the flourishing of postwar Yiddish culture—including the expansion of print, radio, theater, and film industries, greater Jewish participation in civic and cultural life, the ease of travel and cultural exchange—also led Yiddish speakers to take up the languages of the countries in which they were located, such as Polish, Russian, and English. Complicating this situation further was the fact that as Jews were becoming invested in their home states, the dramatic rise in antisemitic incidents from the political right during the 1930s led many Jews to find their new status threatened. In Poland, the Soviet Union, Germany, and the United States, antisemites sought to restrict Jewish participation in civic life, limit Jewish migration and settlement, and contain—or even purge—Jews' political, economic, cultural, and (presumed) racial influence. This complicated set of factors led many Yiddishists to reassert their commitment to the language and to a distinct Jewish national identity.

The Golden Age of Yiddish in Weimar Berlin

The reshuffling of the European order following the war's end in 1918 led not only to new political, geographical, and cultural alignments among Jews, but also to new paths of migration. With the collapse of the Russian, Austro-Hungarian, and German empires and the subsequent emergence of the Soviet Union and new nation-states, economic and cultural opportunities materialized and disappeared at great speed. Often, Yiddish artists and intellectuals found themselves in untenable situations that kept them on the move. Advocates for the Yiddish language briefly converged in Kiev, for example, to conduct significant cultural work under the Kultur-lige (Culture League) until its forced absorption into the Soviet Union's Evsektsiia (Jewish section of the Communist Party) in the first years of the 1920s sent many of its leaders packing.[9] Many found employment elsewhere in the Soviet Union, which provided unparalleled financial resources to produce Yiddish-language theater, art, scholarship, and journalism, yet oftentimes at a severe ideological cost. Although cities such as Warsaw and Vilna in the recently reestablished Poland remained major centers for Yiddish—if not always financially or politically stable ones—throughout the interwar years, intellectuals moved from place to place seeking the cultural autonomy that had been promised to Jews.[10]

In contrast to the tumult in Poland, Berlin at the outset of the 1930s was much calmer for its community of Eastern European Jewish immigrants. The city was home to a substantial number of Yiddish speakers, primarily working-class Jewish migrants and refugees from the Soviet Union and Poland who numbered in the low tens of thousands. For much of the 1920s, Berlin had been the site of a small but vibrant Yiddish publishing center and was a near-compulsory stop for members of the Eastern European Jewish intelligentsia.[11]

For many Jews, Weimar-era Berlin offered a momentary respite from the political turmoil, economic uncertainty, and ideological rigidity found further to the east. Although Germans, including many German Jews, generally viewed Jews from the East with a measure of disdain for their presumed "backwardness," Eastern European Jews of all classes, religious outlooks, and vocations had made their way to Berlin for centuries in search of economic opportunity, physical safety, and political, religious, and intellectual freedom. Most often raised in religious communities, speaking Yiddish, and wearing traditional dress, the *Ostjuden* (Eastern Jews), as they were pejoratively called, occupied a complicated position in German society. To assimilated German Jews, their presence was often an uncomfortable reminder of the recent past that they had overcome in their quest to shed their external markers of difference and be accepted in non-Jewish German circles. Nevertheless, Berlin became a major transit center for Jews migrating to the United States as well as a stopping point for many. Hundreds of thousands of Jews moved through Germany between 1881 and the 1920s, and tens of thousands remained and lived among the larger Russian-speaking community, which after World War I had grown to as many as half a million. Economic migrants were able to find jobs in various trades and industries, or in positions that served the educational and ritual needs of the German Jewish and Eastern European Jewish communities. In the 1920s, Jews from Eastern Europe made up approximately 25 percent of the Berlin Jewish community (which totaled approximately forty-four thousand) and were a numerical majority in other Jewish communities around the country.[12]

In the early twentieth century, some German Jewish attitudes toward Eastern European Jews began to shift. On the one hand, Berlin was growing ever more cosmopolitan and welcoming to immigrants from across Europe and overseas. On the other hand, a growing number of younger German Jews, disaffected by the escalation of antisemitism and the lack of a meaningful Jewish identity, began looking for a way to de-assimilate and forge a "return" to an affirmative Jewish existence. For them, the *Ostjuden* often became a symbol of Jewish authenticity. Eastern European Jews' intimate knowledge of Jewish languages, texts, and traditions was increasingly valued by those German Jews who were looking for keys to their own past. In the years after the war, thousands of German-speaking Jews, including such well-known figures as Albert Einstein, Franz Kafka, and Martin Buber, attended Yiddish- and Hebrew-language cultural events in the city, while German translations of Yiddish literary giants I. L. Peretz, Sholem Asch, and Sholem Aleichem enjoyed great popularity. Yiddish- and Hebrew-language theater troupes were wildly popular among German Jews.[13]

Although contact between German and Eastern European Jews facilitated several important cultural works by German Jews and the level of cultural exchange was often significant, there were few sustained collaborations between the two groups.[14] Settling in the Scheunenviertel and Charlottenburg neighborhoods, most Eastern European Jews lived at a remove from the German Jewish community and focused on their own cultural, political, and social concerns. Since they were not trying to assimilate into the larger society and most of them understood their time in Germany as temporary, they formed their own religious, social, and cultural communities based upon their geographical, political, and occupational affiliations back east. Verena Dohrn has commented that the Berlin Eastern European Jewish community was its own "*Lebenswelt* and a social environment in its own right."[15]

During the first years after the war, Berlin became an important site of Yiddish- and Hebrew-language cultural production by émigrés from the East. Famous Yiddish writers David Bergelson, Der Nister, Moyshe Kulbak, David Einhorn, and Daniel Charney were at one time drawn to its modernist milieu, as were the Hebrew writers Chaim Nachman Bialik, Shmuel Yosef Agnon, Leah Goldberg, Micha Yosef Berdyczewski, David Frischmann, and Uri Tsevi Grinberg.[16] The avant-garde painters Nathan Altmann and El Lissitzky resided there for a time. Berlin was home to branches of the American Jewish Joint Distribution Committee, the US-based Hebrew Immigrant Aid Society (HIAS), the health organization OZE World Union (Obshchestvo Zdravookhraneniia Evreev / Society for the Protection of the Health of the Jews), the Jewish Telegraphic Agency, as well as the headquarters of the World ORT Union (Obchestvo Remeslenogo Truda / Association for the Promotion of Skilled Trades). Berlin was also a prominent site of Jewish migrant radical leftists who used the city as an organizational base.[17] The community of Mensheviks, who were known as the "Delegation Abroad" and were almost all Jews, made Berlin their base while plotting their return to the Soviet Union. The city likewise attracted a number of scholars, including Simon Dubnow, the demographer Jacob Lestschinsky, the historian Elias Tcherikower, the Yiddish linguist Max Weinreich, and the Hebraist Simon Rawidowicz. It was while residing in Berlin that the linguist Nokhem Shtif wrote the programmatic statement that launched YIVO.[18]

Leo Fuks and Renate Fuks have shown that the boom in Yiddish publishing during the first years of the Weimar period was made possible in part by the German mark's hyperinflation.[19] In fact, the heyday of Berlin's Yiddish scene coincided with the most economically tumultuous periods of Weimar-era Germany. Printed on German presses, Yiddish materials were shipped to readers abroad and paid for in foreign currency, which was then generously converted to German marks. Rachel Wischnitzer, the art historian and coeditor of the bilingual Hebrew/Yiddish modernist journal *Rimon/Milgroym* (1922–1924), re-counted this strategy in a 1971 interview: "Well, the trick was this. There was in-flation. Every day a different price on everything. So with a few hundred dollars we could publish. So when you sent issues of *Milgroym* and *Rimon* to New York and we got a few hundred dollars and then could publish the next and so on."[20]

Such arrangements allowed many Yidish writers for the first time to earn a living at their craft. For a brief period, Germany became, in Gennady Estrai-kh's words, a "publisher's paradise, guaranteeing an ideal combination of low prices, high quality, and lax censorship."[21] In the first years after the war, several Yiddish publishing houses were established in Berlin, including the Klal-farlag (which was the renamed Folksfarlag of Kiev's Kultur-lige), Farlag Yiddish, Wostok, Shveln, and Funken. They published hundreds of titles and more than twenty periodicals between 1920 and 1933 and employed many of the writers and cultural activists who migrated to Berlin. Many others worked as foreign correspondents for Yiddish newspapers abroad. Max Weinreich, Ja-cob Lestschinsky, and the Menshevik leader Raphael Abramovitch, for exam-ple, wrote for the New York–based *Forverts* (*Forward*), which paid them in much-coveted dollars.[22]

By mid-decade, however, the stabilization of the German economy meant that Berlin was no longer a financial bargain for those with foreign currency, and Yiddish publishing became unprofitable. The political turmoil and vio-lence in postwar Eastern Europe that had caused so many to take refuge in Ber-lin had eased, and new economic and cultural opportunities in Poland and the Soviet Union enticed many away.[23] The intellectual vibrancy that previously had contributed to the rise of publishing houses and had brought together the much-touted modernist literary circles at the Romanisches Café and the Sholem Aleichem Club, and that had laid the foundation for YIVO, had faded by the end of the 1920s. The economic crisis that facilitated the Nazi Party's increased electoral strength brought on a new period of anxiety for all Jews in the country. The golden age of Weimar Yiddish ended soon after it began.

Notwithstanding the uncertainties facing Eastern European Jews, the activ-ists and intellectuals who assembled in February 1931 to launch the encyclopedia were optimistic about the future of Yiddish-speaking Jewry and had high hopes for its potential to guide Jews into the future. More than a decade had passed since the political emancipation of Russian Jewry, the end of World War I, and the horrific pogroms that occurred during the civil war that followed the Bol-shevik seizure of power. Jewish communities across Europe were settling into the new postwar political realignment. Millions of Yiddish-speaking Jews were experiencing for the first time the opportunity to participate in democratic processes and the right to free political and cultural expression. Those in the Soviet Union were accommodating to a new regime that, in spite of its severe oppression of political opponents, had vowed an end to antisemitism, allowed for broad participation in civic life by Jews, and provided unprecedented levels of state support for Yiddish cultural activities. In addition, the United States was home to a thriving Yiddish-speaking population and was a strong marketplace for Yiddish print, theater, and radio. To the remaining Yiddish-speaking intelligentsia in Berlin, the future looked encouraging enough to take up this bold initiative on behalf of the global community of Yiddish-speaking Jews.

Renewing the Call for a Yiddish Encyclopedia

The February 1931 meeting to launch the *Entsiklopedye* was the result of several years of efforts by Yiddish activists to assert the legitimacy of Yiddish as a language of learning and culture. Much of the credit for the new initiative can be given to Moyshe Shalit, a leader of the Vilna Jewish community and President of the Union of Yiddish Language Writers and Journalists, who had renewed the call for a Yiddish-language encyclopedia in the late 1920s in response to what he perceived as relentless insults to Yiddish by German Jewish scholars. In a 1928 review of the first volume of the German-language *Encyclopaedia Judaica*, which purported to cover all aspects of Jewish culture and civilization, Shalit identified multiple mistakes and a general lack of entries on Eastern European Jewish topics. These errors and omissions were a result, he argued, of the editors' "fundamental error" of refusing to acknowledge "the living spirit of modern Yiddish culture."[24] By focusing almost entirely on the Jewish past, the encyclopedia ignored the living, breathing Eastern European Jews who made up more than half of the world's Jewish population. Such treatment was in contrast to the Russian-language *Evreiskaia entsiklopediia*, which not only took Eastern European Jewry seriously but also dedicated an entire editorial division to Yiddish. Shalit also noted errors in the biographies of the Yiddish authors Sholem Asch, S. An-sky (the pseudonym of Shloyme Zanvl Rappoport), and David Bergelson. The Yiddish writings of the writer Yosef Haim Brenner were ignored in favor of his Hebrew work, as was the pathbreaking Yiddish-language scholarship of the Marxist-Zionist leader and Yiddish scholar Ber Borochov. Eastern European Jewish organizations such as the early Zionist student group BILU and the socialist Jewish Labor Bund were, in his assessment, woefully mischaracterized in the *Encyclopaedia Judaica*.

Frustrated by the lack of respect and care given to Eastern European Jewish topics, Shalit called for an encyclopedia in Yiddish: "And at last, is it not

high time that we should ourselves publish our own encyclopedia, an encyclopedia in the Yiddish language? If not in multiple volumes, at least in one
volume—a Yiddish *Larousse, Pavlenkov,* a small *Brockhaus....* We already
possess a significant amount of preparatory material, terminologies, special
publications and lexicons—and scientific strengths. The foundation has already been laid over the course of the previous ten years. It is necessary at
once to create a proper 'Committee for Publishing a Yiddish Encyclopedia'
with a major press and with plenty of capital."[25] In contrast to a programmatic
statement for a multivolume encyclopedia that he would issue a few years
later, in this 1928 review he envisioned a short-term project that would be accomplished in a two-year period by a staff of five dedicated scholars who
would be supported by a publishing house with access to the necessary funds.

Shalit was not the first to call for a Yiddish-language encyclopedia. In his
February 1931 speech, Dubnow made reference to several unsuccessful attempts to publish an encyclopedia in Yiddish in the early part of the century.[26]
The first of these projects, *Di algemeyne yidishe entsiklopedye* (The general Jewish encyclopedia), was initiated by a group of scholars affiliated with *Der
fraynd* (The friend), the first Yiddish daily newspaper in Russia. According to
the first installment, which appeared in 1904, it aimed to create a compact,
popular, accessible, and affordable encyclopedia that would contain entries on
general *and* specifically Jewish topics. After a weak reception in the Yiddish
press, however, *Di algemeyne yidishe entsiklopedye* ceased publication, stopping
on the word *ultimatum,* which, following the Yiddish spelling, was partway
through *alef,* the first letter of the alphabet.[27]

Other efforts included the 1912–13 undertaking by the publishing house
Tsentral-farlag in Warsaw to publish a single-volume Yiddish encyclopedia
with a Hebrew translation,[28] and the South African Yiddish publisher David
Goldblatt's *Ilustrirte yidishes leksikon* (Illustrated Yiddish lexicon, 1912–1913),
of which a number of fascicles were published, though the lexicon only
reached the word *Azyen* (Asia). After the war, Goldblatt once again attempted
his encyclopedia and published two volumes, in 1920 and 1923, of *Di algemeyne
ilustrirte entsiklopedye* (The general illustrated encyclopedia). Reviews of the
work were universally negative, and no further volumes were published.[29] A
more serious effort was made in 1917 by the writers and editors Hillel Zeitlin
and Shoyl Stupnitski, along with the cooperation of the Warsaw Yiddish daily
newspaper *Moment.* Over the course of that year, the name of the publication,
originally *Ersht yidish entsiklopedish verterbukh* (First Yiddish encyclopedic
dictionary), and its format changed, although it maintained its alphabetical
continuity and was written for an educated audience.[30] Four volumes

appeared in total, and it was offered as a premium to subscribers of the paper. Like Goldblatt's effort, however, this encyclopedia was interrupted, stopping also midway through the letter *alef*. Reactions to this encyclopedia were mixed, with reviewer Yosef Yashunsky blaming its collapse not on the war but rather on the publication's poor organization, lack of consistency and balance (the entry on the czars comprised ten columns, the one on antisemitism was fifty, for example), and frequent changes in format and editor.[31]

Immediately after World War I, there were other attempts that never made it past the planning stage. In 1919, Jacob Lestschinsky, writing on behalf of an initiative of the Kiev-based Kultur-lige, made a renewed call for a Yiddish encyclopedia in which he located the project within the context of the flourishing of Yiddish culture made possible by postwar political realignments. Expressing hope that the encyclopedia would be a "gathering point for our modern Yiddish culture," he ended his proposal by stating that although some had declared that such a massive undertaking was presumptuous in a time of severe economic hardship, "collective presumption is but an expression of a particular level of confidence and certitude."[32]

Two years after Shalit's 1928 appeal for a Yiddish encyclopedia, the editor and cultural critic Nakhmen Meisel took up the task with particular vigor. In a March 1930 issue of the weekly *Literarishe bleter* (Literary pages) that commemorated YIVO's fifth anniversary, Meisel articulated a vision for "a groyse yidishe entsiklopedye" (a great Yiddish encyclopedia).[33] Why was Meisel confident that this attempt would succeed when so many had failed before? He explained that previous efforts suffered on account of the lack of scholarly institutions to support them. Earlier encyclopedias had been the private initiative of a single individual or publisher, and they lacked the resources to sustain such a tremendously complicated undertaking. What was different in 1930 was that not only had Yiddish attained the status of being the premier language of Jewish intellectuals, but the success of YIVO had proved that a Yiddish academic institute could in fact succeed. There was now a community that was broad enough to produce an encyclopedia and engaged enough to support it. Meisel argued that YIVO's five years of accomplishments had fostered the conditions that could make a Yiddish encyclopedia a reality. He pointed to the large number of scholarly volumes produced by its various academic sections, its hundreds of financial supporters across many countries, and the fact that construction on a new building was underway. He saw the first five years as marking the first era in YIVO's history and believed that it was now time to embark upon the next: one marked by a great collaborative project that would showcase the organization's collective strength.

The chief question Meisel posed was whether YIVO was able to commit the necessary resources for the project. In his conception, YIVO was in the best position to realize this long-held dream, given the high esteem with which it was held in the Yiddish-speaking community and its initial success in raising funds for the new building. He also believed that after a period of two years, the encyclopedia would likely become a self-sustaining venture that would not overly tax YIVO's limited resources. Finally, he argued that the project would also be of great benefit to YIVO itself, anticipating that "the Yiddish encyclopedia will be received with great enthusiasm by all friends of the Yiddish word and Yiddish culture in the whole world, and will greatly elevate the esteem and prestige of YIVO."[34]

Previous efforts had also been hindered, he argued, in large part because prior to this time, the Yiddish language had lacked the vocabulary for many scientific and technical terms. Meisel cited a concern expressed by Lestschinsky in his 1919 article in which he claimed that although "[Yiddish-speaking] Jews require access to European scholarship," they are prevented because they "lack the terminology."[35] In the eleven years since Lestschinsky's article was published, however, the word corpus of Yiddish had dramatically expanded as Yiddish experienced an unparalleled period of scientific and cultural growth. A vast catalog of Yiddish materials had appeared on a wide range of scholarly subjects. Schoolbooks on physics, botany, mathematics, and medicine, along with trade journals and newspapers, greatly increased the number of available words, and it was at last possible to present the full range of human knowledge to Yiddish readers. Within five years of its founding, YIVO had published several formidable collections of essays, including volumes of philology, history, bibliography, and ethnography. The success of other reference works, such as Alexander Harkavy's Yiddish-English-Hebrew dictionary and Zalmen Reisen's recently published four-volume Leksikon fun der yidisher literatur, prese un filologye (Lexicon of Yiddish literature, press, and philology), which appeared in 1928 and 1929, as well as the overall popularity of Jewish encyclopedias were further evidence that the time was ripe for a Yiddish-language one.[36]

Ironically, the issue that Meisel predicted to be among the least contentious turned out to be one of the most controversial during its early stages and, in fact, would remain a persistent point of dispute throughout the three dozen years of the encyclopedia's planning and publication. Midway through his call for an encyclopedia, he declared: "As to what sort of character should the Yiddish encyclopedia have—about this there can now be no dispute. Not strictly a yidishkayt [Jewish]-encyclopedia and also not strictly a general encyclopedia mechanically translated into Yiddish."[37] Rather, the encyclopedia would comprise a combination of both general and Jewish subject matter. This was in contrast to other encyclopedias published in recent decades that were dedicated strictly to Jewish subjects but printed in non-Jewish languages.

Meisel argued that the extant Jewish encyclopedias served a fundamentally different purpose from the one he envisioned in Yiddish. Works such as the English *Jewish Encyclopedia*, the Russian *Evreiskaia entsiklopediia*, and the German *Encyclopaedia Judaica* had a twofold purpose. They had the expressed goal of bringing Jewish knowledge to an audience of assimilated Jews who had become divorced from their own history, language, religion, and customs. In presenting an image of Judaism that corresponded to modern sensibilities and the latest scientific understanding, these projects hoped to reacquaint their Jewish readers with their heritage and, in doing so, provide a guide to a restored, if secular, Jewish identity. At the same time, however, these reference works sought to situate Jews within their home countries' historical narratives, to enlighten non-Jewish audiences about the contributions of Jews over the centuries, and to promote positive relations between Jews and non-Jews. By contrast, encyclopedias in Jewish languages were exclusively for Jewish readers who, it was supposed, were less assimilated, already possessed a basic knowledge of Judaism, and presumably were more deficient in knowledge of the larger world.

Following Meisel's 1930 call, YIVO's Central Committee launched a Berlin-based publishing company named the Dubnow Fund (in honor of Simon Dubnow's 70th birthday, which was in September of that year) to oversee fund-raising for the encyclopedia and to decide on its organization. At a meeting in October 1930 that was convened to discuss the issue, Moyshe Shalit stressed the economic opportunities of the project and speculated that an encyclopedia could potentially attract thousands of early subscribers and deliver much-needed funds to the institute. In spite of many reservations as to whether YIVO—which was in fact struggling financially—could afford the undertaking, the Central Committee appointed several of the gathered to oversee the project. The Berlin-based historian Elias Tcherikower assumed the leadership position of the working group. By the early 1930s, Tcherikower, a founder of YIVO and head of its Historical Section, was one of the most highly regarded historians of Eastern European Jewish history and anti-Jewish violence, and had compiled several highly influential reports on pogroms during the civil war that followed the dissolution of the Russian empire. Also appointed to the working group as members were Meisel, Shalit, and Yashunsky. Avrom Kin, who was once active in the Kultur-lige and the Berlin publishing initiative Klal-farlag, also became highly involved in the early planning.[38]

In mid-January 1931, Shalit penned a detailed proposal for the encyclopedia, with the goal of setting the agenda for a major gathering planned for the following month in Berlin.[39] For Shalit, the Yiddish encyclopedia had to be an assertion of Jewish national pride, absent the inherently apologetic stance taken by encyclopedias written in non-Jewish languages. Thus, he wrote, "from the start and for the first time, the Yiddish encyclopedia must be created in a new spirit and in touch with the pulse of a living nation."[40] Ultimately, the encyclopedia would mark the next stage in Jewish national cultural development. "The Yiddish encyclopedia," he stated, "must become the center around which the scientific and intellectual accomplishments and the cultural strengths of the people will be concentrated, and it will lay the foundation for Jewish and general scholarship in Yiddish and thus begin the genuine renaissance of the new Yiddish culture."[41] In his vision, the encyclopedia would be given the rather unwieldy title of "Yidishe entsiklopedye, hantbikher fun yidishe un algemeyne visnshaft, yedies vegn der fargangener un moderner velt" ("Jewish encyclopedia, handbooks for Jewish and general science, information on the past and the modern world"), and was to be a reference work quite different from those Jewish encyclopedias published in non-Jewish languages. Like Meisel, Shalit argued that what was needed was an encyclopedia that focused as much on universal subject matter as on Jewish topics. Additionally, the Jewish entries that would appear should focus on those topics that were particularly relevant to Jews of Eastern European descent, and that reflected their modern sensibilities and the most recent social scientific research. "In none of our current encyclopedias," he wrote, "and certainly in none of the general encyclopedias, is there any reflection of the modern life of the Jewish masses, the social structure of the Jewish population, the economic position of Jewish communities, and even less is there a treatment and illumination of the new Yiddish cultural movement, the Yiddish language, Yiddish literature and Jewish communal life."

In his ambitious plan, Shalit imagined a complex organizational structure of editors, committees, and subcommittees that would be responsible for the encyclopedia's various sections. As a defense against "dilettantism," contributors would write only in their own fields of knowledge. Judging by the lists of topics he provided, the entries would be approximately equal parts universal and Jewish. General topics would include fields such as general history, linguistics, geography, biology, culture, sport, natural and social sciences, psychology, pedagogy, politics, modern problems, socialism, and communism. Jewish topics were listed with greater specificity and included "Jewish history from the Tanakh and Talmud until the twentieth century," ancient Hebrew literature, literature by Jews in other languages, Jewish philosophy, Kabbalah, religious life and movements, Hasidism, Haskalah, Jewish economic history, Jewish communal and worker movements, Jewish political parties, Yiddishism, Hebraism, emigration, Jewish communal associations, and all aspects of the Yiddish language, including philology, folklore, bibliography, press, literature, and theater. Shalit imagined that the encyclopedia would comprise ten volumes plus an index and a supplement. Five thousand copies of each would be published, and the set would contain approximately three thousand illustrations.

The Yiddish Encyclopedia and the Politics of the Yiddish Intelligentsia

On February 14–15, 1931, a month after Shalit made his proposal, the meeting to finalize plans for the encyclopedia convened in Berlin. Among the thirty or so who attended were some of the most notable figures from that city's Russian Jewish émigré community, including the featured guest, Simon Dubnow; ORT leaders Leon Bramson, Iulii Brutskus, and Aron Singalowsky; the Menshevik leader Raphael Abramovitch; the Territorialist activists Avrom Kin and Ben-Adir (pseudonym of Avrom Rozin);[42] the Jewish communal leader Nokhem Gergel, YIVO's Elias Tcherikower and Jacob Lestschinsky; the Yiddish writer Daniel Charney; the art historian Rachel Wischnitzer; and the historian Mark Wischnitzer (who, prior to the war, had been an editor for the Russian-language *Evreiskaia entsiklopediia* and afterward a contributor to the German-language *Encyclopaedia Judaica*). Joining them from Poland were YIVO's Max Weinreich, the publisher Boris Kletskin, and the Yiddish cultural activists Meisel and Shalit.[43]

By the early 1930s, Simon Dubnow was widely recognized as the leading Jewish historian of his era. His conception of Jewish history—which drew heavily from social scientific analysis, in contrast to his predecessors' study of Jewish literary and spiritual transformations—was premised in part upon the belief that Jewish history is best understood as moving through a series of successive migrating centers that extend their influence over the rest of the Jewish world. As he depicted it in sweeping historical surveys, the first center appeared in the historic Land of Israel and then moved through ancient Babylonia, medieval Germany, medieval Spain (while under Islamic rule), and ultimately to Russia and Poland. His work served as an important counterweight to German Jewish historians who tended to disregard the history and contributions of their Eastern European coreligionists. By placing Yiddish-speaking Jewry at the center of his work, Dubnow helped to lay the intellectual foundations for scholarship *on* Eastern European Jewry and *in* the Yiddish language.[44]

In addition, Dubnow was the chief theoretician and symbolic leader of Autonomism, a Diaspora Nationalist ideology that asserted that Jews had the right to live as a national community in the countries in which they resided. A founder of the liberal Folkspartey (Jewish People's Party) in prerevolutionary Russia, Dubnow advocated for the creation of Jewish national assemblies with decision-making power over Jewish communal concerns, for the rights of national minorities to exist within the states in which they resided, and for the right of Yiddish speakers to use their language in the public sphere.[45] Although the Folkspartey did not gain much traction, even in postwar Poland where it was allowed to operate freely, Dubnow's influence was far reaching: Autonomism informed the socialist Jewish Labor Bund's defense of Jewish cultural independence; influenced a decision by Russian Zionists at a 1906 conference in Helsinki to shift the movement's efforts toward *Gegenwartsarbeit* (present-day work) in order to alleviate the dire economic situation of Diaspora Jewry; and led many in the Menshevik camp to sympathize with Jewish national demands.

Although the younger generation at the February 1931 gathering rejected the politically moderate Folkspartey in favor of bolder and less accommodating stances, the vastness of Dubnow's scholarly oeuvre, his engagement with Yiddish intellectual culture, and his commitment to a thoroughly modern Jewish Diasporic existence elevated him to the most eminent position in the Yiddish scholarly world, in spite of having composed relatively little material in Yiddish himself.[46] An encyclopedia of general knowledge in the Yiddish language was, therefore, a fitting tribute to Dubnow, whose life's work was to advocate for the right of Jews to participate collectively in the community of nations as a Diasporic people.

The assembled represented an ideologically diverse and highly prominent segment of the Yiddish-speaking intelligentsia. Many had been instrumental in launching YIVO five years earlier, and most were identified with the Jewish left. With some exceptions, such as Dubnow (b. 1860), Bramson (b. 1869), and Weinreich (b. 1894), they were primarily members of a generation that was born in or around 1880, which was a particularly transformative moment for Jews in the Russian empire. As youths, they had been avid participants in a new Jewish cultural and political environment that had developed in response to pervasive assaults on Russian Jews that followed the Czar's assassination in 1881. Typical of many in their generation, these activists moved regularly among the various socialist, unionist, Diasporist, and Zionist factions and parties that competed for Jewish hearts and minds. In the wake of the 1905 Russian Revolution's collapse and Czar Nicholas II's crackdown on Jewish

FIGURE 1.1 Simon and Ida Dubnow, 1930 (courtesy of YIVO).

political activity, many of them sought to continue their communal engagement by focusing their efforts on Jewish cultural development and self-help
organizations.[47]

Most of those who had gathered together to plan the encyclopedia occupied
a narrow yet highly influential space on the Jewish political spectrum—one
that was located between the Bolsheviks (on their left) and the general Zionists
(on their right) and included former and current Mensheviks, Bundists,

Autonomists, Folkists, Territorialists, and Labor Zionists. Although they held differing stances on the economic, political, cultural, social, and territorial problems facing Jews, they all tended to identify with the general goals of Jewish self-determination, workers' rights, Diaspora Nationalism, and the central role to be played by Yiddish in modernizing Eastern European Jewry and preserving their national cohesion. As nationalists, they were generally opposed to Jews' linguistic and cultural assimilation into the countries in which they were located. As Diasporists and (primarily) socialists, they objected to Zionists' seeming disregard for the immediate material plight of Diaspora Jewry in favor of building a Jewish state. As leftists, they were utterly opposed to the rising fascist movements in Italy, Germany, and (later) Spain. As exiles from Russia and the Soviet Union, they held a profound respect for Russian culture but harbored deep resentment of the Bolshevik assault on Jewish political, religious, and economic life. Several of them, including Abramovitch, Brutskus, and the Jewish communal activist and Yiddish translator Aaron Steinberg, had spent time in Bolshevik prisons. As Yiddishists, they believed that the Jewish future depended on the creation of institutions that responded to the cultural and communal needs of the millions of Yiddish-speaking Jews. They shared a deep respect for Dubnow's authority and his commitment to the possibility of a vibrant postreligious Jewish national life. Coming of age during the tumult of the 1905 Revolution, few of them had opportunities for sustained university training and were, therefore, autodidacts who wrote on a broad range of topics and in a wide range of genres, including scholarly journals, the popular press, pedagogical materials, and political propaganda.

Although he ranks as among the most prominent leaders of the Russian Social Democrat movement, to scholars of Eastern European Jewry and Yiddish, Raphael Abramovitch is today largely unknown. However, more than any other figure, he would become central to launching and maintaining the encyclopedia for most of its three dozen years and its many displacements and relocations. Abramovitch would also be a polarizing figure throughout the history of the encyclopedia. His outright scorn for Zionism was too radical for some and was seen as a threat to the "Jewish" character of the project. For others, his fierce and uncompromising anti-Bolshevism would be the basis of criticism. However, of all the participants at the February 1931 meeting, he was one of the most consistently involved with the encyclopedia—remaining active until the mid-1950s—and the most influential on its content and form.

Born Rafael Rein in 1880 in Dvinsk, Latvia (now Daugavpils), to a family of timber merchants, Abramovitch received religious training in *kheyder* (elementary school) and a secular secondary education from the age of fourteen.[48]

FIGURE 1.2 Raphael Abramovitch, c. 1910 (courtesy of International Institute of Social History, Amsterdam).

In 1899, he attended Riga Polytechnic University to study mechanical engineering, but inspired by the nationalist fervor of his Polish classmates, he became a student activist and joined the (illegal) Jewish Labor Bund in 1901. He was exposed to Marxist texts such as the *Erfurt Program* (1891), the 1891 platform of the German Social Democratic Party written by the Social Democrat leader and Marxist theorist Karl Kautsky,[49] and to the Zionist writings of Max Nordau, and he began to write Yiddish articles for the Bundist *Arbeter-shtime* in 1902. He was expelled from university that same year and thereafter dedicated his life fully to political activism, living underground in what was been called by one biographer an "illegal life."[50] To elude the authorities in Riga, he assumed the name Avram (after his father) and lengthened it to Abramovitch during the 1905 revolutionary upheavals. In 1903, he escaped the country and, after short stays in Berlin and Liège, settled in Geneva to join a community of exiled Bundist activists. He returned to Russia in 1904 to work with the Bund in Warsaw (where he was arrested and held in prison for several months) and became a member of its central committee, representing it in the St. Petersburg Soviet during the 1905 Revolution. In 1906, he joined the central committee of the Russian Social Democratic Workers' Party (RSDWP) following the

Bund's reentry.[51] He spent the period from November 1907 to May 1908 in the United States, on the first of several such trips, raising much-needed money for the Bund. He helped edit Russian-language Marxist journals that were targeted toward Jewish workers and organized party congresses. On account of his illegal political activity, he was arrested in 1910 and sent into exile in the Vologda Province. Upon escaping in January of the following year, he lived in Heidelberg and Vienna, where he was active among the Bundist leadership and wrote for the Russian and Yiddish press. He joined with fellow internationalists in opposing World War I.

Abramovitch returned to Russia in May 1917 to participate in the revolution as a member of the Menshevik faction, which he believed offered the best chance to bring about the emancipation of Russian Jewry, and he served on the central committees of both the Bund and the Mensheviks. Following the Bolshevik Revolution in October, he repeatedly advocated for a multiparty socialist government as a means to thwart Bolshevik hegemony. In July 1918, he was arrested by the Cheka (the Soviet state security organization) for his constant criticism of the regime, in spite of siding with those who encouraged only strictly legal forms of protest. Slated for execution, he was freed after six months in prison on account of pressure from European socialist leaders. Throughout the period of the Russian Civil War (1918–1920), Abramovitch continued with Menshevik and Bundist activity.[52]

Abramovitch left Soviet Russia for Berlin in November 1920 and joined up with his fellow Menshevik Julius Martov, and soon after, they were joined by Fyodor Dan. Abramovitch believed that his stay abroad would be short, having predicted that the Bolsheviks would not be able to maintain their hold on power for long. He would in fact never return to the Soviet Union. Throughout his time in Berlin, Abramovitch adhered closely to the "Martov Line," which insisted that in spite of their opposition to the Bolshevik regime, socialists must not advocate overthrow of the Communist state by bourgeois forces or external armies.[53] With Martov's death, in 1923, leadership of the Mensheviks fell to Dan, in part because there remained a persistent suspicion of those party members who, like Abramovitch, had Bundist ties and who had not been with the party from the beginning. Nevertheless, Abramovitch became the public face of the Menshevik opposition, representing it at international conferences, in its publications, and on international speaking tours. The historian André Liebich notes, "Whereas Dan, the consummate politician, managed the affairs of the party, Abramovitch, with peerless diplomatic skill, represented the party to the outside world. An urbane, witty, and cosmopolitan polyglot, Abramovitch deployed boundless energy in cultivating contacts with foreign socialists, political leaders, and opinion makers."[54] These contacts would prove essential to Abramovitch's 1940 escape to the United States and continued work on the encyclopedia following the German invasion of Western Europe.

In addition to his political work, which included editing and contributing to the Menshevik journal *Sotsialisticheskii vestnik* (Socialist courier), Abramovitch was a prolific author and editor who published Yiddish scholarly essays and several book-length works. In the midst of his early revolutionary period, Abramovitch attempted to publish a Yiddish-language encyclopedia, but he abandoned the project when his sample chapter was rejected by the publisher Saul Ginsburg.[55] In Berlin in the 1920s, he worked as an editor at the Yiddish publishing house Wostok and also wrote a popular history of the Jews (coauthored with Avrom Menes).[56] Abramovitch's primary source of income during his Berlin period was serving as a correspondent for the *Forverts*, having struck up a friendship with its editor, Abraham Cahan, during Cahan's visit to the city in 1921. As Gennady Estraikh relates, Abramovitch's articles served as a counterpoint to the generally sympathetic portrayal of the Bolsheviks that appeared in the newspaper in the early 1920s.[57]

The group that came together to publish a Yiddish encyclopedia in Dubnow's honor was one, therefore, that was both politically and occupationally diverse and represented an influential swath of the Eastern European Jewish landscape. As part of a generation of leaders who had come of age during the upheavals of 1905, they were by the 1930s among the leading architects of the resurgence of modern Yiddish culture. No longer young and less inclined toward advocating for revolutionary change, they looked to this joint venture as a way to advance their shared vision for the Jewish future. As an extension of their political, cultural, and humanitarian efforts, the Yiddish encyclopedia was to be a means by which to further anchor Yiddish-speaking Jews to the modern world and assert their rightful place within it.

"If We Will It . . .": Planning the Encyclopedia

In Dubnow's brief yet rich address at the February gathering, he described encyclopedias not merely as a compendium of knowledge but as a "people's book," a communal project of the nation for whom it was written. In comparing this new Yiddish encyclopedic venture—this "bible for the new age"—with Moses Mendelssohn's "bible in German," Dubnow was referring to the project by the philosopher who, in 1783 as the leader of the Jewish Enlightenment movement known as the Haskalah, was the first to publish the

Hebrew-language Pentateuch (first five books of the Hebrew Bible) into German, along with a commentary known as the *Bi'ur*. The goal of Mendelssohn and his collaborators was to demonstrate that Enlightenment philosophy and loyalty to one's state were compatible with Jewish tradition and law. The controversy that ensued was so profound and the influence of the translation was so powerful that for many—including the historian Dubnow—it marked a new era in Jewish history, comparable to that of Martin Luther's famous sixteenth-century German Bible translation for the history of Christian peoples.

The historians Mordechai Breuer and Michael Graetz have shown, however, that Mendelssohn's decade-long translation likely owed less to Luther than to the French *Encyclopédie* project of Denis Diderot and the French philosophes,[58] whose aim, according to Breuer and Graetz, "was to familiarize the broader public in eighteenth-century France with the rational conceptions of Enlightenment, encapsulated in the form of a collectively authored work presented in a popular style. Taking into account its specific genre and distinctive features, the Bible translation and accompanying *Bi'ur* can nonetheless be viewed as a similar experiment to popularize enlightened conceptions."[59] To Mendelssohn's supporters, his translation made available what was for many acculturated German Jews an otherwise inaccessible Hebrew Bible and helped them to preserve their increasingly strained ties to Judaism as well as to innovate new forms of worship. To his detractors, however, the translation was yet another step on the road to total assimilation by relieving German-speaking Jews of the obligation to learn Hebrew. The *Bi'ur*, in fact, did work bidirectionally. It provided a means for German-reading Jews to become better acquainted with the Hebrew script and became a pathway for some to greater adherence to Jewish law, customs, and identification. Simultaneously, it served many Jews as a guide to the German language.[60] By likening the planned Yiddish encyclopedia to Mendelssohn's translation, Dubnow was in fact drawing attention to the reversed roles of language and content among the two projects. If Mendelssohn's Bible had translated and interpreted Jewish knowledge into a non-Jewish language, the new encyclopedia would then make general knowledge comprehensible to Yiddish readers. In creating a Yiddish-language encyclopedia of general knowledge, the onetime revolutionaries who gathered in 1931 in Berlin were embarking on a decidedly Enlightenment-era project, albeit in the name of Jewish national development.

For Dubnow, an encyclopedia was a vital component of the emerging Jewish nation, a text that, following the model set by other minority groups in

Europe, "each nation must possess." With it, Jews were to be educated not only in self-knowledge—including their own history, language, traditions, and culture—but also in the knowledge of the entire world. Dubnow was largely satisfied that, by 1931, Jews had sufficient access to encyclopedic information on Jewish topics. Overstating the ability of most Yiddish-speaking Jews to read Russian, he declared that, "Today, what one struggles for is no longer information on Jewish questions, for one has recourse to the Jewish encyclopedia in Russian," a reference to the *Evreiskaia entsiklopediia*. What was still lacking was a means by which to move Jews beyond self-knowledge and to an understanding of the larger world, in order to participate in it as informed Jews. For Dubnow, this "bible for the new age" had the potential to unify the Jewish people in a way similar to how the Torah established Jewish peoplehood at Mount Sinai and Mendelssohn's translation began the process of their modernization.

Following Dubnow's opening address, a number of key issues were discussed over the two-day meeting, several of which presaged future debates about the encyclopedia. Topics included organizational questions, such as financing, publication schedule, administrative and editorial control, and the extent to which YIVO would be engaged in the day-to-day affairs of the project. Other topics included issues of outlook and content: the encyclopedia's focus, its length and duration, its target audience, the ratio of general to Jewish knowledge, and the degree to which it would maintain distance—following the example of YIVO—from contemporary politics.

At the end, several resolutions were agreed upon, the first of which was the formal decision by the group to commit to the encyclopedia: "The conference finds that the growing cultural needs of the Jewish masses and the developing state of Jewish scholarship make it necessary and possible to publish a general encyclopedia in Yiddish, and recommends that this undertaking should be the primary task of the Dubnow Fund which was created by the Yiddish Scientific Institute to honor the 70th birthday of S. Dubnow."[61] It was further resolved that the encyclopedia would consist of ten volumes focusing on "all branches of knowledge" and one supplement on specifically Jewish topics. It would be published at a rate of two volumes a year, and would be completed within six to seven years. Funds would be raised by selling shares of $50.00 each with a limit of one thousand shares. A base of $50,000 would be raised immediately and total costs were projected to be approximately $200,000. While YIVO in Vilna would retain control over administrative affairs, the daily work of the encyclopedia would be the responsibility of the Dubnow Fund in Berlin so that YIVO's other scholarly projects and fund-raising would not be overwhelmed. In what may have been a response to the question of what would make this encyclopedia "Jewish" besides the language in which it was written, Moyshe Shalit declared that all of the contributors should themselves be Jewish (with no reported opposition to this curious requirement).

According to Meisel, whose account, "From Dream to Reality," published in *Literarishe bleter* serves as the closest version of an official report of the February 1931 meeting, the plan to create an encyclopedia was nothing less than the fulfillment of a long-held desire of the Jewish people. Writing just days after the meeting, Meisel went so far as to equate the encyclopedia with the dream of Jewish statehood that had been so famously articulated by the Zionist Congress founder Theodor Herzl, as Meisel concluded his report with "If we will it, we will have a Yiddish encyclopedia."[62]

Preparations for the encyclopedia immediately got underway following the February meeting. While administrative work in Vilna seems not to have progressed particularly far, the Berlin-based Dubnow Fund quickly began to organize, opening an office on Uhlandstrasse, in the Charlottenburg district, and printing letterhead. Members of the newly formed "Central Committee," which included Bramson as chair, Abramovitch as vice-chair, and Avrom Kin as secretary, began contacting potential contributors and supporters, while Nokhem Gergel oversaw fund-raising efforts. In May, the committee released an informational brochure about the newly launched project in the hope of attracting investors and subscribers.

As the initial publication of the Dubnow Fund, the brochure was the organization's first attempt to define the project to the public. Drawing upon the prestige generated by the close ties to YIVO and Dubnow, the Central Committee made its pitch to potential subscribers. They spoke of the project as something new and distinct from the earlier encyclopedias marketed to Jewish readers: "We have in mind not only 'Jewish studies,' Jewish history, and 'Judaica,' but in fact an encyclopedia of general knowledge in the Yiddish language."[63] With the title *Algemeyne entsiklopedye* (General encyclopedia), the editors were proclaiming implicitly what they would go on to say directly: the planned general encyclopedia was a recognition that Yiddish-speaking Jewry had reached a new level of maturation and could move beyond its particular interests and engage fully with the larger world, but in their own language: "Our communal and cultural development during the preceding era has paved the way, deepened the importance, and made it possible realize this important national undertaking." They went on to refer to the ways that Yiddish-speaking Jewry had developed since the end of the nineteenth century, producing a generation of Jews who were for the first time capable of participating in

European life and culture. The shift away from a traditional, unsophisticated Jewish life toward engagement with the modern political and culture world has occurred, they argued, not only in the "higher" realms but among the masses of the "lower folk-strata" as well.[64]

At the same time that Jews were participating in European life, they were also developing their own autonomous secular Yiddish-language institutions and creating a broad readership for the encyclopedia: "Indeed, before our eyes our poor *mame-loshn* ["mother tongue," a common term of endearment for Yiddish] has transformed into a mature cultural language." The Central Committee pointed to the fact that only a few decades before, there did not exist even a single daily newspaper in Yiddish, and there now were literally hundreds of newspapers being read by millions. They noted that while in the last decades of the nineteenth century modern Yiddish literature was only making its first tentative steps, by 1931 it was taking its place among the younger European literatures. In response, they declared that "there is now a great camp of writers, who work in the various regions of literature, art, science, and journalism and who together have erected the multistoried building of modern culture in Yiddish."[65] Whereas forty years earlier there had not been a single modern Yiddish school, the authors could point to two thousand Yiddish schools that were currently teaching nearly two hundred thousand students. Consequently, "in several countries there has arisen a new generation who express themselves culturally in Yiddish; a generation that has received their education and upbringing in the Yiddish language." The brochure then repeated the resolutions that had been made at the February meeting and printed a long list of supporters. It included not only many of the luminaries in the Yiddish intellectual world, but also such internationally recognized figures as Eduard Bernstein, Albert Einstein, and Sigmund Freud.

Building upon this momentum, in spring 1931, Gergel, acting as a *sholiekh* (emissary), sailed on the RMS *Majestic* to the United States to raise funds for YIVO and the encyclopedia.[66] The highlight of his tour, which took him to several cities in the Northeast, was a major gathering held in early summer in New York City and chaired by the theater critic Alexander Mukdoni (pen name of Aleksander Kapel) and the playwright David Pinski. At the meeting were assembled over 150 of the leading figures of the New York Yiddish and left-wing intelligentsia, including representatives from YIVO's American Section, the Sholem Aleichem Folk Institute, and labor unions. The opening address was given by Alexander Harkavy, the Yiddish linguist, lexicographer, and author of the first great Yiddish-English dictionary. Dubnow and the German Social Democrat leader Eduard Bernstein sent in telegrams of support, as did many key figures active in the project. Over $2,000 was immediately raised for the encyclopedia and an American Committee of the encyclopedia was soon launched, with Pinski as chair and Mukdoni and the labor activist and editor Joseph Schlossberg serving as vice-chairs. Prominent Jewish leaders, including the Diaspora Nationalist theoretician Chaim Zhitlowsky, the labor leader Baruch Charney Vladeck, and the poet Avrom Reisen served on the organizing committee along with more than a hundred others.

To Ben Zion Goldberg, an editor at the New York Yiddish daily *Der Tog* (The day), the launching of a Yiddish encyclopedia was as momentous as YIVO's founding in the mid-1920s. He recalled that Nokhem Shtif's 1925 plan for the institute had originally received only a lukewarm response by many who thought the proposal was completely unrealizable. Despite the hesitations, there now exists, he extolled, "a beautiful scholarly institute with such professors!" He went on to say that those people who once scoffed at the idea of a Yiddish scholarly institute and were ashamed of Yiddish will no doubt do so once again and will be proven wrong a second time: "One volume will arrive and then a second, and those people who once turned up their noses will see that the Yiddish encyclopedia is not of a lower stature than encyclopedias in other languages. I believe in the encyclopedia."[67]

Fracturing Consensus

Despite Dubnow's great optimism, the appearance of accord and compromise that brought about the resolutions on behalf of the project, and the generally positive reception with which they were greeted in the press, excitement over the encyclopedia was not entirely universal. The *Algemeyne entsiklopedye* would for its entire existence remain a contentious project over which debates on the future of the Yiddish language and Eastern European Jewry were frequently played out. In the fourteen months that lay between the February 1931 planning meeting in Berlin and the publication of a *probeheft* (sample volume) for potential subscribers in April 1932, the project was enmeshed in so much conflict and controversy that it nearly collapsed. Detractors attacked it on the basis of the planners' supposed lack of scholarly objectivity; the extent to which they understood the cultural needs of their intended readers or grasped the theoretical, commercial, and practical complexities of such a massive undertaking; and the appropriate balance between "general" and "Jewish" content.

Criticisms appeared almost immediately. Only days after Meisel's enthusiastic official report of the Berlin gathering, a second, unofficial account appeared, penned under the pseudonym "H. Yulski" and published in the new Bundist literary journal *Vokhnshrift* (Weekly).[68] Based upon the information in the essay, Yulski, who claimed to be reporting from Berlin, likely was either present at the mid-February meeting or closely connected to someone who was. Although Yulski began the critique by saying that the planning meeting was as significant as the late-summer 1908 conference in Czernowitz that played a key role in launching the Yiddish-language movement, he or she went on to raise several concerns about the project, many of which would in fact come to haunt the encyclopedia in future years.

Speaking in the name of the same Yiddish readership on whose behalf the Dubnow Fund's members purported to be working, Yulski expressed concerns that ranged from the relatively trivial, such as complaining about how much time was spent to reach relatively meager decisions, to far more substantial ones, such as asking whether those assembled were too far removed—geographically and ideologically—from the Eastern European Yiddish-speaking masses for whom the encyclopedia was intended. Yulski doubted the extent to which the planners were committed to the long-term goal of realizing the project and chastised them for articulating only vague goals. Yulski attacked Max Weinreich's repeated insistence that the encyclopedia be strictly apolitical and questioned whether such neutrality was even feasible given the participation of such overtly political figures as Abramovitch. "Already at the first meeting," Yulski wrote, "Mr. R. Abramovitch set the tone for the political direction and character of the encyclopedia. Several speakers after him clearly formulated its character as a socialist one, while others [formulated it as] a Social Democratic one." Yulski mockingly described Weinreich, who insisted upon YIVO's maintaining the strictest political neutrality, as an epicurean who arrived at the meeting with his "usual deep fear of the 'sitra achra' [literally "other side," but meaning "immorality"] of politics." Yulski accused the entire Berlin group of elitism and argued that they had not considered the pedagogical needs of those likely to benefit most from an encyclopedia, such as students in the secular Jewish school system in Poland.

Yulski particularly criticized YIVO for its decision to maintain a nonpartisan stance on subjects of immediate concern to Eastern European Jews. Such a position was hotly contested throughout YIVO's pre-World War II existence, with internal tensions among its staff and contributors, many of whom had strong ties to political parties.[69] From its very founding, in 1925, there were disagreements over whether to include prominent pro-Soviet and Bundist activists in its activities. Weinreich was deeply concerned that the inclusion of such scholars would give YIVO the taint of sectarianism. In fact, as

Kuznitz has shown: "In virtually every area of its activity YIVO found this boundary difficult to negotiate, as it was often caught up in the fierce competition among the varied political movements of interwar Eastern Europe."[70] This fear of engaging in any activity that would have the appearance of politics led YIVO's Berlin-based Economic-Statistical Section to hesitate when researching current demographic and economic questions facing post–World War I Jewish communities and prevented it from establishing formal ties to ORT's vocational training program. Similar concerns led the Vilna-based Psychological-Pedagogical Section to decline cooperating with Yiddish schools in producing pedagogical materials or engaging in mutual fund-raising campaigns. Although YIVO's "neutrality" was maintained throughout the interwar years, it would be constantly challenged by those who thought the institution unnecessarily separated itself from the very people it was supposed to serve.

Yulski's concerns likewise echoed an oft-leveled and not unrelated criticism made against the Berlin émigré community throughout the 1920s. Many had settled there to find a respite from the politically charged climate of Jewish Poland, which has been described by Ezra Mendelsohn as ruled by "extreme divisiveness, factionalism, personal hatreds, and the like."[71] This decision to physically distance themselves from the tumult also left the the Berlin émigrés exposed to frequent reproach for abandoning the Jewish masses. For example, writing from Warsaw, the writers Peretz Markish and Melech Ravitch attacked Berlin's café culture, which they saw as a withdrawal from the fight for Jewish culture in Poland, and accused Berlin's Eastern European Jews of being "traitors to their heritage" who had abdicated their responsibility to Yiddish.[72] Similarly, the poet and essayist David Einhorn, who had spent several years in the city in the early 1920s, criticized Berlin's Yiddish literary elite for not re-creating the Kultur-lige community that had briefly flourished in Kiev. Anne-Christin Saß writes, "In [Einhorn's] opinion, the prominent migrants would sit at the 'marble tables' in ... [Berlin's] Romanisches Café, clustering around the 'rich pots' of Jewish philanthropy, drinking coffee, and pretending that from there they could save the whole Jewish nation."[73]

A second critical, albeit less hostile report from a participant at the February conference appeared in early September in *Literarishe bleter* by the North America-based scholar A. A. Roback, who began his essay by agreeing with the basic premise of the February conference that the need for a Yiddish-language encyclopedia was clear and no longer worthy of debate: "Whether from an educational perspective, a cultural one, from a Yiddishist, or even a social-economic one—the Yiddish encyclopedia is a matter of great importance for

Jews."[74] By the time of his report, Roback had been asked to contribute to the encyclopedia. Although he agreed and would eventually provide an entry on the psychologist William James, he expressed several concerns about the decisions reached in Berlin, including the "patently-radical" politics of several of the participants, a clear reference to Abramovitch.

Of most concern to Roback were the brevity of the planned volumes and the seeming rush to completion. It was inconceivable to him that general and Jewish topics could each be adequately covered in only ten volumes and in such a short period of time. Pointing to other European encyclopedias that were much more expansive, Roback argued that the Yiddish encyclopedia must be at least comparable. He recognized that the lack of a central state authority and any territorial contiguity among Jews presented obstacles, but they did not have to be insurmountable ones: "I realize that it is not appropriate to make comparisons with the encyclopedias of other peoples, given that we have no state that can allocate the needed funds for such a cause, and we also do not have access to wealthy and powerful [benefactors] that a Judaistic encyclopedia would attract. While I realize that this is doubtlessly true, it is necessary that the size of the encyclopedia be enlarged, and even if the final volume appears in 20 years, it is better for us to have an equivalent project, than take pride in a symbol of poverty."[75]

A third critique of the project appeared in the pages of the monthly journal *YIVO Bleter* (*YIVO journal*), one of YIVO's own institutional publications.[76] In a long two-part essay, Yosef Yashunsky sought to intervene in the planning of the encyclopedia by injecting a strong dose of pragmatism and advice gained from his own experience. Unlike most of the other participants and critics, Yashunsky had firsthand knowledge of the work and structures that were necessary to the success of such projects. A onetime editor for Brockhaus and Efron's Russian-language *Novyi entsiklopedicheskii slovar'* (New encyclopedic dictionary), which appeared between 1911 and 1916, he had been invested in the idea of creating a Yiddish encyclopedia for over a decade.[77] From his base in Warsaw, where he was a journalist, an ORT leader, and a bibliographer for YIVO, Yashunsky expressed concern that the planners of the encyclopedia were unequipped to manage such a large project. He challenged them to confront a series of practical issues that he considered essential to the encyclopedia's success. Up to that time, public discussions of the encyclopedia were generally marked by ideological discussions and expressions of enthusiasm for its great potential, and tended to avoid the less glamorous but vital editorial, technical, and financial aspects of such a massive undertaking. Yashunsky's essay points to the fact that the lack of a publisher, state-funded research institution, or financially stable organizational support would present nearly impossible problems for the venture.

A decade earlier, in a 1922 *Bikhervelt* essay discussing various failed efforts to publish a Yiddish encyclopedia, Yashunsky had written, "From these [attempts], one can learn a lesson in how *not* to publish encyclopedias, and also how to ensure that such labors are positive."[78] In his *YIVO Bleter* essay, he sought to remedy those past failures by issuing a stern warning to those involved with the new endeavor. Previous attempts were unsuccessful for a variety of reasons, including the absence of a unified purpose, mismanagement, uncertain political and economic environments, and the paucity of Yiddish-language terminology in the realms of science and technology. Above all, past encyclopedias had failed because of the planners' lack of clarity on the sort of encyclopedias they had hoped to publish. Yashunsky's essay, therefore, was intended to be a much-needed systematic examination of the types of national encyclopedias that currently existed, including their size, length, and number of illustrations, and it made several recommendations as to which extant encyclopedias could serve as useful models for the new Yiddish venture.

Reflecting his preference for a general encyclopedia that would contain a relatively small portion of specifically Jewish topics, Yashunsky refrained from analyzing the history of recent Jewish encyclopedias and focused instead on the "great" national encyclopedias such as the English-language *Britannica*, the French-language *Larousse*, the German-language *Brockhaus*, and the Russian-language *Bolshaia sovetskaia entsiklopediia* (Great Soviet encyclopedia), as well as several compact encyclopedic handbooks that were often published as companions to the larger ones. Yashunsky disagreed with many of the Yiddish encyclopedia's strongest advocates about its purpose, size, direction, and imagined audience. Shalit and Robak, for example, had agitated for a long-term, comprehensive multivolume work that would be written at a scholarly level. In their conception, the Yiddish encyclopedia would be a decades-long project that was based upon the model set by the French *Larousse*. Shalit had earlier argued, "We want to create science in Yiddish, not popularizations."[79] However, Yashunsky countered that such "great" encyclopedias reflected an outmoded, nineteenth-century understanding of knowledge that was entirely impractical in the present day. Despite Robak's insistence that there was plenty of time available to produce a multivolume encyclopedia, Yashunsky described how the French *Encyclopédie méthodique par ordre des matières* (1782–1832) stretched to 166 volumes and Ersch and Gruber's *Allgemeine Encyclopädie der Wissenschaften und Künste* (1818–1889) went to 167 volumes. The result was that both projects were many decades in the making, and by the time the later volumes appeared, the information in the earlier ones had become thoroughly obsolete. Compounding the problem was that in the twentieth century, knowledge was growing too vast and was becoming too diverse for such projects to be viable; "present day knowledge," Yashunsky insisted, "has become so ramified that no one encyclopedia is able to encompass it all."[80] Instead, he argued, the new trend in encyclopedias was for specialized encyclopedias written for targeted audiences (such as ones published for those in the trades and professions) and compact encyclopedias for mass audiences. This, he argued, was a consequence of the success of the social changes in the previous decades, "The democratization of cultural life has created large cadres of readers for whom grand encyclopedias are not an appropriate fit."[81] To serve the Jewish masses, he argued, what was needed was a popular encyclopedia for Yiddish readers that followed the current models. He warned, "If we permit the [encyclopedia] not to have a precise scope, the work will grow and grow, and it will likely not be brought to conclusion."[82]

In Yashunsky's view, the new Yiddish encyclopedia, which he hailed as a "grandiose national and cultural publication," should speak to the needs of the broad Yiddish-reading public. He predicted that the audience for the encyclopedia was potentially vast and made up not only of those who regularly read Yiddish books, but also occasional readers and multilingual Jews who typically turned to languages other than Yiddish for scholarly information. To reach this mass readership, he advocated for an encyclopedia that would be compact in size, at no more than ten volumes and thirty million characters; written for a broad reading public; take no more than five years to complete; be reasonably priced at no more than $50 per set (an amount that was in fact out of reach for most Yiddish speakers, especially during the Depression); and contain a ratio of 85 percent general knowledge to 15 percent Jewish.[83] Yashunsky disagreed with an argument made by Abramovitch that the editors should assume a very low level of knowledge among the readers regarding natural science, mathematics, and technologies but a higher level of knowledge of social, political, national, and communal matters.[84] Such assumptions would produce, in his opinion, an unevenly written encyclopedia that would be ripe for failure.

At YIVO's October 1930 meeting, during which plans for the encyclopedia were first discussed, Yashunsky had expressed his doubts as to whether the encyclopedia would be politically neutral enough to appeal to the entire Yiddish-reading public.[85] By late 1931, this concern seems to have been satisfied, for he argued that while the question of political impartiality was

important, he believed that it must not void the encyclopedia of any character whatsoever. Instead, he was concerned with what would become a much
more contested realm: the relationship between general and Jewish knowledge. At the February 1931 meeting in Berlin, it had been decided that the
encyclopedia would contain two-thirds general and one-third Jewish subject matter. Although some argued that the amount of Jewish information
was too low (and in fact some hoped that the Yiddish encyclopedia would be
a wholly Jewish one), for Yashunsky, one-third was much too high. As earlier,
the issue for Yashunsky was one of consistency. Since the general section
would only have room to discuss first-rate artists, writers, and thinkers,
the Jewish section should read similarly. However, to dedicate one-third of
the available space to Jewish subjects would result in the inclusion of entries
on third- and fourth-rate Jewish artists, writers, and thinkers—resulting in
a highly skewed representation.

Yashunsky's most astute observation came, however, when reflecting on an
inherent contradiction within the project, one that would become pronounced as the volumes began to take shape in the coming years. The organizers, he noted, were exclusively comprised of committed cultural and political
activists who were deeply informed of the breadth and depth of Jewish learning, and yet they were attempting to produce a work of general reference, which
rested outside the area of their expertise and experiences. "In their minds they
understand," he wrote, "that an encyclopedia in Yiddish must be a general
one, but in their hearts rest the Jewish parts."[86]

First Crises

Yashunsky's essay appeared just as several crises threatened to derail the
entire undertaking. While many of the subsequent interruptions had external
causes such as the Nazi seizure of power in 1933 and the German invasion of
Paris in 1940, this time the difficulties were strictly internal.

In late November 1931, the Dubnow Fund's chief fundraiser, Nokhem Gergel,
suddenly died of a heart attack, at age 44. An important scholar of the pogroms against Jews in Ukraine in 1919, and an activist long engaged with
Jewish humanitarian causes, Gergel had lived in Berlin since 1921 and been
present at the planning of the encyclopedia since its conception. Gergel was,
according to Meisel, "one of the most energetic, steadfast defenders of the
magnificent project."[87]

Compounding the encyclopedia's challenges was an organizational split
between YIVO and the Dubnow Fund that had been simmering since the

FIGURE 1.3 Nokhem Gergel (courtesy of YIVO).

spring and began to boil over in the final weeks of 1931. Although consensus had been reached in February 1931 as to the encyclopedia's scope and direction, differences of opinion between the Berlin and Vilna groups on how to proceed remained unresolved. Information regarding the schism is scarce, but it appears to have been related to financial constraints within both organizations, questions over the necessity of the *probeheft*, and ideological differences between the two communities of scholars.[88]

The relationship between the Yiddish intellectual communities in Vilna and Berlin had been thorny since YIVO's founding. Although Berlin was the site from which Nokhem Shtif wrote his 1925 plan for the institute, even he had vacillated on the question of where it should be based. Whereas Berlin offered the prestige, wealth, and scholarly resources of a central European city, Vilna provided proximity to the Yiddish-speaking masses and Eastern European Jewish cultural institutions.[89] In the end, the issue was largely decided by the fact that work got underway more quickly and successfully in Vilna than in Berlin and that by spring 1926 the city known as "the Jerusalem of Lithuania" was clearly the winning location. Nevertheless, tensions developed between the two communities as Berlin declined in importance and several of its key figures, including Shtif and Tcherikower, took up residency elsewhere.[90]

There is also little evidence that the encyclopedia's fund-raising efforts secured the monies required to begin the project. Given that by fall 1931, there are no further references to the proposed system by which $50 shares would be sold in exchange for a subscription, it is safe to conclude that it was not very successful. In 1931, $50 was an astronomical price for many members of the encyclopedia's imagined audience, especially for most Polish Jews during the Depression. At the same time, YIVO was suffering from severe financial troubles of its own, in part because of its building project, which taxed the organization's modest resources far beyond expectations. The gap between the organization's ambitions and its resources was growing ever wider. An internal memo in late November 1931 described YIVO as being in a "financially catastrophic condition."[91] Since the earliest discussions of the encyclopedia, Weinreich had been concerned that the project might grow too vast and overwhelm YIVO's other commitments. The original plan to divide the administrative and editorial tasks between Vilna and Berlin was intended to avoid a competition over resources.

As the encyclopedia project and the YIVO building campaign were getting underway, YIVO was also in the midst of publishing its own monthly journal, despite financial constraints. *YIVO Bleter* was launched in early 1931, and from the first issue, it set a new standard for Yiddish scholarly research. As the realization of a vision articulated by Zalmen Reisen at YIVO's 1929 conference, during which much of the institute's agenda was decided, the journal is notable not only for the high quality of its articles and stature of its contributors, but also—in keeping with Weinreich's oft-repeated insistence on YIVO's nonpartisanship—the total absence of articles that directly consider contemporary politics.[92] In the introduction to *YIVO Bleter*'s first issue, the editors articulated the tension between their lofty aspirations and their financial capacity, and rather than providing a full programmatic statement on the journal's aims and standards, they were frank about their doubts as to whether YIVO was able to sustain this "new burden."[93] In spite of these fears, the Central Committee remained committed to the project as it filled an otherwise large void in YIVO's publications, which had up to then either consisted of book-length compendiums of articles from several of its key research sections or shorter articles in its newsletter, *Yedies* (News). At the same time, *YIVO Bleter*'s editors optimistically hoped that it might find an audience beyond the Yiddish-speaking Jewish intelligentsia and "help satisfy the great thirst for knowledge that exists among our broad masses." The structure of the journal was to correspond to YIVO's four sections: philology, history, economics and statistics, and psychology and pedagogy. In addition, it would provide information about YIVO itself and its archival materials and would be a "central tribune for all Yiddish scholarly work."[94]

From one perspective, it seems likely that *YIVO Bleter* and the *Algemeyne entsiklopedye* might have complemented one another. After all, *YIVO Bleter* was created as a forum for journal-length scholarly essays on Jewish topics published for a learned audience, whereas the *Algemeyne entsiklopedye* was to feature encyclopedia-length entries on general topics for a mass readership. However, given the scant funds that were available in this time of economic depression, it was unlikely that they could avoid being in competition. Additionally, the two publications also reflected ideological differences; at stake in the debates was the issue of what sort of information did modernizing, secularizing Jews in the 1930s need most. Did they need to be educated most in the facts of the larger world, or did they need to be acquainted with contemporary research on the Jewish national community? The encyclopedia's planners in Berlin assumed that its Yiddish audience would benefit most from "a Yiddish encyclopedic handbook, from which they will be able to draw the precise scholarly ascertained information that they currently lack in their daily work."[95] As Dubnow stated in his February address, there already was an abundance of sources for those seeking knowledge about Jewish studies. By 1931, Yiddish readers even had access to a Yiddish translation of Dubnow's own ten-volume history of world Jewry, the *Weltgeschichte des jüdischen Volkes* (World History of the Jewish People).[96] By contrast, the mission of YIVO, as reflected in *YIVO Bleter* and its other publications, was primarily to be a source for the latest scientific research on Jewish civilization. In truth, the debate between the encyclopedists and the Vilna circles was less absolute than it was one of emphasis, however, as the Yiddish encyclopedia was planned to contain a significant amount of specifically Jewish content, and YIVO periodically published works drawn from outside of the Jewish world.

The decision, in summer 1932, to publish a *probeheft* to attract potential subscribers and supporters was also a point of contention between the two camps. The idea originated during Gergel's visit to New York, where potential funders repeatedly asked to see a physical sample of the proposed encyclopedia. By midsummer, the editors began to work on a specimen volume, drawing up a list of key terms from a wide range of topics and identifying potential authors. In spite of broad interest, the publication was not approved by YIVO's Central Committee on account of the cost, yet Bramson and the Dubnow Fund nonetheless proceeded to solicit donations for it.[97]

These tensions finally came to a head at a hastily called gathering in Berlin on December 26–27, 1931. At the meeting, Simon Dubnow served as chair, and representatives of the Dubnow Fund included Abramovitch, Bramson, Ben-Adir, Daniel Charney, Kin, Aron Singalowsky, Steinberg, and Mark Wischnitzer. Representing YIVO was the director of the Joint Distribution Committee in Poland, Yitzhak Giterman, along with Lestschinsky, Reisen, Tcherikower, and Yashunsky. Weinreich remained in Vilna on account of illness, which may have been the result of an injury that he sustained in a pogrom in Vilna the month before, during which he permanently lost sight in one of his eyes.[98] The first day was organizational in nature, and it was decided to make the *Entsiklopedye* not only informational, covering all branches of science, but also more deliberately pedagogical. A new compromise between those who wanted the encyclopedia to be general in nature and those who wanted it to stress Jewish topics was also reached: 30 percent of the material would be dedicated to Jewish matters, with the bulk of this content appearing in a supplemental, eleventh volume entitled *Yidn* (Jews).[99]

The second day of the meeting was dedicated to issues of oversight and control. It was decided that the prior arrangement of having two managerial units—one housed at YIVO in Vilna and another housed with the Dubnow Fund in Berlin—would be scrapped. Such a system meant long delays at various stages of a task, and often the duplication of efforts. The *Entsiklopedye* would henceforth become a project entirely of the Dubnow Fund in Berlin, and YIVO agreed to lend its public support and encouragement to the project. A joint communiqué released following the meeting described the decision as due to economic reasons, claiming that the current financial crisis could not allow for two homes for the *Entsiklopedye*. It further stated: "Let it be noted through this statement by the YIVO leadership that they consider the encyclopedia to be an important cultural project and wish to call upon all friends and sympathizers of YIVO to support the Dubnow Fund as much as possible in this enormous task with which it is entrusted."[100]

Despite the appearance of conviviality between the two parties, there is evidence that there was more to the split than economics. Yashunsky's memorandum in *YIVO Bleter* referred to general disagreements among contributors over the scope and size of the project. More pointedly, several letters from Abramovitch and Lestschinsky to supporters in the United States, asking them to contribute to the now-delayed *probeheft*, refer explicitly to "differences of opinion and questions of competence with YIVO" that made it necessary to dissolve the formal relationship.[101] Some supporters, such as Mukdoni, who was a vice-chair of the American Committee, threatened to pull their support for the encyclopedia, since it was no longer going to be a project of YIVO.[102] Nevertheless, members of YIVO in Berlin and Vilna remained intimately associated with the project, participating in editorial matters, contributing entries, and promoting its volumes.

Probeheft

In late April 1932, six months after the Dubnow Fund first announced the *probeheft*, it sent the sample volume to prospective subscribers and supporters. In what was likely one of the last expressions of Jewish optimism about the future of European Jewry, the Central Committee of the Dubnow Fund pointed to its potential to bring about a transformation in the lives of its readers, highlighting its many practical and pedagogical functions. They envisioned their audience as comprising industrious secularized Jews who were searching for information that would allow them to participate more actively and knowledgeably in the political, social, and cultural debates of their time and to learn about their own history, culture, and religion from a modern perspective:

> We read in a newspaper about international events that have excited the
> world, about the conflicts between China and Japan, about war in India,
> about votes in Germany or France—we want to obtain accurate information
> about those countries, about their general situation and political nature; we
> hear on the radio an account about reparations, international debts, or a
> disarmament conference and we lack the necessary knowledge about these
> issues; we have heard a lecture concerning the unemployment crisis or
> about Soviet Russia—and we want to learn the figures and facts. We
> attended a discussion on Zionism and we wanted to get detailed news about

Palestine and Jewish emigration; we visited a theater, a picture gallery, we read a new novel—and we want to be informed about the painters and authors whose work has made an impression on us, about the various movements in poetics and art; our child arrives from school and asks us a question from history or geography—and we cannot give the right answer; we are interested in a medical discovery or technical finding about which we have a brief account; we find in a book a foreign word or a Hebrew word or a name that is unfamiliar to us; we want to write an article, give a speech, take part in a debate—and we lack the necessary facts or statistical data.

Where can we find the essential information, the rigorously verified news, explanations, interpretations, facts, figures?[103]

The *Algemeyne entsiklopedye* would provide accurate and accessible answers to the everyday questions faced by the Yiddish-speaking modern Jew. Drawing from "all branches of science," the encyclopedic set would contain "5000 double-columned pages, 25 million characters, several thousand drawings, diagrams, illustrations, geographic maps, artistic pictures, in black [and white] and in color. Its 40,000 search terms—articles, large and small, biographical notices, brief informative translations, will function as a library for Yiddish readers." Topics were to include "mathematics and astronomy, philosophy and psychology, physics, chemistry and technology, natural science and medicine, hygiene and sport, sociology and anthropology, ethnography and geography, political economy and statistics, history and literature, law and public policy, cultural movements and pedagogy; art: music, theatre, painting and sculpture; politics, social, national and communal movements—all fields of modern human creation will be represented in our encyclopedia." In the encyclopedia's eleven volumes, the *probeheft* promised, "the reader will find answers to all questions. All necessary information will be found there."

The planners recognized that many Jews were also fluent in other languages and might not need a Yiddish-language encyclopedia. For those readers, it was the *Algemeyne entsiklopedye*'s efficient, precise, and readily accessible information that would make it a vital part of their lives since, the editors explained, the speed of modern society no longer permitted the leisure to squander one's precious time researching: "Considering the rapid pace of our lives, the difficult struggle for existence, how many of us have the free time, the opportunity and the desire to sit themselves down for hours in a library and immerse themselves in specialized books about the problems that occupy us? And even if we happen to have a bookshelf of specialized literature at

אַ ל ג ע מ ײ נ ע
ענציקלאָפּעדיע

פּראָבעהעפט

דובנאָװ-פֿאָנד, בערלין 1932

FIGURE 1.4 *Algemeyne entsiklopedye, probeheft* (Dubnov-fond, Berlin, 1932).

home—we may not be able to determine the correct information in that particular moment." As the Dubnow Fund promoted it, the *Algemeyne entsiklopedye* was a reference work designed for the modern age, that of the radio, the telegram, and the newswire. The *Algemeyne entsiklopedye* was to be popular in scope and available to women and men alike, to the rich and poor, to the educated and uneducated.

A general encyclopedia would also fill the gap left by the absence of Yiddish-language universities, reference works, and specialized texts. Although encyclopedias were available in other languages, the *Algemeyne entsiklopedye* would be a means by which those Jews who primarily spoke Yiddish could self-modernize and fully participate in the world outside their own communities:

> The value of a general encyclopedia becomes even greater for that Yiddish reader who is unfamiliar with any foreign language and who lives out his life culturally only in Yiddish. The great libraries can seldom help him, even if he can make use of them: for him, there does not exist a specialized literature of the sort that provides non-Jewish readers with tens and hundreds of works in each region of knowledge. For the Yiddish reader who comprises many social classes in Europe and America, a general encyclopedia in Yiddish is not only the best and shortest, but it is simply the *only way* to expand his range of knowledge, to complete the picture, to receive scientific information.

No longer was a learned Jew one who was proficient in traditional fields such as Torah and Talmud or Jewish laws, rituals, and practices; rather, a learned Jew was one who was informed in "Jewish history, with the social-economic position of Jews from various lands, with the political and communal movements, with literary and cultural creations of the Jewish masses." The eleventh volume, to be dedicated to the topic of "Jews," the editors promised, would provide for the first time "a scientific illumination of all questions. From the prophets until the Tannaim and Ge'onim, from Rambam and Besht until Herzl and Medem, from Elye Bokher until Peretz, Asch, and others, from the struggle between the artisans and the *parnasim* [communal leaders] in the old *kahal* [community] until the rise of the modern classes and modern class struggle—this is the scope of the encyclopedia in the Jewish section."[104]

Making the best of their difficult financial and organizational situation, the Central Committee highlighted the fact that the encyclopedia was not a for-profit venture by a private publishing firm. Instead, they presented their project as an initiative of the Jewish community itself. Identifying the Dubnow Fund as comprising "writers and communal activists from various democratic and progressive movements," they sought to make the case that the encyclopedia was being published for and as a communal good. It thus required the dedication and sacrifice of its transnational audience even in the midst of the economic crisis: "We call upon the Jewish community, all its circles, who are interested in Yiddish mass culture near and far, to become active participants in this great and important cultural undertaking. No one should refuse to help us in this difficult task: each according to his own strength and ability should carry the bricks of this great building." To stress this communal involvement, the editors not only referred twice to YIVO's engagement with the project, but also listed all the Jewish luminaries involved with it.

Although many of the fifty-six entries contained in the *probeheft* are unsigned, the ones that are credited were written by the key figures associated with the project, including Dubnow himself. Also present among the listed authors are some of the encyclopedia's earliest skeptics, including Yashunsky and Roback. Given his early investment in the project, it is not surprising to find Moyshe Shalit present (he wrote an entry on credit cooperatives), but curiously, there are no signed contributions from Meisel, although he is listed among those who were invited to participate in future volumes. Reflecting Shalit's concern for "dilettantism," several of the named entries are drawn from the authors' areas of knowledge; for example, the physician Tsemakh Szabad wrote on insulin, the poet and activist (and Dubnow's daughter) Sophie Dubnov-Erlich contributed a biographical sketch of the Polish novelist and playwright Stefan Żeromski, and the linguist Zalmen Reisen wrote on orthography. Some, however, bear little apparent relationship between author and subject; for example, Yashunsky's own contribution on motors or the entry by the American Jewish labor leader Baruch Charney Vladeck on Abraham Lincoln.

A thirty-six-page soft-cover booklet, the *probeheft* was a significant investment of financial resources and it provides the fullest indication of what the project would have looked like had it followed the stated plan for ten volumes of alphabetically listed entries on general topics plus a supplemental volume on Jewish ones. The *probeheft* included a full-color plate on ceramics; more than a dozen photos, illustrations, and reproductions of modern art, including black-and-white reproductions of two Chagall paintings; and tables and a map of global Jewish migration. The scope of entries departed somewhat from the December 1931 decision that called for a ratio of 70 percent general knowledge to 30 percent Jewish content: of the *probeheft*'s fifty-six entries, forty-five were general knowledge while ten were directly on topics related to Jews,

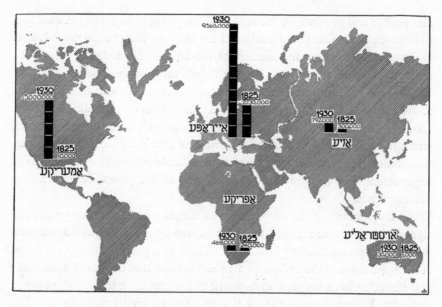

FIGURE 1.5 "Distribution of Jews by Continent in 1825 and in 1930 (in Absolute Numbers)," *Algemeyne entsiklopedye, probeheft.*

FIGURE 1.6 "Dinozaur," *Algemeyne entsiklopedye, probeheft.*

approximately an 80/20 split. A few entries, such as those on orthography and guilds, straddle the two realms, with a general introduction followed by a Jewish subtopic. A disproportionately high number of the longer, multicolumn entries, however, are on Jewish topics, while the subjects of general entries include obelisks, Archimedes, William James, Montessori schools,

פּסח־אינזל – אָדער ראַפּאַנוּי,   קלײנע אינזל
אין פּאַציפישן ים (טשילי) אין דער פּאָלינעזישער גרופּע.
באַרימט געוואָרן דורך
די מערקווירדיקע רי־
זיקע שטיין־בילדער,
וואָס געפינען זיך אויף
אים און וואָס זייער
אָפּשטאַמונג און די
שריפט אויף זיי האָט
זיך דער וויסנשאַפט
ביז איצט נאָך ניט
איינגעגעבן אַפילו אייפ־
צוקלערן.

FIGURE 1.7 "Peysekh-indzl," *Algemeyne entsiklopedye, probeheft.*

saxophones, empirical criticism, dinosaurs, Esperanto, Easter Island, guilds, coffee, and X-rays. Abramovitch contributed lengthy entries on unemployment and the Erfurt Program, the Menshevik leader Grigori Aronson wrote on professional associations, and Mark Wischnitzer wrote on guilds.

Assuming that the *probeheft* does in fact represent how the planners foresaw the encyclopedia as a whole, it is a useful guide to the sort of information they imagined Yiddish readers in the 1930s required. Curiously, and without explanation, the *probeheft* does little to situate Eastern European Jews in their own world, as the editors had advertised in the introduction. It lacks entries, for instance, on the recent global economic collapse, the complicated geopolitical situation following the end of World War I, or on the newly formed Soviet Union, independent Poland, and democratic Germany. Likewise, there are no entries on the League of Nations, the Treaty of Versailles, or the United States. Given the remarkable gains made by suffragists in Europe and the United States in these years, it is notable that while there are nine biographies of men, there exists only one (brief) biography of a woman—the educator Maria Montessori—and no references to the women's movement. The fields of science, medicine, industry, and technology are heavily represented, with entries on Röntgen rays (X-rays), Nikola

Tesla, Josiah Wedgwood, motors, radium, homeopathy, and the epidermis. The arts, literature, and philosophy are also strongly present, with entries on ceramics, Esperanto, Friedrich Nietzsche, modern art, the Russian poet Mikhail Lermontov, and movies.

The entry "Jews" simply refers readers to a "special volume," the planned supplement that would be sent to subscribers. Nevertheless, the 20 percent of specifically Jewish topics include, for example, Dubnow writing on Hasidism, the Bundist leader Franz Kursky (pseudonym of Samuel Kahan) on the Bundist activist and martyr Hirsh Lekert, Lestschinsky on Jewish demography, Ben-Adir on the Zionist leader Max Nordau, Zalmen Reisen on the recently deceased Yiddish writer and activist Hersh David Nomberg, Tcherikower on cantonists (nineteenth-century Jewish forced recruits in the Russian military), and Iulii Brutskus on Turkic Khazars (who were thought to have converted *en masse* to Judaism in the eighth century).

While many of the entries are quite short, at only a few lines, others are much more substantial and run as long as two full pages. A number of entries appear to be straightforward retellings of information that could readily be found available in many general encyclopedias and likely were not specifically researched for the *Algemeyne entsiklopedye*. The brief entry for Easter Island (*Peysekh-indzl*), for example, states simply: "Easter Island—or Rapanui, small island in Pacific Ocean (Chile) in the Polynesian group. Famous for the curious stone structures that are found there and whose origins and script science has been unable to explain." A number of the general entries, however, are more substantial and the product of original research and expertise. Abramovitch's account of the Erfurt Program, for example, reflected his long history with Menshevik politics. Reisen's contribution on orthography is similarly comprehensive. It details the practice of standardizing the spelling and pronunciation of words within different language systems, including a lengthy discussion of the history of Yiddish orthographic standardization. The entry assumes a high level of literacy (and multilingualism) on the part of its readers, as it includes untranslated words in the Cyrillic and Latin alphabets in order to demonstrate the custom of spelling the same word in multiple ways, such as gaol/jail and wódka/водка. Another originally researched and in-depth entry is Zhitlowsky's contribution on empirical criticism, which introduces readers to Richard Avenarius and Ernst Mach's late-nineteenth-century works expounding a philosophical world view based on evidence, observation, and the scientific method.

Given the intellectual, cultural, and political interests of the editors and contributors, the quality and depth of the entries on the topics related to Jews are often substantially more informed and engaging than those that fall into the general category. Among the longest entries in the *probeheft* is Simon Dubnow's two-page contribution on Hasidism, which describes the eighteenth-century Jewish revivalist movement as a spiritual rebellion against the declining conditions of the Jewish masses in the Ukraine. Hasidic Jews are depicted as having lived under "a complicated yoke" of burdens—from the Christian rulers, business and artisan guilds, their village governments, and even their own communal leaders, upper class, and rabbis. Into this context appeared a folk healer by the name of Israel ben Eliezer who was able to mend "not merely the body, but also the souls" of downtrodden Jews with a popular form of Jewish mysticism that usurped rabbinic control. "A simple Jew, an ignoramus, who prays with intention, is to God dearer than the greatest scholar who studies Gemara [rabbinic commentary] for the sake of honor or wealth."[105] Known popularly as the BeShT (from *Baal Shem Tov*, "Master of the Good Name"), the Hasidic movement that he and his disciples initiated marked a revolution in the Eastern European Jewish world, whose struggle, rise, and decline over the course of the nineteenth and early twentieth century Dubnow traces. Similarly, in an entry on Jewish demographics that includes maps, tables, and charts, Jacob Lestschinsky contributed his expertise on the dramatic population growth and migration of European Jews in the nineteenth century.

Reception

Although the *probeheft* was designed for marketing and fund-raising purposes, it was significant enough to garner enthusiastic letters of support and even its own reviews in the Yiddish press.[106] Reactions to it were generally favorable, but not entirely without reservations. Writing in the New York weekly literary journal *Yidish* from his base in Berlin, Daniel Charney spoke of the great celebration that accompanied the release of the sample volume, in spite of the increasing danger faced by Jews in Germany on account of the "slaughtering knife of Hitlerism that waves more and more menacingly over the entire German Jewish community." Charney viewed the encyclopedia as an enormous triumph that had the potential to elevate the status of the Yiddish nation to that of other great civilizations: "If the forthcoming Yiddish encyclopedia will indeed have this elegant an appearance—with such fine printing and with so many color images, drawings, and diagrams—we will really not have anything to be ashamed of in comparison to the other nations of the world, who have published their encyclopedias with state funds.[107] In the Warsaw daily *Haynt*, the Berlin-based journalist and revisionist Zionist Yeshayahu Klinov published a review of the *probeheft* that was generally positive, but wary of some of the editors' choices. As a fellow member of Berlin's Russian Jewish émigré community but of a very different political stripe than the *Entsiklopedye*'s contributors, he had a critical perspective of the effort and intimate knowledge of its context.[108] He began by asking: "How significant is it, when there appears a volume from a leading publishing house, printed on beautiful rare equipment and with interestingly chosen contents? In truth—not much. In our days ... everything is depressed ... one wanders around feeling like a refugee ... on one side there is material poverty and on the other side—the slaughtering knife of the black Nazi hangman."[109] And yet, Klinov argued, even in such uncertain times the appearance of the *probeheft* was cause for celebration. It was "the first step to a genuine cultural undertaking—the first steps of a people's-work." Klinov went on to describe the small community of Russian Jews who had gathered in Berlin at the end of World War I and expressed concern over their relatively thin cultural legacy: "What is the result of this decade-long work? There exists among us a profound pessimism." He saw in the *Entsiklopedye* the potential for validating the émigrés' intellectual efforts in the city: "If the *probeheft* is not left uncompleted, and if there will appear from Berlin the entire encyclopedia, this, in and of itself, will justify our entire Eastern European Jewish Diaspora in Berlin."[110]

Despite his general enthusiasm for the *Entsiklopedye*, he was not without apprehension, including his concern that it was too ambitious an undertaking: "Alongside 'Hasidism' there is 'insulin,' and next to Nomberg—Lermontov. Beside Max Nordau—the Erfurt Program, and next to the word 'Cantonists'—'X-rays.' Is it possible in the ten volumes that are planned to contain so much material without it having a superficial character?"[111] He also raised the ever-persistent question of whether Berlin was the proper place to house the project and wondered if Vilna might be more appropriate. His greatest critique concerned the relative lack of ideological diversity among the contributors. Given that Dubnow, Abramovitch, Tcherikower, Lestschinsky, Ben-Adir, and the others resided in relatively similar ideological camps (pro-Yiddish and pro-Diasporist, the question of socialism notwithstanding), Klinov was concerned the *Entsiklopedye* risked becoming an ideologically narrow project that would reflect the ideas of its initiators and contributors rather than meet the needs of its readers. He acknowledged that while the encyclopedia would of course not be a Zionist one, the Zionist point of view should nevertheless be fairly represented, and by someone with intimate knowledge of the movement. "An article about Max Nordau," he argued, "should be written by a man who was politically close to Nordau's Jewish frame of mind, and really, not Ben-Adir who is not in the Zionist camp." He went on to ask why, given that there were Polish, Russian, German, and Yiddish authors who were the subject of biographical entries, did the editors "not find it necessary to provide in the *probeheft* even one biography of a Hebrew author?" Reminding them of their commitment to scholarly objectivity, he concluded his review by saying, "Let us hope that the wish will be realized. And let us give the editors our best and most heart-felt wishes."[112]

In a review for the Warsaw daily *Moment*, the Berlin-based journalist Herman Svet began by bluntly asking the question, "Is a such a monumental work in Yiddish really necessary?"[113] He went on to say that given the existence of Jewish encyclopedias in several languages, "one must concede that our national need for a Jewish encyclopedia has been more than satisfied."[114] However, in spite of this initial hesitation, Svet was impressed by the fact that what marked the project as unique was the fact that it was not a Jewish encyclopedia, but rather a general encyclopedia in a Jewish language. "It will not be, as are those up to now, an encyclopedia of Jewish studies or only dedicated to *yidishkayt* and Jewish problems, but a work that encompasses, 'all branches of knowledge.'"[115] This fact made the project worthwhile for Svet, who saw it as a potentially substantial contribution for contemporary Jewish life. He was likewise impressed by the physical form of the *probeheft*, and remarked that its "great appearance, printed on fine paper, clean letters, clear and distinct" conveyed its seriousness. His only concern was that some of the entries, like Reisen's contribution on orthography, might be too sophisticated for the average reader and would come across as incomprehensible.

Likely in response to critics of the first *probeheft*, a revised, second edition appeared in January 1933 that contained several revisions, including being longer than the first by two pages.[116] It notes some staffing changes. There were a few minor alterations to entries (such as in Reisen's contribution on orthography and an improved photo for Hersh David Nomberg), and the short entries on the dinosaur, *khumrey-khumres* (a Talmudic term for strict interpretation of the law), and *khay-vekayem* (a term for a simple, ordinary person) were cut. New to the second edition was a full page of black-and-white photographs of sculptures by the artists Wilhelm Lehmbruck, Chana Orloff, Ernst Barlach, and Joseph Bernard, as well as entries on the recently completed Dnieper Hydroelectric Station in Soviet Ukraine and on the Hebrew writer Yosef Haim Brenner.

The inclusion of an entry on Brenner is particularly notable because the first edition of the *probeheft* was strongly criticized by Klinov for the absence of any entries on Hebrew authors. Given that Hebrew literature was experiencing its own dynamic resurgence comparable to that of Yiddish, the absence of any recognition to it opened up the encyclopedia to charges of partisanship. The first half of Nakhmen Meisel's contribution is a straightforward biographical and bibliographical overview of Brenner, concluding with his death in Abu Kabir, Palestine, during clashes between Palestinians, Jews, and British occupying forces.

Possibly in an effort to appease Hebraist critics, the second half of the entry is less encyclopedic than eulogistic. In a break from the otherwise objective tone of the *probeheft*, Meisel lauds Brenner's literary achievements and heaps excessive praise upon his contributions: "B-'s work, both the belletristic and the commentary, depicts the awful hardship and loneliness of Jewish poverty and the suffering and torment, material and spiritual, that so many Jewish intellectuals experienced and endured in the recent age. His sharp artistic eye possessed the tragic ability to see fully the moments of catastrophe and the processes of decay, landlessness and debility." The tribute continues, "With raw nerves and a relentlessly bleeding heart, Brenner, excavates with a measure of cruelty the wounded souls of his heroes."[117] Notably, Meisel's entry on Brenner is limited almost entirely to his Hebrew writing and excludes other aspects of his vast engagement with Jewish political and culture, including his Yiddish writing, his early work with the Bund, his departure from Europe for the Jewish settlements in Palestine, and the scandal he caused within Zionist circles in 1910 by asserting that the trend of Russian Jews converting to Christianity was unproblematic since one's religious conviction held no bearing on one's national affiliation.[118]

The second, revised version of the *probeheft* did not generate the same sort of reviews in the Yiddish press as the first did. The explanation for the difference can be discerned from the title page, which is dated "Berlin, 1933." Appearing as it did in the same month as Hitler's ascension to the German Chancellery, the arrival of the second *probeheft* was quickly overshadowed by much larger historical events. As foreigners, Jews, and figures aligned with the political left, the editors and contributors of the *Algemeyne entsiklopedye* were triply at risk of arrest and deportation. On January 30, the day of Hitler's appointment, Dubnow wrote in his diary: "Just bought the evening edition of the *Voss* [the newspaper *Vossische Zeitung*]. The worst fears of the last days have been realized: it is certain that there will be a cabinet of Hitler-Papen-Hugenberg. Hindenburg, who first promised that he would remain true to the oath to the republic, is now appointing a government of the most bitter enemies of the democratic republic. Recent days bring the same old fears: coup

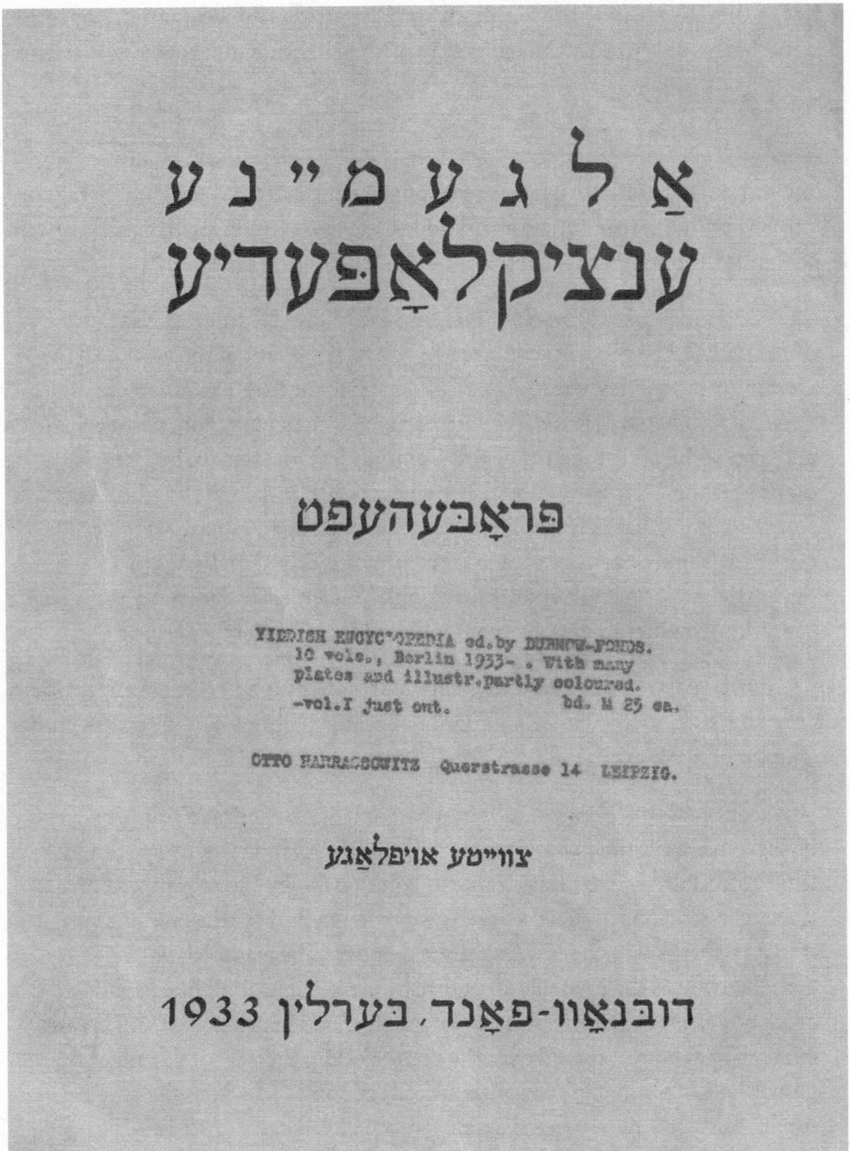
אַלגעמײנע
ענציקלאָפּעדיע

פּראָבּעהעפט

YIDDISH ENCYCLOPEDIA ed. by DUBNOW-FONDS.
10 vols., Berlin 1933- . With many
plates and illustr. partly coloured.
-vol. I just out. bd. M 25 ea.

OTTO HARRASSOWITZ Querstrasse 14 LEIPZIG.

צווייטע אויפלאַגע

דובנאָוו-פאָנד, בערלין 1933

FIGURE 1.8 *Algemeyne entsiklopedye, probeheft,* 2nd edition (Dubnov-fond, Berlin, 1933).

d'état, a dictatorship of the right, an uprising from the left, panic, pogroms. The memories carry me away (thinking of the Kishinev pogrom)."[119]

Flight from the Reich

A few days after the February 27, 1933, fire that destroyed the Reichstag and which Hitler's government manipulated to crack down on leftists and suspend civil rights, Dubnow wrote further:

> The government attributes the Reichstag fire to the Communists; the voice of the people, the government [ascribes] to itself. Terror of the rulers, all the Communist deputies arrested, many Social Democrats, "exceptional decrees" that neutralize the freedom of the individual, freedom of speech and of assembly, banning the entire Communist and even Social Democratic press and election posters. The whole of Berlin is in the hands of Nazi storm columns that perform house searches and shoot leftists. Not a day goes by without dozens of people killed or injured.... Elections are tomorrow, one expects a vote of the people. Yesterday Hitler spoke again on the radio [vowing] to destroy the Republic of the "November criminals."[120]

For several years, Dubnow had been alarmed by the rising antisemitism fueling the Nazi victories. His daughter Sophie Dubnov-Erlich writes in her biography of her father:

> Ten years earlier, Dubnov [Dubnow] had decided to flee revolutionary chaos to preserve the peace necessary for work. Now he was overtaken by a time of troubles, a ferocious counterrevolution fed by the resentment of the upper echelons of society greedy for revenge, and the despair of the impoverished lower classes. A staunch democrat, he was filled with apprehension as the unstable structure of the Weimar Republic began to crack under the relentless pressure of destructive elements. The foul breath of zoological hatred spread over the country from the pages of a vulgar pamphlet distributed in tens of thousands of copies and from the columns of a bloodthirsty newspaper provocatively called *Angriff* (Attack). The main object of this hatred was world Jewry.[121]

In the March 1933 elections, which took place less than a week after the Reichstag fire, the Nazi Party earned nearly 44 percent of the vote, cementing their control over the government in an alliance formed with the German National People's Party (DNVP). The Social Democrats garnered just over 18 percent, and the Communist Party, which earned the third-highest number of votes, came in at just over 12 percent. Over the next several months, Dubnow witnessed the passing of the Enabling Act, which awarded Hitler the power to rule by decree; the April 4 boycott of Jewish businesses; the banning of Jews from government service; and the dissolution of all political parties other than the National Socialists. In August, Dubnow left Germany with his family. Rather than settle in Paris, where his close friends Elias and Riva Tcherikower had relocated, he moved to Riga, Latvia, where he hoped to find peace, solitude, and proximity to family in the Soviet Union.

The Berlin-based Russian Jewish émigré community that had been forged in the wake of the Bolshevik seizure of power and the end of World War I—and that had created the conditions allowing for the creation of the *Algemeyne entsiklopedye*—came to a rapid end in the early months of 1933. Although governments in Germany rose and fell with great frequency following World War I, it was clear to those in the Russian Jewish émigré community that the sanctuary they had found in the country was gone, and they left to find new sites of refuge. Jacob Lestschinsky in particular faced a harrowing departure.[122] He was arrested by German police on March 11 for working as a foreign correspondent for the *Forverts*. He spent four days in prison and was released only following a campaign by the U.S. State Department, which was reported in the *New York Times*.[123] Given two weeks to leave the country, he left via Prague and resettled eventually in Warsaw after being further expelled from Latvia.[124] Soon after his departure, the *Times* further reported that Lestschinsky sent a cable to the *Forverts* alerting them to the fact that dozens of Jews had been killed by the Nazi regime while hundred more were injured and thousands were robbed.

Even in its nascent period, the *Algemeyne entsiklopedye* symbolized and was shaped by the extraordinary instability of its age. The historic importance of its base in Berlin, Germany, notwithstanding, the *Entsiklopedye* was at a geographic remove from the Yiddish-speaking masses of Eastern Europe and the United States, reflecting the increasing displacement of Yiddish and the various ideologies that helped sustain it. This distance only exacerbated the economic uncertainties that were threatening many Yiddish cultural institutions during the Great Depression, including YIVO. Embarking upon a major publishing venture in the early 1930s without major financial backers and with the expectation that it would be sustained by the masses of Yiddish speaking ensured that the Dubnow Fund would be beset by uncertainty and instability. The political climate of the early 1930s was likewise none too welcoming to such ambitious projects. The growing movement of Nazism in Germany led to an escalation of right-wing antisemitic movements across Europe that threatened the status of Jews everywhere. This not only made it all the more unlikely that the encyclopedia would find willing investors, but also led to a hardening of political differences within the Jewish community itself, potentially halting the cooperation that such an ambitious undertaking would require.

Nevertheless, the idea of a Yiddish-language encyclopedia was widely embraced across many ideological divides as a vital tool for the continued modernization of Eastern European Jewry. The figures who came together in honor of their teacher and mentor Simon Dubnow believed that the transnational community of Yiddish speakers was ready to take the next step in its development and become full participants in the world of modern nations. After decades of false starts to realize such a project in Yiddish, by the early 1930s both the language and its speakers had arrived at a point where an encyclopedia was at last widely imaginable. In committing to an encyclopedia as both a tool for their modernization and as proof of it, Yiddish speakers were furthering an Enlightenment-era tradition of publishing encyclopedias in order to encapsulate, disseminate, and assert the authority of scientific knowledge in the face of superstition and ignorance. At the same time, as Jews, they were continuing a millennia-long tradition of shaping and defining the Jewish people through the authority of the book. This was a process that began with the Hebrew Bible itself and continued through the Talmud, a number of legal compendiums composed in the Middle Ages, Moses Mendelssohn's Bible translation and commentary, the English, Russian, and German Jewish encyclopedias, and even through the first major works of Jewish historical scholarship, including Dubnow's own *Weltgeschichte*. As Dubnow remarked in his opening address to the February 1931 meeting, the Yiddish encyclopedia, this "bible for the new age," held the promise of securing the future of the Yiddish nation. In its next phase in Paris, from 1933 to 1940, this promise would be tested repeatedly, as the *Entsiklopedye* would realize some of its greatest accomplishments as well as contend with new challenges that threatened not only its very existence but that of the Yiddish language and its speakers.

MAN PLANS,
AND HITLER LAUGHS

Paris, 1933–1940

A New Home in the City of Light

IN LATE DECEMBER 1934, nearly two years after Hitler's rise to power and almost four years since the February 1931 meeting at which the decision was made to publish a Yiddish encyclopedia, the long-awaited first volume of the *Algemeyne entsiklopedye* appeared in print. In between the first entry, dedicated to *alef*/א (the first letter of the Hebrew alphabet), and the final one, on Atlantic City (אַטלאַנטיק סיטי), 480 columns later, volume 1 provided readers with entries on a wide range of subjects, such as abacuses, automats, Asia, ears, Oman, judicial independence, the Independent Social Democratic Party in Germany, submarines, Uruguay, and the atom hypothesis. The volume was not, as one might expect, published in Warsaw or Vilna or another city with a long reputation as a major Yiddish cultural center. Rather, the home of the relocated project was Paris, the city of the original *Encyclopédie* project of Denis Diderot, Jean le Rond d'Alembert, and the French philosophes. The Dubnow Fund's relocation from Berlin to Paris, more than doubling its distance from Warsaw, marked the continued exile of the *Entsiklopedye* from the historical centers of Yiddish and further into its transnational networks of speakers.

Notwithstanding the delays and the distance, the arrival of volume 1 was met with great fanfare in the Yiddish press. The Vilna daily *Tog* hailed the encyclopedia as a "momentous accomplishment" and expressed joy that while "there are many encyclopedias of Jewish life, all of them are in foreign languages. This is the first one in Yiddish, in spite of many previous attempts."

73

It went on to praise the Dubnow Fund for bringing together people who represented so many different political stances to accomplish this goal.[1] Moyshe Shalit, writing in the Warsaw weekly journal *Literarishe bleter*, hailed it as the realization of a goal "for which people have continually dreamed for more than two decades."[2] Alexander Mukdoni wrote in the New York monthly *Tsukunft* (Future) that "not only is it very beautiful, but it has been the fabulous dream of democratic Jewish intellectuals for the last quarter century."[3] Even the French language *Le journal juif*, which did not typically comment on developments in Yiddish culture, made special note of the volume's appearance and declared that it "filled an incontestable gap" in Yiddish letters.[4]

The twenty-two months between the Nazi takeover of Germany and the release of volume 1 in Paris were filled with challenges for the Dubnow Fund, and the entire project might have ended at the very moment when it was getting underway. The displacement from Berlin interrupted the organizational efforts and planning just when excitement for the project was beginning to build beyond a small community of scholars and language activists. The escape from Germany was filled with peril for some, such as Lestschinsky, who had been arrested, and Abramovitch, who barely avoided it, thanks to being tipped off in advance.[5] There were countless practical concerns that needed to be resolved immediately, such as identifying new resources, offices, presses, and funders. Furthermore, the rising peril of fascism from Germany and the Soviet Union's increasing attacks on the Mensheviks threatened to halt the *Entsiklopedye* entirely, since most of the Dubnow Fund members were also deeply involved in political and social work and threw themselves into antifascist activism. The situation in Poland, where so many of their contributors and supporters lived, was devolving as well. In September 1934, the government renounced the Minorities Treaties at the League of Nations, which added fuel to an already tense antisemitic atmosphere. YIVO was under increased government interference and surveillance, and it still had not recovered fully from its own financial woes.[6]

Another obstacle was the fact that the Berlin-based contributors of the *Entsiklopedye* had scattered after Hitler rose to power and the larger Yiddishist community in Germany collapsed. Dubnow, after remaining in Berlin until the summer of 1933, took up residence in the garden town of Kaiserwald (now Mežaparks), Latvia, near the Baltic coast just north of the capital, Riga. Daniel Charney, with whom Dubnow was in regular contact, also tried to move to Latvia as well as to Poland, but his Soviet citizenship made such a move complicated.[7] Jacob Lestschinsky also returned to the East. He moved to Warsaw, where he continued to work as a correspondent for the *Forverts* for several years. (Later, upon returning to Poland from vacation, he would be barred from reentering on account of writing articles that highlighted rising anti-semitism in the country, and he would move to New York City in 1938.)[8] Aaron Steinberg relocated to London. The largest contingent of encyclopedists, however, resettled in Paris. Among them were Leon Bramson, Raphael Abramovitch (as well as most of the Menshevik Delegation Abroad), Riva and Elias Tcherikower, Ben-Adir, and Avrom Kin. Later in the decade, Daniel Charney and Rachel and Mark Wischnitzer also relocated to Paris.

By taking refuge in Paris, these contributors joined a large community of German émigrés who resettled in the city to escape Nazi persecution. The choice of France (to the extent that it *was* a choice) was relatively straight-forward. Its border with Germany allowed many refugees to maintain connections with family, friends, and businesses back home. It also helped them imagine that a return might soon be possible, especially since many governments had risen and quickly fallen in the postwar German republic. Considering the longstanding tensions between the two countries and France's history as a sanctuary for those escaping political violence, Paris also became a natural site for activists to mount resistance to the new regime. In contrast to Great Britain and the United States, France opened its borders to refugees in the immediate aftermath of Hitler's ascension to power, taking in about twenty-five thousand people by the summer of 1933 out of the sixty to sixty-five thousand who fled that year. Historian Vicki Caron has noted that approximately 85 percent of the refugees arriving in France were Jews. Among France's reasons for accepting so many refugees was a political one, Caron notes, as the Nazi rise to power "was widely perceived as a vindication of France's hardline stance toward Germany. . . . For many French statesmen, a generous reception of the victims of Nazi terror offered the prospect of restoring the anti-German coalition hammered out so painstakingly at Versailles."[9]

The refugees from Nazism joined an already substantial community of exiles from the former Russian empire. Over the course of the 1930s, France became home to approximately three million displaced people, including another thirty thousand German Jews after the 1938 Kristallnacht (Crystal Night, or Night of Broken Glass) pogroms, and half a million refugees from the Spanish Civil War. Although work permits for refugees were severely curtailed (in response to the excess of unemployed laborers due to the Depression), few other restrictions were placed upon them, making France the "foremost nation of asylum in the world" at the time.[10] So many emigrants from the Soviet Union settled in France that, according to historian Marc Raeff, "Paris became the true capital of Russia Abroad," his term for the more than one million Russians who fled the USSR after 1917.[11]

In spite of this seemingly welcome environment, the rush of refugees prompted a severe backlash by the end of 1933, when many government leaders as well as anti-immigrant advocates successfully called for an end to the open-door policy. Along with economic anxieties, this turnabout was prompted by a general dislike of Germans among the French and suspicions over whether some might be in fact working as spies. The result was that for the rest of the decade, many of the refugees who resided in France lived under threat of arrest and deportation. The issue of refugee support, Caron argues, also became deeply politicized and eventually served to help set the stage for the brutal treatment of Jewish refugees under the Vichy regime. Human rights groups, Jewish organizations, socialists, communists, and members of the Radical Party sought to maintain open borders and support refugees by expanding their opportunities to work and protecting them from police abuse and arrest. Right-wing groups and conservative parties rejected refugees' right to work and to engage in political activity and sought to deport as many as possible and maintain closed borders. In response, France looked for international solutions to the growing refugee problem and hoped to pressure Great Britain to allow refugees to settle in Palestine, which was under British control based on a mandate from the League of Nations, and France also appealed to the League to resettle refugees among its member states.[12] These tensions persisted over the course of the 1930s and only grew more palpable as fascists took power across France's border in Germany, Spain, and Italy.

While the encyclopedists were part of a larger group of people fleeing totalitarian regimes for sanctuary in France, they were also continuing a half-century-long tradition of Eastern European Jews resettling in the country. Beginning in the 1880s, more than two-and-a-half-million Jews left the Russian empire, escaping rising political and religious persecution as well as murderous attacks on their communities. The revolutions of 1905 and 1917 in particular prompted vast numbers of Jews to leave. While approximately two million of these émigrés arrived in the United States, about one hundred thousand had settled in France by the mid-1920s. These Jewish migrants tended to be poorer and more proletarian than French Jews, more religiously orthodox, and for the secularized among them, more inclined toward political movements such as socialism, communism, Bundism, Diaspora Nationalism, and Zionism. They were also almost entirely Yiddish-speaking, and many brought with them a commitment to promoting Yiddish culture.[13]

Rather than follow the strategy of acculturation and accommodation chosen by most native French Jews, Eastern European Jews tended to maintain a distinct identity and to form their own mutual aid societies and cultural organizations based upon institutional models they had previously established in Russia. Parisian immigrant neighborhoods of Belleville, the Pletzl ("little square" in Yiddish) of the Marais, and St. Paul became home to Jewish prayer houses, burial societies, and community centers that were run along occupational, political, or geographic ties. Historian Nancy L. Green has shown that these Jews, who worked predominantly in the clothing trades, also became part of the French labor movement at the moment when France was developing into an industrial power. The unions not only served as a means for Jewish workers to improve the conditions of their labor, but also sustained Jewish communal solidarity and provided social services to their members and their families. The Jewish section of the French Communist Party also became a second home for many of its members. Jewish immigrants quickly learned to rely on one another for support, rather than on the state or on native French Jews. By 1913, they founded an umbrella group of immigrant organizations known as the Fédération des Sociétés Juives de France (Federation of Jewish Societies of France).

With the influx of Eastern European Jews that followed the Nazi rise to power, the number of Yiddish-speaking Jews in France grew to approximately 150,000 by the eve of World War II. This put Eastern European Jews on numerical par with native French Jews and made Paris home to the third-largest Yiddish-speaking community in the world, behind New York City and Warsaw. In his study of interwar Yiddish culture in Paris, Nick Underwood demonstrates that although Paris never developed its own distinctive Yiddish cultural legacy, it was an essential site for many Yiddish writers, artists, and activists in the interwar decades.[14] As early as 1922, a Paris office of the Kulturlige was organized to promote Yiddish high culture. In the early 1930s, the city was home to several competing Yiddish-language newspapers and journals, publishing houses, theaters (featuring both "highbrow" and "lowbrow" productions), libraries, cultural centers, and choral groups. In the two decades between the wars, Paris hosted 142 different Yiddish periodicals.[15]

Paris was also home to one of the era's great sensationalist trials, which became a cause célèbre throughout the Yiddish world. At the center was Sholem Schwartzbard, who was born in Russia and moved to Paris in 1910 after many years as a revolutionary activist. He was tried for the murder of the Ukrainian leader Symon Petliura, who was widely viewed at the time as responsible for leading the anti-Jewish pogroms in Ukraine that followed the dissolution of the Russian empire. Tens of thousands of Jews were murdered, including twelve members of Schwartzbard's own family. On May 25, 1926, he got his revenge by shooting Petliura on the street in the Latin Quarter. Schwartzbard immediately admitted to the crime, and Elias and Riva Tcherikower relocated to Paris from Berlin to organize his defense. The French public was generally inclined to support Schwartzbard, who had served France with distinction in World War I, and to despise Petliura, who was widely viewed as a ruthless murderer. After the eight-day trial, he was unanimously acquitted by a jury. The outcome of the trial lent particular stature to the city in the eyes of many Eastern European Jews. A watchmaker by training, Schwartzbard went on to work as a traveling salesman for the *Algemeyne entsiklopedye* in the 1930s and wrote several volumes of Yiddish poetry over his lifetime.

Although some elements of the Yiddish cultural scene were linked to political movements—the *Naye prese* (New press), for example, was a communist newspaper—most had no formal party ties. Instead, as Underwood shows, over the course of the 1930s Yiddish cultural activists, many of whom were affiliated with the Diaspora Nationalist movement, sought to transform their commitment to Yiddish nationalism into a transnational movement that would unite Yiddish-speaking Jews globally *and* participate in the fight against the rising fascist threat. By the mid-1930s, he writes, "Yiddish cultural institutions in Paris [had] laid the groundwork for the mid-1930s French political cohabitation of the French and Jewish Popular Fronts."[16]

Complicating the situation further for Eastern European Jews was a fraught relationship with native French Jews. The first European country to emancipate its Jewish residents, France was often perceived as a beacon of liberty and freedom for Jews around the world, who looked to the country as a site of possible refuge. Yet the equal rights bestowed to Jews came with a price. In a debate on Jewish emancipation in the French National Assembly in December 1789, Count Stanislas de Clermont-Tonnerre famously declared, "The Jews should be denied everything as a nation but granted everything as individuals," a sentiment that helped shape French Jews' relationship to the republican regime for the next century and a half.[17] In exchange for this new status as equal individual citizens before the law, Jews in France strategically fulfilled the expectations placed upon them. Over the subsequent decades, Jews reformed many of their religious practices, communal institutions, names, modes of dress, occupations, national loyalties, and language in order to present themselves as in compliance with French expectations. At the same time, Jews in France reimagined the French ideals of liberty, equality, and fraternity as themselves compatible with Jewish values. In spite of some particularly fierce challenges to their right to be considered French—especially under

Napoleon's regime in the first decade of the nineteenth century and the Drey-fus Affair in the last—French Jews generally experienced peace and prosperity over the nineteenth century. With some exceptions, they conformed to social and cultural codes that allowed them to avoid drawing too much attention to their "Jewishness" and instead to assert their fealty to a liberal French state.[18]

However, beginning with the Dreyfus Affair of the *fin de siècle*, in which France was sharply divided over the case of a Jewish member of the Army's General Staff who was accused of treason, an antisemitic movement began to emerge with particular force.[19] It was laced with racism and accusations that Jews were living as perpetual foreigners who were disloyal to France while ben-efiting from its prosperity. This antisemitism was fueled by many factors, among them the rapidly growing number of Jewish immigrants from Russia. The new arrivals tended to be without many resources and soon found themselves living in overcrowded conditions that quickly turned into unsanitary slums. These mi-grants became targets for French reactionary forces, who blamed them for France's economic, social, and political woes. Historian Paula Hyman writes, "In an age of growing xenophobia and increasing emphasis upon rootedness in French tradition and culture as the prerequisite for claiming French nationality, the foreign origins of close to two-thirds of France's Jews raised anew questions about the assimilability of Jews within French society."[20] The fact that most Russian Jews did not initially intend on staying permanently in France meant that they were less invested in assimilating into French society than in establish-ing their own particular communal institutions rooted in their overwhelmingly working-class status. In the eyes of native French Jews, the immigrants' threat-ened to call into question the "Frenchness" of all Jews, native and immigrant alike, and "disrupted the relative tranquility of native Jewry ideologically, institutionally, and socially."[21] In response, French Jews, wanting neither to lose their status within French society nor to relinquish their control over est-ablished Jewish institutions, vacillated between distancing themselves from Russian Jews and providing social and educational services so as to lessen the immigrants' perceived negative impact on French society.[22]

It was within this land of "uneasy asylum," as Caron has called it, that the Yiddish encyclopedists reestablished their project. For the next seven years, until they were forced to flee Nazism once again, they navigated the shifting political landscape of 1930s Paris as they sought to produce an encyclopedia that would meet the needs of Yiddish-speaking Jews at the very moment when those needs were themselves undergoing a radical transformation.

Restarting the *Entsiklopedye* was a daunting task. It involved recruiting new contributors and editors, contracting with new publishing firms, and securing new sources of financing. The members of the Dubnow Fund attempted to release the volumes as planned, even as they were overwhelmed with resettling their own families and reestablishing their livelihoods. Many encyclopedists spent the next months and sometimes years moving from place to place in search of even a semipermanent home and were focused on earning enough money to keep themselves and the project afloat. The chaos of displacement, this continued exile of Yiddish, which only worsened for most over the course of the 1930s, became reflected in the *Entsiklopedye* and influenced its publishing schedule, the composition of its contributors, and eventually its very contents.

Reconstructing the efforts to rebuild the *Entsiklopedye* after Hitler's rise to power presents particular challenges as well for the historian. The records from the Paris years, 1933–1940, are extraordinarily fragmented because of the encyclopedists' escape from Germany, high degree of mobility, and subsequent flight from France following Germany's invasion in May 1940. Few of the administrative documents, such as financial statements, sales records, minutes of editorial meetings, and advertising materials, survive in the archives. The documents that do exist are primarily in the form of correspondence between editors and contributors and are scattered across the globe—a reflection of the unprecedented displacement of European Jewish intellectuals in the mid-twentieth century. The papers of Simon Dubnow that relate to the *Entsiklopedye*, for example, can be found in collections in Jerusalem's Central Archives for the History of the Jewish People and New York's YIVO Institute for Jewish Research. Those of Raphael Abramovitch were deposited in Amsterdam's International Institute for Social History by his son, Mark Rein, before he went off to fight in the Spanish Civil War. The papers of Aaron Steinberg are located at the University of Southampton in Great Britain, YIVO in New York, and the Central Archives for the History of the Jewish People in Jerusalem. Other materials from the Paris years of the *Entsiklopedye* ended up in archives at the University of Cape Town, Harvard University, the Library of Congress, and the Robert F. Wagner Labor Archives at New York University, among other places. None are to be found in Paris itself.

The materials that do exist from this period, in particular those written just prior to the release of the first volume in late December 1934, convey well the disruption and anxiety of the moment. One key issue for the editors was simply finding one another and the other contributors to the encyclopedia. Many had fled Germany without a clear destination in mind and moved regularly over the subsequent months. A great deal of effort was made to track down Steinberg, for example, who, along with the New York City–based Yiddish cultural leader Chaim Zhitlowsky, was a coeditor of the entries on philosophy. Among his many accomplishments, Steinberg had translated Dubnow's ten-volume history of the Jewish people into German from its original Russian while he was residing in Berlin in the 1920s. For months after he left Germany, editors with the encyclopedia wrote him letters seeking his whereabouts and hoping he would resume his work on the project. As late as February 1934, Ben-Adir was writing Steinberg in Kaunas (the interwar capital of Lithuania, known in Yiddish as Kovne) and only confirmed in March that he had in fact settled in London.[23]

The search for Steinberg also illustrates another complication. With a considerably reduced core of staff located in Paris (Abramovitch, Ben-Adir, and Zelig Kalmanovitch handled much of the day-to-day affairs, and Avrom Menes, Elias Tcherikower, and Iulii Brutskus assisted on editorial matters), much of the work had to be carried out via correspondence.[24] The delays involved in writing requests and waiting for replies, often over the course of protracted negotiations, slowed down an already overdue project. Unlike with a scholarly journal, in which late submissions can appear in a subsequent volume, the alphabetical nature of the Entsiklopedye meant that articles that were submitted late would not appear at all if creative alternatives for entry titles could not be identified. Otherwise, once a volume went to press, there was no going back to include an entry from earlier in the alphabet.

A letter from Ben-Adir to Steinberg written on February 19, 1934, details where the project stood at that time.[25] The encyclopedia was still being imagined as consisting of ten volumes with a supplemental edition dedicated to Jewish topics. Volume 1 was in preparation, with three thousand terms to be included. A firm date of March 20 was set for any remaining entries to be received and a release date was set for late April. A number of scientific articles were on hand, but the volume lacked many articles in Steinberg's area of philosophy. The staff was overworked—"each of us has to do the work of three"—and desperately short of funds. However, by late March, Steinberg still had not responded. Delays such as these (articles from Jacob Lestschinsky and Brutskus also had not arrived on time) pushed back the publication considerably and made the situation "catastrophic."[26]

Ben-Adir's letters to Steinberg were hardly the only ones to document the hardships faced by the encyclopedists at this time; the desperation extended to many Yiddish cultural projects. Letters between Abramovitch and Fishl Gelibter, the executive secretary of the New York–based Arbeter-ring (Workmen's Circle), a socialist-oriented Jewish mutual aid society, highlight these difficulties. In March 1934, Gelibter, who was also a member of the American

Committee of the Yiddish Encyclopedia, sent a few hundred dollars that had been donated by the *Forverts* and the Arbeter-ring. Gelibter wrote that he wished that he was able to send more money and lamented that the *Entsiklopedye* was not the only European Yiddish cause that was raising funds in the United States. Competing with the Dubnow Fund was YIVO and the ORT, as well as secular Yiddish school programs.[27]

An exchange between Abramovitch and Dubnow from April also highlights the financial despair that the encyclopedists were experiencing at the time. To save the project, Abramovitch had written Dubnow, seeking his help. By then, he wrote, the manuscript of the first volume was complete but there were no funds available for publication expenses. He had expected to begin printing that month, but instead was now hoping for June. Abramovitch bemoaned the lack of funds, especially from supporters across the Atlantic. "America let us down miserably," he wrote.[28] They had yet to send a "single dollar," a certain exaggeration. He included several drafts of appeals written as if they had been composed by Dubnow himself and asked for his signature. A week later, Dubnow replied that Abramovitch's letter "makes me sad," and that he had not realized the situation had grown so desperate. He expressed uncertainty about whether the hopes of "our Paris enthusiasts" were attainable. He reported that he signed all three letters and sent them to New York City: "I want to believe that our friends in America will respond to our S.O.S. and will come with help for our enterprise, which will be useful for them as well."[29] He closed with a postscript stating that "out of social and personal grief, I am seeking consolation in my memoirs."

It was not only the Dubnow Fund and other European-based Yiddish projects that were starved for resources; the staff members too had to figure out new ways to make ends meet. Even a figure as prominent as Abramovitch struggled to earn money to support himself, let alone his comrades. Disputes with *Forverts* editor Abraham Cahan over Abramovitch's reporting led to several of his articles being considerably shortened or spiked altogether, and his income was sharply reduced. Fund-raising campaigns in the United States to support European Social Democrats did not generate many contributions. As early as spring 1933, Abramovitch was forced to apply for a loan against his insurance policy with the New England Mutual Life Insurance Company, which he secured with the help of Morris Hillquit, the leader of the Socialist Party of America.[30] Finally, an unidentified "friend" from the United States sent a contribution in August 1934 that allowed the encyclopedia to meet many of its financial obligations.

The First Volumes

Volume 1 finally appeared on December 28, 1934. In the foreword, the Central Committee of the Dubnow Fund discussed how the project had been conceived as a way to celebrate the seventieth birthday of "our great learned Simon Dubnow," and credited YIVO for helping to initiate the project.[31] In a one-sentence paragraph, they characterized succinctly the many delays and misfortunes they had faced: "Extraordinary and unforeseen difficulties befell us and nearly vanquished us over the next three years."

They compared their project to the great encyclopedias of the world, including the English-language *Encyclopedia Britannica*, the French-language *Larousse*, and the German-language encyclopedias *Brockhaus* and *Meyers*. Those initiatives had been launched by powerful and wealthy publishers who were able to invest millions and enlist dozens of directors. Other encyclopedias, such as those published in the Soviet Union, Italy, Czechoslovakia, Latvia, or Lithuania, were published with direct assistance from their national governments. The great Jewish encyclopedias of recent decades, such as those in English, Russian, German, and Hebrew, had the backing of great publishing houses or wealthy patrons (glossing over the many challenges that had actually been faced by the publishers of these encyclopedias). The *Algemeyne entsiklopedye*, by contrast, was a project of the Jewish people themselves.

The foreword then related the many challenges that the Dubnow Fund faced publishing the inaugural volume, including the death of its chief fundraiser, Nokhem Gergel, and the difficulty of creating an encyclopedia that did not simply mimic extant publications but instead contained entries appropriate for the Yiddish-reading public. Most challenging of all, however, was the "Hitler-catastrophe" that forced the project to disband in Berlin and regroup in Paris. The result, the editors declared, was a smaller first volume than was originally planned. They also announced a modification in the publishing schedule in order to reduce the costs of printing individual volumes. The *Entsiklopedye* would now comprise twenty volumes of entries on general topics (instead of the original plan of ten) plus the supplemental volume on Jews. At the new planned rate of one volume every four months, the *Entsiklopedye* was due to be completed in spring 1941.

In a separate introduction, the editors (listed as Abramovitch, Ben-Adir, Menes, and Kalmanovitch) likewise spoke of their project largely in terms of challenges that had to be overcome, although these were not a consequence of the declining situation for Jews in Europe.[32] The issues included questions of format, the lack of a Yiddish scientific vocabulary, and the need to establish new orthographic standards and methods of transcribing words from the Latin alphabet to the Hebrew. The editors also had to work within the perceived educational limits of their audience and to craft an encyclopedia that would appeal to the needs of those readers who "did not undergo a systematic school education." Such readers, they assumed, would not need a reference work to refresh their knowledge but would require more substantial material to impart what they otherwise would have learned in school. Therefore, the volumes were dedicated to what they referred to as *normale* (normal) knowledge entries on a broad range of topics, according to the order of the Hebrew alphabet. The editors also announced that a supplemental, double-sized volume, entitled *Yidn*, would be dedicated to "the field of knowledge that is of special relevance to Jews and Judaism." *Yidn* required a different format altogether and would contain full-length scholarly essays, instead of alphabetical entries, on a range of subjects including Jewish anthropology, history, demography, movement, economics, art, communal movements, political parties, and language.

These introductions, as well as the celebratory reception with which this volume was generally greeted, demonstrate that for its editors and many of its reviewers in the press, the *Algemeyne entsiklopedye* represented a new and momentous chapter in the history of Eastern European Jewry and the modern Yiddish culture that they had created. What differentiated the *Entsiklopedye* from the "great" encyclopedias of the world was not only that the Dubnow Fund did not have a major publishing house, government, or wealthy patron giving it financial backing, but also the simple fact that it was written in the Yiddish language. Yiddish, as a transnational and Diasporic language, lacked state structures (outside of the USSR). Therefore, any project of magnitude— such as the founding of YIVO—had to be a collaborative project of the community of speakers itself. Moreover, a generation earlier it would have been unimaginable to publish such a work in Yiddish, which even at the turn of the century was widely considered to be a "jargon" even by its own speakers and was thought to lack a grammar, a coherent word corpus, and the ability to convey complicated ideas. Whereas previous Jewish encyclopedias, with the exception of the Hebrew-language *Otsar yisrael*, had been written in non-Jewish languages, providing assimilated Jewish readers a means to acquire self-knowledge and asserting Jews' place as a legitimate part of various national frameworks, a Yiddish-language encyclopedia of chiefly *normale* subject matter was an assertion of Jewish self-expression and of Jews' place among the peoples of the world, regardless of the countries where they lived. For the

FIGURE 2.1 *Algemeyne entsiklopedye*, logo.

Dubnow Fund, the *Entsiklopedye* was nothing less than a declaration of the transnational sovereignty of Yiddish and the Jews who spoke it.

Volume 1 of the *Algemeyne entsiklopedye* was handsomely bound in the reader's choice of leather or canvas, and its logo comprised the stylized letters *alef*/א (for *algemeyne*) and *ayen*/ע (for *entsiklopedye*) as well as shafts of wheat and a cog wheel denoting the joining together of the natural and industrial worlds. It contained approximately 1,100 entries, with full-color maps of Australia and Asia, black-and-white photographs, sketches, graphs, tables, and charts. Much of what is included is similar to that of other universal encyclopedias of the period. There are many entries on medical topics and human anatomy, such as a lengthy discussion on abortion by Tsemakh Shabad—a physician and Jewish social and political activist in Vilna (and Max Weinreich's father-in-law)—as well as entries on the aorta, eye, and ear. A great number of entries contend with mechanical and technical innovations, such as automobiles, autoclaves, and automatic telephone systems. The natural world is represented with entries on the eagle and nitrogen, for example.

The volume is particularly heavy on biographical entries, such as the many famous Adlers, including Alfred, Victor, Cyrus, Friedrich (the secretary-general of the Labor and Socialist International who had helped save Abramovitch from being executed by the Bolsheviks in 1918), and another seven less-famous ones. There are entries for the Welsh founder of utopian socialism and the cooperative movement Robert Owen, the former Mexican president Álvaro Obregón, and even one on Abramovitch himself, which was written by Menshevik leader and onetime general secretary of the ORT Grigori Aronson. As in the *probeheftn*, very few famous women receive entries. Among those are Grace Aguilar, an English novelist, poet, and author of works on Jewish history and religion, and Sigrid Undset, a Norwegian novelist and Nobel Laureate.

Reflecting the widely held racial, and racist, perceptions of non-Europeans at the time, there is a sharp difference in the depiction of Western countries and those in Africa and the Far East. Hungary, for example, is described as a modern European state, with rich discussions of its size and demographics, political organization, language, culture, major imports and exports, economy, and technological developments. At the center of the entry's full-page photo spread is a reproduction of the massive and ornate parliament building, surrounded by images of urban and pastoral scenes. A subsection is given over to the history and current status of Hungarian Jewry. Moving further eastward, the images of Ukraine primarily show peasants laboring collectively in fields (the country was part of the USSR at the time) or wearing traditional dress. Given the high number of Jews in the country, a particularly long discussion of section is devoted to Ukrainian Jewry. The entry on Abyssinia (Ethiopia), by contrast, represents Africans as less developed evolutionarily, and even describes Abyssinians' physiognomy. Included among the photographs, next to a shot of Haile Selassie whose caption states only that the person depicted is the emperor, is a closeup of an unnamed woman unclothed from the waist up. The only photos in the entry for Australia are of Aboriginal men, who are depicted almost exclusively in traditional dress.[33]

Likely as a consequence of Abramovitch's commitment to social democracy and his desire to support his exiled comrades, the volume contains many entries written by leftists on topics related to the political left. For example, one of the longer entries, totaling five and a half columns, is by Menshevik activist Petr Garvi on agrarian socialism, bringing the total number of columns on agrarian issues to twenty-eight. There are entries on the Independent Labor Movement in England, the Independent Social Democratic Party in Germany, and the Independent Socialist Workers Party in Poland. Many figures in Abramovitch's political circles, including the Marxist scholar Max Beer and Grigori Aronson, also contributed to the volume.

FIGURE 2.2 Lesser Ury, *Jeremiah* (c. 1897, reproduction from *Lesser Ury: Seine Stellung in der modernen Malerei*, by Adolph Donath, Berlin, 1921).

The volume begins with a black-and-white reproduction of an 1897 painting by the German Jewish artist Lesser Ury (1861–1931) entitled *Jeremiah*. The scholar Chana C. Schütz has noted that the artist was and continues to be known largely for his landscapes and cityscapes of Germany: "He painted Berlin as no other painter did at a time when the small Prussian royal seat was rapidly developing into the capital of the German Reich. The mention of his name instinctively evokes images of scenes in Berlin's cafés and the activity on the streets of the then young metropolis."[34] At the same time, however, as

Schütz reveals, Ury was also painting biblical scenes, "some of them on a gigantic scale." The choice of Berlin-based Ury can be seen as an homage to the city in which the *Entsiklopedye* was first imagined and set into motion, and the painting was first displayed in 1933 at Berlin's Jewish Museum, which opened the week before Hitler's ascension to power.[35] Furthermore and more ominously, Jeremiah, whom Lesser depicts as lying prostrate under the stars, is widely understood to be the "weeping prophet," who bemoans the sins of the people Israel—in particular, worshiping false gods—and warns them of the coming destruction.

A great number of entries are reserved for premodern rabbinical leaders and Jewish religious prayers or texts, including the genre of rabbinic legends known as *Agode* (Legend), a compilation of ethical teachings and maxims entitled *Pirkey oves* (*Ethics of the Fathers*), the Jewish memorial prayer Av Horakhamim (Father, the Merciful), the biblical Abraham, and the Kabbalist Rabbi Avraham Abulafia (1240–1291). Readers are supplied with often lengthy biographical descriptions of premodern Jewish figures such as Abba Mari ben Moses Hayarhi, a thirteenth-century rabbi who resided in Montpellier; the eleventh-century scholar Ibn Ezra; and the Ibn Tibbon family of translators from the twelfth and thirteenth centuries. There are in fact so many entries on Jewish religious life and practice—well over the 10 percent that had been decided upon at earlier meetings—that the volume challenges the *normale* or universal nature of the encyclopedia and gives support to Yosef Yashunsky's 1931 apprehension that a mixed-use encyclopedia would inevitably skew the balance between the entries on general and Jewish topics toward the latter.[36]

Interestingly, many of the Hebrew-language terms, and even some names of rabbinical figures, are written phonetically in Yiddish (which contains vowels) after being provided in Hebrew (which typically does not). For example, the entry for the Hebrew prayer Ovinu Malkeynu (Our Father, Our King) is written according to its Hebrew spelling as אָבֿינו-מלכנו but is also spelled out phonetically as אָווינו-מאַלקיינו so that readers of Yiddish would have the proper pronunciation of the Hebrew. Most of these Hebrew terms, which were derived from Jewish religious life, would have been understood by nearly every Yiddish speaker; however, the reader's knowledge of the correct spelling and pronunciation of them is clearly not something that the editors took for granted.

Nearly all of the entries related to Jews or Judaism from the premodern period are related to religious figures, literature, or liturgy. By contrast, and in a reflection of the encyclopedists' conception of the changes in Judaism over the previous century and a half, nearly all of the entries related to Jews or Judaism in modern times are secular. No rabbinic figures or religious movements from their own time are mentioned. Instead, the focus is on modern Jewish political and cultural movements. Simon Dubnow fittingly contributed an entry on Autonomism in Jewish history, as well as entries on the Hebraist and cultural Zionist leader Ahad Ha'am, the Zionist leader Menachem Ussishkin, and the Russian socialist revolutionary Yevno Azef. Tcherikower contributed an entry on the Hebrew Socialist Union, which formed in London in May 1876 and was the first socialist Jewish group. There are entries on the Hebrew University of Jerusalem, and on cities with a particular Jewish interest, such as Odessa, which was a major center for Jewish political and cultural activity, and Avellaneda, Argentina, which was home to a Jewish community as well as a communist colony.

This division in the encyclopedia between entries on the religious past and the secular present very much reflected the priorities of the encyclopedists themselves. As onetime (and even current) revolutionaries, they maintained a conception of Judaism that insisted upon a stark division between the modern and premodern eras. Although most had been born into religious families, as youths during the tumultuous final days of the Russian empire they broke from tradition and embraced revolutionary movements with an often religious and even messianic zeal. The historian Jonathan Frankel vividly describes this generation of Jewish activists as "extremely young in 1905, utterly committed to the causes of revolution and to that of armed Jewish self-defense against the pogroms. Almost to a man they had become fervent Marxists by 1906, and even those who had not . . . now advocated (philosophically) a monistic determination and (politically) proletarian class war." He continues, "By 1906, the revolution had absorbed their every waking moment, every ounce of strength and every hope. However, to them the revolution meant a struggle not only for social equality and political freedom, but also for national, for Jewish, liberation."[37]

By the 1930s, however, when most of these revolutionaries were in their fifties, their fervor had abated and their utopian hopes for a workers' paradise had faded. Nevertheless, as nationalists committed to modern Yiddish culture, they still understood themselves to be the inheritors of the Jewish tradition and took it as their right to draw from the full scope of the Jewish past as they sought to create secular expressions of Jewish national identity.

The reception of volume 1 in the Yiddish press was overwhelmingly enthusiastic and supportive, and many reviewers hailed it as marking a milestone in Yiddish culture. Letters and telegrams of support poured into the Dubnow Fund's office in Paris.[38] Given the sheer number of collaborators, several of the *Entsiklopedye's* reviewers were also involved in one way or another with its creation. The review that appeared in the *Tsukunft*, for example, was written by Alexander Mukdoni.[39] Based in New York City, Mukdoni had been an early supporter of the project, though he had threatened to disassociate himself from it when YIVO broke with the Dubnow Fund in late 1931. In his review, Mukdoni was largely complimentary about the volume and spoke of it as the fulfillment of a long-held Yiddishist dream. He recounted its history in heroic terms, as very much a product of the tumultuous circumstances in which it was created. He relayed that it was conceived and set forth by Jewish intellectuals who were living in exile from the Bolshevik-ruled Soviet Union. Soon, however, the project was dealt a blow by Gergel's sudden death while in the United States to solicit funds—Mukdoni describes him as having made a "sacrifice" for the *Entsiklopedye*. Worse still, the project "shared the same fate as German Jews," once Hitler began to subject Jews to the "most terrible and bitter violence" and forced the contributors to flee with their "thousands and thousands of index cards" and crates of materials to France. Mukdoni was especially impressed with the *Entsiklopedye*'s entries on Jewish topics, which he described in glowing terms as being lively, original, and authoritative. He was less enamored, however, with the entries on general subject matter, finding them derivative, mechanical, and too often not composed by experts in the field.

Less critical is the March 1935 issue of the Warsaw-based *Literarishe bleter*, which was given over entirely to the volume, and most of the articles were written by figures intimately tied to the project, including Ben-Adir, Zalmen Reisen, Daniel Charney, and Nakhmen Meisel.[40] The issue begins with an overview by Moyshe Shalit, who had penned the 1928 review of the German-language *Encyclopaedia Judaica* that restarted conversations on publishing a Yiddish-language encyclopedia. He began his essay, "The Yiddish Encyclopedia—A Fact," by differentiating the Yiddish encyclopedia from the other Jewish ones that had come before it.[41] What distinguished the *Algemeyne entsiklopedye* from its predecessors most of all, he argued, was that this was the first time that an encyclopedia had been written explicitly for a Jewish readership, in a Jewish language, and with the goal of bringing universal knowledge to its readers. He hailed the work as a "great cultural accomplishment," and gives a brief historical overview and a rich description of the volume and its accomplishments before concluding that the work marks a new era for Yiddish culture and Yiddish-speaking Jewry.

Ben-Adir contributed the essay "A Brief Look 'Behind the Curtain' of the Encyclopedia," which offered insights into the internal working of the Dubnow Fund. He proudly proclaimed that in spite of the many challenges, "the first and most difficult stage is now behind us: the massive and complicated preparatory work has been completed for all twenty volumes. The first volume is already released, and the second volume is nearly ready to be printed, and most of the work is completed on the third."[42] He then went on to outline the many obstacles faced by the organizers. Unlike Shalit's description of the ways in which the larger political crises shaped the *Entsiklopedye*'s first years, Ben-Adir focused on the more immediate financial struggles and other administrative difficulties, such as finding appropriate personnel. It was extraordinarily difficult to recruit (and pay) the right people to serve in the many editorial and administrative positions necessary to execute such a major undertaking. This resulted in many challenges, such as arranging for the many photographic plates, drawings, and maps. Worse still, there were not enough resources to purchase copies of existing Jewish encyclopedias, forcing the editors to pay regular visits to libraries.

In keeping with the regular attacks on Abramovitch and YIVO that stemmed from Soviet Yiddish circles, the Kiev-based journal *Visnshaft un revolutsye* (Science and revolution) issued a complete denunciation of the encyclopedia, which it described as "a bourgeois, clerical-nationalist encyclopedia under the mask of secularism, non-partisanship, and social fair-mindedness."[43] Jerusalem's Hebrew-language *Kiryat Sefer* criticized it for showing favoritism toward revolutionary topics and disregarding religious ones.[44]

Although the arrival of volume 1 in late 1934 was widely embraced as a fresh start for the beleaguered project and a sign that matters had to some extent stabilized, the growing tyranny and antisemitism in Nazi Germany caused disruption far beyond the country's borders and would continually shape the *Entsiklopedye*'s subsequent volumes. Having come to power in January 1933 without a clear electoral majority, Hitler moved quickly to consolidate his position. He eliminated his political opponents within and outside the Nazi Party; those who were not murdered outright were imprisoned in newly built concentration camps. Along with implementing Nazi control over virtually all aspects of society, the regime quickly enacted repressive measures against its Jewish minority, who were less than 1 percent of the country's total population. Jews were subjected to random acts of violence and to organized economic boycotts, and those working within the civil service found themselves dismissed from their posts. These actions, designed to "de-Judaize" Germany, prompted approximately thirty-eight thousand Jews to flee in the first year of Hitler's reign; approximately twenty-five thousand more left each of the next several years.

The situation for Jews in Germany grew dramatically worse with the passage of the Nuremberg Laws in late summer and through the fall of 1935. These laws defined Jews as a racial group (although it was determined by means of their ancestors' religious affiliations), stripped them of their citizenship, and forbade new marriages or sexual relations between Jews and "Aryans." Other laws instituted new checks on hereditary illnesses and outlawed marriage by those ("Aryan" or otherwise) deemed genetically unfit. Many of these laws were soon extended to include Romani people (Gypsies) and people of Black African ancestry. Although some German Jews felt that there might be less uncertainty regarding their status now that it had been codified, the Nuremberg Laws prompted even more Jews to abandon the country.

Outside of Germany, the rest of Europe became increasingly unstable and, in some instances, more threatening to Jews. Britain sped up its munitions production in response to German belligerence and rearmament. France doubled the length of its period of military conscription, from one year to two. Once home to the most liberal immigration and refugees policies on the continent, France saw hostilities toward these newcomers grow markedly.[45] Caron has shown that tensions grew to such an extent that in the summer of 1935, Prime Minister Pierre Laval enacted policies that "limited for the first time the employment of foreigners in artisan trades and peddling," reflecting the growing influence of antisemitism and anti-foreigner sentiment.[46]

In Poland, where the primary audience for the *Entsiklopedye* was located, the government was also turning severely authoritarian. Although after the war it was reconstituted as an independent democratic republic, by the middle of the 1920s Poland had slid into autocratic rule under Józef Piłsudski. Nevertheless, he had sought to keep Poland unified while its status as a Polish national homeland was constantly challenged by its large population of ethnic minorities. In this period, Jewish cultural life flourished in Poland and Jews' economic status generally improved despite their lack of political power.[47] Following Piłsudski's death in May 1935, popular and legal antisemitism rose sharply, and Jews found themselves on the defensive. Quotas on Jews entering universities, professions, and business associations, which had been in place since the 1920s, were sharply lowered, and anti-Jewish violence became more frequent. Across the continent and extending to the United States, authoritarianism, xenophobia, hostility toward refugees, and the persecution of racial, religious, and ethnic minorities was on the rise.

The maelstrom sparked by Nazism notwithstanding, many of the challenges confronting the *Entsiklopedye* in 1935 were much more localized. Having successfully published volume 1 and received generally positive press, the encyclopedia editors were confronted with the challenges of advertising and selling it, as well as with publishing volume 2 within the promised window of only a few months. A significant amount of correspondence from that year, largely letters to and from the Dubnow Fund, and in particular to its secretary Avrom Kin, is preserved in the archives of YIVO. These letters document a range of activities taken up by the fund in the first months of 1935, including Kin's travels to London to identify agents to sell the encyclopedias[48] and Abramovitch's travels to North America (including New York, Miami, Los Angeles, San Francisco, Chicago, and Toronto) for fund-raising and publicity. Very few administrative documents, however, provide clear information on the number of copies sold (likely a few thousand) and balance sheets.

Immediately following the release of volume 1, a banquet was held in Paris to celebrate the *Entsiklopedye*. A similar one was held in New York during a visit by Abramovitch in May and was noticed by the *New York Times*.[49] The volume's arrival was reported widely in the press. Reflecting the increasing dispersal of Yiddish speakers in the two decades after World War I, the archives contain correspondence between the Dubnow Fund and interested buyers from not only France, Poland, and the United States, but also Switzerland, Norway, Canada, Palestine, Great Britain, South Africa, Romania, Latvia, and the Soviet Union. The letters reveal that a price for a leather-bound copy of volume 1 retailed for approximately $5.50 and a canvas-bound copy for approximately $5.00. Early requests for bulk orders came from booksellers in Kaunas (Kovne), Riga, and New York, which alone ordered five hundred copies. In a February 7 letter to the Yiddish linguist and folklorist Alfred Landau, Kin wrote of the editors' anxiety over the volume's reception, "The world of professional critics, who were preparing to sharpen their pens, is pleased with the encyclopedia and have strongly praised it. But the reader, the consumer, the important audiences for the encyclopedia, will they consult it?"[50]

Not only was Nakhmen Meisel, editor of *Literarishe bleter*, a strong supporter of the project, his siblings were as well. His sister, Gitl Meisel, a poet and literary critic who lived in Tel Aviv, offered to spread news of the project to the Yiddish-speaking community in Palestine, and his brother Isaac became the *Entsiklopedye*'s chief sales representative in Poland. In a letter from Nakhmen Meisel to Kin, he warned about the increasing economic difficulties faced by Jewish Poland and how this might impact sales. He was clearly worried that the expansion from ten to twenty volumes would turn off some potential customers, as would the inevitable long amount of time it would take to get the full set published and delivered. However, he offered sympathetically that one cannot "delay the end of the exile" and must push on.[51]

A major obstacle to selling copies in Poland came from what appears to be the mismanagement of sales by Isaac Meisel. As head of Komitet

Dubnov-fond/Stowarzysenie im. Szymona Dubnowa, a firm established to promote the *Entsiklopedye* in Poland, Isaac Meisel was responsible for sales, advertising, and distribution. A series of testy exchanges between Isaac and the Dubnow Fund reveals the fund's dissatisfaction with his efforts. They were frustrated by his tardiness in purchasing advertising space in newspapers, his inability to secure a sufficient number of reviews in the press (Meisel countered that the presses were all demanding free review copies), and with delayed payments for volumes sold. Meisel initially seems not to have accepted much responsibility for many of these issues, blaming them on the "pains of childbirth that are always so difficult."[52] After many exchanges over several months, a stern letter from Kin marked "PRIVATE" in April 1935 seems to have resolved the matter, and Isaac Meisel retained his post.[53]

Abramovitch's correspondence to the Dubnow Fund while on a trip to the United States and Canada also reveals the difficulties of distribution and his concern with protecting the project's viability. For example, it took several months to identify someone in the United States to act as a representative and take responsibility for overseeing sales. Many candidates were ruled out because they were seen as either untrustworthy or politically too vulnerable. Eventually Naftole Faynerman, the executive secretary of the American branch of YIVO, agreed to the task. Shipments of the encyclopedias that were sent to the United States were held up at customs for a full two months, since they were missing a required "printed in France" stamp on them, which entailed a fine of $169. Compounding these difficulties were production problems—most notably with the binding and the method of affixing the color map—which further impeded sales.[54] These obstacles inevitably led to the delay of volume 2, which appeared only in October 1935.

The list of associates (some of whom also contributed entries) was greatly expanded in the second volume from the first, and their names added to the prestige of the project. This list includes the poet David Einhorn as well as the three famous Charney brothers: the labor leader Baruch Charney Vladeck, the writer Daniel Charney, and the literary critic Shmuel Charney. Leon Bramson, the formal head of the Dubnow Fund, is listed, as are the Polish Jewish historians Majer Balaban, Jacob Shatzky, and Emanuel Ringelblum. The second volume contains a full-color map of Europe as well as black-and-white photographs on a variety of subjects. There are significantly fewer entries pertaining to Jewish religious figures and Jewish subjects generally than in volume 1. Those that do exist are on relatively more modern topics, such as Zalmen Reisen's entries on the Jewish Enlightenment leader Isaac Abraham Euchel and the novelist and playwright David Ignatov. There is an entry *on*

FIGURE 2.3 Advertisement for *Algemeyne entsiklopedye* (Sholem Schwartzbard Papers, Courtesy of University of Cape Town).

FIGURE 2.4 "Europe: Political Map," *Algemeyne entsiklopedye*, volume 2.

David Einhorn by the poet Avrom Lyesin (Abraham Liessin), as well as an entry *by* Einhorn on the concept of the "wandering Jew." As a rule, entries on
significant Jewish subjects are allotted far less space than entries on significant
general subjects. For example, the entry on the "wandering Jew" is only three
and a half columns, although the anti-Jewish legend dates back to early Christian times and had been a regular antisemitic trope ever since, including through
the Nazi period. Compared to the first volume, volume 2 also contains a greater
number of entries pertaining to technology and innovation (such as "Iron," "Iron
Industry," "Reinforced Concrete," and "Railroad") as well as to the natural world
(such as "Iguanodon," "Ovum," "Polar Bear," "Impotence," and "Breath").[55]

Like its predecessor, volume 2, which covered "Atlantic Ocean"
(אטלאַנטישער אָקעאַן) to "Interference" (אינטערפערענץ), reflects the particular interests of the encyclopedists themselves, in particular Abramovitch's commitment to social democracy and his antipathy to nationalism. This can be
observed not only in the choice of subjects, but also by the amount of column
space dedicated to them. For example, among the volume's several long
entries are ones on Italy (thirty-four columns with many black-and-white
photos), Europe (twenty-four columns with a full-color map as well as several

subentries), and India (thirty-six columns with more than a dozen black-and-white photos). These entries are of the sort that one would expect to see in a standard encyclopedia and cover topics such as demographics, geography, history, culture, language, economy, and political systems. However, overwhelming the final quarter of the book are nearly one hundred columns on the many international labor movements that, beginning in the mid-nineteenth century, sought to bring together left-wing socialists, anarchists, communists, and unions into one unified organization. Taken as a whole, these entries, many of which were written by Abramovitch himself, are the most comprehensive examination of any topic in the first two volumes and likely one of the most thorough studies of international socialism in *any* general encyclopedia. The entries discuss the prehistory of the socialist movement in London, its founding during the period of reaction following the failed 1848 revolutions, and its many incarnations, with entries such as "International, First," "International, Second," "International in the War Years, 1914–1919," "International, Third," and so on. In addition to the many entries that begin with "international," Social Democracy and labor movements are represented in other ways, such as the long entry on "Individual Psychology" (which was started by Social Democrat Alfred Adler), an entry on "Italian Worker Strikes," and a long discussion on imperialism and its relationship to capitalism.

While the first two volumes are skewed toward topics related to Social Democracy and obscure religious Jewish ones, they also show what the reality for Yiddish-speaking Jews may have looked like in the mid-1930s had they been fully recognized as a national minority group in the societies in which they lived. Published at the very moment when the civil status of Jews across Europe was once again being broadly called into question by extreme nationalists who argued that Jews constituted a profound threat to their societies, *and* by the growing Zionist movement, which insisted that Jews could be safe only in their own homeland in Palestine, these volumes give testament to the persistence of the Diaspora Nationalist vision and the disproportional representation of Eastern European Jews in international socialist movements.

In this sense, these volumes are simultaneously descriptive and prescriptive. They paint a portrait of a world in which Yiddish-speaking Jews constitute their own distinct nation and possess a language that allows them to express and participate in the full range of human affairs. As represented in these initial volumes, which bring Jewish topics such as a rabbinics and Hebrew literature into conversation with "normal" ones like automobiles and explosive matter, Yiddish speakers could be both fully Jewish *and* part of the larger world around them. The volumes represent one of the strongest assertions—and one of the last of its kind—of the Diaspora Nationalist position. They highlight the Jewish contri-bution to the modern world and are a sign to the millions of Yiddish-speaking Jews that their language, culture, and history were as worthy as those of the great civilizations of the world. Since subsequent volumes of the *Entsiklopedye* would be shaped by the growing assaults on Jews as a result of Nazism, volumes 1 and 2 are some of the last attempts to convey what Jewish life in Europe might have looked like had Jews received full rights as a national minority.

Turning Point: Volumes 3 and 4

Volumes 3 and 4, like their predecessors, appeared long after they were initially promised. In addition, both volumes were still on the letter *alef*, a sign of just how slowly the publication was moving through the alphabet.[56] Volume 3, which began with "Intra" (אינטרא) and ended with "Antisemitism" (אנטיסעמיטיזם), was published in December 1936, and volume 4, which began with "Antiseptic" (אנטיסעפטיק) and ended with "Land of Israel" (ארץ-ישראל), appeared in late 1937. A series of letters in 1936 between Abramovitch and Ba-ruch Charney Vladeck, describes the many difficulties faced by the Dubnow Fund as it sought to get volume 3 to press.[57] Almost exclusively, the problems were financial ones. For much of that year, the encyclopedists pursued every means of raising funds, including pressing their American contacts for dona-tions, trying to recover the $169 they paid to the United States Customs Service, and applying (unsuccessfully) for bank loans. They explored the pos-sibility of having the volume printed in Belgium, where publishing costs were lower. As late as the end of October and even after the French government devalued the franc (making foreign currency more valuable), they were still searching for a final $1,000 to publish the work.

The years 1936 and 1937 were difficult for the *Entsiklopedye*, and they were also a period of growing crisis for European Jewry and the continent as a whole. In Germany, the situation for Jews declined even further as Hitler was emboldened by the world's seeming disregard for his continuing violations of the Versailles Treaty. In 1936, a concentration camp for political prisoners was built at Sachsenhausen, reflecting Hitler's continued willingness to punish his opponents and dissidents ruthlessly. That same year, Hitler renounced the Lo-carno Pact among Germany, Belgium, France, Great Britain, and Italy, which called for the international defense of Germany's western border and the de-militarization of the western part of Germany known as the Rhineland. Soon after, he reintroduced troops into the region. German Jews in these years also experienced the effects of the expanding policy of "Aryanization" of Jewish property, which amounted to the state-supported theft of Jewish assets, including bank accounts, homes, land, and businesses. In addition, the Nazi policy known as *Gleichschaltung*, or "coordination," continued to bring organizations, including schools, social clubs, sporting associations, professional societies, and cultural organizations under Nazi control. People labeled as Jews under the law were dismissed from their jobs as well as from social and professional organizations. In 1937, Germany passed laws to prevent Jewish doctors from treating "Aryan" patients.

More broadly, tensions in Europe regularly spilled over into bloodshed. Fascist Italy's invasion of Ethiopia intensified in this period, leading to the spring 1936 fall of Addis Ababa and the country's subsequent defeat and occupation in 1937. This led some Italian fascists to advocate for the resettlement of Italian Jews in the conquered country.[58] Also in 1937, Italy joined the fascist Anti-Comintern Pact, Germany and Japan's alliance against the Communist International (Comintern), thereby bringing together the Axis powers that would go on to wage World War II. In Poland, following the May 1935 death of Piłsudski, anti-Jewish measures increased as many Poles, including government leaders, sought to draw from the German example and revoke Jews' constitutional rights with the goal of pressuring them to emigrate from the country. This led to many fierce clashes between Polish nationalists and Jews. Tensions between Polish and Jewish students escalated to such an extent that in January 1937, the University of Wilno (Vilna) was shuttered for two weeks.[59] In Spain, civil war broke out in 1936 and lasted until 1939. This conflict between Republican supporters of the left-leaning, democratically elected government and nationalists seeking to restore the monarchy and the oversized role of the Catholic Church quickly became representative of the international struggle between the political left (including communists, socialists, and anarchists) and the political right (especially fascists). Many international opponents of the nationalists established brigades that went to Spain to join the fight (including Yiddish-speaking volunteers who formed the Naftali Botwin Company), which helped to shape the image of the conflict as an international struggle against fascism.[60] In April 1937, the German Luftwaffe gave its support to the fascist leader Francisco Franco by bombing the town of Guernica, an act that killed many hundreds of civilians and facilitated Franco's taking of northern Spain.

Outside of Europe, Jewish communities not only were looking upon events in Europe with alarm but also facing their own struggles. The armed revolt of Palestinian Arabs against British rule led to a conflict that lasted from 1936 to 1939 and brought many members of the rapidly growing community of Jewish

Zionists into the fighting. This uprising, which began as a general strike by Arabs against imperial rule, eventually turned into a broad armed conflict that was ruthlessly suppressed by British forces. It also saw increased cooperation between the British and Zionists. In the midst of this conflict, the British released the 1937 Peel Commission Report, which argued for the partition of Palestine, giving much of the arable land to a future Jewish state yet retaining key defensive positions under British control.[61] In the United States, President Franklin Roosevelt easily won reelection in 1936, to the delight of his many Jewish voters, but he would do little to lower the barriers to refugees from Europe until a series of Nazi-instigated crises in 1938. In 1937, the German American Bund, a pro-Nazi organization comprised of Americans of German ancestry, formed and began to operate training facilities in camps in several northeast states. At its zenith in 1939, it held a pro-Nazi rally in Madison Square Garden with twenty thousand supporters in attendance.

Released in 1936, volume 3 at first glance seems to follow the same format as its two predecessors. It opens with a full-color reproduction of the Paleolithic Altamira cave paintings, located in Spain and then thought to date back twenty-five thousand years. In the introductory materials, there is little information provided beyond lists of authors, collaborators, key entries, and errata. Volume 3 includes two full-page color maps, one each of North America and South America, as well as many pages of black-and-white photographs, tables, and maps. There are entries on many countries, including Iran, Iraq, Albania, Ireland, and Algeria. The entry "America" is twenty-two columns long and discusses geography, irrigation, climate, populations, and economics, and also includes a section on Jews in the United States. An entry on Islam receives eight and a half columns and two pages of photographic plates showing the interior of the Great Mosque of Córdoba as well as several examples of Islamic art. Political topics of importance to left-wing movements are once again prominently represented, with the "Anarchism" entry receiving nine and a half columns and a separate, "Anarchist Movements" entry running seventeen columns. There is a five-column entry on the American Federation of Labor and two columns on the movement for an eight-hour workday (akht-shoediker arbetstog). The volume also includes entries on the four different Alexanders who ruled Russia in the modern age, as well as entries on alcohol and alcoholism and on masturbation (onanizm).

Topics of Jewish interest include the Amoraim (literally, "those who say"), the Jewish scholars from approximately 200 to 500 CE whose teachings form the basis of the Talmud. The Renaissance-era writer Elye Bokher, whose sixteenth-century epic poems in medieval Yiddish were a topic of great fascination for interwar Yiddishists looking to establish the historical underpinnings of their movement, receives an entry by Kalmanovitch. An entry on American Yiddish, written by YIVO's Max Weinreich, discusses the creation of a particular American dialect of Yiddish and describes how it combines dialects from Yiddish speakers across Eastern Europe. The civil rights organizations American Jewish Committee and American Jewish Congress each have entries.

What most distinguishes volume 3 from its predecessors is its final entry, "Antisemitism." Although it is alphabetized properly, it is conspicuously out of place as a multiauthored essay (by Ben-Adir, Tcherikower, and Abramovitch) of nearly fifty columns, longer than any previous single entry. It thus marks the first significant format change and the beginning of the encyclopedia's shift in emphasis away from its original vision of transmitting universal, or *normale*, knowledge and toward focusing on particularly Jewish topics as a response to the ever-declining situation of many of its readers. Divided into five sections, the essay covers the "source and essence" of antisemitism; antisemitism as an ideology; antisemitism in the ancient, medieval, modern, and post–World War I periods; "international propaganda and organization of antisemitism"; and "organizations for the struggle against antisemitism." The essay is primarily historical in its disciplinary focus (and, unsurprisingly, strongly Marxist in the sections written by Abramovitch) and concludes with a bibliography. Its length extends the column count of the volume by an additional thirty over the previous two volumes.

Writing on the "source and essence" of antisemitism, Ben-Adir argues that essential to understanding antisemitism is the Jewish people's unique position in the world as the sole group that has preserved its national essence in spite of its constant engagement with other peoples. He writes, "The Jewish *folk* is the only *folk* in the world that have for hundreds upon hundreds of years lived among other peoples, participated in the general processes of historical life, and have not merged themselves with them and who remain an especially distinctive national group."[62] Since the time of the destruction of the second Temple and the dispersal of Jews from the Land of Israel in the year 70 CE, he continues, the Jewish nation has been cut off from its foundation of territorial concentration and unity under a single governing authority. This history has led to Jews' present, unnatural state of dispersion and permanent minority status. Reflecting Ben-Adir's secular understanding of the Jewish past, the section explains that Jews have been able to maintain their coherency, even as they have lived among other peoples, not on account of divine intervention but rather as a consequence of identifiable historical factors. Chief among them is that the survival of the Jewish people stopped becoming a fact and became a "categorical imperative" or, following his understanding of the Jewish religion as a creation of the nation, a "holy commandment" in itself. Antisemitism, he argues, served the paradoxical function of helping to maintain Jewish distinctiveness, since it resulted in Jews' religious, economic, geographical, and political isolation.

Ben-Adir's description of Jews as a distinct national group in possession of an unaltered essence and historical path is consistent with his overall worldview, his sense of the crisis facing European Jews in the middle of the 1930s, and, as of the release of volume 3, his new position as a leader in the movement known as Territorialism. While preparing for the sales and distribution of volume 1, he had traveled to London to attend a meeting of like-minded Territorialists to promote the resettlement of European Jewry outside the Continent, in somewhere other than Palestine. The Territorialist ideology to which he adhered had originally been founded by British Jews in the early twentieth century following a series of deadly anti-Jewish attacks in the Russian empire. Rising antisemitism led Territorialist thinkers to propose that Jews be immediately resettled from hostile places in Europe to sites of European colonial activity, such as in Africa, South America, and Australia. While not initially opposed to Jewish settlement in Palestine, Territorialists in the decades before World War I broke from the Zionist goal of creating a Jewish national homeland in the Land of Israel, believing that not only was it unworkable while Palestine was under Ottoman rule, but that Jews should neither be segregated from non-Jews nor be made to live in a society governed by Jewish religious laws and customs. A powerful alternative to the Zionist movement in the first decades of the twentieth century, Territorialism foundered in the years after World War I and the successful establishment of a Jewish colonial presence in Palestine with British support.[63]

In the mid-1930s, however, the Territorialist idea gained new momentum in response to the growing Jewish refugee crisis and mounting frustrations over the British Mandate for Palestine and increased tensions with Palestinian Arabs. Territorialists feared that Palestine would soon be off limits to Jews seeking sanctuary and began to search for alternative solutions for Jewish resettlement. Unlike the original Territorialists, many new adherents, such as Ben-Adir, did not come out of the Zionist movement and were deeply engaged with furthering Jewish communal life in Europe. As historian Gur Alroey demonstrates, "The nucleus of New Territorialism consisted of Jewish socialists who were disappointed with the Bolshevik Revolution and concerned about rising anti-Semitism in Europe. They no longer believed it possible to integrate into the surrounding society and refused to regard the Zionist solution as the only option."[64] Gathering in London in 1935, organizers from Britain, France, and Poland founded the Frayland-lige far Yidisher Teritoryal-istisher Kolonizatsye (Freeland League for Jewish Territorial Colonization) with the goal of securing territory outside of Europe for collective Jewish relo-cation, ideally within the British Empire.[65] The goal of the Frayland-lige was not the creation of a Jewish state, as the Zionists wished, but the establishment of a Jewish autonomous realm where Jews could live in safety according to the principles of self-determination and could continue to develop Yiddish cul-ture.[66] Writing on antisemitism for the *Entsiklopedye*, Ben-Adir argued that a return to Jewish sovereignty and territorial independence would bring about, if not an end, then at least a profound amelioration of this longest hatred.

The subsequent sections of the entry concern the historical development of antisemitism and were written primarily by Tcherikower, who explains its his-tory not through traditional religious Jewish explanations—as divine punish-ment for Jewish transgressions of the law—but rather through a consideration of Jews' particular status in the world. He traces antisemitism's origins back to the Jewish idea of monotheism during the period of Jewish-Greek encounter and then to Jews' insistence on political and religious autonomy in the Roman era. He goes on to describe Jewish-Christian tensions in the formative period of Christianity and then Jews' geographical, political, and economic isolation in the European Middle Ages. Although Jews, he explains, began to see a reprieve from antisemitism in the modern era following the French Revolution and the gradual granting of civil rights in Western and Central European states, the re-actionary period that followed brought together monarchists, clericalists, and counterrevolutionary forces to undo the liberalizing accomplishments of the Enlightenment and reverse Jews' newly gained rights. In his discussion of anti-semitism in the contemporary period, Abramovitch focused on how the rise of modern capitalism changed the economic and social position of Jews by elimi-nating economic protections and monopolies held by Jews and causing Jews as a group to become overidentified with capitalism and its ill effects on society.

In addition to financial reasons, volume 4 was delayed by world events once again colliding directly with the operations of the Dubnow Fund. In March 1937, Raphael Abramovitch's son, Mark Rein, who was in his late twen-ties, had gone to Spain to report on the war on behalf of the anti-fascists. The next month, he went missing in Barcelona. Highly active in leftist causes, Rein was working as a journalist for publications such as the Stockholm-based *So-cial Demokraten* and the New York *Forverts*. He volunteered on the Catalonian front with the POUM (Workers' Party of Marxist Unification) and had found work in a munitions factory. On the night of April 9, he disappeared. His comrades and, soon, his father, began to suspect that Rein had been kidnapped by Soviet agents. In the midst of the war, Comintern agents had been working behind the Republican lines to conduct a campaign of coercion, harassment, and occasional assassination among socialists and anarchists in an attempt to solidify its authority on the political left and to enlarge the Soviet sphere of control. At times, the clashes led to open fighting. One of those searching for Rein was his friend and fellow journalist Willy Brandt, who would later become chancellor of the Federal Republic of Germany (West Germany) from 1969 to 1974. He commented at the time on the Soviet-led campaign of intimidation and coercion:

> In order to monopolize the leadership, the Communists do not hesitate to use the most vicious means. In a situation when everything depends on the unity of all anti-Franco forces, the methods of the Communist party, the methods of slander and blind terror against their socialist opponents is terribly dangerous to the anti-Fascist war. These methods undermine the morale of the soldiers, they poison the whole international labor movement, they make a mockery of the Popular Front.[67]

Abramovitch himself traveled to Spain in the midst of the conflict to try and find his son, but to no avail.[68] For months, he threw himself into the effort to trace his Mark's whereabouts, writing to socialist colleagues around the world for assistance.[69] Subsequent evidence has led credence to the likelihood that Rein was murdered on Stalin's orders for being Abramovitch's son, and that he had been kidnapped initially either to serve as a hostage or to force him to make public accusations against his father in upcoming political show trials.[70] For the rest of his life, Abramovitch was tormented by the fate of his son, and it fueled his ever-consuming hatred toward the Soviet regime. As for volume 4, it was prepared largely without his input, other than an entry on unemployment (*arbetlozikayt*) that first appeared in the *probeheft* and was subsequently updated.

While this crisis was underway, the Parisian Yiddish world was experiencing two of its greatest cultural achievements: the creation of the Modern Jewish Culture Pavilion at the 1937 World's Fair and, that same year, the First International Yiddish Culture Congress. The scholars Nick Underwood, Matthew Hoffman, and Gennady Estraikh have shown in their respective studies of the pavilion and congress that these events were the culmination of nearly two decades of Yiddish cultural and political organizing among Jewish immigrants from Eastern Europe residing in France.[71] They also provide a helpful glimpse at the state of Yiddish culture and the politics of Eastern European

Jews in the late 1930s as their cultural and political leaders navigated how best to respond to the growing threats of Nazism and Stalinism.

The Modern Jewish Culture Pavilion was one of two pavilions dedicated to Jewish topics, the other being a competing Zionist effort called Israel in Palestine, which displayed the achievements of the Jewish colonial effort in Palestine with an emphasis on its new agricultural settlements.[72] By contrast, the Modern Jewish Culture Pavilion offered spectators a look into the aspirations and accomplishments of European Jews and Yiddish cultural productions in particular. It included copies of thousands of Yiddish-language newspapers and books, items from the Yiddish theater, and materials highlighting the contributions of Jews to the fields of education, arts, science, and pedagogy. The pavilion was initially proposed by the Dubnow Fund, and Abramovitch was named president of the pavilion's committee, although his role was severely curtailed on account of his son's disappearance in Barcelona.[73] The Modern Jewish Culture Pavilion involved contributions from a wide range of Yiddish cultural organizations such as the Vilna-based YIVO, the Warsaw-based Tsentrale Yidishe Shul-organizatsye (Central Yiddish School Organization, known as TsIShO), and the New York–based Arbeter-ring, as well many Jewish luminaries such as the painter Marc Chagall and the writer Sholem Asch. As an assertion of the place of Jews and Jewish culture within modern Europe, the pavilion, Underwood demonstrates, is best thought of not only as an expression of self-pride in the international and Diasporic composition of world Jewry but also as a clear assertion of the Jewish people's place among the nations of the world in light of the rising threats from fascism and antisemitism.

As planning for the World's Fair was underway, other Yiddish activists were organizing the First International Yiddish Culture Congress in an effort led by the Yiddish playwright and writer Chaim Sloves, who had founded a "culture front" to aid in the Comintern-inspired Popular Front's fight against fascism.[74] Given its ties to Soviet communism, the culture front had a difficult time organizing the conference, as it met fierce resistance initially from many of the groups who would go on to participate in the World's Fair pavilion. Hoffman has shown that once Sloves was able to gain the endorsement of the Diaspora Nationalist leader Chaim Zhitlowsky, support for the congress quickly began to grow, although it remained identified in the Yiddish world as largely a communist project. Opponents included organizations such as the Bund and YIVO, newspapers such as the *Forverts* and *Tog*, and prominent Yiddish writers including the poet Jacob Glatstein and I. J. Singer (older brother of Isaac Bashevis Singer), who argued that the goal of the congress was not to promote Yiddish culture but to employ Yiddish to advance Soviet propaganda. Nevertheless, the congress was held in September 1937 in Paris with some four thousand attendees from twenty-three countries. Ironically, the Soviet government objected to Zhit-lowsky's Diaspora Nationalist call for a united international Yiddish commu-nity and did not allow the delegation from the USSR to attend.

The conference's main themes revolved around international Yiddish soli-darity and overcoming internal differences to more effectively wage the fight against fascism.[75] A key outcome of the congress was the formation of the Alveltlekher Yidisher Kultur-farband (International Yiddish Cultural Move-ment, known as IKUF), as well as a new journal, *Yidishe kultur* (Yiddish cul-ture). Although many of the organizers of the pavilion and the congress were at odds with one another politically over the place of Soviet communism within the Yiddish-language movement, they shared a sense of urgency and a deep commitment to the importance of Yiddish culture within the larger fight against the growing threat from fascism. Through their assertion of the integ-rity of Yiddish culture and its role in this fight, they reaffirmed their place within the European community of nations.

Appearing at the very end of that tumultuous year, volume 4 begins with a full-page black-and-white photo of the fourth-century statue *Apollo Belvedere* on display in the Vatican. Among the articles by prominent authors include one on labor (*arbet*) by Benedikt Kautsky, the socialist leader and son of the Marxist theoretician Karl Kautsky. All told, there are more than seventy-five columns dedicated to entries related to the labor movement and labor activ-ism, including a two-page table of the history of the labor movement from the 1786 printers' strike in Philadelphia, Pennsylvania, to the labor unrest at the outbreak of war in 1914. Subjects of other entries include Africa, astronomy, and Armenia. Entries on particularly Jewish topics include Yiddish writers S. An-sky (the pseudonym of Shloyme Zanvl Rappoport) and Joseph Opa-toshu. There were also entries on the Arbeter-ring, Jews in Africa, Jews in Argentina, and the ORT.

Like volume 3, volume 4 ends with a lengthy essay, this time on "Erets-yisroel," the traditional Jewish designation for the territory that was then commonly referred to as Palestine and historically considered by Jews to be their ancestral homeland. The entry is divided into four parts that together span thirty-eight columns. It includes a two-page color map that is titled both "Erets-yisroel" and "Palestine" and shows the region's 1930s-era borders. The entry was composed by four authors: F. Naftali and Y. Shlezinger wrote on the geography, populations, and economics of the region; Ben-Adir wrote the section entitled "Social-Political and Communal-Cultural Life"; and Menes wrote on the region's history.

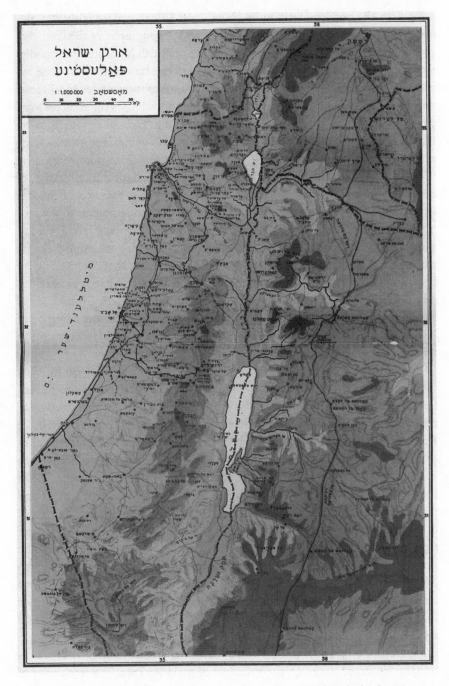

FIGURE 2.5 "Erets-yisroel/Palestine," *Algemeyne entsiklopedye*, volume 4.

At first, the portions written by Naftali and Shlezinger are fairly straight-forward. They provide information regarding the geography of the land, dis-cussed primarily in terms of its borders under the British Mandate, and statistics regarding population and economics. Very quickly, however, the section be-comes dominated by discussions of Jewish immigration under the Zionist movement and Jewish contributions to the economy. It uses the Hebrew word *aliyah* (literally, "ascent"), a Zionist term connoting spiritual elevation, to de-scribe the various waves of Jewish migration. In discussing demographics, the article focuses almost exclusively on the rise of the Jewish population after World War I as the Zionist movement actively facilitated the migration of European Jews to the region. There is no comparable discussion of changes within the Arab community other than statistics that demonstrate the pro-portional shrinking of the population as a result of increasing Jewish coloni-zation. There is little discussion of the religious, cultural, or ethnic diversity among the Palestinian Arab population except to note that the majority of Palestinians were peasants working the land and a small minority were urban dwellers. There is a brief mention of the Bedouin population. Discussions of the economics of the region are limited almost entirely to the contribution of Jewish agricultural workers. In fact, discussions of the non-Jewish majority are nearly entirely absent for much of the first third of the entry.

Ben-Adir's section, "Social-Political and Communal-Cultural Life," is more inclusive of the Arab majority population. He describes the complexi-ties of life in the region, where the British were asserting their authority against the challenges posed by a powerful Zionist movement and a popular Arab uprising against Britain and the Zionists. A great deal of space is allo-cated to the system of British rule and its attempt to identify a permanent solution to the conflict between the competing national movements: "Both the Arabs and the Jews insist that they have been wronged by the other and that each has been wronged by England."[76] He goes on to discuss the history of Arab nationalism in Palestine, locating its origins in the late Ottoman pe-riod and its emergence in force in the immediate postwar period as the League of Nations discussed giving the Mandate over Palestine to the Brit-ish. He writes that the declaration of the Fifth Arab Congress, which was held in 1922 in Nablus in response to the imposition of the Mandate earlier that year, depicts well the platform of the Arab national movement, which argued for the end of British rule, the cessation of Jewish immigration into the region, the implementation of self-rule, and the creation of a constitu-tional democracy based on the principle of majority rule. The remainder of the entry is dedicated primarily to the organization of the Jewish community in Palestine, known in Hebrew and Yiddish as the *yishuv* ("settlement"), including its quasi-governmental bodies and political divisions. The entry also covers Britain's Peel Commission Report, which declared that the Mandate was unworkable and proposed to divide the region into Arab and Jewish states—a plan rejected by both sides (although the Zionist Congress of 1937 did not reject the idea of partition per se as a solution to the conflict).

The final section on the history of the Land of Israel, written by Menes, provides an overview of the many peoples that have inhabited the land and the many regimes that have ruled over it, declaring that "already from the most distant times this small territory was a meeting place for various peoples."[77] Next, Menes discusses the arrival of Israelites as outlined in the Torah and archaeological research dating from the fourteenth century BCE. The article then provides an overview of the Israelite struggles and contributions, as well as those of other ruling societies, including the Assyrians, Babylonians, and Romans. While the historical overview pays particular attention to the Israelite/Jewish presence in the land, it is not overly Zionist, as it does not advocate Jewish hegemony over the land. Rather, the period generally thought of by Zionists as the time of Jewish dispossession, beginning with the Jewish-Roman wars of 67–70 CE, is described in only two short paragraphs. The Middle Ages are examined without much reference to the Jewish presence in the land, other than to mention how Babylonia became a new center of rabbinic thought and the Land of Israel remained home to continued Torah study, with tensions periodically flaring up between Israelite Jews and Babylonian Jews over control of the increasingly dispersed people. The final paragraphs discuss the increase in Jewish settlement in the land in the late nineteenth century, following renewed European engagement and colonial activity in the Middle East. The article ends with the growth in the Jewish population there as a result of the Zionist movement.

As a multi-authored essay that ends the volume, this entry follows a similar format to the one on antisemitism that closes volume 3, and it is listed under the heading "Erets-yisroel" rather than "Palestine," thereby speaking to the Dubnow Fund's growing reconsideration of the *Entsiklopedye*'s function in the mid-1930s. The fact that these two entries, notably located at the conclusion of their respective volumes, were edited by a staff of Diaspora Nationalists who had spent much of their lives working to build a sustainable Jewish life in Europe suggests that the rising anti-Jewish sentiment in Europe was forcing a reexamination of the Diasporist project and original mission of the *Entsiklopedye*.

Born in the last decades of the Russian empire, the encyclopedists in their youth had aligned themselves with (and often helped to found) political parties and labor organizations that not only advocated for the overthrow of the Russian czar, but also hoped to usher in a new era that would allow secular Jewish life to flourish. They were members of groups that bore names such as the Socialist Zionists, the Laborers of Zion, the Jewish Labor Union (Bund), and the Jewish Socialist Workers Party. While these groups at times fought with one another for supporters in the turbulent first years of the twentieth century, when Russia was in the midst of revolutionary upheavals, they were unified in their desire to position themselves in between, on one side, more-mainstream Zionists who wanted to establish a Jewish (and potentially capitalist) homeland outside of Europe and, on the other side, anti-nationalist Marxist revolutionary groups, namely the communists, who wanted to eliminate national identities and movements altogether. As nationalists, the encyclopedists believed that the situation of European Jews in the late-nineteenth and early-twentieth centuries was an abnormal one and a consequence of their landlessness and political powerlessness. As revolutionaries, they committed themselves to overthrowing the autocracy and ushering in a socialist age. Although they asserted the primacy and authenticity of the Jewish nation, they linked their particular national struggle with the cause of liberating all workers and oppressed peoples. With the failure of the 1905 revolutionary movement in Russia, many went on to found the building blocks of modern Yiddish culture and Diaspora Nationalism, including the political organizations, cultural venues, scholarly materials, and artistic and literary forums that sustained it. Following the end of World War I and the breakup of the old European order, the vision of creating a European order that would allow for the unfettered social, cultural, and potentially political development of Jewish life seemed to be realizable for the first time, and they built their names and reputations on this cause. Now in their late fifties and early sixties, they were beginning to watch as the vision they had spent their lives trying to realize—the creation of a Diasporic Jewish nation within the European fold—quickly receded from view.[78]

From the Universal to the Particular: *Yidn alef*

If 1936 and 1937 were years of increasing anxiety over the fate of Jews under German rule, the events of 1938 confirmed the worst fears of many. That year, Hitler instigated three crises that exacerbated the increasingly perilous situation of European Jewry and made a new war seem inevitable. No volumes of the *Entsiklopedye* were published in 1938, as the Dubnow Fund focused its efforts on selling the first three volumes and preparing for what would become a fundamental shift in the project.

The first of the three crises was prompted by Hitler's long-standing aspiration to annex Austria as part of building a greater *Reich* that incorporated lands adjacent to Germany that contained large numbers of ethnic Germans. This aspiration was expressed in the first of twenty-five points laid out in the plan the Nazi Party developed at a 1920 meeting: "We demand the unification of all Germans in the Greater Germany on the basis of the right of self-determination of peoples."[79] A native of Austria, Hitler had long hoped to unite the two countries, a direct violation of the Versailles Treaty. On the morning of March 12, 1938, the German military crossed the Austrian border and was met with no resistance. To the contrary, Austrians flooded the streets in a massive display of approval. Within days, Germany had complete control over the country, which was soon made a part of the German state. As with previous violations of the Versailles Treaty, the Allied governments chose not to interfere so as not to risk getting enmeshed in another world war whose outcome was far from certain.

For the more than 181,000 Austrian Jews, the *Anschluss* (German, "connection"), as it was called, was nothing short of catastrophic. Most Jews lived in the capital city of Vienna, and they immediately fell victim to unimaginable acts of violence and cruelty. Not only did the anti-Jewish laws that had been gradually passed over the previous five years go into effect almost immediately, the euphoria over the German takeover led to assaults on Jewish bodies, homes, businesses, and places of worship. This was the first time since Hitler had come to power in Germany that wide-scale and sustained violence was meted out against a Jewish community. For weeks, Jews were robbed of their possessions, beaten, and subjected to mass public humiliations. They endured detachments of Austrian storm troopers who targeted Jews with ferocious brutality as they looted what they could and destroyed much of what they could not.

The Allied powers met the Nazi takeover of Austria with condemnation but little else. To help ease the refugee crisis of Austrian Jews fleeing the country, President Roosevelt unilaterally combined the visa quotas for German and Austrian Jews, as well as briefly relaxed visa requirements. British prime minister Neville Chamberlain issued regrets, lamenting that short of force, there was little that his country could have done to stop it. France was completely quiet, as the government led by Léon Blum had resigned *en bloc* two days prior, owing to unrelated matters. Austrian Jewish refugees fleeing to France found that the country was no longer so welcoming to Nazism's victims. As Caron notes, "The Daladier government [that replaced Blum's] passed a series of decree laws which imposed harsh restrictions on the entry of immigrants to France and increased police surveillance over those immigrants already there."[80]

In the world of Yiddish letters, the *Anschluss*, coupled with the world's refusal to come to Austrian Jewry's aid, accelerated a crisis in the relationship of
Yiddish-speaking Jews to the modern world. The complete vulnerability of
Jews led many in Europe and the United States to conclude that there remained little future for them anywhere on the continent, and perhaps in the
entire Western world. By the late 1930s, it was clear that the guarantees and
protections that the liberal democracies promised minorities, as articulated in
the Treaty of Versailles and various minorities treaties, were little more than
hollow gestures. Many Jews had invested their hopes for the future in these
agreements, and the optimism that had once defined much of postwar Jewish
life was rapidly turning to despair. Studies by scholars such as Cecile Kuznitz
and Joshua Karlip have shown that many Eastern European Jews who had
once championed Marxist or socialist views alongside their commitment to
Yiddish began to reconsider their political stances and either turn to a politically "neutral" scholarship, embrace a separatist or even Zionist stance, or reject altogether the hope for a Jewish existence based upon the Diaspora Nationalist principles that were Dubnow's legacy.[81]

In late September, the second of three crises unfolded when Great Britain,
France, and Italy, meeting with Germany in Munich, permitted the latter's an-
nexation of a significant portion of Czechoslovakia known as the Sudetenland,
which was home to a large number of *Volksdeutsche*. Historian Wolf Gruner has
shown that this brought yet another round of anti-Jewish humiliation and violence.[82] Germany's late-October decision to expel approximately eighteen thousand Polish Jews from the country, and Poland's initial refusal to accept them,
set off a chain of events that resulted in the third crisis, the state-organized
Kristallnacht pogroms of November 9–10, in which Jewish homes, shops,
houses of worship, and cemeteries throughout Germany, including the recently
annexed Austria and Czech Sudetenland, were violently attacked. A least
ninety-one Jews were murdered (hundreds more likely died of their injuries and
maltreatment later), and as many as thirty thousand Jewish men were arrested
and sent to concentration camps. The German Jewish community was then
billed one billion Reichsmark (worth approximately $400 million in 1938).

Over the course of this turbulent and bloody year, the members of the
Dubnow Fund were preoccupied with the task of selling the first four vol-
umes and identifying a path forward, for both the *Entsiklopedye* and the
Yiddish-speaking Jews it was to serve. By this time, the circulation of the
Entsiklopedye had reached approximately six thousand subscribers, and it had
become financially self-sufficient, with no subsidies necessary to sustain it.[83]
New promotional materials highlighting the accomplishments of the first

FIGURE 2.6 Advertisement for *Algemeyne entsiklopedye*, 1937 or 1938
(Sholem Schwartzbard Papers, Courtesy of University of Cape Town).

volumes were developed to advertise the *Entsiklopedye*. One of these was an eight-page booklet that featured a cover photograph of Auguste Rodin's sculpture *The Thinker* superimposed on a photograph of a (mostly male) crowd of hundreds of people, with the words "*Algemeyne entsiklopedye*" typed above. The image brings together three key elements of the project. The Hebrew letters indicate the Jewish, and specifically Yiddish, readership of the work. Although cast in the early twentieth century, Rodin's sculpture harks back to the Enlightenment origins of the first modern encyclopedia and the quest for knowledge. The throng indicates that this encyclopedia is for and by the *folk*, rather than the elite.

The advertising copy spoke of the *Entsiklopedye* as a tool for the anxious laboring masses to navigate the rapidly changing world:

> The world is filled with problems and events. Non-Jews and Jews alike are
> anxious and distressed, and they yearn to find answers to the questions
> that interest them deeply both for themselves personally and for the world
> at large. Day in and day out, books and newspapers, the radio and telegraph
> bring us an ocean of new facts, reports, and names. How can one orient
> oneself in such a sea of questions, reports, and facts that concern all of us?
> How can the masses, and particularly the working people, for whom the
> toil of laboring leaves them with such little free time, make sense of it all?[84]

The answer to these vexing challenges was of course the *Algemeyne entsiklopedye*, which was an "indispensable compass" and a "people's university" for those Yiddish workers trying to find their way through the dizzying set of world events.

In addition to making the case for the *Entsiklopedye* as a guide to the ever-changing world, the brochure is filled with images displaying the broad range of human accomplishments, such as the recently completed (as of 1931) Empire State Building, an airplane, a rocket, a massive military tank, a totem pole, a pyramid at Giza, Roman ruins, busts of famous men, a photo of two Aboriginal persons with dramatic facial alterations, and a reproduction of Botticelli's *Birth of Venus*. The only recognizably *Jewish* item in the brochure is a frontispiece of an illustrated Hebrew-language religious text. Along with sample entries, the brochure is filled with testimonials from prominent figures and institutions from the world of Yiddish letters, including Dubnow, Sholem Asch, Chaim Zhitlowsky, YIVO, and a wide range of periodicals. A second brochure from this period was addressed in particular to a Polish Jewish audience, and listed the contact person as Szmul Zygielbojm, who was a leader of the Jewish Labor Bund in Poland and a member of the city council in Łódź.

Along with trying to increase sales, the Dubnow Fund spent much of 1938 preparing the *Yidn* supplemental volume. As discussed in chapter 1, the decision to create the *Yidn* volume, which was to cover all aspects of Jewish life, culture, and history, had been the result of contentious discussions held in Berlin during the formative period of the *Entsiklopedye* over the sort of knowledge that Yiddish readers needed most. Did they need universal knowledge to make sense of the larger world or a comprehensive encyclopedia of exclusively Jewish topics like the volumes that had in recent decades appeared in English, Russian, and German? A compromise decision was eventually reached for a 70/30 split between entries on universal topics and those on Jewish ones, with most of the Jewish entries to be included in the supplement.

Officially, this plan was maintained for most of the 1930s. In fact, the decision to publish the supplement earlier than scheduled had been made in private within a few years after the move to Paris. In letters from the first months of 1936, Abramovitch informed Baruch Charney Vladeck of the Dubnow Fund's plan to publish *two* volumes dedicated to Jews and to do so in between publishing volumes 3 and 4, so as to expand the reach of the *Entsiklopedye*. Abramovitch mentioned that many of the articles were already written and that the Dubnow Fund planned to publish the supplemental volumes within half a year's time, a decidedly unrealistic goal.[85] Furthermore, it was the Fund's hope to release them not only in Yiddish, but also eventually in French, English, Russian, and Polish translations. Abramovitch solicited Vladeck's support for a fund-raising effort to generate twenty thousand francs (about $13,000) to cover the costs. Vladeck responded favorably to the change in the plans but noted that raising such a large amount of money in so short of time would be a significant challenge, as American Jewish donors were already giving money to a range of other causes. By 1938, plans for a French-language translation of the supplement were underway (likely to capitalize on the Jewish Pavilion at the Paris World Fair), and a brochure appeared for an *Encyclopédie contemporaine du judaïsme*, to be published in "1 grand volume de 1.200 colonnes."[86] However, given that the *Yidn* volume did not appear until the spring of 1939, and the French version not at all, it is likely that Vladeck was correct about the difficulty of securing the necessary funds.

In the late spring of 1939, the Dubnow Fund published the first of what it announced would be two volumes dedicated to the subject of Jews. In the foreword to what was titled *Yidn alef*, the editors defended the special volume by insisting on the need to create a forum—which they referred to as a "statistical handbook"—that would allow "for a more or less exhaustive enlightening of the sum of Jewish problems that matter to the day-to-day Jewish man

ENCYCLOPÉDIE CONTEMPORAINE DU JUDAÏSME

(EDITION FRANÇAISE)

ASSOCIATION SIMON DUBNOW
76, RUE DES PLANTES, 76 — PARIS (14e)

FIGURE 2.7 Brochure cover for *Encyclopédie contemporaine du judaïsme* (Sholem Schwartzbard Papers, Courtesy of University of Cape Town).

and which he can find in no other place."[87] In particular, the editors imagined that their fellow Jews required knowledge concerning the "material side of the Jewish people, their *'gashmies'* [physical and material existence, quotation marks in original]: their biological structure (meaning racial origins or anthropology), their demographic development, Jewish statistics, Jewish emigration, economic development and the position of Jews in all regions of the world, colonization, cooperative organizations, credit banks, etc., also how the mechanism of Jewish self-governance (various types of communal structures, and so on) became organs of social welfare in many countries."[88] Furthermore, the editors continued, such discussions necessitated a full understanding of the historical development of the Jewish *folk*.

In the foreword, the editors also made special note of the deaths in 1938 of Sholem Schwartzbard and Baruch Charney Vladeck, who were highly prominent in the Jewish world and active with the *Entsiklopedye*. In the first months of the year, Schwartzbard had traveled to Cape Town on behalf of the Dubnow Fund to solicit subscriptions. He did not have much luck, to the great disappointment of the Committee that had formed to support the project. At one meeting convened at the Cape Town Zionist hall, the assembled debated whether Schwartzbard's purpose was to raise money for the Dubnow Fund (along the lines of a charity) or to sell subscriptions, as well as whether there remained any "cultural demand for Yiddish."[89] These debates were apparently settled and the Committee released advertising materials of its own, one of which was an English-language declaration entitled "The Symbol of a Nation's Will to Live." It spoke of the *Entsiklopedye* as a "monumental work that raises the creative forces within the Jewish people" during a time of "tragedies and suffering" and directly addressed the project's critics:

> "Is not an Encyclopaedia in Yiddish too great a luxury in these days of stark
> catastrophe?" some will ask. Others will wonder how our learned men and
> scientists can nowadays find the peace and concentration to sit down
> months and years in the quiet of their room and work so that the odd ten
> million Yiddish-speaking Jews may have a universal encyclopaedia. Surely,
> they will say, in these days when the position of the Jews is being so
> mercilessly assailed, when the freedom they won after centuries of blood
> and tears is threatened, and new Ghettos are being created, how can they,
> our learned men, occupy themselves with a work that does not seem to be
> absolutely necessary and urgent.[90]

In response to these concerns, the Committee argued, the encyclopedia was an assertion of Jews' place within the human fold, "a national expression of

FIGURE 2.8 Sholem Schwartzbard (Sholem Schwartzbard Papers, courtesy of University of Cape Town).

the universal," and an "affirmation that in spite of all the ugly manifestations of the present day, human progress is marching forward."

Within a few weeks of his arrival to South Africa, however, Schwartzbard suddenly fell sick in the middle of the night and died.[91] His death sent shock waves through the world of Eastern European Jewry, and thousands attended his funeral in Cape Town's Maitland Jewish Cemetery. The advertising materials for the *Entsiklopedye* that were among the documents he left behind are the only known copies of any advertising from this stage of the encyclopedia anywhere in the world.

Later that year, Baruch Charney Vladeck also passed away. A close confidant of Abramovitch's and a strong supporter of the *Entsiklopedye* within the American Yiddish world, his death was a particularly powerful blow. Not only was he the managing editor of the *Forverts* for two decades, Vladeck was by far the most prominent labor leader among Jews in the United States. In 1934, he helped form the Jewish Labor Committee, an organization that comprised "the main organizations of the American noncommunist Jewish left," to organize the working-class Jewish response to Nazism, and he persuaded the American Labor Committee to support a highly controversial boycott on German goods.[92] His funeral procession drew a reported five hundred thousand mourners (certainly an exaggeration), and a public housing complex built on New York City's Lower East Side soon after his death was named the Vladeck Houses in his honor.[93]

The editors also announced in the foreword to *Yidn alef* that they would soon publish *Yidn beys*. The volume would cover all cultural matters, in particular those stemming from Jewish languages. Topics would include sacred and rabbinic literature; philosophical, mystical, and messianic literature; the Jewish Enlightenment; liberalism; and radicalism. Particular focus would be paid to Jewish socialist and nationalist movements, including Zionism, Territorialism, and Autonomism. In addition, articles were slated to appear on the Jewish press, publishing, art, architecture, painting, sculpture, music (religious and secular), and theater.

The contributions to *Yidn alef* follow a format entirely unlike the entries in the *normale* series, apart from the entries on antisemitism and the Land of Israel. They are primarily single-author introductory essays on a variety of topics related to Jewish life, history, and culture. Many are composed by figures closely aligned with the *Entsiklopedye*, such as Menes on ancient Jewish history, Steinberg on medieval and modern Jewish history, Tcherikower on Jewish historiography, and Lestschinsky on Jewish emigration. For these contributors, who had for the past four volumes often written entries on subjects far removed from their areas of expertise, these topics must have been a welcome change of pace. Other contributions came from figures such as Arthur Ruppin, a Zionist leader and founder of the Department of Sociology at the Hebrew University, who wrote on Jewish statistics; Liebmann Hersch, a Bundist and professor at the University of Geneva, who wrote on Jewish demography; the archaeologist Eleazar Sukenik (who would later become famous for first identifying the Dead Sea Scrolls) on Jewish archaeology; and Isaac Nachman Steinberg, a Territorialist leader of the Frayland-lige, who wrote on Jewish colonization. In addition, the volume is richly illustrated with dozens of photos, full-color and black-and-white maps, and an assortment of tables and charts. The quality of these works substantiates what Yashunsky (who wrote on Jewish cooperatives for the volume) observed of the encyclopedists in 1931, that "in their minds they understand that an encyclopedia in Yiddish must be a general one, but in their hearts rest the Jewish parts."[94]

Collectively, the essays are a tour de force of Yiddish-language scholarship. Regrettably, they have been overlooked by scholars and reviewers on account of the decline in Yiddish readers after the Holocaust and the fact that the volume was published on the eve of World War II. Taken together, the essays do not reassess the Diaspora Nationalist ideology, nor claim that it was "at a crossroads" along the lines of the 1939–40 journal by the same name (*Afn Sheydveg*) that was edited by Tcherikower, Kalmanovitch, and Yisroel Yefroikin (a leader of the Fédération des Sociétés Juives de France and onetime member of Dubnow's People's Party), in which they repudiated their commitment to Diaspora Nationalism in light of the unchecked peril of Nazism and the refusal of the world's democracies to shelter threatened Jews.[95] In what may have been one of the last such expressions of its time, *Yidn alef* takes a much more defiant stance, insisting upon the integrity of Eastern European Jewish civilization and the Yiddish culture that it produced. For example, Iulii Brutskus's essay on Jewish anthropology, while accepting now-outdated studies of Jewish craniums, hair and eye color, and nose shapes, can be understood as a direct response to Nazism's insistence on racial purity as the primary indicator of a people's worth, as it portrays Jews as a proudly "mixed race" people who cannot be solely defined by their racial "semitism." Although Jews, he argues, "are derived from a common Palestinian origin," the difference between Jewish "types" around the world is a consequence of environmental conditions (such as climate, nutrition, health) and the conversion of non-Jews in Jewish communities.[96] In Brutskus's depiction, Jews' transnationalism and multiracialism are in fact their most defining features.

Yidn alef can also be viewed as a response to the growing influence of the Zionist movement, which had been gathering significant strength following Hitler's rise to power and the world's refusal to take seriously the Jewish refugee crisis that developed in its wake. In spite of contributions from prominent Zionists such as Ruppin and Sukenik, the volume does not concede the Zionist arguments that Jewish life in the Diaspora was a historical error that needed correcting and that the Jewish experience in Europe was marked solely by Jewish powerlessness and humiliation. In I. N. Steinberg's essay on Jewish colonization, the Jewish settlement in Palestine gets its due, but it is placed between discussions of Jewish colonies in Russia and South America and accounts of settlements in the Soviet Union and North America. The essay on Jewish history, written by Menes and Aaron Steinberg, begins in the ancient Land of Israel but treats it as one period among many that make up the Jewish experience over time. Taking up 180 columns, this essay covers the early centuries of Jews in the Land of Israel; the beginning of the Diaspora; the experience of Jews in Islamic countries, Christian Europe, and the Americas; and the modern period. Rather than expressing resignation over the

‏1. מוטיעטילר פֿון אַ ‏ייִדישער‏ פֿרוי (צ ‏י"ה); 2. ספֿרדיש מיידל פֿון ירושלים; 3. תימעןער ייִד; 4. ספֿרדישער
רב פֿון ירושלים; 5—6. מעראָקישע ייִדן; 7—8. ייִדן פֿון בּאַנדאַר; 9. ייִדישע פֿרוי פֿון מאַראָקאָ.

ייִדישע טיפּן

‏10—11. בוכאַרער ייִדן; 12. בּאַרג־ייִד פֿון דאַגעסטאַן; 13. ספֿרבּיאַ־ירושלימישער (ענגלישער) ייִד;
14—15. רוסישע ייִדן; 16. פּוילישער ייִד; 17. ‏היטמער ייִד‏ פֿון פֿאַסטען; 18. ליטװישער ייִד.

FIGURES 2.9 AND 2.10

"Jewish Types," in "Jewish Anthropology," by Iulii Brutskus, *Algemeyne entsiklopedye: Yidn alef.*

future of the Jewish people, *Yidn alef* forcefully defends the Jewish Diasporic experience. As Alexander Mukdoni put it in a review of *Yidn alef*, the volume is best understood as a principled and much-needed Jewish response to the rapidly declining conditions in the world:

> In such a dire time for us Jews, in a time when the world has become simply hooliganized, and we Jews are the victims of this hooliganized world, Jews sit at their desks and labor with great seriousness and with greater responsibility. To the anguished and suffering Jewish folk, one contributes a treasury of Jewish knowledge, a handbook, that will help them in the first place to orient themselves in their own history as well as in their own Jewish world. In the end, such an orientation is the most important. And this book has come at the right time.[97]

Less than six weeks after Mukdoni's review, on September 1, 1939, Germany invaded Poland—home to nearly three and a half million Jews and the center of Yiddish culture—and World War II in Europe began.

Yidn beys

In contrast to Nazi Germany's previous territorial expansions, the seizure of Poland was violent in the extreme. By 1939, Germany had one of the most powerful militaries in the world, and the attack was its first opportunity to demonstrate its full might. Within a few weeks, Germany overwhelmed Poland's ill-prepared defenses through its superior land, air, and sea power. The Polish Air Force was decimated by the German Luftwaffe, and its navy on the Baltic Sea was bombarded by German warships and U-boats. Polish cities were bombed without military justification, and German tanks easily rolled across the border. Poland lost approximately seventy thousand troops fighting the Germans, and as many as two hundred thousand Polish civilians were killed. Poland's Jewish communities, which made up 10 percent of the overall population but which were highly urbanized, suffered terribly during the *Blitzkrieg* (lightning war), as approximately twenty thousand Jews lost their lives in the invasion and tens of thousands of Jewish homes and businesses were destroyed. Once again, the Western democracies failed to intervene militarily, although Great Britain and France declared war on Germany on September 3 (initiating a period widely referred to as the Phoney War).[98]

On September 17, under the pretense of coming to Poland's defense, the Red Army invaded from the east, causing Poland to lose an additional fifty thousand troops in fighting the Soviet forces. On August 23, the mortal enemies Germany and the Soviet Union had publicly signed a nonaggression pact, much to the shock of the world. The treaty also contained secret protocols for the division of Poland and new Soviet and German realms of dominion over lands in east Central Europe. After only two decades of political independence, by the end of September 1939, Poland was once again partitioned out of existence.

Of the areas under German occupation, the western portion of Poland, which was home to approximately six hundred thousand Jews, was annexed to the Reich, while the remainder, which was home to more than one and a half million Jews, was designated the *Generalgouvernement* and treated like an overseas colonial possession. Civilians faced brutal treatment and were often expelled from their homes and businesses. Property was regularly seized without compensation, and military rule was established. The ruling Germans exacerbated existing tensions between ethnic Poles and Ukrainians and elevated the status of ethnic Germans living in the region. The treatment of Polish Jews under German rule in the first months of World War II was particularly vicious, even more extreme than that of Jews in Austria following the *Anschluss*. At least two hundred thousand Jews were deported from the annexed territories into the *Generalgouvernement*, and many of them were subsequently sent across the Soviet border. Within the first few months of the invasion, Jews in the *Generalgouvernement* were compelled to engage in forced labor, wear a Jewish Star of David, and relocate into areas that were eventually designated as ghettos. They were subjected to indiscriminate violence, dismissals from their places of employment, segregation in public spaces, and property theft.[99]

The realms that fell under Soviet rule contained approximately 1.3 million Jews (plus an additional 350,000 others who crossed over from the German side). Those previously residing in the regions that fell under Soviet rule were granted citizenship, while many of the refugees from German-controlled areas were treated as hostile elements and subjected to brutal treatment, such as deportation to the Soviet interior, including Siberia.[100] The city of Vilna and the surrounding regions were transferred to the country of Lithuania.

The occupation of Poland and the transfer of Vilna left YIVO and its many affiliated scholars in a particularly complicated state. On one hand, as historians Kalman Weiser and Cecile Kuznitz note in their studies of interwar Yiddish intellectual culture, for the eight months in which Vilna was under Lithuanian rule, YIVO's output was strengthened by the large number of Yiddish-speaking Jews, including many intellectuals, journalists, and cultural activists, who flooded into the city along with thousands of others who took flight ahead of the German invasion.[101] On the other hand, the leadership was in crisis. YIVO's head, Max Weinreich, was stuck in Copenhagen while traveling with his son

Uriel to a conference in Brussels. Rather than seek to return, he made plans to relocate to the safety of New York, where YIVO had an American branch.[102] Zalmen Reisen, one of YIVO's central academic and administrative leaders, was arrested soon after the Soviet takeover of Vilna, likely for his role as editor of the daily newspaper *Tog*. Dubnow, who still resided in Latvia (which remained neutral at this point in the war), spent his time deeply concerned over the fate of his family and friends, most of whom were in Poland. He briefly considered moving to Vilna, where his daughter, Sophie, and his grandsons had found refuge. He even explored starting an English-language weekly with Aaron Steinberg to inform Americans about the events unfolding in Europe but rejected suggestions that YIVO should relocate to the United States.[103]

For members of the Dubnow Fund in Paris, the invasion and partition of Poland prompted another set of crises, personal and professional. Not only were they cut off from many of their family members, but a number of their colleagues and collaborators were missing as well. The archival documents from this period are particularly spotty, but the few letters that do survive are filled with queries as to the whereabouts of *Entsiklopedye* contributors. For example, Kalmanovitch, who had returned to Vilna after working on the *Entsiklopedye* during the Dubnow Fund's first year in Paris, was unaccounted for. Ben-Adir desperately searched for him in the hopes of receiving the remaining portion of his entry for *Yidn beys*, since the volume was otherwise ready to go to press by late winter 1940.[104] Most important, with Poland isolated, the masses of Polish Yiddish readers who made up the majority of the readers and subscribers of the *Entsiklopedye* were entirely out of reach. Like the staff of YIVO, the members of the Dubnow Fund (with which there was much overlap) entered into a period of crisis, struggling with the immediate disarray of their own organization while continuing their role as intellectual and cultural caretakers of a Yiddish-speaking community that was effectively cordoned off at the center and increasingly dispersed on the periphery. As they would describe later, the editors realized that after the occupation of Poland, Paris was "the last free Yiddish center on the European continent."[105]

Yidn beys finally appeared in print in early May 1940. In the brief foreword, which has the dateline "Paris, March 1940," the editors spoke of the "difficult atmosphere" that surrounded the release of the first *Yidn* volume and the "blaze of world-fire" that accompanied this second one.[106] They also discussed the new set of administrative and psychological hindrances to their work that were a consequence of the war. Polish Jewry, the main audience of the *Entsiklopedye*, was now divided between Nazi and Soviet authorities, and those in the Nazi sphere of control were being subject to ever more brutal treatment. Not only were Polish Jews at risk, but the great institutions of Jewish culture, such as libraries, galleries, and scientific institutions, were closed and access to their materials cut off: "The greatest Jewish center in Europe—Poland—is being obliterated entirely, along with almost all of its scientific and literary strength and resources."[107] In response to these challenges, the editors committed themselves to continuing the project, but announced that they were forced to divide volume *beys* into two, although it was unclear whether or not a third volume, *giml*, would appear later in 1940 as hoped, given the mounting crisis. The abridged *Yidn beys* is limited to Jewish languages, religion, literature (through the Enlightenment), theater, art, and music. *Yidn giml*, they announced, would cover recent Yiddish and Hebrew literature, the press, past and current Jewish cultural and educational activity in all countries, and the history of the Jewish worker movement, "which has played a monumental role in modern Jewish life."

More so than *Yidn alef*, which was focused on social scientific essays describing the history and contours of world Jewry, the second volume in the *Yidn* series is an accounting of Jews' religious and cultural developments and contributions. The volume contains the expected assortment of essays from figures closely associated with the Dubnow Fund and the circle of scholars around YIVO, including Kalmanovitch writing on the Hebrew and Aramaic languages,[108] Weinreich on Yiddish and Yiddish philology, Menes on the origins of Jewish religion, and Steinberg on late medieval Jewish messianism. Rachel Wischnitzer (writing as Rachel Wischnitzer-Bernstein) contributed a richly illustrated four-part essay on Jewish art that spanned the ancient period of Jewish settlement in the land of Israel, the Middle Ages, the Renaissance, and the Baroque period. Ben-Adir did not contribute to the volume, perhaps because that same April he published a book-length essay entitled *Farn geshikhtlekhn yom-hadin, dos yidishe folk tsvishn toykhekhe un geule* (Toward the historic day of judgment, the Jewish people between condemnations and redemption), which made the case for a Territorialist solution to the ongoing crisis.[109]

At the same time, *Yidn beys* also contains a significantly larger number of essays from scholars outside of Europe and several from figures outside of the Yiddishist community, including some unlikely ones. Reflecting the broad range of Jewish topics and the increasing dispersion of European-born Jewish intellectuals, a large number of essays were composed by scholars who had migrated to Palestine, Britain, or the United States. The second volume of the *Yidn* series, therefore, marks another important shift in the project. Whereas contributors to the general encyclopedia's first four volumes were primarily Yiddish-speaking intellectuals who were to some extent affiliated with the Diaspora Nationalist movements and tended to be located between the communists (on the left) and the Zionists (on the right), the contributors to the *Yidn* volumes were drawn from a significantly wider range of ideological viewpoints.

Most prominently, the historian Gershom Scholem contributed two essays to *Yidn beys*, one on Jewish mystics in Kabbalah and the other on messianic movements among Jews after the 1492 Spanish expulsion. Born in 1897 in Berlin, into an assimilated Jewish family, Scholem was among those Jewish youths in the first decades of the 1900s who found themselves questioning whether German Jewry had sacrificed too much over the previous century to be part of a society that was increasingly antisemitic. He took up the study of Hebrew and the Talmud and aligned himself ideologically with Zionism. Studying in Munich in 1915, at the age of seventeen, he became friends with Walter Benjamin, who was twenty-three at the time. Eager to join the growing Zionist colony in Palestine, Scholem made his way to Jerusalem in 1923, a year after completing his doctoral dissertation on a Jewish mystical text. When the Hebrew University in Jerusalem opened its doors, in 1925, he became a lecturer in Jewish mysticism and was later appointed professor. In the ideology of Zionism and its redemptive hope for the restoration of the Jewish people in their imagined homeland, Scholem identified a Jewish messianic impulse whose study became the focus of his life's work. His field-defining *Major Trends in Jewish Mysticism*, which was based on a series of lectures given in New York in 1938, would be published (first in English) in 1941 and would propel him to the upper echelons of Jewish historical scholarship.

A passionate Zionist, Scholem was an unlikely choice for the Dubnow Fund, yet given the shifting nature of the volumes and the crisis facing European Jewry, the ideological differences that once divided many Jewish intellectuals, especially those living outside of the major Jewish centers that were under assault, no longer carried the same weight. Scholem was by no means the only figure outside of Yiddishist circles to contribute. The Polish-born and (in 1940) England-based Hebraist scholar Simon Rawidowicz contributed a piece entitled "Hebrew Literature in the Time of the Jewish Enlightenment," and the renowned Berlin-born and Palestine-based Jewish pianist and music critic Alice Jacob-Loewenson provided an essay on the history of Jewish music. The Talmudist Boaz Cohen (who taught at the Jewish Theological Seminary of America, in New York City) contributed one essay on Talmudic literature and a second on rabbinic and liturgical literature. The Paris-based Polish Jewish art critic Chil Aronson wrote on the history of Jewish art, and the Russian-born and Jerusalem-based historian Victor (Avigdor) Tcherikover wrote on the Jewish Hellenistic period.[110]

The publication of *Yidn beys* marks an abrupt shift from the *Algemeyne entsiklopedye*'s central mission of providing universal knowledge to Yiddish-speaking Jews, in the name of their modernization, toward conveying a much more particularistic body of knowledge that spoke directly to a Jewish community in the midst of profound crisis. In the process, the encyclopedia also moved from its narrow ideological perspective to reach across the political and cultural divisions that had defined much of modern Jewish civilization.

Unfortunately, *Yidn beys* barely saw the light of day in its original form. On May 10, 1940, only a few weeks after its release, the German military ended the Phoney War and quickly conquered Western Europe.

Flight

The rapidity with which German troops swept through the Netherlands, Belgium, Luxembourg, and France, and the constant stream of reports and rumors about atrocities they committed, sparked a panic among civilians and prompted millions to flee southward in a desperate attempt to stay ahead of the advancing troops. Scholars estimate that in the first weeks of the assault on Western Europe, as many as eight million people took to the roads in what became one of the largest mass migrations in history.[111] Grabbing whatever they could and traveling by whatever means available, including train, car, bicycle, animal, or foot, a disorganized stream of refugees poured out of Paris, mostly heading south with no clear destination in sight.

In a memoir written immediately following his flight from Paris, the French Jewish author Léon Werth describes the evacuation as a time of utter chaos and desperation:

> The caravan of cars is overtaken by cyclists, male and female, and by
> limping pedestrians. Their heads seem pulled toward their feet. Some carry
> a travel bag; others have one or two suitcases in hand. Imagine how
> exhausting this walk is with a valise at the end of your arm. Others push
> baby carriages—loaded with children, bundles or their most important
> possessions—or the strangest vehicles cobbled together by handymen out
> of wooden planks and old bicycle wheels. A woman is seated on the lid of a
> three-wheeled delivery cart, which a man pedals. An old man on a bicycle,
> alone, is leading his dog on a leash.[112]

Evacuees often spent weeks on the road, crawling along in traffic jams that at times moved only a few kilometers a day. Those with automobiles quickly ran out of fuel and had to trek on foot or pay to have their vehicles towed by farm animals. They faced hunger, thirst, and exhaustion, as well as occasional aerial attacks by German planes. Werth describes that the roads soon became littered with discarded possessions that were abandoned because they simply could not be carried any longer.

By the end of June 1940, nearly all of Western and Central Europe was in the hands of Germany and its allies. France signed an armistice with Germany on June 22, and the country was split into two. The northern half, including Paris, and all Atlantic coastal regions came under full German occupation. The southern half, including the Mediterranean coast, was placed under French military rule and became known alternatively as the Free Zone or Vichy France, after its provisional capital. Until France was fully occupied by Germany in November 1942, the southern zone served as a proxy state for Germany and was headed by a government that collaborated with the Nazi leadership.

Rightfully anxious about their fate, Jews, especially the foreign born, were among the first to take flight. Historian Hanna Diamond estimates that in 1940, approximately 90 percent of all Jews in France resided in Paris. Many had come to Paris as refugees from Nazism in Germany, Austria, Czechoslovakia, and Poland, and they had very little in the way of support networks or knowledge of how to manage outside of the capital. For months prior to the invasion, France's Daladier administration had harassed and imprisoned many of them out of fears that they were potential spies for Germany. Native-born French Jews perceived the presence of foreign-born Jews as a threat to their own hard-won status and offered them only meager support. Following the armistice, most native French, including many French Jews, returned to Paris under the impression that they would be relatively safe back in their homes. Foreign Jews and political and cultural opponents of the Nazi regime, by contrast, generally stayed in Vichy France and tried to flee the country.

A small number of documents detailing the flight of the members of the Dubnow Fund have survived in archives. Through them it is possible to reconstruct in part the story of their escape from Paris and eventual arrival in New York. This group includes Abramovitch, Kin, Ben-Adir, Menes, and Tcherikower (and their families), and they were joined by several close colleagues such as Leon Bramson (who had been in Paris during the 1930s as leader of the ORT and remained the titular head of the Dubnow Fund), the ORT activist Aron Singalowsky, the poet David Einhorn, and a number of Abramovitch's Menshevik associates, some of whom would later come to write for the *Entsiklopedye* in America.

In addition to whatever personal property they could carry, members of the Dubnow Fund managed to take the manuscripts for *Yidn giml* with them, as well as a small portion of their administrative materials and correspondence. However, they were forced to abandon most of the editorial and financial documents, the printing plates of the extant volumes, printing paper, photos, maps, and the full set of index files of the entries, all of which remain lost to this day.[113] In addition, the fund's stockpile of copies of all published volumes, approximately twelve thousand in number, had to be abandoned.[114] Making matters worse, approximately one thousand recently published copies of *Yidn beys* had disappeared en route to America, with one later report suggesting that they were lost at sea, speculating that "presumably the ship was sunk by a Nazi submarine," although there is no confirmation of this.[115]

By mid-July, most members of this group had found shelter in Vichy France in the city of Toulouse, about four hundred miles south of Paris. They had been running for their lives and realized immediately that nowhere in France would be safe. Of the states bordering France, Italy and Germany were Axis powers, Belgium and Luxembourg were occupied, Switzerland was neutral and refused to accept most refugees lest it too risk invasion, and with the 1939 victory of the nationalists in the civil war, Spain was now in the hands of the fascist leader Francisco Franco. For most refugees, leaving the country meant leaving the Continent.

The last available port in France was Marseille, and the city, which was home to many foreign consular offices, including that of the United States, drew a steady stream of panicked refugees seeking to book passage on a ship, often regardless of the destination. Getting to Marseille was not simple, as authorities at times insisted that aliens carry a *sauf-conduit*, a "safe conduct" pass, or risk police harassment or arrest. Furthermore, arriving in Marseille was no guarantee of safety. Not only were the very few available passenger ships in high demand, but as the war progressed, few vessels of any sort arrived or disembarked from Marseille. Refugees were susceptible to arrest and imprisonment by French authorities on the slightest suspicion, and many were turned over to German authorities.

Since the onset of war, in September 1939, only a small number of countries were willing to open their borders to refugees from Nazism. Long-standing immigration restrictions born of post–World War I nativist and isolationist concerns were tightened further on security grounds. Few countries in fact had specific policies for refugees, and as a result most of those seeking to escape France had to find sanctuary via normal immigration processes. Finding sanctuary in the most desired sites, such as the United States, Great Britain, or Palestine, was nearly impossible. In the United States, for example, the wait for a much-coveted visa through the regular channels was often years away, as the applicant list had grown impossibly long. Great Britain likewise clamped down on refugees to Britain itself as well as to Palestine, which it continued to control. To get nearly anywhere, one had to obtain a complicated set of documents, including an exit visa to depart France, an entry visa to arrive into the country of one's final destination, a transit visa simply to pass through other countries, and a ticket on a departing ship. Refugees seeking to acquire a residency or visitor's visa to the United States had to secure an affidavit testifying to their financial, physical, and moral fitness, as well as demonstrate that they had the means to support themselves and not become a financial liability to their new host country. Most of these documents carried an expiration date that often had passed by the time that they arrived, and the process would have to start all over again. For many, Marseille was less a transit point than a trap.

A July 19 letter from Abramovitch (signed using his given name, Rein) to Nathan Chanin—his onetime Bundist ally and an Arbeter-ring leader, who was by then working with the Jewish Labor Committee (JLC) in New York—indicates that by mid-July Abramovitch had arrived in Marseille and was coming to understand the nearly insurmountable obstacles to acquiring a U.S. visa. Abramovitch wrote:

> A member of the Consulate explained to me the situation as follows: the existing regulations about visitor visas to USA demand that the applicant should be in possession: 1. Of a passport enabling him to return to France; 2. Of an affidavit issued by an American citizen of means; 3. Of a visa to a third country, enabling him to go there after the expiration of the USA-visitor visa (in case that his return to Europe or in France should be impossible).
>
> None of my friends can fulfill the point 3, and very few of them can have an affidavit. Under these circumstances how can we get visas? That's the point of view of the Consulate. The following steps must be taken: 1. Provide for all of us a *financial guaranty*, sufficient under the existing regulations, as to make unnecessary the affidavits. 2. Get for all of us canadian, san-domingoan or other visas as visas to a "a third country." Or if that is not possible have the State Department *officially* advise the Consulate, that for a *certain list of persons* the point 3 has to be dropped (in this case the Immigration officers of New York must be especially informed of that exceptional measure).

If these administrative roadblocks were not enough, Abramovitch went on to explain that the documents alone did not secure passage aboard a ship to the United States. In fact, by July, most ships bound for America were no longer departing from France, as its Mediterranean port was subject to blockade by the British Navy. Instead, refugees had to make their way to Lisbon, nearly one thousand miles away overland.

> On the other side you must realize, that we need not only visas, but also money for the passage and so on. And that is not all: you can have a ship to America only in Lisbon but you can get to Lisbon only through Spain, and the Spanish authorities do not grant transit visas to people without regular passports. That is the main difficulty for the most of us, save a few, who are in possession of a polish passport. . . . I have no idea, how we are to meet that obstacle, but we'll try our best. But to try we must have before all the american visas, and some money.[116]

Moreover, the anti-fascists among the refugees, such as those in Abramovitch's circle, were liable to be arrested at any moment, and in that event would be turned over to the German authorities. Although the systematic mass murder of Jews had not yet begun, the arrest, torture, and execution of political opponents of the Nazi regime was widely known. While Abramovitch's high-profile stature made him and those in his circles particularly vulnerable, his international profile also meant he had political contacts in the United States who could advocate for emergency visas on their behalf. In fact, within a few days of the French surrender, efforts were underway to aid those prominent refugees who were most vulnerable to capture and arrest. A group of writers, journalists, political activists, and labor figures gathered in New York to found the Emergency Rescue Committee (ERC) to petition the United States government to issue emergency visas for refugees thought to be most at risk. The ERC received support from writers, artists, and intellectuals associated with the political left, such as the journalist Dorothy Thompson, Alvin Johnson of the New School for Social Research, and the novelists Upton Sinclair and Thomas Mann. First Lady Eleanor Roosevelt gave her support to many of the ERC's initial efforts.[117] As early as June 25, Eleanor Roosevelt, writing from New York City, was petitioning State Department officials on behalf of imperiled political activists and intellectuals trapped in various parts of Europe, many of whom were leaders in the Jewish community, such as the Vilna-based Yiddish cultural activist and educator Shloyme Gilinsky, who would later become the executive secretary of the *Algemeyne entsiklopedye*, and the now-Toulouse-based Avrom Menes.[118]

At the same time as the ECR was forming, the JLC was organizing on behalf of its Social Democratic and Bundist allies who were trapped in Vichy France and Soviet-controlled Vilna. Abramovitch's previous contact with the

JLC, fostered during his 1935 trip to the United States, helped facilitate his rescue and that of several of his encyclopedist and Menshevik colleagues and their families. Historian Catherine Collomp explains that the long-standing ties between the JLC and the Abramovitch group ensured that the JLC was well positioned to act on the group's behalf.[119]

On July 2, JLC executive director Isaiah Minkoff, American Federation of Labor president William Green, International Ladies' Garment Workers Union president David Dubinsky, and *Forverts* general manager Alexander Kahn met with Secretary of State Cordell Hull and Assistant Secretary of State Breckinridge Long to petition on behalf of emergency visitor visas for labor leaders in southern France and Vilna. In a memorandum of the conversation that Long drafted later that day, he recounted that Green described the endangered figures as "intellectual men who had been a force in legitimate labor movements and who had been advocates of a democratic form of government and opposed to the totalitarian systems." Long accepted a list of names with the caveats that each person would have to be certified "as being desirable from their point of view to save as representatives of the labor movement" and that Green would assume responsibility for guaranteeing the conditions of their stay. Long indicated as well that it was expected that as visitors, the grantees would "not engage in any political activity during their presence within the jurisdiction of this country."[120]

On July 3, Minkoff provided Long with an expanded version of the list that Eleanor Roosevelt had sent to the State Department the previous week. Among those added were figures trapped in Vilna, including Kalmanovitch, who ended up being confined in the city's ghetto, which Germany established following its July 1941 invasion of the Soviet Union, and who in September 1943 was deported to an Estonian concentration camp, where he was later murdered. On the list of those trapped in France, several encyclopedists are mentioned, including Abramovitch, Bramson, Einhorn, Daniel Charney, Grigori Aronson, Menes, Ben-Adir, Kin, Tcherikower, and Singalowsky. Circumventing the standard immigration procedures, a telegram sent on July 6, 1940, from Washington to the consul in Marseille ordered, "Should any of the outstanding intellectual leaders listed below and members of their families apply for visas within the next two weeks, their cases should receive immediate consideration without regard for office hours or holidays."[121] Word traveled quickly to the Dubnow Fund regarding their good fortune. (Within six weeks, as Collomp notes, the State Department began to insist upon a higher level of scrutiny of each applicant, and by October, Long put a near-complete end to visas granted to prominent Europeans under emergency situations.[122])

A July 13 letter from Kin (in Toulouse) to Ben-Adir (location unknown but likely nearby) states that Abramovitch traveled from Toulouse to the U.S. Consulate in Marseille because he had received word that the visas had been approved, but Kin was unclear as to whether they were limited to political figures or included cultural activists like themselves.[123] A week later, he again wrote to Ben-Adir with great relief, stating that he had learned from Abramovitch that the consul in Marseille provided him with a list of names of people who were slated for visas, including the two of them.[124]

A version of the list also exists in the files of the New York–based JLC and indicates that most of the figures named either were in Toulouse or could be contacted through Abramovitch. The list provides the name of the person in need of a visa and a brief biography, and notes which family members were accompanying him or her. In the margins, there are handwritten notes indicating how many people were in each group and other pertinent information. Curiously, a note beside Daniel Charney's name states "will not go."[125]

Two separate letters composed on July 29, one from Kin to Ben-Adir and another from Abramovitch simply to "my dear friend," relay the good news. The United States would be issuing tourist visas to the members of the list and Minkoff had provided the necessary financial guarantees. Yet as Abramovitch cautioned, still remaining were the "difficulties with the transit visas, shipping possibilities, and so on. But we'll try to overcome all the obstacles in our way to the USA."[126] Records in the JLC archives also indicate that it sent over $3,000 to Abramovitch for travel expenses.[127]

Archival materials for the encyclopedists during the first weeks of August are nearly nonexistent. It is clear, however, that the members of the Dubnow Fund and many of their allies on the list were able, after three tortured weeks of delays, to obtain *sauf-conduits* that allowed them to travel from Toulouse to Marseille to collect their visas. They left Marseille on August 16 and arrived in Lisbon by August 20.[128] While the details of their journey are unknown, the vast majority of arrivals in Lisbon from France traveled via rail through Spain. The members of Abramovitch's group were fortunate that in the first two months following the occupation of France, Spain had not put up many administrative obstacles to refugees passing through on their way to Portugal.[129] By mid-July, the city had been receiving hundreds of refugees daily. The *New York Times* and the *New Yorker* were reporting that Lisbon was filling with thousands of people seeking to make the trip, by sea or by air, to any point of refuge off the Continent.[130] For some, the barriers to escaping the grip of the Nazis seemingly proved insurmountable, and they took their lives during the journey. These included Walter Benjamin, who is widely believed to have committed suicide, on September 26, after being thwarted in his attempt to cross the Pyrenees.

For the members of the Dubnow Fund and many of the political figures in Abramovitch's circle, their stay in Lisbon—measured in weeks and months— was comparatively brief. Others were trapped for years; some died while waiting in limbo.[131] On August 28, Abramovitch, along with his wife, Rosa, his daughter, Lia, and several others, departed Lisbon with the help of the Jewish Labor Committee and the refugee assistance group HICEM.[132] They sailed on the U.S. passenger ship *Excalibur* and arrived in New York on September 6. Abramovitch, Rosa, and Lia are listed on the ship's manifest as holding Nansen passports (an indication of their status as stateless) and, following the standards of the time, as members of the Hebrew race.[133] On September 3, Ben-Adir, Einhorn, Tcherikower, and Aronson departed on the Greek ship *Nea Hellas*, arriving in the United States on September 12. Kin and Menes were among the last of the group to remain in Lisbon.[134]

In a letter to Ben-Adir dated September 15, Kin wrote that he expected to depart on September 28, also on "the 'famous' Greek ship *Nea Hellas*." He went on to state, "We are not that upset about the delay. We can rest from our travels. After all, we've been on the road for three months already." He asked Ben-Adir about his first impressions of America and whether he had managed to connect with their Territorialist allies. He also spoke of his sadness at having to leave friends behind in Marseille. He closed his letter by relating a bit of good news: "I am bringing a great present to America. I tore almost by force the first and second volume *Yidn* from our subscribers in Marseille. . . . Your sea journey was probably not an easy one and it won't be for us either. But after having gone through so many bad journeys already, this last leg doesn't worry us too much."[135] Kin and Menes arrived on October 13. With them was Petr Garvi, a Menshevik leader who would contribute several entries to volume 5 (1944) of the *Entsiklopedye*. Leon Bramson, as head of the ORT, stayed to oversee its operations aiding imperiled Jews, first in the ORT's relocated headquarters in Vichy, and then again when it moved to Marseille in November.[136]

A few months after arriving to New York, Ben-Adir wrote to Mukdoni regarding the current state of the *Entsiklopedye*.[137] He spoke of his joy over his son's success at finding work in a chemical laboratory, the work that he was undertaking to prepare the *Yidn giml* volume, and his efforts on behalf of the Frayland-lige. He then wrote of the plans to reestablish the encyclopedia and solicited Mukdoni's help as an emissary. A campaign was underway to raise the funds necessary to publish the forthcoming volume and relaunch the project in America. In spite of these intentions, he realized that the current situation was deeply unstable and that plans could change at any time, quipping wryly, "A mentsh trakht—un Hitler lakht" ("A man plans—and Hitler laughs"), substituting "Hitler" for "*Got*" (God) in the common proverb.

In coming to America in the late summer and early fall of 1940, the encyclopedists avoided the fate of their colleagues who remained in Europe. World War II had begun, but the major centers of Yiddish life in Europe, while now occupied by hostile and antisemitic powers, were not yet battlegrounds or sites of forced ghettoization, enslavement, and murder. Jews in German-occupied Poland were facing horrific discrimination and segregation, the theft of their property, and the persistent threat of violence, but the systematic murder of Jews that would start the following summer had not yet begun and was still unimaginable. At this point, the encyclopedists did not know that in coming to the United States, most would never be returning and would become some of the last remaining exemplars of Yiddish culture and Eastern European Jewish political life. In saving what they could of the *Entsiklopedye*, in bringing the manuscripts for the next volume, in reestablishing their headquarters, and in recommitting themselves to their project's success, they were demonstrating their determination to continue their work on behalf of the still-living millions of Yiddish readers.

However, now in their third country of exile, they also were coming to realize that an encyclopedia of general knowledge along the lines of what they had envisioned a decade earlier was no longer what those millions of readers required. Nevertheless, they remained steadfast in seeing the project through. After all, how else to defend a culture except through cultural works? What other weapons did they have at their disposal? As Ben-Adir had written to Shmuel Charney in the fall of 1939 after the invasion of Poland, "Especially now in what are these wholly tragic times, our duty is even greater to prove that our culture possesses an eternal value for which there can be no greater sacrifice."[138]

The turbulence of the 1930s is well reflected in the Paris volumes of the *Algemeyne entsiklopedye*. By the time of their flight from France, the Dubnow Fund had published six volumes in some of the most difficult conditions. Four fell under the *normale* series, and reached only partway through the first letter of the alphabet, to "Erets-yisroel." Two volumes from the *Yidn* series had been published. What the editors could not know at the time was that they were still more than twenty-five years away from completing their task.

3

SPINNING THE
HISTORICAL THREADS

New York, 1940–1966

Refuge in America

WHEN THEY ARRIVED in New York in 1940, the encyclopedists entered a city that was home to the largest and most successful Jewish population in the world. Approximately 1,785,000 Jews lived in New York City, far surpassing the 350,000 who resided in Warsaw, the city with the next-largest number of Jews.[1] The United States as a whole had a population of nearly 5 million Jews, well beyond Poland's 3.3 million. Jews in New York belonged to all economic classes, resided in many parts of the city, skewed to the left half of the political spectrum, and maintained a broad range of religious observance, from deeply observant to radically secular. American Jews were generally economically successful and often outpaced other European migrant groups in terms of their affluence. This was in part a consequence, Hasia R. Diner argues, of "Jewish trade unions, the general prosperity of the 1920s, and continuing Jewish investment in the education of their children," but also "by virtue of having been in the right place at the right time."[2] They were underrepresented in those sectors of the economy that were hit particularly hard by the Depression, such as agriculture and heavy industry, and overrepresented in those areas that were better positioned to absorb the financial shock, such as the garment industry.

Especially in and around New York City, the vast majority of Jews in 1940 were of Eastern European descent and either had some fluency in Yiddish or were no more than one or two generations removed from the language. The city was the major center of Yiddish-language cultural production in all of the

Americas. Although usage of Yiddish was in steep decline among American-born children of Yiddish speakers, it remained an integral part of the city's landscape. It was a common language of the home, workplace, market, and union hall. The city was the site of a vibrant Yiddish press, radio, and theater. Organizations such as the Arbeter-ring and the Central Yiddish Culture Organization (CYCO, pronounced *tsee-ko*) were dedicated to promoting and preserving Yiddish culture, a task that often went hand in hand with defending the rights of the Jewish working class. Although down from its height of 275,000 subscribers in the 1920s, the Yiddish-language daily *Forverts* in 1940 could still claim 170,000 subscribers.[3]

The mass migration of Jews from Eastern Europe that began in the early 1880s and lasted until the mid-1920s brought approximately two million Jews to the United States, and by 1940 they, together with their descendants, made up the majority of Jews in America. Although many left Eastern Europe (in particular the Russian Empire) to escape escalating antisemitic violence, they also came to the United States as part of a much larger migration of twenty million people who arrived mainly from Southern and Eastern Europe. Like so many immigrants before them, they came to the United States for economic opportunity and to experience political and religious freedom. Unlike previous waves of migrants, who tended to settle throughout the country, these arrivals populated northeastern and midwestern cities, where they joined the new and rapidly growing industrial labor force.

They also arrived in a country with a preexisting racial color line that separated whites from African Americans. Historian Eric L. Goldstein has demonstrated that the newly arrived Jews learned quickly that "making it" in America was contingent upon engaging in a range of economic, cultural, and linguistic practices that would establish their compatibility with whiteness.[4] Following patterns long repeated in their history, Jews modified their names, dress, forms of worship, language, and family structures in order to fit better with the expectations of the surrounding society. Jewish newcomers believed that their newly adopted country provided the opportunity to assimilate into the majority white society and to enjoy the full range of privileges afforded to it. In response, many of the institutions that they founded, such as Jewish presses, loan societies, labor unions, fraternal organizations, and houses of worship, were concerned with fostering Jewish self-help and communal support as a means to move into the middle class. While Jews' long history of experiencing antisemitism and strong ties to the political left led many to challenge the country's policies of racial segregation and its broader culture of white supremacy, others demonstrated their affinity with white America by seeking access to racially exclusive institutions and neighborhoods, hiring African American women as domestic servants, and refraining from "interracial" marriages. They pursued higher education vigorously and sought to climb the economic ladder quickly. After federal legislation passed in the early 1920s reduced the flow of new immigrants entering the country to a trickle, the absence of new arrivals, who often brought with them the Yiddish language, religiously orthodox ways, and radical politics, accelerated this process of "whitening" even further—an explicit goal of the new immigration restrictions.

Notwithstanding the historically unprecedented opportunities available to Jews, antisemitism remained a persistent barrier to their progress and at times risked becoming physically dangerous. Some of the hatred that Jews experienced was rooted in Christian religious antipathies that dated back more than a millennium and persisted into the contemporary era. In addition, Jews regularly found themselves stereotyped as dishonest in commerce, as political radicals determined to overthrow the capitalist system, and ultimately as a people who were unassimilable and therefore a risk to the nations in which they resided. A May 1939 public opinion poll of Americans found that only 39 percent of respondents believed that Jews "have the same standing as any other peoples and they should be treated in all ways exactly as any other Americans." Nearly 32 percent believed that "Jews have some different business methods and, therefore, some measures should be taken to prevent Jews from getting too much power in the business world." Ten percent stated that Jews should not "mingle socially where they are not wanted," while another 10 percent stated that "we should make it a policy to deport Jews from this country to some new homeland as fast as it can be done without inhumanity."[5] These attitudes toward Jews were, by and large, imported from Europe but were not nearly as virulent when manifested in the United States. There were no pogroms threatening Jewish neighborhoods or laws explicitly restricting Jews' citizenship, housing, business, or religious affairs. The one murderous episode of antisemitic violence to occur in this period, the 1915 lynching of Leo Frank in Georgia, while deeply unsettling to southern Jews in particular, did not incite further attacks on Jews around the country.[6]

The country in which the encyclopedists found refuge in 1940 was, therefore, one replete with contradictions and paradoxes concerning its Jewish citizens. They were the largest and most economically well-off Jewish community in the world but possessed little political power to effect change in the country's draconian immigration laws. They encountered historically low levels of antisemitism but resided in a country that still bore deep suspicions about their compatibility with white Christian America. They maintained strong ties to liberal and even radical politics but were increasingly participating in practices that reinforced the color line for their own racial and economic "advancement." Most were relatively recent arrivals to the country but were rapidly distancing themselves from their Eastern European roots.

Throughout the fall of 1940 and the first half of 1941, it remained unclear whether the encyclopedists would be returning to Europe or if their time in America would be permanent. The persecution of Jews under Nazi rule was intensifying and reports of the establishment of ghettos in the East were appearing in the Jewish press with greater frequency. However, the wholesale murder of Jewish civilians that would soon begin was still unimaginable, and the possibility of rebuilding a vibrant European Jewish life after the war still conceivable. The United States remained out of the war, the Soviet Union was in a pact with Germany, and the rest of Europe was occupied. One question for the encyclopedists was whether they could continue their project with even more limited means, a further reduced staff, and European Jewry under increasing assault. Another was whether their Yiddish-language project could find a readership—now primarily American—who would be responsive to their mission.

The *Entsiklopedye* in the Years of War and *Khurbn*

In fleeing to America, the encyclopedists found themselves in a setting that was utterly foreign to most of them and yet in circumstances that were all too familiar. New York City, with its subways, tenements, and skyscrapers, looked nothing like the cities of Europe. It was sprawling and densely packed with people of diverse ethnicities, nationalities, languages, and cultures. At the same time, the experience of flight and resettlement was by this point a defining characteristic of their lives. Many of the encyclopedists were now in their third country of exile. They had arrived in Berlin in the 1920s after the Bolshevik Revolution in Russia. They had found refuge in Paris following the Nazi rise to power in Germany in 1933. Now in New York after the fall of France, in 1940, they again had to restart their cultural and political work, while somehow earning enough money to support themselves and their families.

They were well aware that the move from Berlin to Paris had not gone smoothly for their project. The *Entsiklopedye* was just gaining momentum and they had to rebuild it almost entirely anew. The editors and contributors who had scattered across Europe had to relocate and recommit to the work. New financing had to be secured, and new offices, printers, and suppliers had to be identified. The entire printing schedule of the project had to be readjusted. It took nearly two years from the time they left Germany for the first volume to appear in print. Chastened by that experience and now fully immersed in their work, the encyclopedists—Abramovitch, Kin, and Ben-Adir in particular— took up the task of seeing to its quick restoration in New York. Undoubtedly, they were highly conscious of the precarity of not only the *Entsiklopedye*'s status, but also their own. As refugees in a country that was generally hostile to immigrants (even if New York City was not) and that insisted that new arrivals demonstrate their loyalty in large part through self-sufficiency, they understood the necessity of getting back to work. They also saw their intellectual and cultural labor as a moral imperative. Forbidden by the terms of their visas from engaging in overt political activity, writing and research became the primary means by which they could participate in the struggle against fascism and serve the Jewish community they had left behind in Europe and the one they now joined in America. They were also no longer young. Most had been born in the 1880s, and the time left remaining to them to complete this work was beginning to run out.

Fortunately, much of what they lacked in Berlin and Paris was present in New York. They had physical safety from war and from the threats of Nazism and Soviet totalitarianism. Crucially, they also had access to a sophisticated and expansive network of Jewish communal support. They had arrived upon a scene where there existed decades' worth of institutions and organizations that could potentially provide resources in support of their venture. It was home to refugee resettlement groups, emergency rescue committees, Yiddish cultural societies, a dynamic Jewish press and arts community, and Jewish labor groups.

Within weeks of arriving, the encyclopedists had already begun to reconstitute the project. Their temporary address (as indicated on letterhead that they had printed immediately after arriving) was Abramovitch's new apartment on Manhattan's Upper West Side, near Columbia University.[7] Working at what must have been a furious pace, they managed to republish *Yidn beys* in December 1940 with the financial support of CYCO, which would come to fund the project entirely for several years. A new title page indicates that the reprint was a second edition published by CYCO, the copyright was held by the American Committee of the Yiddish Encyclopedia, and it was printed in a union shop. The print run was an ambitious three thousand copies.[8] The foreword to the second edition states:

The volume *Yidn beys* was published in Paris at the beginning of May 1940.[9] The events of the following weeks and the occupation of Paris and much of France by the Germans made further work on the encyclopedia in Europe impossible. A massive shipment of the encyclopedia volumes that was shipped from Paris to us in New York at the end of May was lost on the way. Only a small number of copies of the volume *Yidn beys* that were sent from Paris through the mail arrived in America.

The Central Yiddish Culture Organization (CYCO), which is the representative of the Yiddish *Algemeyne entsiklopedye* in the United States and Canada, believes that it should not permit this monumental work to be lost to our cultural world. It has decided therefore to republish the volume *Yidn beys* without alteration here in America. This also allows subscribers of the encyclopedia in the United States, in Canada, Mexico, and also South America to receive the volume, which is the sixth of the *Algemeyne entsiklopedye*.

Nearly all of the editors of the encyclopedia have emigrated from Paris to New York. This great work, which began in Berlin and was relocated to Paris on account of the triumph of Hitlerism, has taken its next step and is now based in America.

CYCO is convinced that with the support of the larger Jewish community and through the strength of Yiddish culture, this vital publication will continue until its conclusion.[10]

CYCO's support indeed proved invaluable to the reestablishment of the *Entsiklopedye* in New York. Founded in 1938 as a "non-partisan Yiddish organization" with chapters "across the U.S. and as far away as Argentina," CYCO focused its efforts on Yiddish publishing and distribution, and later became the publishing arm of the Alveltlekher Yidisher Kultur-kongres (World Congress for Jewish Culture).[11] In 1948, CYCO would publish reprints of both the *normale* (1–5) and *Yidn* (*alef–giml*) volumes.

To mark the momentous occasion, a celebration was planned for late February 1941 at the Grand Street Boys' Association building in midtown Manhattan. The invitation announced that the project had come to the United States to stay, having made "substantive steps towards planting the publication of the encyclopedia here in American soil," an indication that its editors perhaps believed the United States was not simply a temporary layover until the war's end.[12] The invitation was sent out on newly printed letterhead that gives the address of the *Entsiklopedye* as 425 Lafayette Street (Astor Place), which was then home to HIAS, YIVO, and several Jewish publishing ventures.[13] The list includes many luminaries of the New York Yiddish political, cultural, and scholarly communities, such as Chaim Zhitlowsky, the labor leader David Dubinsky, the writers Joseph Opatoshu and Avrom Reisen, and YIVO-based scholars Max Weinreich, Jacob Lestschinsky, Elias Tcherikower, and Jacob Shatzky.[14]

Maintaining their momentum was of primary importance. Doing so while contending with the absence of many of the contributors and colleagues who were left behind in Europe was especially painful, given the alarming news reports of life under Nazi occupation. Even correspondence with Aaron Steinberg in London during the Blitz was extraordinarily difficult. As he did in early 1934, Ben-Adir sent endless letters inquiring about his whereabouts and beseeching him for a response, which arrived only after a long silence.[15]

Following the successful republication of *Yidn beys*, by spring 1941, the encyclopedists were fully at work preparing *Yidn giml* for publication.[16] They also managed to reprint three thousand copies of *Yidn alef* to replace the stock they were forced to abandon when they fled Paris. Most of the essays for *Yidn giml* had been received when they were still in Paris, and the manuscripts were among the few materials that they managed to take with them to America. The editors and several staff members received regular stipends of $60 a month for most of 1942 and 1943 from the National Refugee Service, an organization that provided millions in support to Jewish victims of Nazism who had taken shelter in the United States.[17] A stipend of $2,294 from the National Refugee Service allowed them to return Avrom Menes to the staff and hire several others, including Abramovitch's Menshevik colleague Grigori Aronson, the Bundist activist and expert on the Jewish labor movement Israel Sadowski (who wrote under the pen name Victor Shulman), and a young mathematician and physicist named Lipman Bers, who also worked for YIVO as it was reestablishing itself in New York. Further financial support came from the sale of subscriptions and individual volumes and donations from supporters in the United States, Mexico, and Canada ($14,772.25), a grant from the Jewish Labor Committee ($6,000), and a loan of $3,125.75.[18]

Yidn giml, the third volume in the *Yidn* series and the seventh volume overall, was published in April 1942. In the time between the December 1940 rerelease of *Yidn beys* and the publication of *Yidn giml*, European Jewish life—along with the rest of life on the Continent—had been entirely upended. On June 22, 1941, Germany broke its pact with the Soviet Union without warning and invaded the country. In an assault it named Operation Barbarossa, Germany sent four million soldiers into battle along a front line that extended more than 1,800 miles. Reflecting the Nazi belief that Slavic peoples were subhuman, German forces acted with unrelenting brutality against the military forces they encountered and the civilian populations in their path. Within weeks, Germany had conquered much of the territory taken by the USSR at the start of the war in September 1939 and was pushing into Russia itself. Having taken Poland and Western Europe so quickly, Hitler had assumed that

Stalin's forces would also swiftly fall. Germany's goal had been to destroy communism entirely and force the Russians into total subjugation, likely by starving the majority of the population and preserving a small percentage to serve as forced laborers for a future German Reich. By December 1942, German forces had captured nearly 4 million Soviet prisoners of war and deliberately starved 2.8 million of them to death.[19]

The territories between Germany and Russia were home to Jewish communities that dated back centuries and that, taken as a whole, made up the largest population of Jews in the world. From the northern Baltic states of Estonia, Latvia, and Lithuania, and moving south through Belorussia, Poland, and Ukraine, these lands were the traditional home of Eastern European Jewry. They were the cradle of modern Yiddish culture, the birthplace of diverse religious customs and dynasties, the center of Jewish politics, and the home to the *shtetlekh* of small-town Jewry as well as the cosmopolitan cities of the most urbanized Jews. Within weeks of the German invasion, these regions became the killing zone where the Nazi Holocaust against Jewish people began. By late July 1941, German forces had begun systematically murdering men of fighting age, and then, throughout the fall, started hunting Jews regardless of age and gender. This was accomplished often with the help of members of the local non-Jewish population, many of whom welcomed the Germans as liberators from the Soviets and saw the invasion as a chance to inflict horrific violence against their Jewish neighbors.

By spring 1942, the inhabitants of the Warsaw ghetto—numbering over four hundred thousand, almost all Jews—had long been sealed off from the rest of the world and were facing starvation and epidemics. Further ghettos were established throughout Poland and other German-occupied lands. The extermination camp at Chełmno had become operational. In Western Europe, Jews were facing repeated acts of violence, segregation, property theft, and especially for foreign Jews, mass incarceration in camps. When the editors were writing the foreword to *Yidn giml*, Jews from German-annexed Upper Silesia had already been deported to Auschwitz and murdered with Zyklon B. The United States, long sitting on the sidelines, was gearing up to enter the fighting, having declared war on the Axis powers following the December 7, 1941, bombing of Pearl Harbor. Although the encyclopedists in America did not know it yet, many of their friends and colleagues had already been murdered, and several great Yiddish cultural institutions had been destroyed or dismantled.

Unable to effect real change in the lives of their family, comrades, and communities left behind in Europe, they threw themselves into their work. Along with working on the *Entsiklopedye*, Abramovitch restarted the *Socialist*

Courier and in 1944 published a two-volume set of memoirs, *In tsvey revolutsyes* (In two revolutions), a work of more than 750 pages that recounts his child-hood from his earliest political activity through the Bolshevik seizure of power.[20] Ben-Adir, having just published *Farn geshikhtlekhn yom-hadin* imme-diately prior to fleeing Paris, founded a new Territorialist journal named *Afn shvel* (On the threshold) in 1941 and wrote many of its initial articles. Tcheri-kower finished editing a two-volume study of French Jewry, *Yidn in frankraykh: shtudyes un materyaln* (Jews in France: Studies and materials), which was pub-lished by YIVO in 1942.[21]

Although few of the specifics regarding the fate of European Jews were yet known to the editors of the *Entsiklopedye* in spring 1942, it was clear that the future would bear little resemblance to the past. They also began to realize that the *Entsiklopedye*'s mission would likewise need to shift in response to the worsening conditions. Once imagined by its editors as a resource that would "serve practical and scientific ends," the *Entsiklopedye*, they announced in the foreword to *Yidn giml*, would move toward the goal of creating a "literary monument that would make permanent the experiences and accomplish-ments of the material and spiritual development of the Jewish folk until the beginning of the historical rupture of the second world war."[22] Sensing the magnitude of the destruction, the editors imagined the *Entsiklopedye* as an instrument with which to preserve the past in preparation for a diminished and transformed postwar Jewish life:

> It is clear that after the war the life of the Jewish masses in Europe will look
> entirely different from how it was in the nineteenth and in the first third of
> the twentieth centuries, just as European development in general after the
> war will not be a simple continuation of the earlier age. But with each
> historical rupture, elements from the past are found in the new period.
> Moreover, in many areas of Jewish spiritual and ideological life the lines of
> development and continuation will not be torn. And so, it is worthwhile to
> continue spinning the historical threads, so that the new age should benefit
> from the experience of the previous era, and it is necessary first of all for
> everyone to know what was created in the past and which of its elements
> can be worthwhile building blocks for the future.[23]

Reflecting this imperative, *Yidn giml* is very much a project of Jewish émigrés and exiles who maintained intimate ties to Eastern European Jewry. It in-cludes essays from contributors who had recently arrived from Europe, such as Abramowitz, Ben-Adir, Menes, and the journalist Leyb Shpizman, as well as from scholars who had emigrated to North America previously but who had long been associated with the encyclopedia, such as the literary critic Shmuel Charney, who wrote on the history of Yiddish literature, and the historian Jacob Shatzky, who wrote on the Yiddish-language press. Although the editors had brought the manuscript for this volume with them from Paris, it does not contain entries by any of their colleagues trapped in Europe, they note in the foreword, but do not explain why. There are likewise no contributions from Aaron Steinberg, who remained incommunicado. All authors whose works do appear were born in Eastern Europe. Most had strong ties to the Yiddish cultural world, to modern Jewish politics, or to both, such as the writer, editor, activist, and teacher Nokhem-Borekh Minkoff; the linguist Judah Joffe; the scholar, journalist, and YIVO librarian Mordecai Kosover; and the Winnipeg-based Yiddish school director and author Avrom Golomb. The volume also features a contribution by the Bundist leader and member of the Polish Government in Exile Szmul Zygielbojm, who would prominently take his life in London on May 11, 1943, after the Warsaw ghetto uprising, in an act of protest against the world's indifference to the fate of European Jews under Nazi rule.[24]

Yidn giml, which was thought of at the time as the conclusion of a three-part "detour" of the encyclopedia written in response to the increasing assaults on Eastern European Jewry, has four primary areas of focus: the history of Yiddish and Hebrew literatures, an overview of the Jewish press, a history of Jewish communal and nationalist ideological movements, and the history of Eastern European Jewish labor and socialist movements (including their offshoots in the United States). Of the many contributions, two stand out for their breadth and scope: Shmuel Charney's "Yiddish Literature from the Mid-eighteenth Century until 1942" and Ben-Adir's "Modern Social and National Currents among Jews."[25]

For the encyclopedists, Charney's essay represented something of a coup for their project. Since the earliest stages of the venture, they had sought to gain his support and participation, but he had limited himself only to lending his name to the editorial board. By the early 1940s, Charney's stature in the world of Yiddish letters was incomparable. Through his criticism and stewardship of several foundational periodicals and collections, Charney played a central role in the cultivation of modern literary Yiddish. As a young man, he had been an active member of the Zionist Socialist Workers Party in the heady days of the 1905 Russian Revolution, when he was jailed and tortured.[26] The party had argued that Jews required their own independent territory to develop sufficient class consciousness to create a Jewish proletariat and overthrow the capitalist system. Following the failure of the

FIGURE 3.1 Shmuel Charney (courtesy of YIVO).

revolution, he turned his attention fully to literary criticism. In his twenties and thirties he played a central role in either launching or editing works such as *Di literarishe monatsshriftn* (The literary monthly), *Di yidishe velt* (The Jewish world), *Der pinkes* (The record), and *Leksikon fun der yidisher literatur un prese* (Lexicon of Yiddish literature and the press), which helped set the stage for a national renaissance in Yiddish letters. The violence that followed the Bolshevik rise to power made the situation in Russia untenable for him. An incident in April 1919 in which his houseguest and onetime collaborator in *Di literarishe monatsshriftn*, A. Vayter, was murdered by Polish soldiers compelled Charney to leave Europe permanently. By late summer of that year he had resettled in New York City. Charney shifted toward a more politically moderate stance after coming to the United States and focused his efforts on literary criticism and building Yiddish cultural institutions. He published essays in the newspaper *Der tog* and in the monthly *Di tsukunft* (The future), and was a highly acclaimed public lecturer, editor, and teacher. Following the establishment of an American section of YIVO in 1925, he played a central role in its organization and development. Charney's participation in *Yidn giml* bestowed his unmatched authority upon the encyclopedia.

Charney's essay is a wide-ranging three-part survey of Yiddish that draws from his by then four decades of criticism. At over one hundred columns long, it is the lengthiest entry in the work. It covers the period in which Yiddish began to take on increased symbolic meaning during the growing Hasidic movement of the mid-eighteenth century, through the Jewish Enlightenment in the nineteenth, when the pressure on Jews to assimilate to their host countries led to a decline in the usage of Yiddish in Western Europe, through the stirrings among Eastern European Jews of a new Yiddish renaissance in the late nineteenth century, to the triumph of Yiddish as a national language of the Jewish people in the twentieth. His essay reflects Charney's lifelong commitment to overturning the assimilatory legacy of the Jewish Enlightenment, his dedication to promoting sophisticated expressions of literature that would serve the interests of the Jewish nation, and his championing of modernist Yiddish literary forms.

The bulk of the entry is dedicated to the twentieth century as the period in which Yiddish literature achieved its greatest heights, even as "language wars" were fought between advocates for Yiddish, who tended to lean toward Diasporist political movements, and those for Hebrew, who tended toward Zionist ones. In the essay—which presents itself as comprehensive yet has very little consideration of women Yiddish writers—Charney moves chronologically and geographically in an effort to demonstrate how modern Yiddish was shaped by the chaotic political events of World War I and the collapse of the Russian empire, which had been home to millions of Yiddish speakers and several major Yiddish cultural centers. Charney's essay, like many in the volume, is marked by a sense of mourning and the author's awareness that much of the world he is describing has been forever diminished. In his discussion of Yiddish during the time of the Republic of Poland (1919–1939), Charney writes:

> Yiddish writers in Poland gathered into various, more or less organized
> groups. . . . In spite of the enormous poverty, want, and hunger on one side,
> and antisemitism on the other side that led both writers and readers to
> leave the country at the first opportunity and forced those left behind to
> loneliness, worry, and despair—in spite of this they continued to enrich
> Yiddish literature. . . . After the Hitler invasion, Polish Yiddish writers were
> scattered and spread to the corners of the world, so that the greatest

portion of Yiddish writers who lived in Eastern Europe came to America on visas. Only a smaller number remain in Poland, condemned—for a time—to hardship, enslavement, and silence.[27]

Ben-Adir's sweeping essay, "Modern Social and National Currents among Jews," is an extensive discussion of modern Jewish nationalism from its first stirrings in the mid-nineteenth century to the eve of World War II. Prior to the emancipation of European Jews, he explains, Jewish communities tended to live isolated from the non-Jews around them because of broadly held anti-Jewish attitudes as well as internal Jewish communal desires to live in closed societies. This wish for self-isolation ended, he argues, with the rise of the European Enlightenment and capitalism, twin forces that pushed all members of a society to transform themselves into useful citizens of the state and incentivized them to participate in a modern economy. The failure of the Enlightenment and capitalism to make Jews equal members of the states in which they were a part expressed itself in chauvinistic and antisemitic forms of nationalism and prompted the first stirrings in Jews of their own national self-conceptions.

As a Territorialist who stood outside of mainstream Zionist politics, Ben-Adir asserts the possibilities of an authentic Jewish life lived in the Diaspora. Written prior to the creation of the State of Israel and the wide embrace of Zionism among Jews worldwide, it reflects much of the diversity and possibilities of Jewish nationalism that were still present in the early 1940s, and conveys well the vast range of competing ideological perspectives, visions for the future, and organizational efforts that shaped the Jewish national project for decades. In spite of a deep pessimism that runs through the essay, Ben-Adir remains hopeful that Jewish Diasporic life will continue to thrive. Written just prior to the wholesale slaughter of European Jews, it is among the last expressions of the vast possibilities of Jewish nationalism and a recognition of its many cultural, political, economic, and spiritual dimensions.

Among the many strengths of Ben-Adir's survey is that it describes fully the importance of the contributions of Eastern European Jewry to the development of Jewish nationalism. While not dismissing the central role of Theodor Herzl and the Zionist Congress, which Herzl founded and which gave direction and an organizational frame to the movement, Ben-Adir explores the contributions of early national groups such as Khibat Tsiyon (Love of Zion) and the cultural Zionist leader Ahad Ha'am. Significant space is given to the Territorialist movement, of which he was a leader. Ben-Adir also stresses the pivotal role that the 1905 Russian Revolution played in the development of the movement. In this attempt to overthrow the czar, which drew support from across the political spectrum and prompted hundreds of thousands of workers to strike, Jews participated at a rate far beyond their numbers in the overall population. Jewish self-defense organizations and labor groups joined the strikes and took part in street battles with police.[28] In particular, Jewish radicals, Ben-Adir among them, formed several political parties that sought to synthesize the often-conflicting demands of socialism and nationalism. In doing so, they helped pave the way for a Labor Zionist movement to form and become dominant within the larger Zionist movement, including among those Zionists who settled in Palestine and established a quasi-Jewish state there after World War I.

After discussing several "experiments" in Jewish colonization in the interwar period, including those in Palestine and in the Soviet Union's Birobidzhan region, he concludes by reflecting the anxiety of the present moment, when it is clear that terrible events are occurring but the impacts are not yet known:

> What will come of these just-described developmental processes after this horrific catastrophe, which is now raining over the heads of European Jewry, in which entire Jewish communities are being uprooted from the earth, are now facing theft, enslavement, and torture, and are now being confined in ghettos and concentration camps?[29]

This essay was one of the last of Ben-Adir's compositions. Since arriving in the United States, he had thrown himself into the work of the *Entsiklopedye* and the Frayland-lige's *Afn shvel*. He died on November 14, 1942, after a difficult illness. In an entry dedicated to Ben-Adir in the subsequent volume of the *Entsiklopedye* (1944), Jacob Lestschinsky hailed him as one of the founding members of a new radical Jewish politics that flourished during the period of the 1905 Revolution, and as someone who "truly believed in the fundamental idea of the necessity of an independent Jewish life."[30] Lestschinsky then memorialized him as a figure who, after laboring for decades to realize this vision, "underwent a transformation from maximal Diaspora-optimism to extreme Diaspora-pessimism," on account of the worsening fate of European Jewry following the rise of Nazism: "He changed his opinion not under the influence of a purely theoretical skepticism but under the weight of the reality of Jewish existence."

Most reviews of *Yidn giml* that appeared in the Yiddish press were strongly supportive. Writing in the English-language journal *Jewish Social Studies*, however, the historian Bernard D. Weinryb was far more critical in a 1942 review of the *Yidn* series.[31] Born in Turobin, Poland, in 1900 and educated in

FIGURE 3.2 Ben-Adir (Avrom
Rozin) (courtesy of YIVO).

Breslau, Germany (today Wrocław, Poland), Weinryb had been a member of
the editorial staff of the *Encyclopaedia Judaica* before moving to Palestine, and
then to New York City in 1939. After locating the *Algemeyne entsiklopedye*
within a larger trend of Jewish encyclopedias that began in the early the twentieth century, Weinryb curiously states that "while the editorial board does
not admit it, the separate publication of the articles on Jews [the *Yidn* volumes
under review] is in itself a reflection of the changed situation of the Jews since
the encyclopedia was first launched a dozen years ago," a shift that was in fact
discussed openly in the forewords to the *Yidn* volumes themselves. After providing a brief summary of the tumultuous events experienced by the editors
of the *Entsiklopedye* since its founding in the early 1930s, he credits the upheavals as the reason for the "disjointed effect of the whole," and points to several
inconsistencies within the formatting of the articles. While Weinryb was
somewhat forgiving of these defects, he was much more critical of the editors'

initial decision to publish the *Entsiklopedye* from Berlin and Paris, which put them at a far remove from the Yiddish-speaking masses on whose account they worked. The result of this distance was that the editors, he claimed, put themselves out of touch with the shifting needs of their audience, especially with the *Entsiklopedye*'s continued emphases on Diaspora Nationalism and Yiddishism and its general disregard for Zionism and Hebraism. Anticipating a criticism that would be leveled against the *Entsiklopedye* in later years, he ended his review with a warning for the editors that they needed to publish volumes that would speak to the needs of American Jews if they were to remain relevant. "In this country the struggles of Yiddishism have reached an extremely critical stage," he wrote. "The average reader of this *Encyclopedia* is more or less sympathetic toward Hebrew and Zionism or, in any case, not opposed to the movement. The editors of the *Encyclopedia* must take this fact into account if it is to meet the needs of Yiddish readers in the United States."[32]

Following the release of *Yidn giml*, the encyclopedists remained committed to realizing the original vision of the project: the creation of an encyclopedia of universal knowledge in Yiddish. In a May 1942 draft of a funding proposal for a grant from the National Refugee Service, they declared their intention was still to publish an encyclopedia of twenty volumes and explained that much of their work since arriving to the United States had been consumed by preparing "for the second time the files, the catalogue of entries (i.e., the alphabetical index of the items—about 40,000—divided in sections according to various sciences and disciplines—all arranged in a well-organized system)."[33] They also undertook a widespread subscription campaign and solicited funds in the United States, Canada, and Mexico. With support of the Jewish Labor Committee, they managed to raise approximately $28,000 (the equivalent of more than $500,000 in 2021 dollars) and paid more than two dozen contributors and staff members. Repeating a line of argument they had made when they first began the project, they pressed their appeal by explaining that "none of the serious national encyclopedias in Europe was ever accomplished without a substantial financial contribution by the state (i.e., the Polish, Czech, Italian or Greek) or of some rich private Maecenas [a benefactor to Horace and Virgil]." Their intention was to publish the fifth volume in the *normale* series in 1943, as well as to republish the first four volumes of that series. Privately, they also believed that it was essential to the continued existence of the project that they publish at minimum two volumes a year from now on.[34]

It perhaps unsurprising that the *normale* series volume 5, which covers entries from the Eastern Roman Emperor Flavius Arcadius (ארקאדיוס) to animals/living things (בעלי-חיים), appeared only in early 1944, a year later than predicted in

1942 and a full seven years after the publication of volume 4. In the foreword to
the fifth volume, which was published jointly by the Dubnow Fund and
CYCO, the editors (listed as Abramovitch, Ben-Adir, Tcherikower, Lestschinsky, Kin, and Brutskus) addressed the many hardships facing the project.[35]
Most painfully, the masses of Yiddish-speaking Jews in Eastern Europe were
being slaughtered. Closer to home, two of its central contributors passed away
in New York (Ben-Adir and Tcherikower, who died suddenly in August 1942).[36]
For the first time, the editors employed the term *khurbn* (catastrophe) to
describe the slaughter of the Jews, although the full extent of the genocide was
still not fully understood. In subsequent years, the word *khurbn* would come
to serve as the Yiddish equivalent of the English term *Holocaust* and the
Hebrew term *Shoah*. The editors wrote:

> This volume was prepared and issued in conditions that were enormously
> difficult for scholarly and publishing work. The second half of 1942 and the
> entire year of 1943 were not only a period of savage bloodshed for the entire
> world, but also a time of the greatest catastrophe in the entire history of
> the Jewish people: these were the months in which came the horrible
> *khurbn* in the Jewish ghettos of Poland, in the German-occupied cities and
> towns of the Soviet Union, and in all other occupied countries.
>
>   In the time when the entire Jewish community of an entire continent
> was being exterminated—that community, which was the originator and
> the backbone of Yiddish culture—in that time it was psychologically and
> morally extremely difficult to secure the peaceful and calm work that is
> demanded for the further publication of this encyclopedia.[37]

Further difficulties, they noted, were the lack of available young staffers—
many had gone off to fight in the war—and the painful absence of their colleagues in Europe and the Land of Israel who had contributed to the encyclopedia's earlier volumes. The editors lamented the number of readers who were
cut off from them and they thanked CYCO and American Jewish cultural institutions for giving them the "courage" to continue with their difficult task.
Most important, they announced another shift in the publication schedule.
Rather than end the *Yidn* series with *giml*, they announced that planning was
underway for a *Yidn daled* that would cover the "organization of internal Jewish life and Jewish folk culture."

The editors did not need to enumerate the sufferings of European Jewry.
Although the full horrors of the genocide would only be understood after the
war, readers of the *Entsiklopedye* would have been well aware of the reports
of Nazi atrocities, which were followed closely in the Yiddish press. These

included mass shootings of Jews following the German invasion of the Soviet Union, the deportation and slaughter of more than a quarter of a million Jews in the Warsaw ghetto in the summer of 1942 and the armed uprising that took place there from mid-April to mid-May 1943, the mass deportation of Jews from Western Europe to camps and ghettos in the East, the forced starvation of Jews in ghettos, and even rumors of death camps.[38]

Notably, volume 5, which begins with a full-page black-and-white reproduction of Venus from Botticelli's painting *Venus and Mars* (c. 1485), finally completes the letter *alef* and makes it to nearly the end of the letter *beys*. Unlike the third and fourth volumes, the fifth does not end on an essay-length topic related to Jewish life and history. However, in a clear reflection of the shifting emphasis of the *Entsiklopedye*, volume 5 contains an exceedingly high number of entries related to specifically Jewish subjects.[39] Alongside relatively brief entries on *normale* topics such as population, Belgium, and baseball, there are many biographical entries on major Eastern European Jewish writers and leaders as well as key figures of the European political left.[40] These include entries on the modern Yiddish writer Sholem Asch by Shmuel Charney, on the Social Democratic leader Otto Bauer by Abramovitch, on the Labor Zionist founder and Yiddishist Ber Borochov by the Labor Zionist leader Abraham Revusky, on Chaim Nachman Bialik by the Hebrew poet Avrom Regelson, on Ben-Adir by Lestschinsky, and on the Zionist leader David Ben-Gurion by the Zionist journalist and publicist Leyb Shpizman. Volume 5 also includes entries on Jewish labor and nationalist organizations such as the early Zionist student group BILU, the Jewish Labor Bund, and the Soviet Jewish settlement in Birobidzhan.

The editors, who had largely dropped the name Dubnow Fund from their official correspondence, referring to their venture in correspondence simply as the "Yiddish Encyclopedia," still planned in 1944 to continue publishing volumes in the *normale* series. However, volume 5 would be the final one. As they would come to understand fully in the months and years that followed, millions of Yiddish speakers in Europe had been murdered by the Nazis and their collaborators. From their vantage point in New York, the future of the Yiddish language—whose development their encyclopedia of general knowledge was to help foster—was bleak beyond comprehension.

Furthermore, so many of the readers, editors, contributors, fund raisers, booksellers, and reviewers of the encyclopedia had perished in the *khurbn*. Simon Dubnow, in whose honor the *Algemeyne entsiklopedye* was launched and who had inspired a generation of Eastern European Jewish scholars and activists, was murdered on December 8, 1941, during an action that left 25,000 inhabitants of the Riga ghetto dead. In the final year of his life, he had endured terrible isolation. He was alone, his wife, Ida, having died of illness soon after their arrival in Latvia. Not wanting to be farther away from his children or abandon the people and lands for whom he had devoted his life's work, he turned down several offers to emigrate to the United States.[41] Little news reached him of his Yiddishist colleagues who had fled to Paris and were by then in New York. He was deeply concerned about saving YIVO and its treasures from destruction.[42] Soon after the German occupation of Latvia, he was briefly imprisoned for not turning over his scholarship to the authorities. He came out of prison "completely broken" and moved into the ghetto, where he attempted to continue writing. There are conflicting reports regarding the exact circumstances of his death, but it is likely he was shot while waiting to board a bus during a mass deportation of ghetto inhabitants to the nearby Rumbula forest, where they were to be executed by a Nazi *Einsatzgruppe* with the help of local collaborators of the Latvian Auxiliary Police. He was buried in a mass grave. As his daughter Sophie Dubnov-Erlich writes, after his death a rumor began to spread (which has since made its way into folklore) that as he was about to be murdered, Dubnow beseeched his fellow Jews, "People, do not forget. Speak of this, people; record it all."[43]

Leon Bramson died in Marseille on March 2, 1941, of unknown causes. Yosef Yashunsky, who had become a prominent member of the Warsaw ghetto Judenrat (Jewish council) and had organized classes and workshops for imprisoned Jews, was killed in the Treblinka death camp, where an estimated 925,000 Jews were exterminated. Moyshe Shalit was murdered in a massacre at Ponary, in which tens of thousands of Jews from Vilna alongside thousands of Poles and Soviet prisoners of war perished. Majer Balaban was murdered in the Warsaw ghetto. Zalmen Reisen had been arrested in October 1939 by the Soviet secret police and was executed in the summer of 1941. After being confined in the Vilna ghetto, Zelig Kalmanovitch was deported to the Vaivara concentration camp in Estonia, where he died in winter 1944.

Eastern European Jewish scholarly institutions also faced nearly wholesale destruction. In the city of Vilna, for example, the famous Strashun Library, home to tens of thousands of Jewish texts and rare Judaica and for decades an ecumenical site for learning and study (welcoming women and men, religious and secular alike), was plundered first by the Soviets and then by the Germans. In the eight months of Lithuanian control over the city, the library had become a sanctuary for the thousands of refugees from Poland who had taken shelter in the city. Scholar Dan Rabinowitz has shown that following the Soviet takeover of the city in June 1940, the library fell under control of the new regime.[44] It was closed and soon purged of many materials that ran counter to Soviet ideology, which included most works written in Hebrew, while most Yiddish works were left intact. YIVO experienced a similar fate under the Soviets. Cecile Kuznitz describes that with Max Weinreich out of the country, Zalmen Reisen arrested, and Zelig Kalmanovitch pushed aside, leadership was temporarily turned over to "a staff member with communist sympathies."[45] The institute was subsequently absorbed into the Institute of Lithuanian Studies and renamed the Third Museum and Library of the Institute of Lithuanian Studies, with the linguist and former Folkspartey leader Noyekh Prilutski as its head.[46] Under Soviet control, YIVO was purged of any staff members who held Bundist or Zionist views, but its holdings were left undisturbed, and even grew as it added collections from Jews who had fled or been killed.[47]

Within weeks after the German invasion in June 1941, the Strashun Library and YIVO were targeted by the Einsatzstab Reichsleiter Rosenberg (Reich Leader Rosenberg Taskforce), a Nazi agency whose mission included plundering Jewish cultural treasures for a planned museum in Frankfurt that was to be dedicated to the study of the Jewish people following their destruction. The Nazis forced many staff members to create lists of materials—collected over decades and representing some of the most valuable archives, sacred texts, and artifacts of Eastern European Jewry—and then required them to sort and pack the items for shipment or destruction. Staff from both organizations debated whether to resist (and risk losing their lives), smuggle the materials out of the institutions for safekeeping, or cooperate in the hope that the items would be preserved if sent to Germany and away from the fighting (with the possibility of recovering them after the war). After slaughtering thousands of the city's Jews in early September, the Nazis formed two ghettos, into which they forced more than twenty thousand of the Jews who remained. The Strashun Library was located in the smaller ghetto, which was liquidated in October. Over the winter that followed, staff members and other volunteers began to hide books and cultural artifacts in a variety of spots, including a bunker dug in the library basement and other locations throughout the ghetto. In spite of their efforts, the Germans sent more than twenty-three thousand library books to Frankfurt, while many others went to Berlin.[48]

The Gestapo arrested Prilutski on August 1 and allowed him to leave only in order to perform his work at YIVO. He was severely beaten and killed on August 18, 1941. In March of the following year, the Nazis forced several former YIVO members and others from the ghetto, including Kalmanovitch, to disassemble YIVO's collection in order to determine which materials would be sent to Germany.[49] The YIVO building was turned into a massive sorting station for materials from a variety of libraries and museums in the city and region. Historian David E. Fishman tells of how several members of this group formed a *papir-brigade* that successfully smuggled thousands of Jewish books and materials into the ghetto, including many works of incalculable importance, such as diaries of Theodor Herzl, a record book used by the Vilna Gaon, and letters and manuscripts by Leon Trotsky, the Hebrew poet Bialik, and the Yiddish writer Sholem Aleichem. The YIVO building also became a site for partisan resistance activity, as several members of the brigade used the building to transfer weapons into the ghetto. In spite of these efforts at rescue, the Nazis destroyed a tremendous amount of material. Fishman reports that the librarian and Bundist activist Herman Kruk, who meticulously kept a diary while confined in the ghetto, lamented this loss by noting: "YIVO is dying; its mass grave is the paper mill."[50]

At the end of the war, a core group of encyclopedists was still alive and primarily living in New York, including Abramovitch, Lestschinsky, Kin, and Menes. Others who had contributed in various ways, such as Daniel Charney, Max Weinreich, Shmuel Charney, David Einhorn, Nakhmen Meisel, Iulii Brutskus, and Rachel and Mark Wischnitzer, were also safe in America. Aaron Steinberg remained in London. It was left to them to remember the dead and chart a course forward.

Recovering the Past to Build for the Future

The destruction of European Jewry was an inconceivable loss that was unprecedented in Jewish history and memory. Not only were millions exterminated in a years-long campaign of murderous violence, but the political, economic, social, and cultural structures that had sustained Jewish lives were brought to a near-total end. For the community of Eastern European Jewish émigré intellectuals and activists who had found shelter in America and spent their entire lives fighting on behalf of the right of Jews to live freely as a national group, the Holocaust left them searching for a new direction. In the immediate postwar years, the destruction seemed so complete that the very future of Jews as a people seemed in doubt. The Diasporist beliefs that had shaped their efforts and insisted that Jews could live autonomously as Jews among other nations no longer seemed possible in a post-*khurbn* world. The European Jewish worker and social democracy movements, which had long fought for the right of workers, Jewish and otherwise, to organize collectively and determine the conditions of their labor, were utterly shattered, having lost most of their leaders and rank and file. The Yiddish language and culture were dealt a severe blow. Outside of a small number of Hasidic Jewish speakers and an even smaller community of secular Jews ideologically committed to the continuation of Yiddish as a medium of day-to-day speech, it appeared that the language no longer had a population substantial enough to sustain it beyond the current generation. The fear of so many of these émigrés was that not only would Jewish life be inextricably altered, but that their life work had suddenly and brutally lost its relevance.

This despondency was expressed in several works by Jacob Lestschinsky, who had long since relinquished his Diaspora Nationalist beliefs. In a 1944 essay entitled "Vuhin geyen mir? Yidishe vanderung a mol un haynt" (Where are we going? Jewish migration past and present), Lestschinsky describes Jews as existing on the precipice of disaster, with little choice but to emigrate to Palestine or face near-total destruction through assimilation into the larger societies in which they were located.[51] In the 1948 study, *Crisis, Catastrophe and Survival: A Jewish Balance Sheet, 1914–1948*, which was written for the World Jewish Congress, he argues that the "Hitler catastrophe" "cut off sharply and irrevocably a thousand-year thread of Jewish history."[52] Furthermore, he explains, the extermination of the wellspring of Ashkenazic Jewry accelerated a process of assimilation that had begun in the late eighteenth century with civic emancipation and continued with increasing rapidity following the rise of the Soviet Union. By the time of this essay, Lestschinsky had been in the United States for a decade and was deeply pessimistic about the continuation of Jewish life in the country absent the "fortress" of Eastern European Jewry: "With the sudden destruction of the national fortress, the Jewish people has all at once lost the ground from under its feet. From the point of view of our survival reservoir, we have been reduced to the position of paupers."[53]

In his analysis, world Jewry had shifted from being predominantly European in its composition to being predominantly American. In the United States, the twin forces that had historically maintained Jews' group cohesion—internal Jewish nationhood and external hatred—were comparatively nonexistent. In the absence of these traditional barriers to assimilation, American Jews, he feared, were quick to embrace the standards and expectations of the dominant society and were uninterested in fostering the development of Jewish languages. They were thus unable to transmit a Jewish cultural legacy to future generations. Furthermore, the near-complete extermination of the Jewish working class, which had historically resisted the assimilation that was all too common among petit bourgeois Jews and which had strengthened "Jewish economic structure and [made] Jewish life more creative," diminished severely "the Jewish capacity for survival."[54] Writing in early 1948, on the eve of the establishment of the State of Israel, Lestschinsky saw that the task ahead was to preserve as much of the European Jewish tradition as could be recovered from the ruins of the *khurbn* and to direct it toward the goal of building up Jewish life in the community in Palestine. Another decade would pass before he finally took his own advice and moved, in 1959, to Tel Aviv, residing on a street named after Simon Dubnow.[55]

Amid their anguish and despair, the Eastern European Jewish intelligentsia who found themselves in the United States after the war took up four interrelated tasks that they saw as central to the reconstruction of Jewish life, several of which gave shape to the future mission of the *Algemeyne entsiklopedye*. First and most immediate was preserving the cultural legacy of European Jewry through recovering the Jewish artifacts and texts scattered across Europe. Some remained behind in cities and towns after the Jewish communities that had once possessed them had been deported or murdered. Others remained hidden, having been secreted away in the hopes that they would later be recovered. Still others had been collected by the Nazis as part of their campaign to plunder Judaica in order to study their victims and commemorate their victory over the Jewish people. These included hundreds of thousands of Jewish volumes held at the Offenbach Archival Depot outside of Frankfurt, Germany, which the Americans had established after the war to collect the several million books and archival materials that the Nazis had looted from the countries they had occupied.

Whereas most of the items in the depot were returned to their countries of origin, those from destroyed Jewish communities, families, and institutions—such as the collections of YIVO and the Strashun Library—needed to be rehoused. This sparked a great and often highly contentious competition between Jewish institutions and organizations in England, Palestine, and the United States, each of which presented itself as the successor to the great institutes of Jewish learning in Europe. As Lisa Leff and Dan Rabinowitz have shown in their separate studies, these efforts at recovery led at times to subterfuge and deception, as institutions, including and perhaps especially YIVO, struggled mightily to take possession of the seized materials so that they would not be returned to the now-Soviet-controlled lands from which they were taken or turned over to competing Jewish repositories. In many instances, the preferences of the surviving members of the Jewish communities in which the materials had been located before the war were not factored into the deliberations.[56] Although these efforts at recovery did not directly involve the work of the *Entsiklopedye*, several of its contributors and editors played key roles, most prominently Max Weinreich, who labored to establish New York as YIVO's new center, and Columbia

University historian Salo W. Baron, who would become an editor for the *Entsik-lopedye's* English-language volumes and who sought to distribute the treasures to Jewish institutions around the world. At times, the two found themselves in competition with each other over the fate of the materials.[57]

A second task of the Yiddish émigré community in the United States was to restore the frayed bonds of the transnational community of Yiddish speakers. Although millions of Yiddish speakers still remained after the war, they were severely diminished in number and were now scattered across the globe in locations that were inhospitable for the wide transmission of the language, such as in Allied-controlled displaced persons camps in central Europe, inside the Soviet Union, and in Palestine/Israel, the United States, Canada, Mexico, Argentina, South Africa, and Australia. For Yiddish activists, these communities of speakers were the surviving remnant of a shared linguistic national culture on whose behalf they had worked since they were youths. Unwilling to concede that their generation would be the last of its kind, they made maintaining and preserving this community a chief priority.

With the institutions and structures that had for so long supported secular Yiddish culture in Eastern Europe nearly completely destroyed, many surviving Yiddish intellectuals, activists, and writers sought ways to come together and unite around the cause of restoring their mother tongue. Historian Rachel Rojanski has shown that this often meant abandoning the now-unrealizable political aspects of the Diasporist and Autonomist agendas, to which so many of them had once adhered, and concentrating their efforts on fostering Yiddish cultural development.[58] This impetus was most directly articulated in the founding of the Alveltlekher Yidisher Kultur-kongres in 1948. Formed by several luminaries in the Yiddish world, including Jewish Labor Committee leader Jacob Pat, Shmuel Charney (who would serve for a time as the organization's president), and Pinkhos Schwartz (the executive secretary of YIVO and brother of the librarian and Vilna ghetto diarist Herman Kruk), the Kultur-kongres, as it was known, developed ties with Yiddish-speaking communities wherever they could be found. After merging with CYCO in 1953, it held annual conferences asserting the continued importance of the Diaspora, advocated for Yiddish in the newly formed State of Israel, and assumed responsibility for publishing the monthly journal *Tsukunft*. This imperative to "breath[e] life back into the Jewish people" also gave new meaning to the work of the encyclopedists, as they sought out ways to reorient their project to help unite Yiddish speakers around the globe.[59] They reached out to scattered Yiddish communities and eventually published a volume in the *Yidn* series that was dedicated to exploring Jewish life in the Americas.[60]

A third task was to document and memorialize the Jewish people and communities destroyed in the *khurbn*. In the years immediately after the war, the details of the Holocaust (a term which would not come into wide use until many years later) remained murky. Much of Europe was in ruins, many of the killing sites were destroyed, eyewitnesses had been murdered, survivors were suffering the trauma of their experiences, and so much evidence remained to be sifted through that relatively little was known about the Nazi killing process or the response of Jewish victims. The impetus to record the murder of European Jews was one that was widely felt even in the midst of the destruction. Dubnow's purported cry to "record it all," the countless thousands of diaries kept by prisoners in ghettos and camps and by those living under occupation or in hiding, the massive archival effort led by the historian Emanuel Ringelblum in the Warsaw ghetto (much of which was retrieved after the war), the reports smuggled out of Europe in the hope of alerting the world, the records kept and secreted away by the slave laborers in the gas chambers of Auschwitz—Jews across Europe had chronicled their experiences under the Nazis.[61]

After the war, the investigations continued as a way to establish a historical record of what had occurred, memorialize the murdered, and gather evidence of Nazi crimes. Historian Laura Jockusch has shown that immediately following the end of fighting, Jews across Europe began to document the *khurbn*:

> Immediately after their liberation from Nazi rule and with the end of combat, Jews in fourteen European countries founded historical commissions, documentation centers, and projects for the purpose of documenting and researching the recent annihilation of European Jews. These initiatives of Jewish Holocaust documentation arose as grassroots movements impelled by the survivors' own will and with no government backing. . . . Out of fear that the Nazis' efforts to destroy all evidence of their murderous crimes would condemn the Jewish cataclysm to oblivion before its full scope was even known to the world, activists in the documentation initiatives furiously collected every vestige of the past that they could get their hands on.[62]

Jockusch and the historian Mark L. Smith have demonstrated that for these investigators and scholars who worked in Europe, Palestine/Israel, and the United States, documenting the Jewish experience under Nazi rule was utterly necessary to understand the larger tragedy.[63] This meant recording survivors' experiences and taking their testimonies seriously as historical sources. In contrast to subsequent scholars who often rejected the diaries and personal writings of victims and survivors of the Holocaust as too subjective in their orientation to be of historical or legal value, these initial efforts at survivor documentation were widespread and ultimately provided the foundation for the academic discipline of Holocaust studies.

Along with gathering evidence and writing the first histories of the *khurbn*, mourning the murdered six million Jews and the destruction of the thousands of communities in which they resided became a task of chief importance. This was expressed, as Hasia R. Diner has shown, in countless ways, including new liturgies recited and services held in synagogues, the construction of makeshift memorials, commemorative concerts and theater performances, and the publication of special editions of Jewish newspapers and magazines.[64] Survivors of the Holocaust compiled memorial books, known in Yiddish as *yizker-bikher*, as a monument to destroyed Jewish communities. Hundreds of these works appeared in the first decades after the war and contain necrologies (lists of those killed), descriptions of communal life, photographs, maps, and illustrations.[65]

The *Algemeyne entsiklopedye* would take on the dual obligations of documenting and memorializing the Holocaust in its postwar volumes. Individual members among the encyclopedists likewise committed themselves to these tasks. In 1947, for example, Abramovitch, with the support of the *Forverts*, published a memorial book to Eastern European Jews. Entitled *Di farshvundene velt/The Vanished World*, this bilingual Yiddish/English work contains nearly six hundred pages of photographs, descriptions, and memories of Jewish life before the *khurbn*. In the introduction, Abramovitch describes the long history and legacy of Eastern Europe as the true center of modern Jewish life, the "cradle of all Jewish national political movements" where "the rich neo-Jewish culture in Yiddish, Hebrew, and other languages was created, with a literature and modern press that has gained for itself a world reputation." He spoke of the contribution of Eastern European Jewry to world civilization and how it continually seeded Jewish communities around the globe. Abramovitch then turned to the importance of memorializing and establishing a permanent record of the destroyed world, noting the profound difficulty of such a task:

> Yet we, both those who are tied irrevocably to the past epoch as well as those who are beginning to write this new chapter in the history of our people, are confronted with the responsibility of immortalizing for future generations our common Eastern European heritage. This cannot be accomplished merely by bowing our heads before the mass grave of our

sacred martyrs. It is necessary also to reflect on the past, to experience it emotionally, to record and interpret it, so that future generations may learn from it. Thus we shall erect a dignified monument to it and at the same time render a service to the future.[66]

Abramovitch's introduction to *Di farshvundene velt* also points to the fourth task of this community of émigré intellectuals and activists: as some of the last representatives of a destroyed civilization, they understood themselves to be responsible for bequeathing a legacy to postwar Jews—particularly those in the United States—that could form a foundation for a restored and renewed Jewish future. They shared Lestchinsky's pessimism about the ability of American Jewry to manage this burden on its own, believing that the pressures and opportunities to assimilate were so great that they themselves were required to take deliberate steps to ensure the Jewish people's survival. So much about America was impressive, including its size, economic might, democratic traditions, religious and political freedoms, openness to European peoples, and comparatively low levels of antisemitism. Yet these were the very factors that would permit American Jews to abandon the bonds that tied them to the world of their ancestors in Eastern Europe. They feared that in the hope of making Judaism compatible with American expectations, Jews would reduce their association with it to an exclusively religious expression, and in the process strip it of its rich linguistic, cultural, historical, labor, and political heritage.

These activists also believed passionately that the long history of Eastern European Jewry held elements that were vital for postwar Jewry in the United States, as it assumed its role as the preeminent Jewish community in the world. As Kalman Weiser has framed it in his discussion of YIVO's reassessment of its mission in the postwar United States, "Would American Jewry, a relatively young settlement whose emotional maturity and identity as a national collective many eastern European Jewish intellectuals on both sides of the Atlantic deemed still underdeveloped, be suited for the task that stood before it?"[67] In October 1940, Max Weinreich and Naftali Feinerman wrote Jewish Labor Committee leader Adolph Held (while trying to rescue YIVO staff from Vilna) of the need to study American Jewry according to the same scholarly methods that YIVO had applied to Eastern European Jewry: "Jewish life in America itself needs evaluation not only by speeches and newspaper articles. It is important that the roots of the facts be probed as closely as possible by social research, which, though developed in the United States more than anywhere else, has been barely applied to Jewish life in this country."[68]

In response to the impulse to "make the Eastern European Jewish past usable for the American Jewish present and future," as Markus Krah has characterized it, and to study the problems of American Jewish life, émigré intellectuals and activists sought to represent the recently destroyed world in ways that would render it familiar and accessible for American Jewish audiences.[69] This undertaking occurred in a wide range of ways, some of which began during the war itself. In 1940, for example, YIVO published A. A. Roback's *The Story of Yiddish Literature*, a comprehensive, if often uneven, survey of Yiddish writing from its origins in medieval German lands to its flourishing in the late nineteenth century as a fully modern language.[70] That same year, as Weiser explains, the annual conference of the American section of YIVO focused on expanding its role to include "a research agenda addressing the unique history and culture of American Jewry."[71] After the war, YIVO embarked upon an ambitious program to make Eastern European Jewish history and culture accessible to American Jews, the stated goal being "to transplant and foster, wheresoever Jews live, the creativity of Eastern European Jewry which revealed itself in traditional Judaism, in Yiddish and in Hebrew literature, in the struggles of the people for their cultural, political and economic emancipation, in the upbuilding of Palestine and of the settlements overseas."[72] Such efforts manifested themselves in projects such as raising a new generation of Yiddish speakers through a renewed effort at building Yiddish secular schools, conducting social scientific research into American Jewish youths, publishing research and pedagogical materials in Yiddish and English, and training a new generation of scholars.[73] In 1946, YIVO began to publish an English edition of its flagship journal, entitled *YIVO Annual of Jewish Social Science*, which featured translations of Yiddish-language materials and, eventually, original work composed in English.

Eli Lederhendler has shown that YIVO was hardly alone in this project to recover and repackage Eastern European Jewish life for American audiences, most often in the English language. The two decades after the Holocaust in particular saw the publication of dozens, if not hundreds, of popular and scholarly historical accounts, anthologies and collections of essays by leading intellectuals and political figures, translations of modern Yiddish literature and poetry, as well as several Jewish encyclopedias, dwarfing the number of such works published before the war. Taken together, they constituted "a vestige and a remembrance: at least as much an evocation of an earlier generation of Jewish immigrants in America as they were a symbolic homage to the old Europe."[74]

This fourfold set of tasks—salvaging the cultural treasures of Eastern Europe, maintaining a transnational community of Yiddish speakers, documenting and memorializing the Holocaust, and transmitting Yiddish culture to American Jewish audiences—guided the work of the *Entsiklopedye* until its final volume was published in 1966. The goal of the project as it was envisioned at the start of the 1930s, to serve as a vehicle for the modernization of Yiddish-speaking Jewry so that they could assume their place among the family of nations, was by the end of the war utterly transformed. Although the editors never abandoned their commitment to the form of the encyclopedia, their vision to impart universal knowledge gave way to the imperative to make an archive of their recently destroyed world that would be accessible to future generations.

The Jewish People: Past and Present

In 1946, in response to these new imperatives, a publishing group made up of members of the Dubnow Fund and referring to itself as Jewish Encyclopedic Handbooks Inc., released the first volume of what was initially planned to be a three-volume English-language encyclopedia based upon the *Yidn* series of the *Algemeyne entsiklopedye*. Publishing a translated edition of the *Yidn* volumes had been the vision of the encyclopedists since the mid-1930s, and it took on renewed significance during the war. Preparations for an English translation were underway at least by 1944, as correspondence from Kin and Abramovitch to contributors, reviewers, and readers makes clear.[75] Given that the volume's title page lists Ben-Adir, who died in 1942, and Tcherikower, who died in 1943, among the editors (along with Abramovitch, Brutskus, Kin, Lestschinsky, Menes, and Steinberg), it is likely that work on it began several years earlier.

The Jewish People: Past and Present (hereafter, *JPPP*) was a sustained attempt by the encyclopedists to branch out to the non-Yiddish-speaking world. Volume 1, which comprised sixteen essays by twelve scholars that covered Jewish historical and social scientific topics, contained a mix of English-language articles translated from the prior *Yidn* volumes and contributions composed especially for this work. The editorial advisory board, which had a more symbolic than actual role, included such American Jewish intellectual giants as Salo W. Baron, the theologian and rabbinical leader Mordecai M. Kaplan, the Reform Jewish leader and rabbi Solomon B. Freehof, and the scholar and rabbinical leader Jacob Rader Marcus. This merger of the surviving leaders of the "old" Jewish world with the luminaries of the "new" bestowed upon *JPPP* a robust measure of authority in the postwar era.

In a short opening preface to volume 1, the publishers spoke directly to the encyclopedia's central aim of linking the European Jewish past to the American Jewish future:

Two-thirds of European Jewry has been annihilated and the Old World's most important centers of Jewish culture and spiritual creative forces are no longer in existence. At so tragic a moment in the three-thousand-year old history of our people, it is of greater importance than ever before to acquaint the readers of the English-speaking world—the present home of the majority of the Jews—with the past and present of the Jewish people as well as with its achievements in the various fields of cultural life and with the complex problems of Jewish life in our times.

The Jewish community in America—the greatest and most influential today—is the bearer of the heaviest responsibility, of the keenest duty to save and preserve the cultural treasures of our people and to keep up our spiritual creative work.[76]

Volume 1 contains articles that cover a wide range of historical, religious, demographic, and economic aspects of Jewish life. Many are edited translations of works that appeared in the first *Yidn* volume, such as Brutskus's "The Anthropology of the Jewish People" (which, although unacknowledged, was significantly revised by Claude Lévi-Strauss), Sukenik's "History of Jewish Archaeology," Menes's "The History of the Jews in Ancient Times," and Steinberg's "The History of the Jews in the Middle Ages and Modern Times," as well as essays by Tcherikower and Lestschinsky.[77] Gershom Scholem's "Jewish Mysticism and Kabbala," which appeared in *Yidn beys*, also appears here, much to the dismay of Scholem himself, who had not given permission for his work to be translated into English and republished.[78]

The opening essay, "Race Theory in the Light of Modern Science," stands apart from the other contributions in the volume by not focusing exclusively on Jews. Written by M. F. Ashley Montagu (pen name of Israel Ehrenberg), this essay was one in a series of scholarly and popular broadsides he wrote to challenge eugenicist thinking, which had dominated anthropology since the late nineteenth century and undergirded the programs of extermination in Nazi Germany and segregation in the United States. Drawing heavily from his 1942 pathbreaking work, *Man's Most Dangerous Myth: The Fallacy of Race*, which had launched him to prominence, Montagu's article rejects the notion of race as a biological construct and argues that it can be dated back to nineteenth-century American proslavery advocates seeking to identify a scientific basis for their claims of white racial superiority.[79] These notions of race, he goes on to show, were adopted and expanded upon by European thinkers, such as Arthur de Gobineau and Houston Stewart Chamberlain, who sought to undermine the gains made in the nineteenth century toward universal human equality. Their

THE JEWISH PEOPLE

PAST AND PRESENT

VOLUME 1

JEWISH ENCYCLOPEDIC HANDBOOKS

CENTRAL YIDDISH CULTURE ORGANIZATION (CYCO)

NEW YORK

FIGURE 3.3 *The Jewish People: Past and Present*, volume 1 (1946).

writings, he asserts, "may be regarded as the spiritual progenitors of Hitler's *Mein Kampf*, a work in which the concept of 'race' reaches its final theoretic development, in preparation of that dreadful consummation of its principles which has led to the deliberate murder of more than 5,000,000 Jews, millions of Poles, and millions of others throughout the continent of Europe."[80] In place of notions of "race," Montagu advances the idea of "ethnic groups," a concept that resists claims of purity and exclusivity and instead acknowledges the intermixing between groups that has always occurred and allows for shared attributes to be studied. At the end of the brief essay, he argues strongly against any notions of a "Jewish race" and, given the broad diversity of Jews in the world, also resists the idea that Jews make up a single ethnic group. If Jews share attributes with one another, he argues, "this quality is not due to any inherited characters of the persons in question, but rather to certain cultural acquired habits of expression, facial, vocal, muscular, and mental."[81]

As the opening essay in volume 1 of *JPPP*, Montagu's study sets the tone for the encyclopedia as a compendium rooted in the most current scholarly thinking and profoundly shaped by the recent war and *khurbn*. Published for an English-language audience and therefore accessible to Jewish and non-Jewish readers alike, volume 1 is a bold assertion of Jews' long-standing contribution to the larger world and a repudiation of the racist and antisemitic ideologies that had sought to constrain them. By tackling the thorny subject of race at the outset, the work draws connections between the experiences of African Americans and Jews as victims of similar ideologies of white supremacy. It foreshadows much later studies that examine the strong ties between American and German policies of racial separation and the high degree of interwar cooperation between eugenicists and lawmakers in both countries.[82]

Several reviews of volume 1 appeared. Writing for the *New York Times*, Rabbi Louis L. Mann was wholly favorable. "These volumes, judging by the first, should find their place not only on the library shelves but also in homes," Mann's review declared, and recommended that Jewish and Christian authors alike keep them nearby so as to correct widespread disinformation on topics related to Jews.[83] The Jewish popular press was likewise generally favorable, with strong reviews appearing in the *National Jewish Monthly* and *Jewish Frontier*.[84] Many reviews were published in academic publications, an indication that *JPPP*, although clearly aimed toward a popular readership, was taken seriously as a scholarly work. These reviews are decidedly more mixed than Mann's, with some praising the work as a strong beginning for the new series while others attacked it for advancing outmoded ideas. A review in the *Journal of Biblical Literature* by Theophile Meek, a scholar of Mesopotamian literature

and the Old Testament at the University of Toronto, praised the work for its
objectivity and overall contribution but felt that the form of the encyclopedia,
as a compendium of introductory essays, generally left too much unad-
dressed.[85] In a review in the *Quarterly Review of Biology*, the geneticist Bentley
Glass praised the volume, in particular Montagu's and Brutskus's contributions, for challenging the still widely accepted notion that Jews were a racial
group and for offering welcome insights into Jewish history and religion.[86]

Other reviews, written by Jewish scholars and intellectuals of a younger
generation—precisely those whom the *JPPP* was intended to influence—were
more skeptical of its overall contribution and skeptical of its intention to guide
the Jewish future in America. Writing in the *Jewish Quarterly Review*, Ellis
Rivkin, then in his early thirties and on the cusp of beginning what would become an illustrious career as a historian at the Hebrew Union College in Cincinnati, characterized the contributions by Menes and Steinberg, which were
the sole focus of his review, as failures. Each, he argued, held "a preconceived
notion as to the meaning of Jewish history" while lacking "a sound methodological approach."[87] Further, Rivkin criticized what he saw as the authors'
overt Jewish nationalism and the whole project's driving concern to instill that
nationalist ethos in American Jewry: "To a very great extent this cavalier disregard of verifiable facts stems from the bias and subjectivity of the authors.
Committed to a Jewish nationalist program in the present, Menes and Steinberg cannot avoid finding support for it in the past. They impose their subjective interpretation on the past and measure it by their own standards. Nation,
national autonomy and state are used with an almost talismanic reverence. All
positive movements in Judaism were national and, of course, democratic. . . .
National chauvinism and historic reality are indeed poor bedfellows!"[88]

Milton Himmelfarb, who would later become a major figure in American
letters and a leading voice of neoconservatism, wrote a lengthy, at times di-
gressive review in the journal *Commentary* in which he credited *JPPP* with
being a major "contribution of a school of Jewish learning relatively new to
these shores" and "an event of some magnitude in one area of the social sciences."[89] He continued, "This is doubly true if those prophets are right who
see the tradition that produced it as destined to occupy the leading role in
Jewish scholarship in America in the decades ahead, now that it has begun to
strike root here." Eastern European Jewish scholarship, he noted, stood at
odds with the German Jewish scholarly approach known as *Wissenschaft des
Judentums* (Science of Judaism), which had begun in the early nineteenth
century and had concerned itself chiefly with the critical study of Jewish (especially rabbinic) literature and culture. *Wissenschaft des Judentums* had also

dominated Jewish scholarship in America for the previous century. Himmelfarb understood clearly that the impetus behind *JPPP*, YIVO, and the larger social-science-inflected approach to scholarship from which it stemmed was to shape the future of American Jewry: "Those who believe that the future of institutional Jewish scholarship in this country lies with the tradition represented by *The Jewish People* argue that it is a tradition that seems to share the interests, tastes, and insights of the mid-20th century, and is therefore readily adaptable to American needs."

Himmelfarb was more hopeful in his assessment of volume 1 than Rivkin was, and remained optimistic that subsequent volumes would make a strong contribution to American Jewry. He held the editing in great disdain, however, describing it as sloppy and imbalanced, and an injustice to the authors. He praised the contributions by Scholem, Menes, and Steinberg as "models of sensitive and imaginative scholarship," but attacked others, such as Lestschinsky's, on the basis of methodological flaws and "not reaching the high level of the others."[90] In spite of the acclaim that he occasionally bestows on the volume, he is severe in his skepticism over the extent to which the culture from which it stemmed could inform postwar life in America: "Now they must know that Yiddish, the language of East European Jewry, may soon survive only as an ancient tongue like Aramaic."[91]

Volume 2 of *JPPP* differs significantly from its predecessor. Although the board of editors and the editorial advisory board remained largely the same (each was expanded by one member: Mark Wischnitzer joined the first and Abram L. Sachar, head of the recently founded Brandeis University, the second), the orientation of volume 2 is much more focused on the Jewish present than the past. Moreover, the majority of contributions are not translations of essays from the *Yidn* volumes by Eastern European Jewish scholars but are original commissioned pieces. Roughly the same length as volume 1, at about 430 pages, volume 2 contains more than twice as many individual contributions and covers a broader range of topics, although little ties the various sections together. The volume is abundantly illustrated with nearly one hundred photographs and reproductions.

This uneven volume begins with articles on Jewish demographics in Europe, the United States, Canada, and Palestine and then moves on to a series of essays on "Jewish colonization" that discuss the Jewish agricultural settlements in Russia, the Americas, and Palestine that were established in the last decades of the nineteenth century. It continues with nine articles on aspects of modern Jewish education, several of which first appeared in *Yidn giml*. One of these essays, "Yiddish Secular Schools in the United States," was penned by

the education leader Salman Yefroikin, brother of Yisroel Yefroikin, who together with Tcherikower and Kalmanovitch had edited *Afn sheydveg* before
the war. Some of the volume's entries cover secular and religious school movements, such as those in Hebrew and Yiddish, while others examine Jewish
schools in the United States, Latin America, the British Commonwealth, and
Palestine. Curiously, several introductory articles on Judaism are located in
the middle of the work rather than at the beginning or in the first volume in
the series. These pieces cover broad topics such as Jewish law, Jewish morals,
and "Jewish ways of life." The final essays are derived mainly from *Yidn giml*
and include Ben-Adir's thorough "Modern Social and National Currents
among Jews" and articles on the Jewish socialist movements in Russia and
Poland by Menes and Abramovitch. The volume ends with an essay by J. C.
Rich on the Jewish labor movement in the United States.

Appearing in late 1948, volume 2 also includes a chronology of events and a
series of documents related to the Zionist movement and the founding of the
State of Israel, which occurred on May 14 of that year. However, other than a
half sentence referencing "an up-to-date chronological table of the Zionist
movement," there is little recognition in the preface of this monumentally historic occurrence. Although it is likely that the founding of the state occurred
just as this volume was going to press, Ben-Adir's essay contains a photograph
of Chaim Weizmann, identifying him as the first president of Israel, and one of
David Ben-Gurion as "prime minister of the provisional government of Israel,"
indicating that there was time to make at least some last-minute changes.
While the timeline is comprehensive, the documents included in this section
are disjointed and likely reflect the haste with which they were assembled. It
begins with the 1882 "Manifesto of the BILU, the Pioneers of Modern Zionism" and then leaps three and a half decades to a reprint of the 1917 Balfour
Declaration, in which the British government stated its support for the establishment of a national home for the Jewish people in Palestine. It next includes
the Zionist manifesto released in response to the Balfour Declaration; the 1922
League of Nations Mandate for Palestine, which gave Britain control over the
territory; the 1921 resolution of the United States Congress in support of a Jewish national home; the 1937 Peel Commission Report, which suggested partition as a solution to the Arab-Jewish conflict; and the 1942 Biltmore Platform,
in which several major American Jewish organizations and leaders aligned
themselves with the goal of forming a Jewish "commonwealth" in Palestine.
The timeline concludes with the 1947 resolution for Palestine adopted by the
General Assembly of the United Nations and the May 1948 proclamation of the
State of Israel (in Hebrew and English). Missing from these sources are many

key documents of the Zionist movement, especially those that demonstrate the broad ideological diversity of its early decades. There are no documents, for example, from the Zionist Congresses, which helped to build the infrastructure of the Zionist movement, nor are there any writings by Theodor Herzl. Likewise absent are documents from the 1906 meeting of Russian Zionists in which the delegates declared that Zionists should shift their efforts toward *Gegenwartsarbeit* (German, "work in the present day") in order to ease the suffering of Diaspora Jewry, documents related to Ber Borochov's efforts to lay the foundation of a Labor Zionist movement, and documents that represent any non-Territorialist manifestations of Zionism (such as the writings of Ahad Ha'am). Nor is there any material representing critics of Zionism, either from Jewish groups or Palestinian Arab organizations.

Reviewers of volume 2 generally commended the work as a significant contribution to American Jewish letters. Louis L. Mann, who had praised volume 1 in the *New York Times*, remained supportive, declaring that it would be "welcomed not only by Jewish people but also by seekers of culture belonging to other faiths, and by scholars generally," but criticized the work for being "uneven" in terms of the level of scholarship.[92] Religious scholar Carl E. Purinton referred to it as a "valuable reference work" that will be of "interest chiefly for members of the Jewish community or other students of Jewish community life," and in fact applauded the selection of documents on Zionism as "welcome."[93] The Jewish educator Mark M. Krug generally hailed the essays on Jewish education as a "signal service" and "informative and authoritatively written," but expressed disappointment at the seeming commitment of the authors to limit themselves "to an objective recital of facts" in order "to steer clear of controversial issues."[94]

Volume 3, originally intended as the last of the series, appeared in 1952. Shmuel Charney is listed as among the editors, while the names of Ben-Adir, Tcherikower, Brutskus (who died in 1951), and Lestschinsky are absent. "Shlomoh F. Gilinsky," whose first name was more commonly spelled "Shloyme," is listed as executive director. Before the war, Gilinsky was the director of the Medem Sanatorium, a renowned institution with strong Bundist ties in Międzeszyn, Poland, near Warsaw, which treated thousands of children and young adults with, or at risk for, tuberculosis. He was among those Jewish political activists and communal leaders who in 1940, with the help of the Jewish Labor Committee, had fled Vilna for the United States by way of Japan. By the summer of 1946, he was working on the encyclopedia, gradually taking over many administrative duties from Avrom Kin. In the preface, the editors explained that volume 3 was the culmination of a project that began more than six years prior (in truth, it was nearly a decade) and whose reception had surpassed all expectations. They proudly announced their intention to publish a second set of three English-language volumes "which will make a systematic presentation of the history of Jewish communities in the various continents and countries of the world," stating that the preparation for the first of these was already underway.

Volume 3, which is focused on Jewish literature with additional articles on art and music, is a much more cohesive compendium than its predecessors. Seven of its thirteen articles are translations (often revised and expanded) from the *Yidn* volumes. Eleven are on the theme of Jewish literature and move chronologically from biblical times to the present, covering literature written in Hebrew, Aramaic, and Yiddish, as well as Jewish literature written in non-Jewish languages, such as English, German, and Russian. The essays include Menes's survey "Jewish Literature in Biblical Times" and Shmuel Charney's sweeping survey "Yiddish Literature in the Past Two Hundred Years," as well as articles by Boaz Cohen and Joseph Heller. Simon Dubnow's daughter, the poet and activist Sophie Dubnov-Ehrlich, who had arrived in the United States in 1942, contributed an essay on Jewish literature in Russian. Rachel Wischnitzer's "Jewish Art" is revised from *Yidn beys* in a much-expanded form. Previously, the essay ended with the Baroque period and confined itself primarily to Jewish art in the Land of Israel in the ancient period and to art in the European Middle Ages. In volume 3 of *JPPP*, more than half of the essay surveys Jewish art and architecture (Wischnitzer's specialization) in the modern period in Europe, the United States, and Israel. The article contains black-and-white and color plates of works by well-known Jewish artists, such as Marc Chagall and Amedeo Modigliani, and ones now largely forgotten, such as Isaac Lichtenstein and Ilya Schor. The final article, on Jewish music, is by the composer Abraham Wolf Binder and surveys music from the biblical period, the period of European Jewish history, and the United States and Israel. The book ends with a long-awaited—by several reviewers, at least—index to the three volumes. The price of the volume was $10 for a regular edition and $15 for the "De-luxe" edition with gold-colored edging.

Reviews of volume 3 were brief but generally enthusiastic. An unsigned review in the *Journal of Bible and Religion* declared that "the publishers are to be congratulated upon the success of this scholarly undertaking" and expressed its enthusiasm for the forthcoming series.[95] In the *Journal of Biblical Literature*, the Bible scholar and translator Harry M. Orlinsky was highly complimentary of the volume and stated that the entire series "should be in every school and public library."[96]

True to form, the editors revised their plans for a second three-volume set. In 1955, a fourth and final volume in the *JPPP* series appeared as part of widespread commemorations of the 1954 tercentenary of Jewish life in America. That year, Jewish communities across the United States celebrated the occasion, proud that what began as a small settlement made up of a handful of Jewish refugees fleeing from the Inquisition in Portuguese-held Brazil grew into the largest Jewish community in the world, in a country that permitted Jews an unprecedented amount of religious freedom and acceptance. The highlight of that year's activities was a National Tercentenary Dinner held in New York City with President Dwight D. Eisenhower serving as a guest of honor.[97] Volume 4 of *JPPP* reflected this sense of triumph and accomplishment. In the preface, the editors announced that the publication of the volume marked the "great interest exhibited by a considerable sector of American Jewry in the 300th anniversary of Jewish life in the United States."[98] In particular, the volume would consider the "unique role of the Jewish community in the economic and social life of the country" and its impact on the "American way of life."

By 1955, the number of editors had shrunk considerably, and the remaining ones—Abramovitch, Kin, Lestschinsky, Menes, Shmuel Charney, and Wischnitzer—were all, with the exception of Menes, in their mid- to late seventies. Gilinsky is still listed as executive director. Milton Himmelfarb, the *Commentary* editor who had written a cautiously optimistic review of volume 1, is listed as holding the new position of literary editor, along with Israel Knox, a professor of philosophy at New York University and a former director of the English-speaking division of the Arbeter-ring.

Volume 4 comprises eleven essays, beginning with a survey of American Jewish history by Anita Libman Lebeson, author of the recently published *Pilgrim People*, a survey of Jewish life in America.[99] Like Lebeson's book, the essay locates Jews within American history, with particular attention to the various contributions, great and small, of Jews at key moments in the country's development. The essay begins, in a section entitled "A Dream Is Born," by noting the contribution of Jewish crewmen to Christopher Columbus's voyage of 1492. In line with the triumphalist conceptions of the country that were in wide currency in the decade after World War II, Lebeson writes of an America that was largely empty of civilization and thus a blank slate upon which to build a new society. The absence of a legacy of antisemitism, Lebeson argues, made it possible for Jews to come to the "new world" as "pilgrims" or "pioneers" in their own right, and find religious freedom and tolerance. In America, Jews were able—in spite of occasional barriers erected by their enemies—to overcome hardships, establish congregations, participate in commerce and westward expansion, and help shape and realize the benefits of the American dream. The history of American Jews, as Lebeson endeavors to demonstrate, is intimately intertwined with the larger history of American progress and expansion and America's position as a beacon of democracy, liberty, and freedom.

Lebeson declares, more aspirationally than was the case, that the "American Jew was integrated." The essay prominently displays reproductions of portraits of major American Jewish leaders such as Gershom Mendes Seixas, the cantor at New York City's Congregation Shearith Israel in the eighteenth century, and the nineteenth-century educator and philanthropist Rebecca Gratz, as well as images of "founding fathers" George Washington and Thomas Jefferson, the signing of the Declaration of Independence, and the Liberty Bell. President Washington's letter to the Hebrew Congregation in Newport, Rhode Island, in which he famously proclaimed the centrality of religious tolerance in the new American government, "which gives to bigotry no sanction, to persecution no assistance," is reproduced over two pages. By contrast, Lebeson describes Europe as a site of ever-present danger for Jews, where there was "no end to Jewish martyrdom and no limit to their heroism," and where Jews were "hunted and pursued." Lebeson's essay glosses over many periods of American history—the section on American Jews and slavery, for example, hardly addresses the issue at all. The essay ends with the Civil War, with a coda on the late-nineteenth-century Hebrew-language poet and educator Emma Lazarus, whose words adorn the pedestal of the Statue of Liberty. Without explanation, Lebeson stops immediately before the last decades of the nineteenth century, when waves of migration brought more than two million Jews to the United States and new questions arose concerning their level of integration.

The remaining essays in the volume focus more heavily on the twentieth century, although there are scant direct references to the Holocaust. Setting aside his general pessimism regarding Jewish life in the Diaspora, Jacob Lestschinsky contributed a lengthy study, "Economic and Social Development of American Jewry," which portrays Jews in the United States as being socially integrated and far more urbanized than any Jewish community previously, and generally wealthier than Americans as a whole. It is clear from the essay that in spite of his disillusionment with the potential for a flourishing Jewish life outside of Israel, he is impressed by the unparalleled number and diversity of Jews within the United States. He writes: "Before our eyes there is taking place a gigantic amalgamation of over five million Jews in a country of a size and strength unexampled in Jewish history. In the United States there have met Jews from all parts of the world: from some thirty European countries and about half a score Oriental lands."[100] This amalgamation, he argues, has acted according to "the principle of majority rule," in which more-populous Jewish groups have integrated smaller ones (for example, German Jews absorbing Northern and Western European Jews in the mid-nineteenth century, and Eastern European Jews absorbing German Jews in the beginning of the twentieth). The long-term prospects of American Jewry remained in doubt, however, as the twin threats of low birthrates (two children or fewer per family) and intermarriage between Jews and non-Jews threatened to slow its growth. Other essays in the volume touch on a range of subjects. The Conservative rabbi and theologian Jacob Agus wrote about denominationalism in Jewish religious life, the historian Philip Friedman wrote about Jewish political and social movements, the historian Joshua Trachtenberg discussed American Jewish scholarship, Mark Wischnitzer contributed an essay entitled "The Impact of American Jewry on Jewish Life Abroad," and Shmuel Charney contributed "Yiddish Culture in the United States."

Considering the lofty aspirations of the *JPPP* volumes, which included above all bequeathing a legacy of the prewar Eastern European Jewish experience to postwar American Jewry, it is challenging to assess the extent to which they achieved their goals. The editors, almost all of whom were autodidacts with little formal training in their fields of expertise, came of age in a world in which European Jewry was undergoing a profound transformation. That world, which had seemed to be on the cusp of revolutionary change, was one of crumbling empires, working-class insurrections, fatally explosive antisemitism, and deep national pride. The editors' visions for the future assumed that Jewish communities would generally live lives that were distinct—socially, religiously, linguistically, and in some cases, even geographically—from non-Jews. By contrast, American Jews in the immediate postwar era were highly educated and professionalized, swiftly moving out of the working classes, suburbanizing, and proclaiming their affinity with American values in large part by downplaying their distinctiveness while stressing their religious compatibility with Christians.

Nevertheless, there are some means by which the volumes' success can be measured. Approximately twenty thousand sets and at least three thousand individual copies were eventually sold.[101] This is not surprising, given that the postwar English-reading Jewish community in the United States was far more economically well off than prewar Yiddish readers. More than five hundred libraries in the United States continue to hold volumes of *JPPP* in their collections. Hundreds of previously owned volumes are available for resale through book dealers. A database search of academic journals reveals more than two hundred references to the four volumes of *JPPP*: some of the references are to reviews, but the majority are to articles that cite scholarly essays in the encyclopedia.[102]

Along with the Yiddish volumes, publishing *JPPP* resulted in formidable expenditures. Particularly burdensome were the up-front costs, including payroll for an expanded staff, payments to authors, fees for permissions for photographs and reproductions, production and printing costs, advertising expenses, and office space rent. The cost of the paper alone for just one of the volumes was $7,000. Publishing volume 4 of *JPPP* and *Yidn hey*, which appeared in 1957, together cost a reported $80,000.[103] Although the archival records remain spotty, sources indicate that the English and Yiddish ventures raised funds not only from subscribers but also through often hefty bank loans, donations and loans from philanthropists (in particular the real estate developer Mendel Racolin and, following his death in 1950, his son, the lawyer and theater producer Alexander Racolin), and grants from Jewish agencies.[104] In addition, several "friends of the Jewish Encyclopedia" committees were formed, sometimes in conjunction with YIVO, to raise funds and promote the project, often in Jewish communities far from New York City, such as in Winnipeg, Montevideo, and Cape Town.[105] Among the early "honorary sponsors" of the project was Albert Einstein. However, as with the prewar volumes of the *Algemeyne entsiklopedye*, the economic uncertainty was a constant source of anxiety and led to delayed and, at times, even unrealized plans.

JPPP was one of the most sustained efforts by the surviving remnant of Eastern European Jewish scholars in America to shape the Jewish future through the transmission of the complicated, multifarious, and culturally rich Jewish world that had been so recently destroyed. Having played major roles in forging the political, intellectual, and cultural world of Eastern European Jewry for the first half of the twentieth century, the editors launched *JPPP* as a means to translate their work, literally and figuratively, for English-reading audiences, Jewish and otherwise, who were contending with vastly different questions and challenges from the ones that the editors had confronted in their lifetimes. Unsurprisingly, the generation to whom they bequeathed their legacy had other ideas about this "handoff" from one Jewish center to another, following Dubnow's framework for Jewish history. American Jews after the war were interested less in inheriting a legacy than in what Lederhendler refers to as a "culture of retrieval," a mining of the past to fashion new identities as American Jews. They could draw from the Eastern European Jewish legacy as it suited them, but they did not necessarily feel bound to it.[106]

A Great and Tragic *Mekhitse*:
The Yiddish *Entsiklopedye* after the Holocaust

The publication of *JPPP* did not mean an end to the Yiddish volumes of the *Entsiklopedye*. While the English-language volumes were being prepared, plans were also underway to continue the *Yidn* series, even as its primary audience of Eastern European Jewish readers had been nearly entirely exterminated and the number of remaining Yiddish speakers continued to diminish. They could still be found around the globe, living primarily in communities that had been established prior to World War II during the period of mass emigration from Eastern Europe, many of which subsequently received tens or even hundreds of thousands of refugees from Nazism or survivors of the Holocaust. After the war, these communities did not face the same antisemitic, structural, or nationalist barriers that had prevented or slowed their linguistic assimilation, and fewer Yiddish speakers were passing the language down to their children. The number of Yiddish speakers in cities such as Buenos Aires, Moscow, Montreal, Paris, Cape Town, Tel Aviv, Paris, and New York, therefore, steadily declined as speakers adopted the dominant language of the country in which they resided.

To counter this assimilationist trend, many remaining Yiddish writers and activists threw themselves into the task of ensuring the postwar continuity of the language and culture that had sustained generations of Eastern European Jews. Jan Schwarz has demonstrated that in contrast to popular contemporary images of Yiddish as having been utterly destroyed during the Holocaust and consigned to "crumbling old books that nobody outside the Yiddish world was able to read," for the quarter century after the end of World War II, "the Yiddish cultural world was in constant, dynamic flux, maintaining a staggering level of activity in the form of publications, cultural performances, collections of archival and historical materials, and the launching of young literary talents."[107] This drive to preserve, protect, and even expand a transnational Yiddish culture after the war resulted in a burst of creative productivity. Gennady Estraikh has noted that the twelve daily Jewish newspapers that were published outside of the State of Israel a decade after the end of the war were all in Yiddish, while many attempts to publish Jewish dailies in non-Jewish languages failed.[108] In Buenos Aires, the book series *Dos poylishe yidntum* (Polish Jewry) published more than 175 volumes from 1946 to 1966. In Israel in 1949, the poet and former prisoner of the Vilna ghetto and partisan fighter Avrom Sutzkever founded the literary quarterly *Di goldene keyt* (The golden chain), which helped spark and sustain interest in Yiddish in a country that was often less than accepting of the language. The journal lasted until 1995. In Warsaw, the publishing house Yidishbukh (Yiddish Book) published more than three hundred works in the 1950s and 60s. In Montreal, the Yidishe Folks-biblyotek (Jewish People's Library) and Komitet far Yidish (Committee for Yiddish) promoted Yiddish-language activity to a community of tens of thousands of speakers, many of whom were Holocaust survivors. In Paris, Yiddish speakers organized commemorations of Jews murdered in the Holocaust, drawing thousands of participants. In Melbourne, members of the Jewish Labor Bund continued to support Yiddish cultural projects, and Yiddish theater, radio programming, and publications lasted for decades. In New York City, a broad array of new initiatives appeared after the war, not only the renewed activities of YIVO, CYCO, and the Arbeter-ring, but also the founding of the Kultur-kongres and its massive *Leksikon fun der nayer yidisher literatur* (Lexicon of new Yiddish literature), which ultimately resulted in eight volumes and remains to this day a key reference work of modern Yiddish culture. The commitment to Yiddish was present in the staging of Yiddish poetry readings at New York's 92nd Street Y and in the burst of literary activity by writers and poets such as Jacob Glatstein, Kadya Molodovsky, Chaim Grade, and Isaac Bashevis Singer.

In 1950, eight years after the publication of *Yidn giml*, the fourth volume of the *Yidn* series appeared in print following a strenuous effort to raise the necessary funds and locate writers to contribute.[109] The financial situation was in fact so dire that Abramovitch explained to Steinberg that if *Yidn daled* did not appear by January of that year, "we will be ruined and lost."[110] Although it was originally slated to have been on the "organization of internal Jewish life and of Jewish folk culture," the editors announced that *Yidn daled* would be the first of a new three-volume series.[111] The initial three *Yidn* volumes, they wrote, existed on the one side of a vast divide that signified the end of an era:

> The first series was conceived and carried out in the years 1938–1942, which were a great and tragic *mekhitse* [the partition separating women from men in traditionally orthodox synagogues] between the epochs of emancipation and *khurbn* תש״א–תש״ה [Hebrew calendar 5701–5705].
>
> After the second world war and the catastrophe of European Jewry, there began a new period in Jewish history. The European period—that epoch of the political and intellectual leadership of Eastern European Jewry in the Jewish world—has ended together with the near total *khurbn* of the great Jewish communities in the old world.[112]

Although the editors overstated the extent to which Jewish life in Europe had come to an end, in deciding to continue their project, they provided one of the very few links between prewar Europe and postwar America.[113] They viewed their encyclopedia as a means by which to aid the "new" Jewish communities in the United States and Israel as they assumed their positions of leadership in the Jewish world:

> Not for the first time in the history of the Jewish people was decline and khurbn in one land accompanied by the growth and ascent in other centers. "Accompanied" does not mean compensated or equalized: the six million murdered Jewish lives cannot be returned. The sudden disappearance of the Eastern European centers in the course of a long historical period will be felt in the Jewish world.
>
> But the emerging communities in the new world and the young government in the birthplace of the Jewish people are an omen of the ever-lasting living strength of our "eternal people" that has already experienced so many catastrophes and khurbones.

The second volume of this new series, Yidn hey, they announced, would cover the history of Jewish communities in the rest of the world, including the Americas, Africa, Australia, and Israel. The third, Yidn vov, would describe the extermination of European Jewry in the years 1939–1945.

Yidn daled may best be described as a type of scholarly yizker bukh for European Jewry, providing readers with a comprehensive overview of two thousand years of European Jewish history, country by country, with a particular focus on the period immediately prior to World War II. As the first Yiddish-language volume of the encyclopedia that was compiled and edited fully in the postwar United States, the work contains richly illustrated and documented essays by many of the surviving original editors and contributors to the project, including Lestschinsky, Abramovitch, Menes, and Shatzky, each of whom wrote sweeping essays charting vast swaths of history and territory.[114] Lestschinsky's "Economic Rise and Fall of European Jewry," for example, comprises a broad analysis of the economic conditions of Jews across Europe, and is not limited to a single country or region. The essay contends with the changing economic roles of Jews across Europe, examining Jews' economic shift to early capitalism, the development of a Jewish bourgeoisie and petite bourgeoisie, the development of Jewish laboring classes and the proletariat, and so on, noting how these developments differed by region. In the final section of the essay "The Crisis of European Jewry," Lestschinsky discusses how World War I and the geopolitical changes that occurred in its wake led to a severe economic decline for European Jews, primarily in the East, where many faced Sovietization and, in Poland, an increasingly hostile climate. Abramovitch's survey of the history of Jews in Poland, Lithuania, and Russia begins with the earliest Jewish settlements in Eastern Europe, in the fourteenth and fifteenth centuries, and charts their vast growth and rocky development over the subsequent centuries as Eastern Europe's Jews came to occupy, in the Dubnowian sense, the preeminent position in the Jewish world. Shatzky's "Jewish Politics in Poland between the Two World Wars" discusses how interwar Jewish politics were inflected by tensions that emerged in the newly independent Poland between secular and religious Jews, Marxist and liberal Jews, and Diasporists and Zionists. Menes contributed the longest and most sweeping piece in the volume, "The Eastern European Age in Jewish History." At more than one hundred and fifty columns, the entry examines the broad history of Jewish religious and social life since the earliest Jewish settlements in the late thirteenth century. The remaining essays in the volume concern various European countries. The entry on the history of Jews in Luxembourg is, appropriately, the shortest essay, running just over four columns in length.

The work also contains essays by several surviving luminaries of the European Jewish world, many of whom had experienced Nazi persecution. These include an essay on the Jews of Yugoslavia by Isaac A. Alcalay, who had been the first Jew to serve as a senator in the Yugoslavian parliament and who became chief rabbi of the Central Sephardic Jewish Community of America shortly after coming to New York in 1942. Max Wiener, a leading figure of Germany's Reform Jewish community who left Germany for the United States in 1939 (and who passed away as the volume was going to press), contributed two articles, "Jews in Germany and Austria" and "Jews in Scandinavian Countries." Michael Molho, who contributed an essay on the Jews of Greece, was a descendant of distinguished rabbis in the Greek port city of Salonica, where he had been a business and Jewish community leader, as well as an editor for a Ladino-language press and a scholar. He escaped Greece while it was under German occupation and managed to stay alive with help from the Greek resistance. After the war he returned to Salonica and served as the chief rabbi to the Jewish community there for several years before resettling in Buenos Aires.[115] Adolf Kobler, who wrote on the Jews of Holland, was a rabbi and historian who had been a leader of Cologne's Jewish community before finding refuge in New York in 1939. With *Yidn daled*, these contributors had the opportunity to memorialize the world they once knew.

In a 1951 review of *Yidn daled*, Philip Friedman was effusive that the encyclopedia had been sustained in spite of the assault on European Jewry.[116] A trained historian, Friedman was himself a Holocaust survivor, and his daughter and wife did not survive. He spent the war years hidden in Lwów

FIGURE 3.4 Philip Friedman (courtesy of YIVO).

(then in Poland, now Lviv, Ukraine), and after its liberation in the fall of 1944, he immediately went to work with a small group of colleagues, known as the Central Jewish Historical Commission, to collect documents and testimonies from the Holocaust. He then spent two years in Germany helping to prepare for and testify in the Nuremberg trials. In 1948, he and his new wife, the scholar Ada June Eber-Friedman, arrived in the United States with the assistance of Salo W. Baron. Philip Friedman would go on to become a research associate and archivist at YIVO and to teach and write extensively about the *khurbn*. In 1960, he coauthored a bibliography of all known scholarship on the subject, published by YIVO.[117]

Published in *Tsukunft*, Friedman's review spoke not only of the many merits of *Yidn daled*—which for him included the contributions of Menes, Wiener, and Shatzky—but also of the historical significance of the *Entsiklopedye's* very existence. He was less impressed by Lestschinsky's essay, in which he found many errors, and Abramovitch's, which he found unsophisticated. In particular, he praised the *Yidn* volumes for having continued in spite of the *khurbn* and claimed that *Yidn giml*, published in 1942, would serve as a "beam of light" to "a future historian of our age in their dark, desperate, and lost search," a testament to the resolve of Yiddish scholars and their refusal to succumb to despair.[118] He also spoke positively of the changing mission of the *Entsiklopedye* as it moved away from its original goal of providing universal knowledge to Yiddish readers and toward a focus on the history, contributions, and fate of world Jewry.

Turmoil and Transitions:
The Yiddish Encyclopedia in the 1950s

There are few financial records of the *Entsiklopedye* in the archives. However, several of those that do exist cover the period from the early 1940s through the early 1950s, and they provide insights into the financial health of the venture and highlight the extent to which it struggled. They also provide details of the sales of the Yiddish and English volumes. The balance sheet "Income and Expenditure Totals from November 1943 to December 1952" indicates that Jewish Encyclopedic Handbooks Inc. took in $101,779.25 in contributions.[119] Sales of the Yiddish volumes amounted to $324.897.31 and sales of the English totaled $170,574.12. Subtracting losses "on Exchange" (the exact meaning is unclear but it is likely related to losses that were a result of currency exchanges) and "amounts due to us," the "Income in Cash" came to $555,011.50. As impressive as this number may appear, the fact that it covers a period of more than a decade indicates that the sales and contributions were quite modest. Expenses from this period included the 1948 reprinting of 50,500 copies of the eight Yiddish volumes (volumes 1–5 of the *normale* series and *Yidn alef, beys*, and *giml*). Making matters even more difficult, the expenditures, which included "Editorial Salaries & Expenses & Authors' Fees," "Physical Production" of the volumes, "Commission & Tour Expenses," "Administrative Salaries," and "Packing & Shipping, Publicity and Business & Office Expenses" came to $600,131.50, for a loss of $45,120. The volumes sold in this period amounted to 52,000 in Yiddish and 20,000 in English "in round figures."

Other documents in this period relate that Jewish Encyclopedic Handbooks Inc. survived on a combination of loans from banks (including one for $25,000 from the Public National Bank and Trust Company of New York) and individual backers, donations from its worldwide network of supporters, and most of all, from subscriptions and sales of individual volumes or sets.[120] A list of subscribers from June 1951 indicates that volumes were sold in 31 countries and in 45 of the 48 states in the United States, as well as in Washington, DC, and Honolulu. Hundreds of sets were also sold to universities, public libraries, synagogues, Jewish community centers, and bureaus of Jewish education across the country.[121]

Yidn hey did not appear in print until 1957. By the time it was published, many of the original members of the Dubnow Fund, then in their mid- to late seventies, had stepped down from the project or otherwise scaled back their engagement, and several others had passed away. For several years, Avrom Menes only occasionally attended meetings, although he still wrote the introductory essay for *Yidn vov* (1964). Lestschinsky had retired to Miami Beach, Florida, although he continued writing and in fact contributed several more pieces to the *Entsiklopedye* and continued to be listed as an editor. Aaron Steinberg, who in 1948 took on the role of head of the Cultural Department of the World Jewish Congress, still maintained ties, although his contributions as editor lessened. In October 1955, Mark Wischnitzer, who, after arriving in New York, had worked closely with YIVO and Jewish social welfare organizations and taught history at Yeshiva University, died of a heart attack while in Tel Aviv. Shmuel Charney died suddenly, on December 24, 1955, on his way home from a YIVO Executive Committee meeting. He had participated frequently in editorial and administrative meetings of the *Entsiklopedye* up to the month in which he passed away. Following his death, thousands of notices were published in his honor, and YIVO published a *Festschrift* in his honor in 1958.[122]

In a move that is dramatic for the history of the *Entsiklopedye* and yet not much remarked upon at the time, Raphael Abramovitch formally ended his affiliation with the project in early 1955. Although he was listed as one of the editors of volume 4 of *JPPP*, which appeared that same year, there are no other references to him in any of the subsequently published volumes. The surviving administrative records from the 1950s are spotty, but minutes from a meeting of the Encyclopedia Committee of April 30, 1955, state that a month earlier, "friend R. Abramovitch" had "resigned from the managing committee."[123] It is likely that Abramovitch's resignation was a formal recognition of his lessening involvement with the *Entsiklopedye* since the early 1950s in favor of his political projects. In addition, his eyesight, which had been failing since the early 1940s, was by then nearly completely gone.[124]

The Menshevik-inflected Social Democratic movement that Abramovitch had at one time led had been shattered during the war, and he dedicated much of his remaining years to reestablishing its influence and relevance. He was still broadly respected in labor circles. In 1941, soon after arriving in the United States, a banquet held in honor of his sixtieth birthday drew more than six hundred attendees.[125] That same year, Abramovitch restarted his journal

Sotsialisticheskii vestnik with the help of the Bundist philanthropist Frank Z. Atran, whose foundation later gave significant sums to the *Entsiklopedye*.[126] In 1947, Abramovitch had assumed editorship of the short-lived but influential journal *Modern Review*, which was published by the American Labor Conference on International Affairs Records, a group that had been founded during the war and "included American labor leaders, American and European scholars, and representatives of the European labor movement who lived in the United States."[127] Its executive secretary for a time was Varian Fry, and its members included the leader of the American Federation of Labor, William Green, and the head of the International Ladies' Garment Workers Union, David Dubinsky, as well as leaders from steelworker, railway, and clothing unions. Historian Howard Brick explains that Abramovitch looked to *Modern Review* to maintain the movement as it sought to reconstitute itself. Almost immediately, however, the journal itself fell into an ideological crisis as it unsuccessfully sought "to span the gap between extreme right and extreme left in the socialist movement."[128] Abramovitch, whose animosity toward the Soviet Union only increased as the Cold War took hold, had backed the United States in the war between the two global superpowers rather than join those who sought to carve out a "third way" between them. In the fight that followed, the managing editors of the *Modern Review* were dismissed, leaving Abramovitch to take on new staff, including the sociologist Daniel Bell. Although the journal published works by luminaries of the political left, such as the former three-time French prime minister Léon Blum and the Spanish Marxist Víctor Alba, it collapsed within a few years.

Subsequently, Abramovitch—who remained, in the words of the historian André Liebich, "the uncontested Menshevik patriarch"—threw himself into writing what would become his most widely read work in English, *The Soviet Revolution, 1917–1939*, which appeared in 1962 with an introduction by the philosopher Sidney Hook.[129] Abramovitch provided a Menshevik interpretation of the period just prior to the 1917 Revolution in Russia and the Bolshevik takeover of power until the beginning of World War II. Although the work received several critical reviews in the press, it was hailed by George Kennan and Isaiah Berlin.[130] The historian Robert V. Daniels welcomed it as a "valedictory [that] will stand as a fitting climax to a life of struggle in the cause of humanity."[131]

Abramovitch passed away in April 1963. For nearly a quarter century, he had been one of the most visible and, given his political position, most contentious figures associated with the *Entsiklopedye*. His participation and leadership had brought the encyclopedia alternating measures of prestige and suspicion. His international connections led some of the towering leaders of the political left to contribute to the *Entsiklopedye*, and his contacts in the world of Jewish labor not only helped the project acquire much-needed subsidies but also facilitated the rescue of many members of the Dubnow Fund as they fled Europe. His quiet departure from the project remains a mystery—even his death went unmentioned in the volume that appeared the following year—but may be attributed to the political divisiveness that defined so much of his life's work and to the fact that by the mid-1950s there was little place for his politics in the shrinking American Yiddish scene.

With Abramovitch's departure in the mid-1950s, the final links between the *Entsiklopedye* and the world of prewar Jewish politics were almost entirely dissolved. Now a decade removed from the end of World War II, the project went through one final transformation. Rather than aiding in the modernization of Yiddish-speaking Jews or trying to shape and inform American Jews as they assumed responsibility for leading world Jewry into the new era, the encyclopedia, with its final Yiddish volumes, took on the dual tasks of maintaining the fraying bonds of Yiddish communal life and documenting the destruction of European Jewry.

By the mid-1950s, the *Entsiklopedye* had long since dropped the name "Dubnow Fund," other than in Yiddish on the title page, and referred to itself either by its publishing arm, Jewish Encyclopedic Handbooks Inc., or more simply as the "Yiddish Encyclopedia." The active members of the group included, among others, Nathan Chanin, a onetime Bundist activist who had served nearly eight years in prison in Siberia for revolutionary activity before escaping. In the United States, he was the secretary-general of the Arbeter-ring, and after retiring from that position, he served as chairman of the board for the encyclopedia. Emanuel Pat, son of Jewish Labor Committee executive secretary Jacob Pat, was also deeply involved and took on much of the administrative work.[132] Emanuel had been among those who had escaped Vilna after the German invasion, and traveled to the United States by way of Japan. A physician by training, he served with the US military's medical corps in Europe and was one of the first Jewish writers who reported on Nazi death camps.[133] The labor activist and CYCO manager Iser Goldberg, who had thrown himself into Yiddish cultural activism after arriving in New York in 1941, took responsibility for much of the sales of the *Entsiklopedye*, visiting more than thirty Jewish communities in the Americas, including a much-celebrated trip to Cuba in the summer of 1949.[134] Leyzer Ran, who had arrived in New York in 1953 after spending several years in Cuba working with the ORT, took on an administrative role with the *Entsiklopedye* for several years. From 1928 to 1936,

Ran had been a student and researcher with YIVO. He and his wife, Basheva, were arrested in Moscow and spent the war years first in a Soviet gulag and then in exile in the Uzbek city of Samarkand. They were repatriated in 1946.[135] Shloyme Gilinsky continued to fulfill the role of executive secretary, overseeing administrative affairs.[136] Of the original members of the Dubnow Fund, only Avrom Kin remained intimately tied to the project, performing as much of the day-to-day administrative and editorial work as his health would allow.

With offices now housed at 25 East 78th Street, in a building that was purchased by Frank Z. Atran, renamed the Atran House for Jewish Culture, and donated to the Jewish Labor Committee, the encyclopedists were busy with ambitious plans for the future.[137] As a result of their broad outreach efforts and support from philanthropists such as Atran, the encyclopedists were able to claim close to ten thousand subscribers in twenty-nine countries for the Yiddish volumes.[138] Sales, however, were weaker than anticipated, and the encyclopedia was, as always, under continual threat of collapse. At one meeting, Chanin noted in exasperation that the encyclopedia had existed in a state of permanent crisis since coming to the United States, and he raised the possibility of turning the project over entirely to YIVO or the Kultur-kongres.[139] Along with sales, donations from the Jewish Labor Committee, the Joint Distribution Committee, the Atran Foundation, and the Conference on Material Claims against Germany (a reparations program funded by West Germany that assisted many Jewish cultural institutions destroyed during the Holocaust) kept the organization afloat.[140] Undaunted, the encyclopedists were busy finalizing *Yidn hey*, which would be a volume about Jewish life in the Americas, as well as completing a multivolume study of the Nazi *khurbn*.

At some point in the mid-1950s, they also made the extraordinary decision to restart the *alef–beys* volumes, the last of which had appeared in 1944 and ended with "Animals" (בעלי-חיים). However, instead of continuing with entries on universal, or *normale*, matters, a new, ten-volume *alef–beys* series would be dedicated exclusively to Jewish topics. This marked a profound shift in the *Entsiklopedye* and the final blow to its founding vision of transmitting knowledge of the larger world to Yiddish readers. Instead of producing a Yiddish encyclopedia on the model of the English-language *Britannica*, the French-language *Larousse*, or the German-language *Brockhaus and Efron*, the editors now sought to publish a work of original contributions in the tradition of other scholarly Jewish encyclopedias of the twentieth century.[141] The number of such works had grown significantly in recent decades, especially in English and Hebrew; most notably, the ten-volume *Universal Jewish Encyclopedia* had been published in New York between 1939

FIGURE 3.5 Simon
Rawidowicz, 1949
(courtesy of Benjamin
C. I. Ravid).

and 1943, and in Tel Aviv, the Hebrew-language *Encyclopaedia Hebraica*, which would eventually run to thirty-two volumes, had begun publishing in 1949.[142]

To lead this initiative the encyclopedists turned to a figure outside of Yiddishist academic or political circles, the Hebraist Simon Rawidowicz. It is unclear why Rawidowicz was chosen for this project, although there were few Jewish scholars working in the United States who carried the same intellectual weight as did he. Along with his attachment to forging modern Hebrew culture, he remained deeply committed to the continuation of Jewish life in the Diaspora.[143] He also deeply admired Simon Dubnow, and in 1954 had edited a Hebrew-language edition of Dubnow's letters that begins with a long series of tributes from scholars and friends.[144] Rawidowicz had also previously written for the *Entsiklopedye*, contributing an essay for *Yidn beys* entitled "Hebrew Literature in the Time of the Jewish Enlightenment."

Born in 1897 in Grajewo, Lithuania (then part of Russia), Rawidowicz moved to Berlin in 1919 and studied at the University of Berlin, where he was a leader of the growing Hebrew-language movement and founded the Ayanot publishing house to make classical Hebrew works available to a wider reading public. He also briefly coedited a Yiddish newspaper that was published by the Labor Zionist movement. He was on the cusp of receiving an academic appointment when Hitler assumed power, and the offer was rescinded. Soon after, his wife was dismissed from her position as a cancer researcher. Rawidowicz sought to secure a position in Palestine, but unable to do so, he emigrated to England, where he taught at Jews' College, in London, and at Leeds University. In 1948, he arrived in the United States. Within a few years, he joined, and soon became chair of, the Department of Near Eastern and Judaic Studies at Brandeis University, which had been founded in 1948 in Waltham, Massachusetts. In spite of his deep ties to the Hebrew language and culture, he was at odds with many leaders of the Zionist movement for his refusal to accept that the new state was to be the exclusive spiritual center of Judaism and that the age of the Jewish Diaspora had reached its end. He famously had a dispute with Israeli prime minister David Ben-Gurion over whether the new state should be called "Israel," since it was the historic name of the Jewish people. Rawidowicz protested that the two should not be synonymous. He also spoke out against the systemic maltreatment and dispossession of Palestinian Arabs.[145]

It took several months of correspondence (and one personal visit) between Rawidowicz and Jacob Pat—the two had been on opposite sides of disputes between Hebraists and Yiddishists in 1918—to reach an agreement over the terms of Rawidowicz's participation.[146] What seems to have convinced him to serve as editor-in-chief of the project (for a trial period of one volume) was the encyclopedists' commitment to the highest academic standards, as well as a payment of $2,500, which would allow him to continue working on his own scholarship. His son Benjamin C. I. Ravid writes in the introduction to Rawidowicz's collected works:

> His motivation was twofold. First and foremost, he believed that the Eastern European past could be adequately described only in Hebrew or Yiddish, and that if this task were not done then by those of his generation who knew Eastern Europe still at firsthand, it could never be adequately done later; hence he felt that since it was decided that he was the person best suited to undertake this task, he had the moral responsibility to accept and to erect this monument to the past. Second, he hoped that the income from the encyclopedia would enable him to finance the publication of his Hebrew writings, for which he could find no publisher in the United States.[147]

Immediately after committing in early 1957, just as *Yidn hey* was going to press, Rawidowicz went to work. He used his clout to bring Salo W. Baron to the editorial advisory board (though Baron acknowledged that his Yiddish was "quite rustic [sic]" after many years of disuse).[148] Over the next several months, Rawidowicz edited dozens of entries that must have been written in the year or two before he assumed the post. However, his health had been failing him. He had suffered three heart attacks—two since arriving to the United States—and on July 20 of that year, he had two more and died. Rawidowicz's passing was a tremendous blow to the world of Jewish letters, the Hebrew-language movement, and the Yiddish encyclopedia. After his death, there was little mention of continuing with the *alef–beys* series. Instead, all efforts were put toward publishing what would become the final volumes on the *khurbn*.

In 1950, in the introduction to *Yidn daled*, the editors stated that the next volume would contend with the history of Jewish communities outside of Europe, including those in the Americas, Africa, Australia, and Israel. When *Yidn hey* finally appeared, in 1957, it was limited to the Americas, with entries appearing on the United States, Canada, Argentina, Brazil, Mexico, and Cuba. Furthermore, a third of the essays, most of them concerning the United States, are in fact translations of ones that first appeared in *JPPP*, primarily volume 4. The brief foreword to the volume, written in the name of the "Encyclopedia Committee," did not address the crossover from the English-language editions but declared that other regions of Latin America would be covered in subsequent volumes. The editors also announced the impending return of the *alef–beys* volumes, which they stated would appear regularly, although they did not reveal that the volumes would be limited to Jewish topics. Of all the *Yidn* volumes, *Yidn hey* may be the least ambitious and therefore the least successful. Perhaps reflecting the limited resources that were available, this volume was the first that did not feature any full-color reproductions or any artwork on the frontispiece.

Among those essays reprinted from *JPPP* were ones that were likely initially composed in Yiddish, making their inclusion in this volume particularly effortless. Such essays included Jacob Lestschinsky's "Jews in the United States," Philip Friedman's "Social and Political Movements [in the United States]," Shmuel Charney's "Yiddish Culture in America," and Mark Wischnitzer's "American Jewish Aid to World Jewry."[149] One of the few original essays in the section on the United States is "The Jewish Labor Movement in America," by the Socialist Party activist Samuel Weiss, which examines the movement's rise from the 1880s through the late 1940s.

Some of the most engaging essays in the volume are on Jewish communities outside of the United States. Louis Rosenberg, the esteemed social statistician and author of the highly regarded 1939 study *Canada's Jews*, contributed a piece on the Canadian Jewish community. Rosenberg, who had been born in Poland and spent his childhood in Leeds, England, had immigrated to Canada just prior to World War I. He had been inspired to work in farming communities in western Canada by the Labor Zionist ethos of building up the Jewish nation through agricultural work.[150] His essay, which examines birth and death rates, marriage rates, employment, politics, and educational trends among Canadian Jewry (in just twenty pages, including photographs), locates the Jewish presence deep within the country's history, dating back to the mid-eighteenth century. The piece details the Jewish contribution to Canada and asserts the right of Jews to exist as a minority group within the multinational, multilingual country. A second, very brief essay by the acclaimed Yiddish poet and onetime Autonomist activist Melech Ravitch surveys Jewish culture in Canada, including schools, the press, Yiddish literature, and libraries and theater.

The volume contains three essays on Argentina, including an overview of the country's Jewish community by the highly respected journalist and onetime Labor Zionist activist Aharon Leyb Schussheim, who had died two years earlier. Schussheim's contribution, which surveys the Argentinian Jewish population from the period of the first settlements in the mid-nineteenth century to the present, commemorates the success of that community's social, cultural, educational, and economic growth.[151] The essay also discusses at length the violence inflicted upon the Jews of Buenos Aires during the infamous riots of the Semana Trágica (Tragic Week) of January 7–14, 1919, when a series of increasingly violent clashes between striking workers and the police sparked mob attacks on institutions throughout the city. Right-wing vigilante groups associated with the newly created Argentine Patriotic League began wantonly attacking Jewish neighborhoods, believing that Russian Jewish radicals were chiefly responsible for the strikes in the name of establishing a Bolshevik-inspired "Argentinian Soviet." Jews were assaulted randomly on the streets and dragged out of their homes, and dozens were murdered.[152]

The other two essays on Argentina are on its Yiddish literature, by the Yiddish novelist and journalist Yankev Botoshansky, and its Jewish schools, by the writer Shmuel Rozansky. The final, brief essays in the volume are "Jews in Brazil," by the writer and journalist Elye Lipiner; "Jews in Mexico," by the Bundist leader and Yiddish activist Tuvye Meisel; and "Jews in Cuba," by Leyzer Ran, drawn from his time spent there before arriving in the United States.[153] Together the entries on Jewish communities outside the United States make up less than 25 percent of the work, diminishing further the volume's impact and its ability to maintain ties between the increasingly diffuse community of Yiddish speakers globally.

Considering the barriers that the encyclopedists faced, including profoundly insecure funding, the loss of many of its central members, administrative chaos, the diminishing number of readers, and the shifting relationship of American Jewry to the Yiddish language, its culture, and the lessons that it might offer, the 1950s can still be considered a time of moderate success. The encyclopedists managed to publish four volumes, two in Yiddish and two in English—a profound accomplishment given the many constraints under which they had to work. It was clear, however, by the end of the decade that the financial, intellectual, and cultural resources that had sustained this project for three decades were all but expended. Following Rawidowicz's sudden death, all efforts were focused on releasing the final volumes, which would be dedicated to the *khurbn* that brought the world of Yiddish nearly to its end.[154]

Khurbn

The original publication schedule for the *khurbn* volumes was for two volumes each in Yiddish and English to be published in 1961, the bulk of the material having been collected, edited, and translated by early 1960. However, the two Yiddish-language volumes on the Holocaust did not appear until 1964 and 1966, once again a result of delays caused by financial challenges and the passing of several key members of the editorial board.[155] Neither of the English-language volumes, which were to have been titled "The History of the Jewish Catastrophe under the Nazis" (and were to have cost nearly $80,000 to produce), ever made it to press.[156] The editorial committee for the *khurbn* volumes was chaired by Philip Friedman, who had been one of the first to research the Jewish experience of the Holocaust, especially in the East, where most ghettos, concentration camps, killing fields, and extermination centers had been located.[157] Other members of the editorial board included Kin, Lestschinsky, Steinberg, and Kosover, as well as several of the first scholars to research and write on the Holocaust and the postwar reconstruction of European Jewry, such as Judah J. Shapiro, Joseph Tenenbaum, and Isaiah Trunk.[158]

By the early 1960s, when the volumes were being prepared, a great deal was already known and understood about the murder of European Jewry. Among American Jewish communities, the Holocaust was a focus of intense commemoration and memorialization.[159] The Nuremberg trials, which took place soon after the war, served, as Lawrence Douglas has shown, an important didactic function by teaching many Americans about Nazi crimes against

Jews.[160] Similarly, the 1961 prosecution of Nazi leader Adolf Eichmann in Jerusalem, which placed the suffering of European Jews at the center of the trial, was covered closely in the United States. The years immediately following the Holocaust also saw many efforts to collect and publish the testimonies of survivors, in both Europe and the United States.[161] Hundreds of *yizker bikher* appeared as survivors of destroyed communities sought to create a monument to their history. An English translation of Anne Frank's *Diary* was published in 1952 and quickly became a best seller and the basis of a 1955 Broadway play and a 1959 Hollywood film.[162] Campaigns on behalf of Jewish survivors who resided in displaced persons camps were featured widely in the press.[163] Journalistic accounts of Nazism, such as William L. Shirer's 1960 best-selling work, *The Rise and Fall of the Third Reich*, kept Nazism at the center of public discussions. Hannah Arendt's 1963 account, *Eichmann in Jerusalem: A Report on the Banality of Evil* (based on her reporting in the *New Yorker*), set off a widespread controversy over the role of Jewish leadership during the genocide and the nature of Nazi evil, but also served to keep the extermination of European Jews during the war in the public eye.

Scholarship on the Holocaust was growing as well, much of it written in Yiddish and Hebrew by those who, like Friedman, had a direct relationship to the event.[164] Mark L. Smith has shown that Yiddish-speaking scholars in particular often had an early awareness of the catastrophe and access to sources that were unavailable to other scholars. This generation of survivor scholars tended to draw upon victim and survivor accounts to investigate Jewish life and actions under Nazi rule. They were deeply invested, Smith argues, in locating the study of the Holocaust within the larger sweep of Jewish history, leading them "to their study of Jewish life, rather than death, under Nazi occupation."[165] They were also driven by an overwhelming urge to "to dispel the accusations of cowardice and passivity that arose in the early years following World War II against the Jewish victims of Nazism."[166]

Working in another vein were scholars, several of whom were émigrés from Nazi Germany, such as Gerhard Weinberg, Henry Friedlander, and Raul Hilberg who focused their studies on German perpetrators. Drawing primarily from German-language documents, they sought to reconstruct *how* the Nazis had imagined, planned, and carried out the Holocaust.[167] Most influential was Raul Hilberg's 1961 study, *The Destruction of the European Jews*, which was the first to systematically examine the genocide in its broadest scope, explaining it as a methodical campaign of extermination that was distinct from the war effort.[168] Hilberg noted in a lecture delivered a few months before he died, in 2007, that he constructed his groundbreaking study almost entirely from

scratch, following a decade's worth of research among documents seized by
Allied forces: "I was transported into a world for which I was totally unpre-
pared. I would read a document, but I would not understand what it meant.
The context had to be built record by record."[169] In spite of the success of Hilberg's work and its monumental impact on establishing the field of Holocaust
studies, it was met with criticism by those who challenged its exclusive depen-
dence upon German documents and Hilberg's disparaging remarks concerning the seeming lack of Jewish resistance to Nazi aggression. Hilberg's lack of
attention to Jewish life under Nazi rule was all the more noteworthy given
that Philip Friedman had served as a reader of his doctoral dissertation at Columbia. Friedman strongly criticized Hilberg's approach to the Holocaust.
However, the two continued to associate, and when Hilberg struggled to find
a press in the United States for his work, Friedman sought (unsuccessfully) to
have Jerusalem's Yad Vashem publish it.[170]

It was, therefore, with the twofold intention to provide a thorough overview
of the Holocaust and to do so through the experience of Jewish survivors that
Friedman and the rest of the *Entsiklopedye* editorial committee prepared the two
khurbn volumes. As the editors explained in a funding application from 1960:

> Hitherto, hundreds of memorial books have appeared that deal with single
> communities that have been destroyed or with individual topics. However,
> a full, comprehensive history that would acquaint the Jews as well as the
> non-Jews with all the facts relating to the annihilation of six million Jews,
> among them one and half million Jewish children, is still lacking.
>
> There can be no doubt that such a comprehensive history, rendered
> objectively by scholarly historians of our generation, is urgently needed.
> The work, furthermore, must appear in the near future, since five or ten
> years hence it may be too late. Unfortunately, the generation of the
> catastrophe is rapidly disappearing.
>
> There is another matter of great importance: up to now, all attempts that
> have been made to issue comprehensive works on the destruction have
> brought forward the side of the murderers, of the Nazis. The Jewish side,
> however, is lacking. It is urgently necessary to record the life of the Jews,
> Jewish suffering and martyrdom under the Nazis in all its phases, particu-
> larly, the Jewish resistance.[171]

The editors were not exaggerating the urgency: by the time the first of the two
Yiddish volumes arrived in 1964, the encyclopedia had suffered a profound
number of losses, which they acknowledged in the foreword. Gone were Simon Rawidowicz, Philip Friedman, Isaac Schwarzbart, Joseph Tenenbaum,

and Shloyme Gilinsky. By the time the second volume was published, Jacob Lestschinsky, Nathan Chanin, and Louis Sigal, a labor leader and Jewish communal activist who had been a vice-chair of the *Entsiklopedye* board, had also passed.

The two volumes together contain twenty-eight essays written by twenty-three scholars. Each volume is well over four hundred pages, and while the first of them, *Yidn vov*, contains more than seventy-five illustrations (most of which are photos), the second volume, *Yidn zayen*, contains none at all, an indication of the financial straits of the project in its final days. The authors of the essays include only a small handful of the regular contributors to the *Algemeyne entsiklopedye*, such as Avrom Menes, who wrote the introductory essay, "Problems of Life and Resistance in the Ghettos," and Lestschinsky, who contributed the essay "Polish Jewry on the Eve of the Hitler-Catastrophe." The majority of entries are from scholars who were survivors of the Holocaust or émigrés from Nazi Europe and who had been researching the genocide for years. These include the historian and bibliographer Joseph Gar, who wrote on Jewish life in the Baltic states; the refugee advocate and World Jewish Congress leader Aryeh Tartakower, who wrote on Jewish culture and politics in Poland between the two world wars; the editor and political activist Mordechai Wolf Bernstein, who wrote on the destruction and resistance of Jews in Poland; the historian Isaiah Trunk, who contributed the essay "The Destruction Process of European Jews in the Nazi Era"; the historian Léon Poliakov, who wrote on the fate of French Jewry; and the survivor and author of the first major study of the Theresienstadt ghetto, H. G. Adler, who wrote on the destruction of Jews in Czechoslovakia.

Along with this impressive list of contributors, among those who are acknowledged as readers of the manuscripts are a number of illustrious figures who were also survivors and émigrés. These include the Zionist activist, journalist, and essayist Robert Weltsch, the journalist and refugee advocate Leyb Gorfinkel, the displaced persons advocate and early scholar of the Holocaust Samuel Gringauz, the historian Erich Goldhagen, and the journalist and advocate for refugees and survivors Kurt Grossman. Most surprising, but a sign of the interconnectedness of the first scholars to work within the emerging field of Holocaust studies as well as the editor's wish to publish works that met the highest scholarly standards, the final figure thanked in the foreword, for serving as a consultant, is Raul Hilberg.[172]

The *khurbn* volumes, which were published in part with funding from the Claims Conference, were among the most comprehensive studies of the Holocaust from the point of view of its Jewish victims to date. They stand as a powerful repudiation to those studies that focus solely on the perpetrators of the genocide, to those historians who dismissed Jewish sources in their research, and to those writers who condemned Jewish victims for not resisting forcefully enough. The volumes cover nearly every aspect of occupied Europe and draw their material from sources in more than a dozen languages, including Yiddish, Hebrew, German, Polish, English, Russian, Dutch, Greek, Italian, Norwegian, Romanian, Serbo-Croatian, and Hungarian. Most the essays are organized by country, and although they differ from one another on account of the varying experiences of each country during the war, many follow a similar pattern that begins with a discussion of the social, economic, religious, and cultural positions of Jews within those states. The essays then speak of the degree to which antisemitism had been present in the state and its acceleration with the rise of Nazism and the outbreak of war. They discuss the initial anti-Jewish laws that came into effect, the measures to isolate and concentrate Jews, the theft of Jewish property, and the deportation and subsequent extermination of Jews.

Most essays give particular attention to the issue of Jewish life under Nazi occupation, including methods of Jewish survival, self-help, and armed resistance. To refute claims of Jewish passivity that had emerged during the Holocaust and became common in Israel and elsewhere after the war, the first volume contains a two-page map entitled *The Network of Resistance*, highlighting the many labor camps, concentration camps, and extermination centers where Jews took up arms against their oppressors.[173] In fact, the issue of Jewish resistance is prominent throughout the volume, from Menes's opening essay to lengthy discussions of the 1943 armed uprising in the Warsaw ghetto and other sites in Poland, with photos of Jewish partisans. The volume even includes a reprint of one of the rare photographs taken by a member of the Auschwitz *Sonderkommando*, the Jewish workers forced to dispose of corpses, with the goal of making Nazi crimes known to the world.[174]

The *khurbn* volumes were received extraordinarily well and reviewed widely in the Yiddish press. In a review of the first volume in *YIVO Bleter*, the historian William Glicksman (who was also a Holocaust survivor) was enthusiastic, stating that since the literature on the destruction had grown significantly, an encyclopedic overview would allow readers to stay up to date on recent developments. Although he praised the volume heavily, in particular for the great effort that went into compiling the many contributions, he expressed disappointment that the essays by Wiener, Lestschinsky, and Tartakower were either reprints or revisions of earlier works they had already published.[175] While expressing his appreciation for Menes's efforts to depict

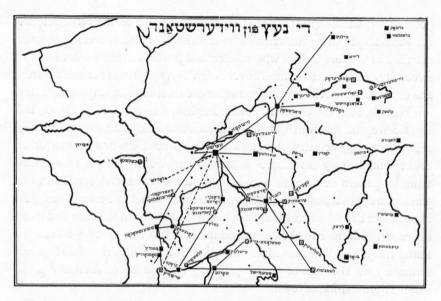

FIGURE 3.6 "The Network of Resistance," in *Algemeyne entsiklopedye: Yidn vov*.

Jewish life in the ghettos, he criticized what he saw as Menes's overly sympathetic view of the complicated role of the Jewish councils. Under Nazi rule the
councils were forced to run the day-to-day administration of the ghettos, and
prompted many ethical and moral debates about whether they were agents of
collaboration or providers of much-needed social services and organization.
Glicksman hoped that the subsequent volume would contend more directly
with the difficult issue of the Jewish ghetto police, which in many ghettos
were tasked with rounding up Jews for deportation, often to extermination
camps. Nevertheless, he credited the work as a great accomplishment for
bringing together so much of what was known about the Holocaust in one
place.

  In 1967, the editors of the second *khurbn* volume, *Yidn zayen*, which appeared in 1966, received the prestigious Jewish Book Award's Leon Jolson
Award for best book on the Nazi Holocaust, bringing the encyclopedia committee a $500 prize, which likely was very welcome. Unfortunately, Avrom
Kin never got to receive his honor. Six weeks before it was granted, he passed
away.

  As earlier, there exist few archival records to document the financial health
of the organization in its last days. One report relates that from the period
of September 1961 until the end of 1966, when the final volume of the

Entsiklopedye appeared, contributions related to the two *khurbn* volumes amounted to $27,435.[176] More than half of this was a result of a donation from the Atran Foundation, with other monies coming from the chapters of the International Ladies' Garment Workers Union (Locals 66 and 62), the Jewish Labor Committee, the Forward Association, and other Jewish labor and philanthropic groups. A sum of $15,000 is listed as being held in a "Conference Account," reflecting a contribution from the Conference on Material Claims. Total receipts from this period are listed as $52,100.92 and total disbursements are listed as $51,983.27, leaving a remaining balance in December 1966 of $117.65. The cost of preparing and publishing each of the *khurbn* volumes was approximately $16,750, and nearly $18,500 was spent on administrative expenses from June 1963 through July 1966.

In the foreword to the final volume, Iser Goldberg, who then was the executive director of CYCO, writes, "We bring this volume to the thousands of readers and subscribers in Jewish communities all over the whole world and we hope that with it, we have made an important contribution to the growing *khurbn* literature."[177] This ambition was far more modest than the one Simon Dubnow had expressed at the founding meeting of the *Entsiklopedye*, when he spoke of the "ten million of whom speak Yiddish, [who] must have an encyclopedia in their own language." However, even this hope of Goldberg's was unattainable. By the mid-1960s, the encyclopedia committee had run its course. It was out of funds, out of energy, and without the means to sell the final volumes. In early 1968, Goldberg himself died, and by then there were few people left to promote the work, and not many buyers for it.

CONCLUSION

WHEN I BEGAN researching the *Algemeyne entsiklopedye*, I telephoned the offices of CYCO, then based in the relocated Atran Center for Jewish Culture, on East 21st Street in Manhattan, looking for any documents that they might have in their archives or collections.[1] CYCO's director, the actor and singer Hy Wolfe, answered my call. When I explained to him what I was looking for, he was surprised, to say the least: "You're calling about the Yiddish encyclopedia? In all of my years, no one has ever called asking about the encyclopedia. Come over, my basement is full of them. I can't give 'em away!" When I arrived, he took me to the basement, and there, stacked floor to ceiling on bookshelves, neatly and perfectly arranged, were hundreds upon hundreds of copies of the final two volumes, untouched and unsold.

The reason for this state of affairs is not hard to fathom, but it is perhaps more involved than one might surmise. The *Algemeyne entsiklopedye*, which was by 1966 more than three and a half decades removed from its founding in Weimar-era Germany, relied for its survival on an audience of Yiddish readers that was both sharply diminishing in number and that no longer looked to the *Entsiklopedye* to situate themselves in the world or learn about their past. Given that producing the *Entsiklopedye* involved vast financial resources as well as dozens of authors, editors, managers, clerks, and sales representatives, the venture could no longer be sustained beyond its last volume on the *khurbn*. Having charted a path that began with the hope and promise of Yiddish culture to bring Eastern European Jews fully into the modern era (a "bible for the new age," as Dubnow called it) and that ended with desperate efforts to salvage what remained of its legacy, the *Entsiklopedye* had at last run its course.

However, as much as the *Entsiklopedye* can serve as a means for under-standing the history of modern Yiddish culture and the ideologies that sus-tained it in the mid-twentieth century, it would be incorrect to assume that Yiddish also came to end in this period; it most decidedly did not. Rather, even as the community of native speakers of the language continued to de-cline, Yiddish culture divided into dual but intertwining lines that continue to this day.

Along one strand, scholarly activity in and on behalf of Yiddish-language development continued. A recent study by Alec Eliezer Burko explains how in the decades after the Holocaust, scholars worked assiduously on Yiddish-language planning and increasing the number of speakers.[2] Focusing in particular on the work of Yiddish linguists based primarily (although not ex-clusively) at YIVO in New York City, Burko's research reveals that a small group of ideologically committed Yiddishists sought to rescue the language from disappearing as a medium of communication among Jews, as well as to compile a body of knowledge that could serve as a resource for future speakers and scholars of the language. These efforts included creating and maintaining a Yiddish secular school system, as well as producing comprehensive Yiddish-language scholarly journals, pedagogical materials, dictionaries, a thesaurus, and several important lexicons of Yiddish culture. Not all of these works made it to completion. The multivolume *Great Dictionary of the Yiddish Language*, for example, made it only partway through the letter *alef*, and Max Weinreich's magnum opus, the four-volume *Geshikhte fun der yidisher shprakh* (History of the Yiddish language), which appeared after his death, never included the much-longed-for bibliography.[3] Yiddish secular school systems have since dis-appeared, yet popular and academic Yiddish-language programs continue to be offered around the world, although few children outside of religiously or-thodox circles are raised in the language. Yiddish remains a medium for schol-arly work, although it is almost entirely restricted to the topic *of* Yiddish and appears infrequently. By contrast, scholarship *on* all aspects of Yiddish (including linguistics and sociolinguistics, history, literature, theater, and film) is thriving, albeit in languages other than Yiddish, and Yiddish Studies continues to be a dynamic academic discipline in its own right.[4]

In a second strand, which by all measures is far more influential than the first, Yiddish by the mid-1960s was finding its way into American popular cul-ture and language. As the number of native speakers was declining, Yiddish began to take on a new symbolic meaning for American Jews as they fash-ioned hybrid identities that allowed them to distance themselves from the obligations of religious traditions without threatening their place within the white American majority culture. Jeffrey Shandler has identified this shift as one in which the primary function of Yiddish transformed from being a vernacular language—one of day-to-day communication—to a "post-vernacular" one, in which its "meta-level of signification" became dominant over its primary functions.[5] Stripped of the ideological associations that were so central to Yiddish intellectual culture before the war, Yiddish-inflected English (sometimes referred to as Yinglish) in the decades after the war increasingly became a cultural marker of one's Eastern European Jewish roots, and was often played for laughs or nostalgia. This was present, for example, in the routines of the comedian Lenny Bruce, in the Broadway success of the musical *Fiddler on the Roof,* and in the films of Mel Brooks and Woody Allen. Several scholars have noted the importance of Leo Rosten's 1968 best seller, *The Joys of Yiddish,* a comedic compendium of Yiddish phrases for English readers, in bringing Yiddish words and phrases into American colloquial English. Ilan Stavans has remarked that *The Joys of Yiddish* served as "a thermometer showing how 'cool' American Jews can be, how successful their journey from immigration to assimilation has been."[6] Appearing in the same year as Uriel Weinreich's *Modern English-Yiddish Yiddish-English Dictionary* (and with the same publisher), Rosten's lexicon received no end of opprobrium from Yiddishists and scholars of Eastern European Jewish culture, who resented its success and feared that it would reduce the status of Yiddish—which for them symbolized the richness and promise of their entire civilization—to an assortment of lowbrow and off-color jokes. Worse still from this perspective, Rosten's *Joys* not only has been revised and expanded many times but has also spawned a subgenre of popular Yiddish-English lexicons that range from the sincere to the prurient and that make little effort to follow the scholarly and orthographic standards set by YIVO.[7]

This relationship of Ashkenazi Jews toward Yiddish allowed them to simultaneously distance themselves from the perceived obligations of prewar Yiddish culture while embracing its lighter aspects as a marker of their ethnic identity. Today, however, these two strands increasingly intersect, as the study of the Yiddish language and culture has become deeply engaged with its popularization. The last several decades have witnessed an international flowering of Yiddish cultural projects that are both broadly popular and deeply informed by scholarship. This includes Yiddish cultural festivals, translation projects, digital scholarship, musical productions, Eastern European Jewish heritage tours, and innumerable efforts to recover and preserve the lost and forgotten cultural treasures of the pre-Holocaust era. At the same time, the work of CYCO, the Congress for Jewish Culture (the renamed

Kultur-kongres), the Workers Circle (the renamed Arbeter-ring), and of course YIVO continues. Although the number of native speakers of Yiddish outside of religiously orthodox communities remains small, widely repeated claims of Yiddish's "death" are greatly exaggerated. Yiddish is being taken seriously again, not only for the way it can help Jews navigate their relationship to the majority culture, but as a topic worthy of study in itself and a means to affirm new Jewish identities. As Shandler has convincingly argued in a recent study, this "interest is rooted in a desire to engage a form of Jewishness understood as arcane or lost; it is envisioned as organic, authentic, and comprehensive, realized in the intense expressivity of vernacular speech."[8]

One prominent sign of the merger between the scholarly and popular engagements with Yiddish is the 2008 publication of *The YIVO Encyclopedia of Jews in Eastern Europe*, an impressive two-volume English-language compendium that stretches 2,400 pages and provides a comprehensive guide to Jewish life and culture in the "regions east of the German-speaking realm, north of the Balkans, and west of the Urals."[9] This ten-year effort involved 450 contributors and teams of editors and administrative staff and resulted in a work comprising 1,800 entries, nearly 1,200 illustrations, and several dozen color plates and maps. Compared to the *Algemeyne entsiklopedye*, which was so often defined by its poverty and by the fact that its editors and contributors were largely autodidacts, *The YIVO Encyclopedia* is impressive in large measure for its abundant resources (as witnessed by the lengthy list of donors who are thanked at the outset) and its scholarly professionalism.

As described by its editor in chief, the historian Gershon David Hundert, the aim of *The YIVO Encyclopedia* is to "recover and represent the civilization of the ancestors of the majority of Jews in the world." In contrast to the overly prescriptive *Algemeyne entsiklopedye*, which sought to impart a strongly Diasporist and socialist vision of the Jewish past, present, and future, *The YIVO Encyclopedia* endeavors instead to be wholly descriptive and "is intended to be an ecumenical work: nondenominational, nonideological, and nonconfessional."[10] Whereas the *Algemeyne entsiklopedye* presented itself as a project of and on behalf of the Yiddish *folk*, *The YIVO Encyclopedia* seeks a wider and less-defined audience of "anyone interested in the history and culture of Jews in Eastern Europe." In spite of these significant differences, both works share an imperative to establish an archive of knowledge that will be of service to Jewish readers. Likewise, they reflect the fact that the encyclopedic impulse remains deeply embedded within the world of Yiddish culture and scholarship. Curiously, *The YIVO Encyclopedia* includes no indication that its editors were aware that in its earliest years, YIVO itself had launched a Yiddish encyclopedia. References to the *Algemeyne entsiklopedye* are present only a handful of times, either as part of biographical entries or within footnotes.[11]

As exemplified by *The YIVO Encyclopedia*, there has been little place for the *Algemeyne entsiklopedye* within either the scholarly or popular strands of contemporary Yiddish culture. It is too popular in its orientation for most scholars and too scholarly for popular audiences. Other than occasional references to individual entries that appear in academic works, the *Entsiklopedye* has not received attention from scholars since its final volume appeared in 1966. As I note in the introduction to this book, complete sets are difficult to obtain and the contrasting classification systems make it challenging to engage with. Unlike the many Yiddish academic dictionaries, grammars, and lexicons that appeared in the 1950s, 60s, and 70s and continue to be published today, the *Entsiklopedye* has not served the many efforts to "revive" Yiddish culture or aid in its scholarly investigation. As with all encyclopedias, its perceived utility fades with age as new knowledge and information replace the old.

However, as I hope the preceding chapters have demonstrated, the *Algemeyne entsiklopedye* is much more than a disjointed collection of obsolete information. Its volumes contain snapshots of how many of the leading Jewish intellectuals of the twentieth century interpreted the Jewish past, present, and future in what were some of the most tumultuous decades in all of Jewish history. Taken as a whole, it is an unrivaled depiction of how Yiddish cultural and intellectual activists tenaciously responded to the hopes, traumas, and triumphs of the middle decades of the twentieth century, when they went from achieving their greatest accomplishments to suffering their most profound losses, and then sought to chart a new path forward to the future.

ACKNOWLEDGMENTS

My interest in the *Algemeyne entsiklopedye* was sparked by a 2006 request by Gennady Estraikh to contribute to a special edition of the *Journal of Modern Jewish Studies* on the theme of Jewish encyclopedias. Although I had previously referenced the *Entsiklopedye* on occasion, I hadn't until then stopped to look at it in its entirety. Reading through the forewords of the individual volumes, I immediately became transfixed, having realized that the *Entsiklopedye* told a unique story of the continuity of modern Yiddish culture in the middle decades of the twentieth century, when nearly every other collaborative Yiddish project either came to an abrupt end on account of the Nazi Holocaust or was begun in response to it. While the *Algemeyne entsiklopedye* is not a lost text per se, it nonetheless seemed worthwhile to set upon this task of historical recovery, as it became clear to me that the possibilities and promises of prewar Yiddish culture and Diaspora Nationalism are revealed in its pages, as are the near-complete destruction of these twin phenomena in the Holocaust and their afterlives in the decades following the end of World War II. Above all, the story of the *Algemeyne entsiklopedye* is one of the tenacity of a culture that is all too often spoken of exclusively in terms of its fragility.

For reasons both wonderful and terrible, and which I have written about in a brief essay ("A Mentsh Trakht, Un Covid-19 Lakht," *AJS Perspectives: The Unfinished Issue*, Fall 2020), completing *The Holocaust & the Exile of Yiddish* took many years. Rather than recount that history here, I would like to thank the many people and institutions that made it possible.

I am indebted to Elisabeth Maselli of Rutgers University Press for expressing interest in this work several years ago and being patient with me while I completed it. My thanks to her and the entire staff at RUP and Westchester Publishing Services for seeing it through to publication.

I am deeply grateful to Gennady Estraikh, who, along with sparking my interest in this topic, was willing to share his historical and linguistic expertise with me at many stages of the project, including reading a draft of the completed manuscript and offering many helpful suggestions. Cecile Kuznitz has unparalleled expertise in this period and I am grateful for her willingness to read the full manuscript and offer insightful criticisms and helpful edits that improved the work significantly. Individual chapters were generously read by Mirjam Gutschow, Lisa Leff, Nick Underwood, and Kalman Weiser, each of whom offered very valuable suggestions and corrections.

The initial archival research for this project was supported by a 2008 Summer Research Grant from the National Endowment for the Humanities. In spring 2009, I was fortunate enough to be a Fellow at the Frankel Institute for Advanced Judaic Studies at the University of Michigan, Ann Arbor. From my time there, I am grateful in particular for conversations on this project with Anthony Bale, Amir Banbaji, Mikhail Krutikov, Deborah Dash Moore, and Timothy Phillips. Nick Block, then a graduate student, kindly helped locate many hard-to-find reviews of the *entsiklopedye*'s first volumes in the Yiddish press. Travel funds from the Frankel Institute also allowed me the opportunity to conduct research at Amsterdam's International Institute of Social History. A month-long fellowship in 2013 at the Kiev Judaica Collection at George Washington University proved to be extraordinarily helpful, not the least on account of Brad S. Hill's and Shelly Buring's bibliographic expertise. Since then, Brad has generously and regularly provided me with crucial bibliographical source material, for which I remain very appreciative.

At the University at Albany, SUNY, where I was on faculty from 2003 to 2016, this project received support from the university's Faculty Research Award, the State of New York/United University Professions Joint Labor-Management Committees' Individual Development Award, the College of Arts and Sciences, and the Center for Jewish Studies. Conversations with colleagues, graduate students, and friends in the Judaic Studies Department, the History Department, and the Albany Chapter of the United University Professions, in particular Bret Benjamin, Joel Berkowitz, Carl Bon Tempo, Arthur Brenner, Kori A. Graves, Paul Stasi, Stacy Veeder, and Meredith Weiss, helped shape and sustain this project.

At Wake Forest University, where I hold the Michael H. and Deborah Rubin Presidential Chair of Jewish History, I received generous support from the Humanities Institute in the form of a Summer Writing Grant and Book Development Grant (particular thanks to Dean J. Franco, Aimee Mepham, and Kimberly Scholl). The provost's office and the Department of History generously awarded travel funds that allowed me to visit archives at the University of Cape Town, and a grant from the Archie Fund for the Arts and Humanities made it possible for me to conduct research at the New York Public Library. A Reynolds Research Leave in spring 2020 allowed me much-needed time to write. I am deeply grateful for conversations regarding this book with my colleagues Lisa Blee, Simone Caron, Ben Coates, Dean J. Franco, Thomas Frank, Annalise Glauz-Todrank, Alisha Hines, Michael Hughes, Jeff Lerner, Monique O'Connell, Leann Pace, Nate Plageman, Jessica Richard, Jake Ruddiman, Susan Z. Rupp, Penny Sinanoglou, Charles Wilkins, Mir Yarfitz, and Qiong Zhang.

I thank Robert Ambaras, Victor Gilinsky, Peter Gourevitch, and Benjamin Ravid, all of whom were generous in their willingness to share anecdotes, memories, and materials regarding their family members' involvement with the *Entsiklopedye*. Hy Wolfe, of the Central Yiddish Culture Organization, was instrumental in helping me locate several hard-to-find volumes of the *entsiklopedye* and consistently championed this project. I am grateful as always to Rebecca Erbelding of the United States Holocaust Memorial Museum for her willingness to share with me her unparalleled expertise in the United States' response to the refugee crisis of the 1930s and 40s. Conversations on this project with friends and colleagues over the years have been invaluable. I am grateful for the wisdom and insights of Natalia Aleksiun, Doris L. Bergen, Roger Brooks, Sarah Cushman, Anja von Cysewski, Anna Hájková, Paul B. Jaskot, Shifra Kuperman, Eddy Portnoy, Rachel Deblinger, Allison Schachter, Jeffrey Shandler, Andrea Sinn, and Gerben Zaagsma.

I have had the opportunity to present this research on several occasions, many of which stand out as having been very beneficial to thinking through this work and its many implications. These include presentations at the Yiddish Symposium at the University of Amsterdam (thanks to Shlomo Berger, ז"ל), YIVO (Paul Glasser), the Simon Dubnow Institute for Jewish History and Culture (Arndt Engelhardt), Georgia State University (Jared Poley), the North Carolina Jewish Studies Seminar (Malachi H. Hacohen), and the Wake Forest University Department of History Seminar (Nate Plageman). My most embarrassing professional moment (so far) was when I nearly passed out while presenting on the *Algemeyne entsiklopedye* at the Jewish Museum Berlin. I am deeply grateful for Michael Brenner's willingness to read my paper to the audience while I recovered. For his generosity, Michael is welcome to tease me for the rest of our lives.

I thank the staff at the following libraries and archives for their generous assistance as I sought to find the scattered remnants of the *Entsiklopedye*: Sharona Wachs of the University Library of the University at Albany, State University of New York; Kaeley McMahan, Kathy Shields, and Melde Rutledge of the Z. Reynolds Smith Library at Wake Forest University; Mary Cockerill of the University of Southampton; Amanda Seigel of the New York Public Library's Dorot Jewish Division; Hans Luhrs of the International Institute of Social History-Amsterdam; Gunner Berg, Leo Greenbaum, Paul Glasser, Sara Belasco, and Vital Zajka of the YIVO Institute for Jewish Research and the Center for Jewish History; Gail Malmgreen of the Tamiment Library/Robert F. Wagner Labor Archives of New York University; Elliot H. Gertel of the Hatcher Graduate Library at the University of Michigan; Veronica Belling and Clive Kirkwood of the University Cape Town Libraries; the staff of the African and Middle Eastern Reading Room of the United States Library of Congress; the staff of the Widener Library at Harvard College Library; Natalia Krynicka at the Maison de la culture yiddish-Bibliothèque Medem; and the staff at the Bibliothèque nationale de France.

I am deeply grateful to Barbara Ann Schmutzler and Marisa Elana James, who were extraordinarily helpful in tracking down archival sources at the Central Archives of the History of the Jewish People. Nina Warnke kindly translated some very hard-to-read Yiddish-language handwriting. Dovid Braun—one of my very first teachers of Yiddish—helped me solve a number of difficult transliteration puzzles. The editorial expertise of Allison Brown of Henry St. Editing improved this work immensely.

There is no one I would rather be with in a pandemic-induced lockdown than Jennifer Greiman and Harley Simone Trachtenberg. As trying and difficult as this period was, it was a joy and a gift to spend each day of it with the two of you. Ditto for our lives together.

Days before my last book appeared in print, my father, Harvey Trachtenberg, ז"ל (1936–2017), passed away. I dedicate this book to his memory and in honor of my mother, Eleanor P. Trachtenberg.

NOTES

Introduction

1. See, for example, Michel Foucault, *The Order of Things: An Archaeology of the Human Sciences* (New York: Pantheon Books, 1970); Richard Yeo, *Encyclopaedic Visions: Scientific Dictionaries and Enlightenment Culture* (Cambridge: Cambridge University Press, 2001); and Ann M. Blair, *Too Much to Know: Managing Scholarly Information before the Modern Age* (New Haven: Yale University Press, 2010).

2. A complete listing of the *Algemeyne entsiklopedye*, including reprints and re-issues, can be found in the bibliography.

3. The historian Philip Friedman noted the symbolic value of the *Entsiklopedye* in a 1951 review of *Yidn daled*, in which he wrote that "the encyclopedia itself already has its own history—in essence—a fragment of the Jewish fate in Europe over the past ten years." See Friedman, "Di yidishe entsiklopedye—a kapitl kultur-geshikhte fun undzer dor," *Tsukunft* 56 no. 3 (March 1951): 130.

4. Other Yiddish ventures that also successfully transitioned from prewar Europe to postwar North America include YIVO's journal *YIVO Bleter* and Zalmen Zylber-cweig's *Leksikon fun yidishn teater*.

5. Tony Michels, "Exporting Yiddish Socialism: New York's Role in the Russian Jewish Workers' Movement," *Jewish Social Studies* 16, no. 1 (Fall 2009): 1–26.

6. Spelling the last name of the three "טשאַרני" brothers who appear in this work in a consistent way poses significant challenges. Shmuel wrote under the name "Shmuel Charney," or at times "Shmuel Tsharni," (and was at times addressed as "Tscharny") but regularly published under and was most often referred to by the pen name "Shmuel Niger" ("ניגער") from an early age. In this work, I use the name

"Shmuel Charney," other than in footnotes and the bibliography. Daniel's last name is at times spelled "Tsharni." I refer to him here as "Daniel Charney." Baruch took up the name "Vladeck" as his *nom de guerre* in his youth. His name is often rendered "Baruch Vladeck Charney," or simply "Baruch Vladeck." In this work, I refer to him as "Baruch Charney Vladeck." On the problematics of Shmuel Charney's pen name, see Eli Bromberg, "We Need to Talk about Shmuel Charney," *In geveb* (October 2019), accessed October 31, 2021, https://ingeveb.org/articles/we -need-to-talk-about-shmuel-charney.

7. Shimeon Brisman, *A History and Guide to Judaic Encyclopedias and Lexicons* (Cincinnati: Hebrew Union College Press, 1987), 1; Madeleine Herren, "General Knowledge and Civil Society: An Accurate and Popular View of the Present Im- proved State of Human Knowledge," in *Allgemeinwissen und Gesellschaft: Akten des Internationalen Kongresses über Wissenstransfer und Enzyklopädische Ordnungs- systeme, vom 18. bis 21. September 2003 in Prangins*, ed. Paul Michel, Madeleine Herren, and Martin Rüesch (Aachen: Shaker Verlag, 2007), 491. Robert Darnton explains that "philosophers had rearranged mental furniture since the time of Ar- istotle." In Robert Darnton, "Philosophers Trim the Tree of Knowledge," chap. 5 in *The Great Cat Massacre and Other Episodes in French Cultural History* (New York: Vintage, 1984), 193. On initiatives in ancient China, see Jun Wenren, *Ancient Chinese Encyclopedia of Technology: Translation and Annotation of Kaogong Ji, the Artificers' Record* (New York: Taylor & Francis, 2012). I thank Qiong Zhang for this reference. On Islamic encyclopedia practices, see Elias Muhanna, *The World in a Box: Al-Nuwayri and the Islamic Encyclopedic Tradition* (Princeton: Princeton University Press, 2018). I thank Charles Wilkins for this reference.

8. Kathleen Hardesty Doig, "Encircling Encyclopedias," *Eighteenth-Century Studies* 36, no. 3 (Spring 2003): 442.

9. By the time Diderot and his colleague Jean le Rond d'Alembert came to edit the *Encyclopédie* (a collaborative project with over a hundred individual contribu- tors), there existed a tradition of "modern" encyclopedias that stretched back nearly a century. The original prospectus for what became the *Encyclopédie* called for the project to consist of a French translation of Ephraim Chambers's 1746 English-language *Cyclopaedia, or an Universal Dictionary of Arts and Sciences*. See Yeo, xii–xiii.

10. Denis Diderot, "Encyclopédie," in *The Portable Enlightenment Reader*, ed. Isaac Kramnick (New York: Penguin Books, 1995), 17–18.

11. John H. Lienhard, "Diderot's Encyclopedia," in "Engines of Our Ingenuity," episode 122, accessed October 31, 2021, http://www.uh.edu/engines/epi122.htm.

12. Yeo, xii.

13. Herren, 489.

14. The title of the first Brockhaus was *Conversations-Lexikon mit vorzüglicher Rücksicht auf die gegenwärtigen Zeiten*.

15. Herren, 490.

16. Robert Collison, *Encyclopaedias: Their History throughout the Ages* (New York and London: Hafner Publishing Company, 1964), 1–20.

17. Herren, 495. Also see Benedict Anderson, *Imagined Communities* (London: Verso, 1983), in particular, chap. 10, "Census, Map, Museum."

18. On the *Encyklopedia Powszechna*, see "Polish Encyclopedias," University of Illinois Library, accessed October 31, 2021, https://www.library.illinois.edu/ias/spx/slavicresearchguides/encyclopedias/poland/polency2/. Like the *Algemeyne entsiklopedye*, the *Encyklopedia Powszechna* had its publishing schedule interrupted several times, in particular on account of the failed 1863 Polish national uprising against Russia. On the "Encyclopedia Africana," see W. E. B. Du Bois and Guy B. Johnson, *Encyclopedia of the Negro: Preparatory Volume with Reference Lists and Reports* (New York: Phelps-Stokes Fund, 1945) and Kwame Anthony Appiah and Henry Louis Gates Jr., eds., *Africana: The Encyclopedia of the African and African American Experience*, 2nd ed. (Oxford: Oxford University Press, 2005), xi–xv. Philip Mattar, ed., *The Encyclopedia of the Palestinians*, rev. ed. (New York: Facts on File, 2005).

19. Theodore Wiener, "Encyclopedias," in *Encyclopaedia Judaica*, 2nd ed., ed. Fred Skolnik (Detroit: Thomson Gale, 2007), 399. Also see Brisman, 1–21.

20. Beer Perlhefter and Bella Perlhefter, *Be'er Sheva: An Edition of a Seventeenth Century Yiddish Encyclopedia*, ed. Nathanael Riemer and Sigrid Senkbeil (Wiesbaden: Harrassowitz Verlag, 2011). On whether the Perlhefters' volume can accurately be considered an encyclopedic work, Riemer and Senkbeil argue that "*Be'er Sheva* . . . wants to cover essential aspects of Jewish knowledge from the secular to the future world, and from earth's creation to the resurrection of the dead. With this in mind, the manuscript can be considered to be an encyclopedia that replaces a library for the reader who has not mastered the Hebrew language," xxix.

21. Ibid., vii.

22. See Brisman, "Introduction."

23. Their outline was also published the following year. See David Cassel and Moritz Steinschneider, *Plan der Real-Encyclopädie des Judenthums, zunächst für die Mitarbeiter* (Krotoschin: B. L. Monasch & Sohn, 1844).

24. Arndt Engelhardt, "Moritz Steinschneider's Notion of Encyclopedias," trans. William Templer, in *Studies on Steinschneider: Moritz Steinschneider and the Emergence of the Science of Judaism in Nineteenth-Century Germany*, ed. Reimund Leicht and Gad Freudenthal (Leiden, Boston: Brill 2012), 109–153.

25. For representations of Jews and Judaism in German encyclopedias of the nineteenth century, see Kirsten Belgum, "Translated Knowledge in the Early

Nineteenth Century: Jews and Judaism in Brockhaus' *Conversations-Lexikon* and the *Encyclopaedia Americana*," in *Simon Dubnow Institute Yearbook* 9 (2010): 303–322.

26. Engelhardt, 120–122.

27. Ibid., 122.

28. Ibid., 124.

29. Adam Rubin, "Jewish Nationalism and the Encyclopaedic Imagination: The Failure (and Success) of Ahad Ha'am's 'Otsar Hayahadut,'" *Journal of Modern Jewish Studies* 3 (2004): 247.

30. Ibid., 254. Rubin here is quoting Ahad Ha'am himself.

31. Ibid., 259.

32. Ibid., 263.

33. There is a wide body on the literature of the efforts to collect and preserve Jewish national treasures in this period. See, for example, Samuel Kassow's discussion of interwar Poland in *Who Will Write Our History?: Emanuel Ringelblum, the Warsaw Ghetto, and the Oyneg Shabes Archive* (Bloomington: Indiana University Press, 2007), in particular chap. 3, "History for the People"; Jeffrey Veidlinger, *Jewish Public Culture in the Late Russian Empire* (Bloomington: Indiana University Press, 2009), in particular chap. 8, "The Jewish Historical and Ethnographic Society: Collecting the Jewish Past"; and Cecile Esther Kuznitz, *YIVO and the Making of Modern Jewish Culture: Scholarship for the Yiddish Nation* (Cambridge: Cambridge University Press, 2014), in particular chap. 1, "'Language Raised to the Level of a Political Factor': Yiddish Scholarship before YIVO."

34. On the making of modern Hebrew, see Robert Alter, *The Invention of Hebrew Prose: Modern Fiction and the Language Revolution* (Seattle: University of Washington Press, 1988); Benjamin Harshav, *Language in Time of Revolution* (Berkeley: University of California Press, 1993); and Todd Hasak-Lowy, *Here and Now: History, Nationalism, and Realism in Modern Hebrew Fiction* (Syracuse: Syracuse University Press, 2008).

35. On the making of modern Yiddish culture, see, in addition to Kassow, *Who Will Write Our History?*, and Kuznitz, *YIVO and the Making of Modern Jewish Culture*, Sarah Abrevaya Stein, *Making Jews Modern: The Yiddish and Ladino Press in the Russian and Ottoman Empires* (Bloomington: Indiana University Press, 2004); David E. Fishman, *The Rise of Modern Yiddish Culture* (Pittsburgh, University of Pittsburgh Press: 2005); Barry Trachtenberg, *The Revolutionary Roots of Modern Yiddish, 1903–1917* (Syracuse: Syracuse University Press, 2008); and Kalman Weiser, *Jewish People, Yiddish Nation: Noah Prylucki and the Folkists in Poland* (Toronto: University of Toronto Press, 2011).

36. Isidore Singer, ed., *The Jewish Encyclopedia* (New York: Funk and Wagnalls, 1901–1906). Also Joseph Jacobs, *The Jewish Encyclopedia: A Guide to Its Contents,*

an Aid to Its Use (New York and London: Funk and Wagnalls, 1906). The history of the *Jewish Encyclopedia* has been told by Shuly Rubin Schwartz in *The Emergence of Jewish Scholarship in America: The Publication of the Jewish Encyclopedia* (Cincinnati: Hebrew Union College Press, 1991) and by Yaakov Ariel in "A Proud Announcement: *Jewish Encyclopedia* and the Coming of Age of Jewish Scholarship in America," in *Simon Dubnow Institute Yearbook* 9 (2010): 381–404. The biographical information on Singer is drawn from Schwartz, 19–24. Also see Jessica L. Carr, "Reconstructing History: The *Jewish Encyclopedia*," chap. 4 in *The Hebrew Orient: Palestine in Jewish American Visual Culture, 1901–1938* (Albany: State University Press of New York, 2020), 133–170.

37. Ariel, 385.

38. Ibid., 393. Also Henry D. Shapiro, "Review of *The Emergence of Jewish Scholarship in America: The Publication of the Jewish Encyclopedia*," *AJS Review* 19, no. 1 (1994): 112–113.

39. Ariel, 390.

40. Yehudah Leib-Binyamin Katzenelson et al., eds., *Evreiskaia entsiklopediia* (St. Petersburg, Brokhaus-Efron, 1906–1913). Jeffrey Veidlinger, "'Emancipation: See Anti-Semitism'—The *Evreiskaia entsiklopediia* and Jewish Public Culture," in *Simon Dubnow Institute Yearbook* 9 (2010): 405.

41. Veidlinger, *Jewish Public Culture in the Late Russian Empire*.

42. Veidlinger, "'Emancipation: See Anti-Semitism,'" 408.

43. Jacob Klatzkin, Nahum Goldmann, and Ismar Elbogen, eds., *Encyclopaedia Judaica* (Berlin: Eshkol 1928–1934).

44. Michael Brenner, *The Renaissance of Jewish Culture in Weimar Germany* (New Haven: Yale University Press, 1996).

45. Arndt Engelhardt, "The *Encyclopaedia Judaica* (1928–1934): A Cultural Arsenal of Knowledge at an Existential Junction," trans. William Templer, in *Simon Dubnow Institute Yearbook* 9 (2010): 428. Also see Engelhardt, *Arsenale Judischen Wissens: Zur Entstehungsgeschichte der* Encyclopaedia Judaica (Göttingen: Vandenhoeck and Ruprecht, 2013). Also see Brisman, 52–59.

46. "Tsu di lezer," *Di literarishe monatsshriftn* 1 (February 1908): 7–8.

47. For a general overview of Yiddish-language school systems in the early twentieth century, see S.T., "Dos yidishe shulvezn," in *Algemeyne entsiklopedye: Yidn giml*, cols. 383–424 (New York, 1942). On Yiddish schools in Eastern Europe, see Ezra Mendelsohn, *The Jews of East Central Europe between the World Wars* (Bloomington: Indiana University Press, 1983); and Joshua D. Zimmerman, "TSYSHO," in *The YIVO Encyclopedia of Jews in Eastern Europe*, ed. Gershon David Hundert (New Haven: Yale University Press, 2008), 1919–1920. On Yiddish schools in the Soviet Union, see Arkadi Zeltser, "Soviet Yiddish-Language

Schools," trans. Yisrael Cohen, in *The YIVO Encyclopedia*, 1790–1791. On Yiddish schools in the United States, see Fradle Pomerantz Freidenreich, *Passionate Pioneers: The Story of Yiddish Secular Education in North America, 1910–1960* (Teaneck, NJ: Holmes & Meier Publishers, 2010) and Naomi Prawer Kadar, *Raising Secular Jews: Yiddish Schools and Their Periodicals for American Children, 1917–1950* (Waltham, MA: Brandeis University Press, 2016). On Soviet Yiddish institutions, see David Shneer, *Yiddish and the Creation of Soviet Jewish Culture, 1918–1930* (Cambridge, Cambridge University Press, 2004), 60–87. On the pre–World War II history of YIVO, see Kuznitz, *YIVO and the Making of Modern Jewish Culture.*

48. Brisman, 36. For overviews of Yiddish encyclopedic projects, see Nakhman Meisel, "A groyse yidishe entsiklopedye," *Literarishe bleter* 13 (1930): 242–244; Meisel, "Mir hobn keyn mazl nisht tsu a yidisher entsiklopedye," *Yidishe kultur* 5 (May 1954): 5–11; and Brisman, 34–36, 44–48, and 59–61.

49. David E. Fishman, *Embers Plucked from the Fire: The Rescue of Jewish Cultural Treasures in Vilna* (New York, YIVO Institute for Jewish Research, 1996); ibid., *The Book Smugglers: Partisans, Poets, and the Race to Save Jewish Treasures from the Nazis* (Lebanon, NH: ForeEdge, University Press of New England, 2017), Alexandra Garbarini, *Numbered Days: Diaries and the Holocaust* (New Haven: Yale University Press, 2006); and Kassow, *Who Will Write Our History?*

50. Annette Wieviorka, *The Era of the Witness*, trans. Jared Stark (Ithaca, NY: Cornell University Press, 2006); Laura Jockusch, *Collect and Record!: Jewish Holocaust Documentation in Early Postwar Europe* (Oxford: Oxford University Press, 2012); Lisa Moses Leff, *The Archive Thief: The Man Who Salvaged French Jewish History in the Wake of the Holocaust* (Oxford: Oxford University Press, 2015); and Dan Rabinowitz, *The Lost Library: The Legacy of Vilna's Strashun Library in the Aftermath of the Holocaust* (Waltham, MA: Brandeis University Press, 2019).

51. Roni Stauber, "Laying the Foundations for Holocaust Research: The Impact of Philip Friedman," *Search and Research Lectures and Papers* 15 (Jerusalem: Yad Vashem International Institute for Holocaust Research, 2009); Natalia Aleksiun, "Philip Friedman and the Emergence of Holocaust Scholarship: A Reappraisal," in *Simon Dubnow Institute Yearbook* 11 (2012): 333–46; ibid., "An Invisible Web: Philip Friedman and the Network of Holocaust Research," in *Als der Holocaust noch keinen Namen hatte: Zur frühen Aufarbeitung des NS-Massenmordes an den Juden / Before the Holocaust Had Its Name: Early Confrontations of the Nazi Mass Murder of the Jews* (Vienna: New Academic Press, 2016), 149–165; and Jan Schwarz, *Survivors and Exiles: Yiddish Culture after the Holocaust* (Detroit: Wayne State University Press, 2015).

52. Eli Lederhendler, "The Eastern European Jewish Past and Its Historians: Cultural Interventions in Postwar America," ed. Eliyana R. Adler and Sheila E.

Jelen, in *Reconstructing the Old Country: American Jewry in the Post-Holocaust Decades* (Detroit: Wayne State University Press, 2017), 23–43; Markus Krah, *American Jewry and the Re-invention of the East European Jewish Past* (Berlin: De Gruyter Oldenbourg, 2018); Mark L. Smith, *The Yiddish Historians and the Struggle for a Jewish History of the Holocaust* (Detroit: Wayne State University Press, 2019); and Alec Eliezer Burko, "Saving Yiddish: Yiddish Studies and the Language Sciences in America, 1940–1970," (PhD diss., The Jewish Theological Seminary, 2019).

53. David Engel addresses this in *Historians of the Jews and the Holocaust* (Stanford: Stanford University Press, 2009).

54. An exception is Brisman, who dedicated several pages to the *Algemeyne entsiklopedye* in his *History and Guide*, pages 62–70.

1. A Bible for the New Age

1. Simon Dubnow, "Vi azoy zaynen mir gekumen fun yidishe entsiklopedye tsu an entsiklopedye in Yidish," Central Archives of the History of the Jewish People (CAHJP), Simon Dubnow Papers, folder 1; Tsaytvaylike komisye farn Dubnov-fond baym yivo, "Seder-hayom fun der baratung: april, dem 14–15 februar," YIVO Archives RG 1.1, folder 15, Dubnov-fond, items returned to Vilna. See also the reference in "Barikhtn: entsiklopedye af yidish," *YIVO Bleter* 1, no. 3 (March 1931): 285–86.

2. Dubnow, "Vi azoy."

3. On the efforts to ensure the protection of national minorities after the war, see Carole Fink, *Defending the Rights of Others: The Great Powers, the Jews, and International Minority Protection, 1878–1938* (Cambridge: Cambridge University Press, 2006).

4. Ezra Mendelsohn, *The Jews of East Central Europe between the World Wars*, 14.

5. Figures from Martin Gilbert, *Atlas of the Holocaust* (London: Michael Joseph Limited, 1982), 32.

6. The Minorities Treaty guaranteed legal rights to all inhabitants without regard to nationality, race, religion, or birthplace. Its goal was to protect minority populations in several of the nation-states that formed after World War I. See Fink, *Defending the Rights of Others*.

7. Ezra Mendelsohn, "Jewish Politics in Interwar Poland: An Overview," in *The Jews of Poland between Two World Wars*, ed. Yisrael Gutman et al. (Hanover and London: Brandeis University Press, 1989), 12. Also see Kassow's discussion of interwar Poland in *Who Will Write Our History?*, in particular chaps. 1–3.

8. See the discussions in Stein, *Making Jews Modern*; Trachtenberg, *The Revolutionary Roots of Modern Yiddish*; Weiser, *Jewish People, Yiddish Nation*; and Kuznitz, *YIVO and the Making of Modern Jewish Culture*.

9. Hillel Kazovsky, "Kultur-lige," in *YIVO Encyclopedia*, 953–956.

10. On the lack of a single Yiddish "center," see Kalman Weiser, "The Capital of 'Yiddishland'?," in *Warsaw. The Jewish Metropolis: Essays in Honor of the 75ᵗʰ Birthday of Professor Antony Polonsky*, ed. Glenn Dynner and François Guesnet (Leiden and Boston: Brill, 2015), 298–322.

11. On Eastern European Jewry in Weimar-era Berlin, see the essays in *Transit und Transformation: Osteuropäische Migranten in Berlin 1918–1939*, ed. Verena Dohrn and Gertrud Pickhan (Göttingen: Wallstein Verlag, 2010). See also Tobias Brinkmann, "From Hinterberlin to Berlin: Jewish Migrants from Eastern Europe in Berlin before and after 1918," *Journal of Modern Jewish Studies* 7, no. 3 (November 2008): 339–355.

12. Brenner, *The Renaissance of Jewish Culture*, 33. See also Delphine Bechtel, "Cultural Transfers between 'Ostjuden' and 'Westjuden': German-Jewish Intellectuals and Yiddish Culture 1897–1930," in *Leo Baeck Institute Year Book* 42 (1997): 69. Bechtel writes, "The number of Eastern European Jews in Germany swelled from 15,000 in 1880 to 78,000 in 1910. It reached 90,000 in 1914 and 107,000 in 1925."

13. Elias Tcherikower, "Di ranglenishn fun yidish in Daytshland," *Literarishe bleter* 20 (1932): 309–311. Also see Brenner, *The Renaissance of Jewish Culture in Weimar Germany*, in particular part 3, "In Search of Authenticity," and David N. Myers, "'Distant Relatives Happening onto the Same Inn': The Meeting of East and West as Literary Theme and Cultural Ideal," *Jewish Social Studies* 1, no. 2 (Winter 1995): 75–100.

14. A discussion of one such collaboration can be found in the essay by Heather Valencia, "A Yiddish Poet Engages with German Society: A. N. Stencl's Weimar Period," in *Yiddish in Weimar Berlin: At the Crossroads of Diaspora Politics and Culture*, ed. Gennady Estraikh and Mikhail Krutikov (Oxford: Legenda Press, 2010), 57–72.

15. Verena Dohrn, "Diplomacy in the Diaspora: The Jewish Telegraphic Agency in Berlin (1922–1933)," in *Leo Baeck Institute Year Book* 54 (2009): 224. Also see Verena Dohrn and Anne-Christin Saß, "Einfürung," in *Transit und Transformation: Osteuropäisch-jüdische Migranten in Berlin 1981–1939*, 9–22; Arthur Tilo Alt, "Yiddish and Berlin's Scheunenviertel," *Shofar* 9.2 (1991): 29–43; and the essays in Stiftung Jüdisches Museum Berlin, *Berlin Transit: Jüdische Migranten aus Osteuropea in den 1920er Jahren* (Göttingen: Wallstein Verlag, 2012).

16. On the cultural interaction between German and Eastern European Jews, see Shachar M. Pinsker, "Berlin: Between the Scheunenviertel and the Romanisches Café," chap. 6 in *Literary Passports: The Making of Modernist Hebrew Fiction in Europe* (Stanford: Stanford University Press, 2011); Allison Schachter, "Yiddish Modernism in Weimar Berlin," chap. 3 in *Diasporic Modernisms: Hebrew*

and Yiddish Literature in the Twentieth Century (Oxford: Oxford University Press, 2012); and Marc Caplan, *Yiddish Writers in Weimar Berlin: A Fugitive Modernism* (Bloomington: Indiana University Press, 2021).

17. See Gerben Zaagsma, "Transnational Networks of Jewish Migrant Radicals: The Case of Berlin," in *Transit und Transformation: Osteuropäische Migranten in Berlin 1918–1939*, 218–233.

18. N. Shtif, "Vegn a yidishn akademishn institut," in *Di organizatsye fun der yidisher visnshaft* (Vilna: Tsentraler Bildungs-komitet and Vilbig, 1925): 3–33.

19. Leo Fuks and Renate Fuks, "Yiddish Publishing Activities in the Weimar Republic, 1920–1933," in *Leo Baeck Institute Year Book* 30 (1988): 421–422. Also see Marc Raeff, *Russia Abroad: A Cultural History of the Russian Emigration, 1919–1939* (Oxford: Oxford University Press, 1990), 75.

20. See the interview with Rachel Wischnitzer in Francesco Melfi, "A Rhetoric of Image and Word: The Magazine *Milgroym/Rimon*, 1922–1924 and the Jewish Search for Inclusivity," (PhD diss., Jewish Theological Seminary, 1996), 225–226. Later in the interview Wischnitzer stated, "The main thing was to send to America" (ibid., 228).

21. See Gennady Estraikh, "Vilna on the Spree: Yiddish in Weimar Berlin," *Aschkenaz—Zeitschrift für Geschichte und Kultur der Juden* 16 (2006), 109–110. On Yiddish journalism in Berlin, also see Estraikh, "Weimar Berlin—An International Press Centre," in *Transit und Transformation: Osteuropäisch-jüdische Migranten in Berlin 1981–1939*, 77–92.

22. Amy Blau, "Max Weinreich in Weimar Germany," in *Yiddish in Weimar Berlin: At the Crossroads of Diaspora Politics and Culture*, ed. Gennady Estraikh and Mikhail Krutikov (Oxford: Legenda Press, 2010), 163–178; and Gennady Estraikh, "Jacob Lestschinsky: A Yiddishist Dreamer and Social Scientist," *Science in Context* 20 (June 2007): 222–225.

23. A parallel phenomenon occurred within Berlin Hebrew literary culture. See Arnold J. Band, "From Diaspora to Homeland: The Transfer of the Hebrew Literary Center to Eretz Yisrael," in *Studies in Modern Jewish Literature* (Philadelphia: Jewish Publication Society, 2003), 143–156.

24. Moyshe Shalit, "Entsiklopedyes," *Bikhervelt* 1 (April 1928): 38. Perhaps in a reflection of the animus he held for the *Encyclopaedia Judaica*, Shalit also published an equally critical review of the inaugural volume in *Di yidishe velt* 6 (September 1928): 457–470.

25. Ibid., 46.

26. These attempts included F. F. Pavlenkov's 1899 release of a one-volume encyclopedic dictionary that was reprinted four times prior to the 1917 revolution. Florentii Fedorovich Pavlenkov, *Entsiklopedicheskii slovar'* (St. Petersburg: Brockhaus-Efron, 1899).

27. Brisman, 36. The first two volumes are held at the Jewish National and University Library in Jerusalem. Although some have asserted that three, and even four, were published, no fascicles beyond the first two are known (Brisman, 384, n. 55).

28. The project fell through when, reportedly, co-compiler Khaim Tshemerinski failed to complete his task, as reported by Reisen to Yashunsky. See Yosef Yashunsky, "Pruvn fun yidishe entsiklopedyes," *Bikhervelt* 2 (1922): 127.

29. Brisman, 44–45.

30. Hillel Zeitlin and Shoyl Stupnitski, *Ersht yidish entsiklopedish verterbukh* (Warsaw: Farlag Hantbikher, 1917).

31. Yashunsky, "Pruvn," 130–131.

32. Jacob Lestschinsky, "Di yidishe entsiklopedye," *Bikhervelt* 2–3 (1919): 14.

33. Nakhmen Meisel, "A groyse yidishe entsiklopedye," *Literarishe bleter* 13 (1930): 242–244.

34. Ibid., 244.

35. Lestschinsky, 14.

36. Alexander Harkavy, *Yidish-english-hebreisher verterbukh* (New York: Alexander Harkavy, 1925); Zalmen Reisen, ed., *Leksikon fun der yidisher literatur, prese un filologye*, 4 vols. (Vilna: Boris Kletskin, 1926).

37. Ibid., 243.

38. Minutes of Central Board, 14–16 October 1930, YIVO Archives, YIVO Administrative Records, 1925–1941, RG 1.1, Lithuanian addendum, folder 5. Also see *Yedies fun YIVO* 34 (July 3, 1931), which states, "In association with Simon Dubnow's jubilee, a special Dubnow Fund with the purpose of publishing scientific work and supporting young researchers was established." קין is alternately rendered "*Kihn*" or "*Kin*." For consistency, I use *Kin* throughout this work.

39. Moyshe Shalit, "Vegn an entsiklopedye af yidish," *Literarishe bleter* 3 (1931): 37–40.

40. Ibid., 37.

41. Ibid.

42. Ben-Adir is the commonly used pseudonym of Avrom Rozin (ראָזין). In this work, I use *Ben-Adir* consistently (other than in citations where appropriate) to avoid confusion, although he often alternated between the two names in his published works and correspondence. At times, his name is rendered by others as *Rosin* or *Rozen*.

43. Nakhmen Meisel, "Fun troym tsu virklekhkayt: A baratung vegn a yidisher entsiklopedye, Berlin 14–15 februar," *Literarishe bleter* 27 February 1931, 157–60.

44. On Dubnow's contribution and influence on subsequent Jewish scholarship, see Benjamin Nathans, "On Russian-Jewish Historiography," in *Historiography of*

Imperial Russia: The Profession and Writing of History in a Multinational State, ed. Thomas Sanders (Armonk, NY: M. E. Sharpe, 1999), 411–424.

45. Kalman Weiser, "Folkists," in *YIVO Encyclopedia*, 520–521.

46. On Dubnow's role in the Yiddish intellectual world, see Kuznitz, "YIVO's 'Old Friend and Teacher': Simon Dubnow and His Relationship to the Yiddish Scientific Institute," in *Simon Dubnow Institute Yearbook* 15 (2016), 477–507. On Dubnow's relationship to scholarship in the Yiddish language, see Smith, *The Yiddish Historians*, 9–10.

47. See the essays in Stefani Hoffman and Ezra Mendelsohn, eds., *The Revolution of 1905 and Russia's Jews* (Philadelphia: University of Pennsylvania Press, 2008).

48. The biographical information on Abramovitch is drawn from the following: Raphael Abramovitch, *In tsvey revolutsyes: di geshikhte fun a dor* (New York: Arbeter-ring, 1944); Arkadi Zeltser, "Abramovich, Rafail," in *YIVO Encyclopedia*, 1–2; Y[itskhok] Kh[arla]sh, "Abramovitch, Raphael," *Leksikon fun der nayer yidisher literatur*, ed. Shmuel Niger and Jacob Shatzky, vol. 1 (New York: Alveltlekher yidisher kultur-kongres, 1956–81), cols. 12–16; and Estraikh, *Transatlantic Russian Jewishness: Ideological Voyages of the Yiddish Daily* Forverts *in the First Half of the Twentieth Century* (Boston: Academic Studies Press, 2020), 119–127.

49. Karl Kautsky, *Das Erfurter Programm in seinem grundsätzlichen Theil* (Stuttgart, J.H.W. Dietz, 1892).

50. Kh[arlas]h, 12–13.

51. In 1903, the Bund split with the RSDWP over the former's insistence on holding the exclusive right to organize the Jewish proletariat and to have Jews be considered a cultural nation within a federative structure in the Party. See Henry Tobias, "The Bund and the First Congress of the RSDWP: An Addendum," *Russian Review* 24, no. 4. (Oct. 1965): 396.

52. See Gennady Estraikh, *Transatlantic Russian Jewishness*, 124–125.

53. André Liebich, *From the Other Shore: Russian Social Democracy after 1921* (Cambridge, MA: Harvard University Press, 1997), 83–84.

54. Ibid., 23.

55. Gennady Estraikh, *Transatlantic Russian Jewishness*, 120.

56. Raphael Abramovitch and Avrom Menes, *Leyenbukh tsu der geshikhte fun yisroel* 1 (Berlin: Wostok, 1923).

57. On Abramovitch and Cahan's relationship, see Gennady Estraikh, "The Berlin Bureau of the *Forverts*," in *Yiddish in Weimar Berlin: At the Crossroads of Diaspora Politics and Culture*, ed. Gennady Estraikh and Mikhail Krutikov (Oxford: Legenda Press, 2010): 151–4; and Estraikh, "Raphael Abramovitch's Menshevik Voice in the *Forverts*," chap. 4 in *Transatlantic Russian Jewishness*, 119–149.

58. Mordechai Breuer and Michael Graetz, *German-Jewish History in Modern Times*, ed. Michael A. Meyer, assist. ed. Michael Brenner, trans. William Templer, vol. 1, *Tradition and Enlightenment 1600–1780* (New York: Columbia University Press, 1996), 304–312.

59. Ibid., 304.

60. After Hitler's rise to power, some prominent German Jews were rethinking Mendelssohn's translation, criticizing it for having facilitated the Jewish flight from the "ghetto" and the end of traditional Judaism. See Guy Miron, *The Waning of Emancipation: Jewish History, Memory, and the Rise of Fascism in Germany, France, and Hungary* (Detroit: Wayne State University Press, 2011), 34–38 and, for a counter-response, 60–66.

61. Meisel, "Fun troym tsu virklekhkayt," 159.

62. Herzl's original quote was "Wenn ihr wollt, ist es kein Märchen" ("If you will it, it is no dream"), in the epilogue of his 1902 Zionist utopian novel, *Altneuland*.

63. Tsentral-komitet fun Dubnov-fond, "Algemeyne entsiklopedye" (Berlin, 1931): 3.

64. Ibid.

65. Ibid., 4.

66. Leon Bramson, letter to Chaim Zhitlowsky, April 24, 1931, YIVO Chaim Zhitlowsky Papers RG 208, folder 1076. Also see the account by A. B., "Di yidishe amerike far der yidisher entsiklopedye," *Literarishe bleter* 26 (1931): 499–500.

67. "An entsiklopedye af yidish," *Der tog* (May 9, 1931).

68. H. Yulski, "Di entsiklopedye af yidish," *Vokhnshrift far literatur, kunst un kultur* 7 (March 6, 1931): 102–103.

69. The most thorough discussion of these tensions can be found in Kuznitz, *YIVO and the Making of Modern Jewish Culture*, in particular "The Dilemmas of Political Engagement," 99–109.

70. Ibid., 99.

71. Mendelsohn, "Jewish Politics in Interwar Poland: An Overview," 13, 14.

72. See Glenn S. Levine, "Yiddish Publishing in Berlin and the Crisis in Eastern European Jewish Culture 1919–1924," in *Leo Baeck Institute Year Book* 42 (1997): 92–93. On the role of Berlin's coffeehouses as a meeting place for Jewish artists and writers, see Shachar M. Pinsker, *A Rich Brew: How Cafés Created Modern Jewish Culture* (New York: New York University Press, 2018), 173–185.

73. Anne-Christin Saß, "Reports from the 'Republic Lear': David Einhorn in Weimar Berlin 1920–24," in *Yiddish in Weimar Berlin: At the Crossroads of Diaspora Politics and Culture*, ed. Gennady Estraikh and Mikhail Krutikov (Oxford: Legenda Press, 2010), 182.

74. A. A. Robak, "A bisl mer vaytzikhtikayt," *Literarishe bleter* 37 (1931): 709.

75. Ibid.

76. Yosef Yashunsky, "Tsu der diskusye vegn an algemeyner entsiklopedye af yidish," *YIVO Bleter* 2 (Dec. 1931): 289–307 and "Farnem un kharakter fun der yidisher entsiklopedye," *YIVO Bleter* 3 (1932): 121–39.

77. K. K. Arsen'ev, ed. *Novyi entsiklopedicheskii slovar'* (St. Petersburg, Brock-haus and Efron: 1911–1916).

78. Yashunsky, "Pruvn fun yidishe entsiklopedyes," *Bikhervelt* 2 (1922): 132. Stress in the original.

79. Yashunsky, "Tsu der diskusye," 289. He also cites Shalit: "The Yiddish ency-clopedia must become the center around which the scientific and spiritual cre-ations of all cultural strengths should be concentrated."

80. Ibid., 290.

81. Ibid., 292.

82. Yashunsky, "Farnem un kharakter," 126.

83. Yashunsky, "Tsu der diskusye," 289.

84. Yashunsky, "Farnem un kharakter," 127.

85. Kuznitz, *YIVO and the Making of Modern Jewish Culture,* 165.

86. Yashunsky, "Farnem un kharakter," 133.

87. Nakhmen Meisel, "Afn frishn keyver fun Nokhem Gergel," *Literarishe bleter* 48 (1931): 889–890. Also see Robak, "A bisl mer vaytzikhtikayt," 709; and the letter of the American Committee of the Yiddish Encyclopedia, September 25, 1931, YIVO Archives, Chaim Zhitlowsky Papers, RG 208, folder 1076.

88. For example, see the partial letter of May 12, 1931, from the Tsentral-komitet, Gezelshaft Dubnov-fond, to YIVO, which discusses organizational differences be-tween the two groups, YIVO Archives, RG 1.1, folder 15, Dubnov-fond, items re-turned to Vilna. Also see the letter of September 19, 1931, from Bramson and Kin to YIVO in which they appeal for a "harmonious" relationship between the Dubnow Fund and YIVO, in YIVO Archives, RG 1.1, folder 15, Dubnov-Fond, items returned to Vilna.

89. See the discussion in Kuznitz, *YIVO and the Making of Modern Jewish Cul-ture,* 44–70.

90. Ibid., 126.

91. Minutes of Central Board 1930–1935, YIVO Archives, RG 1.1, Lithuanian addendum, folder 13.

92. See Yidisher Visnshaftlekher Institut, *Barikht fun der konferents fun dem yidishn visnshaftlekhn institut: opgehaltn in Vilne fun 24tn bizn 27tn oktober 1929* (Vilna: YIVO, 1930).

93. Di tsentral-farvaltung fun yidishn visnshaftlekhn institut, "Aroyslozndik di YIVO-Bleter," *YIVO Bleter* 1 (January 1931): 1.

94. Ibid., 3.

95. Tsentral-komitet fun Dubnov-fond, "Algemeyne entsiklopedye," 5.

96. Simon Dubnow, *Weltgeschichte des jüdischen Volkes*, trans. Aaron Steinberg (Berlin: Jüdischer Verlag 1925–1929). The first Yiddish translation was published in an abridged three-volume format as *Di nayste geshikhte fun yidishn folk fun di alte tsaytn biz tsu hayntiker tsayt*, trans. Nokhem Shtif and Khaim-Shloyme Kazhdan (Warsaw: Kultur-lige, 1931).

97. Leon Bramson to Shmuel Niger, July 29, 1931, YIVO Archives, Shmuel Niger Papers, RG 360, folder 589.

98. Kuznitz, *YIVO and the Making of Modern Jewish Culture*, 141.

99. "Komunikat fun Dubnov-fond un YIVO," YIVO Archives, Chaim Zhitlowsky Papers, RG 208, folder 1076, and YIVO Archives, Jacob Shatzky Papers, RG 356, folder 32.

100. Ibid.

101. Letter to Chaim Zhitlowsky from Raphael Abramovitch and Jacob Lestschinsky, January 23, 1932, YIVO Archives, Chaim Zhitlowsky Papers, RG 208, folder 1076; letter to Jacob Shatzky from Raphael Abramovitch and Jacob Lestschinsky, January 23, 1932, YIVO Archives, Jacob Shatzky Papers, RG 356, folder 32; and letter to Alexander Mukdoni from Raphael Abramovitch and Jacob Lestschinsky, January 23, 1932, YIVO Archives, Alexander Mukdoni Papers, RG 227, folder 23. Also see the exchange between Kalmanovitch and Yashunsky from January 1932, YIVO Archives, RG 1.1, folder 34. Meisel's February 1931 report in *Literarishe bleter* indicates that even at the outset, there was concern over whether YIVO would be able to dedicate the time and energy to such a large undertaking. "Will not the encyclopedia paralyze the work of YIVO?," Meisel, 158.

102. See the letter to Alexander Mukdoni, February 20, 1932, YIVO Archives, Alexander Mukdoni Papers, RG 227, folder 23. Abramovitch makes the case that in spite of YIVO's formal disengagement with the Dubnow Fund, many of its key members, such as Lestschinsky, Tcherikower, Yashunsky, and Weinreich, remain involved.

103. For this quote and those that follow in this section, see the untitled introduction to *Algemeyne entsiklopedye: probeheft* (Berlin: Dubnow Fund, 1932), unpaginated [all stresses in the original].

104. "Tannaim" and "Ge'onim" refer to generations of rabbinic sages. "Rambam" and "Besht" are acronyms for famous rabbinic leaders: Rabbi Moses ben Maimon (1138–1204) and Rabbi Israel ben Eliezer (ca. 1698–1760, who was also known as the Baal Shem Tov, or Master of the Good Name). "Herzl" refers to the Zionist leader Theodor Herzl (1860–1904) and "Medem" refers to the Bundist leader Vladimir Medem (1879–1923). Elye Bokher (aka Eliahu Levita, 1469–1549)

was an author of Yiddish romantic epic poetry, and Yitskhok Leybush Peretz (1852–1915) and Sholem Asch (1880–1957) were major modern Yiddish writers.

105. Simon Dubnow, "Hasidut, Hasidism," *Algemeyne entsiklopedye: probeheft*, 25.

106. Support to the Dubnow Fund even came from faraway places, such as the letter from A. Dembo, a Johannesburg-based seller of Jewish books. Correspondence from A. Dembo, January 18, 1933, YIVO Archives, RG 1.1, Records of YIVO (Vilna): Administration folder 15.

107. Daniel Charney, "Der onheyb iz gemakht (a briv fun berlin)," *Yidish: Vokhnshrift fun der yidisher kultur-gezelshaft* (May 27, 1932): 13.

108. Klinov had been present at the February 1931 meeting. See Meisel, 158.

109. Yeshayahu Klinov, "Shekheyonu," *Haynt*, May 2, 1932.

110. Ibid.

111. Ibid.

112. Ibid.

113. Herman Svet, "Der ershter aroysfor fun der Dubnov-entsiklopedye," *Moment*, May 13, 1932.

114. Ibid.

115. Ibid.

116. *Algemeyne entsiklopedye: probeheft*, 2nd ed. (Berlin: Dubnow Fund, 1933).

117. Nakhmen Meisel, "Brener, Yosef-Khaim," in *Algemeyne entsiklopedye: probeheft*, 2nd ed., 23.

118. See Matthew Hoffman, *From Rebel to Rabbi: Reclaiming Jesus and the Making of Modern Jewish Culture* (Stanford: Stanford Univ. Press, 2007), 90–116.

119. Dubnow, "30. Januar," *Buch des Lebens* 3, 162–163. Franz von Papen was the recently ousted Chancellor who convinced President Hindenburg to appoint Hitler to the Chancellery. Alfred Hugenberg was head of the German National People's Party (DNVP).

120. Ibid., "6. Februar," 163.

121. Dubnov-Erlich, 209.

122. Estraikh, "Jacob Lestschinsky: A Yiddishist Dreamer and Social Scientist," 227.

123. "Asks Berlin Report in Leschinsky [*sic*] Case: State Department Instructs Embassy to Get Data on Arrest of Newspaper Correspondent," *New York Times*, March 14, 1933; "Special Cable to the New York Times," *New York Times*, March 14, 1933; and "Writer Attacks Germany: Correspondent of Jewish Paper Here Tells of Alleged Terrorism," *New York Times*, March 26, 1933.

124. "Latvia Said to Ban Anti-Nazi," *New York Times*, November 5, 1933.

2. Man Plans, and Hitler Laughs

1. "Ershter band fun algemeyner entsiklopedye af yidish aroys fun druk," *Vilner tog* (January 11, 1935): 3.

2. Moyshe Shalit, "Di yidishe entsiklopedye—a fakt," *Literarishe bleter* 11 (March 15, 1935): 161.

3. A. Mukdoni, "An algemeyne entsiklopedye in yidish," *Tsukunft* 40, no. 5 (May 1935): 298.

4. "Une encyclopédie universelle en yiddisch," *Le Journal Juif* (March 1, 1935): 4. I am grateful to Nick Underwood for alerting me to this source.

5. Estraikh, *Transatlantic Russian Jewishness*, 175.

6. Kuznitz, *YIVO and the Making of Modern Jewish Culture*, 142.

7. Gennady Estraikh, "Tsharni, Daniel," in *YIVO Encyclopedia*, ed. Gershon David Hundert, 1913–1914.

8. Gennady Estraikh, "Jacob Lestschinsky: A Yiddishist Dreamer and Social Scientist," *Science in Context* 20 (June 2007): 230–31.

9. Vicky Caron, *Uneasy Asylum: France and the Jewish Refugee Crisis, 1933–1942* (Stanford, CA: Stanford University Press, 1999), 14–15.

10. Caron, 2.

11. Raeff, *Russia Abroad*, 37.

12. See Caron, 33, and chap. 3, "The Conservative Crackdown of 1934–35," 43–63.

13. On Eastern European Jews in Paris in the period before World War I, see Nancy L. Green, *The Pletzl of Paris: Jewish Immigrant Workers in the Belle Epoque* (New York: Holmes and Meier, 1986), from which much of this description is drawn. Also see David H. Weinberg, *A Community on Trial: The Jews of Paris in the 1930s* (Chicago: The University of Chicago Press, 1977); Jonathan Boyarin, *Polish Jews in Paris: The Ethnography of Memory* (Bloomington, IN: Indiana University Press, 1991); Richard I. Cohen, *The Burden of Conscience: French Jewish Leadership during the Holocaust* (Bloomington: Indiana University Press, 1987); Leff, *The Archive Thief*; Paula Hyman, *From Dreyfus to Vichy: The Remaking of French Jewry, 1906–1939* (New York: Columbia University Press, 1979); and Nick Underwood, *Yiddish Paris: Staging Nation and Community in Interwar France* (Bloomington: Indiana University Press, 2022). I am grateful to Nick Underwood for sharing his book manuscript with me.

14. See Underwood, *Yiddish Paris*. Also see the discussion in Jean Baumgarten and Alan Astro, "Yiddish in France: A Conversation with Rachel Ertel," *Shofar: An Interdisciplinary Journal of Jewish Studies* 14, no. 3, (Spring 1996): 125–137, as referenced in Underwood, *Yiddish Paris*.

15. Zosa Szajkowski, "150 yor yidishe prese in Frankraykh—biblyografye fun der yidisher prese in Frankraykh un in di kolonyes," in *Yidn in Frankraykh: shtudyes un materyaln*, ed. Elias Tcherikower (New York: YIVO, 1942), 1:236–308. Also see the rich description of interwar Yiddish Paris in Gennady Estraikh, "A Quest for Yiddishland: The 1937 World Yiddish Cultural Congress," *QUEST Issues in Contemporary Jewish History* 17 (September 2020): 96–117.

16. Nicholas Lee Underwood, "Staging a New Community: Immigrant Yiddish Culture and Diaspora Nationalism in Interwar Paris, 1919–1940," (PhD diss., University of Colorado, 2016), 40.

17. The French National Assembly, "Debate on the Eligibility of Jews for Citizenship," in *The Jew in the Modern World: A Documentary History*, 3rd ed., ed. Paul Mendes-Flohr and Jehuda Reinharz (Oxford: Oxford University Press, 2011), 124. Originally cited as Achille-Edmond Halphen, ed., J. Rubin, trans., *Recueil des lois: Décrets, Ordonnances, avis du Conseil d'Etat, arrêtés et règlements concernant les israélites depuis la Révolution de 1789* (Paris, 1851).

18. See Paula E. Hyman, *The Jews of Modern France* (Berkeley: University of California Press, 1998), 17–52; Ronald Schechter, *Obstinate Hebrews: Representations of Jews in France, 1715–1815* (Berkeley: University of California Press, 2003).

19. See Pierre Birnbaum, *The Anti-Semitic Moment: A Tour of France in 1898*, trans. Jane Marie Todd (New York: Hill and Wang, 2003).

20. Hyman, *From Dreyfus to Vichy*, 1. Also see Weinberg, 6.

21. Ibid., 63.

22. Cohen, 6–11.

23. See the letters from Avrom Rozin to Aaron Steinberg, February 5, 1934, February 19, 1934, and March 14, 1934, and from Avrom Kin to Aaron Steinberg, February 5, 1934, CAHJP Aaron Steinberg Papers, P159.

24. Avrom Kin would soon once again take on an expanded role. Joshua Karlip writes that in 1933, Zelig Kalmanovitch relocated to Paris to work on the *Entsiklopedye*, since "YIVO endured a severe economic crisis as a result of the worldwide depression and no longer could pay Kalmanovitch's salary." Joshua Michael Karlip, "The Center That Could Not Hold: *Afn Sheydveg* and the Crisis of Diaspora Nationalism," (PhD diss., Jewish Theological Seminary, 2006), 341.

25. Avrom Rozin to Aaron Steinberg, February 19, 1934, CAHJP Aaron Steinberg Papers, P159.

26. Avrom Rozin to Aaron Steinberg, March 27, 1934, CAHJP Aaron Steinberg Papers, P159.

27. See the exchanges between Fishl Gelibter to Abramovitch and Kin, March 3, 1934, and March 10 (or 19, obscured), 1934, IISG Raphael Abramovič Papers, folder 2.

28. Raphael Abramovitch to Simon Dubnow, April 18, 1934, Internationaal Instituut voor Sociale Geschiedenis (IISG) Raphael Abramovič Papers, folder 4. I am grateful to Prof. Mikhail Krutikov for his assistance with the Russian.

29. Simon Dubnow to Raphael Abramovitch, April 25, 1934, IISG Raphael Abramovič Papers, folder 4.

30. See the correspondence between Abramovitch (R. Rein) and Morris Hillquit, April 21, 1933, May 10, 1933, and June 30, 1933, IISG Raphael Abramovič Papers, folder 2.

31. Tsentral-komitet fun "Dubnov-fond," "Hakdome," *Algemeyne entsiklopedye,* vol. 1 (Paris: Association Simon Dubnow, 1934), unpaginated.

32. "Fun der redaktsye," *Algemeyne entsiklopedye,* vol. 1., unpaginated.

33. The entries for Auburn, New York, and Auburn, Maine, defy explanation.

34. Chana C. Schütz, "Lesser Ury and the Jewish Renaissance," *Jewish Studies Quarterly* 10 (2003): 360.

35. Ibid., 369–370. The painting did not survive the Nazi era and "has been missing since the forcible closing of the Jewish Museum in November 1938." Chana C. Schütz, "Lesser Ury: Images from the Bible," in *Lesser Ury—Images from the Bible* (Boca Raton: Boca Raton Museum of Art, 2003), 20. Exhibition catalog.

36. Mentioned in chap. 1. Yashunsky himself was very pleased with the first volume, and praised it effusively in a letter to the Dubnow Fund in February 1935: "Y. Yashunsky to Dubnow Fund," February 3, 1935, IISG Raphael Abramovič Papers, folder 38.

37. Jonathan Frankel, *Prophecy and Politics: Socialism, Nationalism, and the Russian Jews, 1862–1917* (Cambridge: Cambridge University Press, 1981), 329.

38. See the letters of support (along with some criticisms) in IISG Raphael Abramovič Papers, folder 38.

39. A. Mukdoni, "An algemeyne entsiklopedye in yidish," 298.

40. *Literarishe bleter* 11 (March 15, 1935).

41. Shalit, "Di yidishe entsiklopedye—a fakt," 161.

42. Ben-Adir, "A bisl 'makhoyre-haparged' fun der entsiklopedye," *Literarishe bleter* 11 (March 15, 1935): 164.

43. B. Slutski, "A burzhuaze, klerikal-natsyonalistishe entsiklopedye unter der maske fun veltlekhkayt, umparteyishkayt un 'sotsyal-gezonenkayt,'" *Visnshaft un revolutsye* 2, no. 6 (1935): 163.

44. Review of *Algemeyne entsiklopedye,* vol. 1, *Kiryat Sefer* 12 (1935/36): 311–312. In fact, there were concerns among the editors that the volume *not* be too political. Abramovitch rejected a submission by the anarchist leader Alexander Berkman on "The Anarchist Movement Today," for its strong subjectivity. See Alexander Berkman to R. Abramovitch, January 21, 1934, IISG Alexander Berkman Papers, folder

219; and Raphael Abramovič Papers, Paris Folder II Correspondence 1931, 1933, 1934 A-J.

45. Vicki Caron, "The Politics of Frustration: French Jewry and the Refugee Crisis in the 1930s," *The Journal of Modern History* 65, no. 2 (Jun. 1993): 314.

46. Ibid., 316.

47. See Ezra Mendelsohn, "Poland," chap. 1 in *The Jews of East Central Europe between the Two World Wars*, 11–83.

48. Documents testify that in at least one instance, Kin was unsuccessful at finding a distributor. The Home Library Book Company was concerned that its agents would be unsuccessful in selling the encyclopedia with only one volume in print as of early 1935. See Home Library Book Company to J. Pomerantz, March 5, 1935, IISG Raphael Abramovič Papers, folder 38.

49. "Jews Here to Dine in Honor of a Book," *New York Times*, May 12, 1935.

50. Avrom Kin to Alfred Landau, February 7, 1935, YIVO *Algemeyne Entsiklopedye* Papers, RG 1149, folder 72.

51. Nakhmen Meisel to Avrom Kin, February 17, 1935, YIVO *Algemeyne Entsiklopedye* Papers, RG 1149, folder 73. Also see the exchanges between Gitl Meisel and Avrom Kin, in ibid.

52. Isaac Meisel to Dubnov-fond, January 6, 1935, YIVO *Algemeyne Entsiklopedye* Papers, RG 1149, folder 75.

53. Avrom Kin to Isaac Meisel, April 10, 1935, in ibid.

54. See the letters from Abramovitch to "Dear Friend," April 11, April 26, and May 4, 1935, YIVO *Algemeyne Entsiklopedye* Papers RG 1149, folder 55.

55. Few reviews of volume 2 appeared in the Yiddish press. Among them is Menakhem Shapiro, "A por bamerkungen vegn der algemeyner entsiklopedye in yidish," *Haynt*, April 3, 1936, 7, which criticized several errors found in historical articles. A review by the poet B. Alquit (the pen name of Eliezer Blum) in the journal *Inzikh* (Introspectivism) criticized volume 2 in part for not including an entry on "Inzikh" as a poetic movement and suggested that it could be remedied in volume 3 with an entry on "Introspective," which did not ever appear. See B. A-T, "Refleksyes: notitsn af der zayt fun umshterblekhkayt (Reflections: Notes on the margin of immortality), *Inzikh* 21 (February 1936): 108–112.

56. In fairness, the Yiddish language contains an inordinately high number of words that begin with *alef*. For example, in Uriel Weinreich's *Modern English-Yiddish, Yiddish-English Dictionary* (New York: Schocken Books, 1977), the number of Yiddish words beginning with *alef* make up nearly 18 percent of the total. Additionally, the dictionary does not account for the high number of proper nouns that also begin with the letter *alef* but which are included in the encyclopedia.

57. See Raphael Abramovitch and Baruch Charney Vladeck correspondence, IISG Raphael Abramovič Papers, folder 9.

58. Richard Pankhurst, "Jewish Settlement in Ethiopia: Plans for Mass Jewish Settlement in Ethiopia (1936–1943)," accessed October 31, 2021, https://tezetaethiopia.wordpress.com/2005/04/20/plans-for-mass-jewish-settlement-in-ethiopia-1936-1943br-smallby-richarch-pankhurst/.

59. Emanuel Melzer, *No Way Out: The Politics of Polish Jewry 1935–1939* (Cincinnati: Hebrew Union College Press, 1997), 74–76.

60. See Gerben Zaagsma, *Jewish Volunteers, the International Brigades and the Spanish Civil War* (London: Bloomsbury, 2017).

61. The commission was formally known as the Palestine Royal Commission. See the study by Penny Sinanoglou, *Partitioning Palestine: British Policymaking at the End of Empire* (Chicago: University of Chicago Press, 2019).

62. Ben-Adir (Avrom Rozin), "Moker un mehus fun a'" in "Antisemitzm," *Algemeyne entsiklopedye*, vol. 3, ed. Raphael Abramovitch et al. (Paris, Dubnov-fond, 1936), 453.

63. Gur Alroey, *Zionism without Zion: The Jewish Territorial Organization and Its Conflict with the Zionist Organization* (Detroit: Wayne State University Press, 2016).

64. Ibid., 264.

65. See also Yankl Salant, "Frayland-lige," in *YIVO Encyclopedia*, ed. Gershon David Hundert, 545–547.

66. Alroey, 272–273.

67. Willy Brandt and Leo Lania, *My Road to Berlin* (London: Peter Davies, 1960), 87. Brandt is here quoting himself from a pamphlet written in 1937. Also see pages 86–89.

68. Jeremy Adelman, *Worldly Philosopher: The Odyssey of Albert O. Hirschman* (Princeton: Princeton University Press, 2103), 136–137. Also see Boris Volodarsky, *Stalin's Agent: The Life and Death of Alexander Orlov* (Oxford: Oxford University Press, 2015), 245–250.

69. For example, see "Correspondence between Rafail Abramovich and Emma Goldman," June 28, 1937, August 6, 1937, and August 12, 1937, *Columbia University Libraries Online Exhibitions*, accessed October 31, 2021, https://exhibitions.library.columbia.edu/exhibits/show/melting-pot/item/500.

70. Walter G Krivitsky, *In Stalin's Secret Service: An Expose of Russia's Secret Policies by the Former Chief of the Soviet Intelligence in Western Europe* (New York: Harper and Brothers, 1939), 172–173.

71. Nick Underwood, "Exposing Yiddish Paris: The Modern Jewish Culture Pavilion at the 1937 World's Fair," *East European Jewish Affairs* 46, no. 2 (2016): 160–175; Matthew Hoffman, "From Czernowitz to Paris: The International Yiddish Culture

Congress of 1937," in *Czernowitz at 100: The First Yiddish Language Conference in Historical Perspective*, ed. Kalman Weiser and Joshua A. Fogel (Lanham, Maryland: Lexington Books, 2010), 151–164; and Estraikh, "A Quest for Yiddishland."

72. Tzafrir Fainholtz, "The Jewish Farmer, the Village and the World Fair: Politics, Propaganda, and the 'Israel in Palestine' Pavilion at the Paris International Exhibition of 1937," *MODSCAPES 2018*, accessed October 31, 2021, https://www.shs-conferences.org/articles/shsconf/pdf/2019/04/shsconf _modscapes2018_10004.pdf.

73. Underwood, "Exposing Yiddish Paris," 164.

74. Hoffman, "From Czernowitz to Paris."

75. The proceedings of the Congress were collected and printed as *Ershter alveltlekher yidisher kultur-kongres: Pariz 17–21 Sept. 1937, stenografisher barikht* (Paris, New York, Warsaw: Tsentral-farlag fun alveltlekhn yidishn kultur-farband IKUF, 1937).

76. Ben-Adir, "Erets-yisroel," in *Algemeyne entsiklopedye*, vol. 4 (Dubnov-fond: Paris, 1937), col. 499.

77. Menes, in ibid., 516.

78. On this reevaluation of Diaspora Nationalist ideologies, see Joshua M. Karlip, *The Tragedy of a Generation: The Rise and Fall of Jewish Nationalism in Eastern Europe* (Cambridge, MA: Harvard University Press, 2013).

79. "The Program of the NSDAP," The Avalon Project of Yale Law School, accessed October 31, 2021, https://avalon.law.yale.edu/imt/1708-ps.asp.

80. Caron, "Prelude to Vichy: France and the Jewish Refugees in the Era of Appeasement," *Journal of Contemporary History* 20, no. 1 (January 1985): 158.

81. See Kuznitz, *YIVO and the Making of Modern Jewish Culture*; and Karlip, *The Tragedy of a Generation*.

82. Wolf Gruner, *The Holocaust in Bohemia and Moravia: Czech Initiatives, German Policies, Jewish Responses* (New York: Berghahn Books, 2019).

83. "General Encyclopedia in Yiddish: History," May 15, 1942, YIVO A. Kin Papers RG 554, folder R.

84. Association Simon Dubnow, "Algemeyne entsiklopedye" (Paris: I.C.C. undated). The only extant copy of this brochure is located in the University of Cape Town archives, Sholem Schwartzbard Papers BC 1155, folder 7.

85. See the January-February 1936 exchanges between Raphael Abramovitch and Baruch Charney Vladeck, IISG Raphael Abramović Papers, folder 9.

86. Association Simon Dubnow, "Encyclopédie contemporaine du judaïsme" (Paris: Undated). The only extant copy of this brochure is located in the University of Cape Town archives, Sholem Schwartzbard Papers BC 1155, folder 7. There are also letters announcing the impending volume in the papers of Aaron Steinberg.

See CAHJP Aaron Steinberg Papers P159. As for the English translation of *Yidn alef*, there is a reference in a January 11, 1939, letter from Abraham Kin/Kine of the American Branch of the Yiddish Encyclopedia to Mukdoni that it is "almost secured," although the meaning of this is unclear. An English translation, with additional articles, did not appear until 1946 (and is discussed in chapter 3). A. Kin to A. Mukdoni, YIVO Alexander Mukdoni Papers RG 227, folder 12.

87. "Hakdome," *Algemeyne entsiklopedye: Yidn alef* (Paris: Dubnov-fond, 1939), unpaginated first page.

88. Ibid.

89. Meeting notes, February 14, 1938, University of Cape Town archives, Sholem Schwartzbard Papers BC 1155, folder 7.

90. "The Symbol of a Nation's Will to Live," University of Cape Town archives, Sholem Schwartzbard Papers BC 1155, folder 7.

91. See the exchange between Hilda Purwitzky and Anna Schwartzbard, March/April 1938, University of Cape Town archives, Sholem Schwartzbard Papers BC 1155, folder 5.

92. Catherine Collomp, "The Jewish Labor Committee, American Labor, and the Rescue of European Socialists, 1934–1941," *International Labor and Working-Class History* 68 (Fall 2005), 115.

93. "Half Million See Vladeck Funeral," *New York Times*, November 3, 1938, 23. On the Vladeck Houses, see "The Future of NYCHA," accessed October 31, 2021, https://eportfolios.macaulay.cuny.edu/nycha/infrastructurebuilt-environment /welcome-to-fulton-houses.

94. Yashunsky, "Farnem un kharakter," 133.

95. See Karlip, *The Tragedy of a Generation*. Also see Karlip's "At the Crossroads between War and Genocide: A Reassessment of Jewish Ideology in 1940," *Jewish Social Studies* 11, no. 2 (Winter 2005): 170–201.

96. Brutskus, "Yidishe antropologye," in *Algemeyne entsiklopedye: Yidn alef*, 29.

97. Alexander Mukdoni, "A velt mit visn vegn yidn," *Der Tog*, July 21, 1939.

98. See the descriptions in Richard J. Evans, "Lightning War," in *The Third Reich at War* (New York: Penguin Press, 2008), 1–28.

99. See the description in David Engel, "Poland since 1939," in *YIVO Encyclopedia*, ed. Gershon David Hundert, 1404–1405, from where this description is drawn.

100. "German Invasion of Poland: Jewish Refugees, 1939," in *Holocaust Encyclopedia*, United States Holocaust Memorial Museum, accessed October 31, 2021, https://encyclopedia.ushmm.org/content/en/article/german-invasion-of-poland -jewish-refugees-1939.

101. See Weiser, *Jewish People, Yiddish Nation*, 244–248, and Kuznitz, *YIVO and the Making of Modern Jewish Culture*, 181.

102. In correspondence between Ben-Adir and Weinreich of March 1940, Ben-Adir discussed his efforts to send desperately needed money to Weinreich in payment for his contributions to *Yidn beys*. Ben-Adir to Weinreich, March 1, 1940, YIVO Max Weinreich Papers RG 584, folder 604.

103. Sophie Dubnov-Erlich, *The Life and Work of S. M. Dubnov: Diaspora Nationalism and Jewish History*, ed. Jeffrey Shandler, trans. Judith Vowles (Bloomington: Indiana University Press, 1991), 237–239. Also see Kuznitz, "YIVO's 'Old Friend and Teacher,'" 491–494.

104. Rozin to Weinreich, March 1, 1940, YIVO Max Weinreich Papers RG 584, folder 604.

105. "Hakdome," *Algemeyne entsiklopedye: Yidn giml* (New York, 1942), unpaginated.

106. Di redaktsye, "Hakdome," *Algemeyne entsiklopedye: Yidn beys* (Paris, 1940), unpaginated.

107. Ibid.

108. The essay "Aramish" by Kalmanovitch is less than three columns long, suggesting that the Dubnow Fund never received his remaining work for the volume, and instead went to press with what they had on hand.

109. A. Rozin, *Farn geshikhtlekhn yom-hadin, dos yidishe folk tsvishn toykhekhe un geule* (Paris, 1940).

110. I am grateful to Professor Mark Slobin and Professor Michael Lukin for the information on Alice Jacob-Lowenson, and to Professor Albert Baumgarten for the information on Victor (Avigdor) Tcherikover.

111. Hanna Diamond, *Fleeing Hitler: France 1940* (Oxford: Oxford University Press, 2007), 150.

112. Léon Werth, *33 Days*, trans. Austin Denis Johnston (Brooklyn: Melville House Publishing: 2015), 9.

113. See the discussions in YIVO A. Kin Papers RG 554, folder R.

114. In 1946, a number of these volumes were recovered and offered for sale by the remaining representatives of the Dubnow Fund in Paris. See "Fun der yidisher entsiklopedye," *Undzer shtime*, January 5, 1946. I am grateful to Nick Underwood for sharing this article.

115. Harry M. Orlinsky, review of *The Jewish People: Past and Present*, vols. 3 and 4, ed. Raphael Abramovitch et al., *Journal of Biblical Literature* 75, no. 1 (March 1956): 80–82.

116. Raphael Rein to Nathan Chanin, July 19, 1940, Tamiment Library and Robert F. Wagner Labor Archives (TL/RWLA), Jewish Labor Committee Records, box 39, folder 1, "Abramovitch Letters." Emphases and typos are in the English-language original.

117. See Nancy Brown, "No Longer a Haven: Varian Fry and the Refugees of France," in *The Memory of the Holocaust in the 21st Century: Yad Vashem Second International Conference on the Holocaust and Higher Education* (Jerusalem: Yad Vashem International Task Force on Holocaust Education, Remembrance and Research, 1999).

118. See the letter and accompanying list from Eleanor Roosevelt to Adolf A. Berle, June 25, 1940. RG-59, Department of State, General Visa Correspondence, 1940–1944, box 147, 811.111 Refugees/139. I am grateful to Dr. Rebecca Erbelding of the United States Holocaust Memorial Museum for sharing this document with me. Gilinsky eventually managed to arrive in the United States in March 1941, by way of Siberia and Japan. I am grateful to Victor Gilinsky for sharing the story of his family's flight from Vilna.

119. Collomp, 123. For a detailed study of the efforts of the JLC to rescue European Jews, see Collomp, *Rescue, Relief, and Resistance: The Jewish Labor Committee's Anti-Nazi Operations, 1934–1945,* trans. Susan Emanuel (Detroit: Wayne State University Press, 2021), 88–128.

120. Breckinridge Long, Department of State Memorandum of Conversation, July 2, 1940. RG-59, Department of State, General Visa Correspondence, 1940–1944, box 147, 811.111 Refugees/127. I am grateful to Dr. Rebecca Erbelding of the United States Holocaust Memorial Museum for sharing this document.

121. Department of State telegram to American Consul, Marseille, France, July 6, 1940. RG-59, Department of State, General Visa Correspondence, 1940–1944, box 147, 811.111 Refugees/127.

122. Collomp, "The Jewish Labor Committee, American Labor, and the Rescue of European Socialists, 1934–1941," 123.

123. Avrom Kin to Ben-Adir, July 13, 1940, YIVO Ben-Adir Papers RG 394, box 2.

124. Avrom Kin to Ben-Adir, July 20, 1940, YIVO Ben-Adir Papers RG 394, box 2. On the activities of the United States Consulate in Marseille during this period, see Melissa Jane Taylor, "American Consuls and the Politics of Rescue in Marseille, 1936–1941," *Holocaust and Genocide Studies* 30, no. 2 (Fall 2016): 247–275.

125. TL/RWLA Jewish Labor Committee Archives, box 38, folder 24, July–August 1940. Daniel Charney eventually arrived in the United States in 1941.

126. A. Kin to Ben-Adir, July 29, 1940, YIVO Ben-Adir Papers RG 394, box 2; Raphael Abramovitch to "My dear friend," July 29, 1940. TL/RWLA Jewish Labor Committee Archives, box 39, folder 1, "Abramovitch Letters."

127. See the records in "JLC—France," Jewish Labor Committee Archives, box 39.

128. Raphael Abramovitch to "My dear friend."

129. Ronald Weber, *The Lisbon Route: Entry and Escape in Nazi Europe* (Lanham, Maryland: Ivan R. Dee, 2011), 7–8.

130. Ibid., 9. Also see Lillian Mowrer, "Fiesta in Lisbon," *New Yorker*, July 20, 1940: 36–42; and Alva E. Gaymon, "Portugal Holding Delicate Position," *New York Times*, July 28, 1940.

131. Marion Kaplan, *Hitler's Jewish Refugees: Hope and Anxiety in Portugal* (New Haven: Yale University Press, 2020).

132. HICEM is an acronym of three Jewish migration assistance organizations that merged in 1927: the New York–based HIAS (Hebrew Immigrant Aid Society), the Jewish Colonization Association (JCA), and Emigdirect (United Jewish Emigration Committee).

133. See the ship manifest at Ancestry.com. "New York, Passenger and Crew Lists (including Castle Garden and Ellis Island), 1820–1957." For the original data, see Passenger Lists of Vessels Arriving at New York, New York, 1820–1897. Microfilm Publication M237, 675 rolls. NAI: 6256867. Records of the U.S. Customs Service, Record Group 36. National Archives at Washington, D.C.

134. See the records in TL/RWLA Jewish Labor Committee Archives, "JLC—Rescue, September 1–15, 1940," box 39.

135. Avrom Kin to Ben-Adir, September 15, 1940, YIVO Ben-Adir Papers RG 394, box 2.

136. On ORT activities in France during World War II, see Leon Shapiro, *The History of ORT: A Jewish Movement for Social Change* (New York: Schocken, 1980), 190, 195–197.

137. A. Rozin to Alexander Mukdoni, February 20, 1941, YIVO Alexander Mukdoni Papers RG 227, folder 12.

138. Ben-Adir to Shmuel Niger, October 26, 1939. YIVO Shmuel Niger Papers RG 360, folder 589.

3. Spinning the Historical Threads

1. Paul Ritterband, "Counting the Jews of New York, 1900–1991: An Essay in Substance and Method," in *Papers in Jewish Demography*, ed. Sergio Della Pergola and Judith Even (Jerusalem: Avraham Harman Institute of Contemporary Jewry, 1997), 199–228. In providing these numbers, I recognize that counting Jews is an exceedingly difficult and often fraught enterprise, especially in the United States, where Jews have not historically been identified as a category under the law. As I discuss below, the adaptability of American Jewish identity was one of the many challenges facing the encyclopedists as they sought to determine the function of the *Algemeyne entsiklopedye* in this new landscape.

2. Hasia R. Diner, *The Jews of the United States* (Berkeley: University of California Press, 2004), 230.

3. Christopher Gray, "Streetscapes/The Jewish Daily Forward Building, 175 East Broadway; A Capitalist Venture with a Socialist Base," *New York Times*, July 19, 1988.

4. Eric L. Goldstein, *The Price of Whiteness: Jews, Race, and American Identity* (Princeton: Princeton University Press, 2006). Also see David R. Roediger, *Working toward Whiteness: How America's Immigrants Became White* (New York: Basic Books, 2005).

5. Hazel Gaudet Erskine, "The Polls: Religious Prejudice, Part 2: Anti-Semitism," *Public Opinion Quarterly* 29, no. 4 (Winter 1965–1966): 653.

6. For a standard overview of the history of antisemitism in the United States, see Leonard Dinnerstein, *Antisemitism in America* (New York: Oxford University Press, 1994).

7. Abramovitch to A. Ruth & Sons, Real Estate, November 18, 1940, YIVO A. Kin Papers RG 554, folder R. Yearly rent for 511 W. 113th Street, apartment 61, was $936.

8. "General Encyclopedia in Yiddish: History," May 15, 1942, YIVO A. Kin Papers RG 554, folder R.

9. Although May 1940 does seem to be the correct month for the initial publication of *Yidn beys*, in the foreword to *Yidn giml*, the editors give the month as March.

10. Tsentrale yidishe kultur-organizatsye, "Hakdome tsu der tsveyter uflage," in *Algemeyne entsiklopedye: Yidn beys*, repr. (New York: Central Yiddish Culture Organization, 1940), unpaginated.

11. "About CYCO," accessed October 31, 2020, http://www.cycobooks.org/about.php.

12. Nokhem Khanin, Binyumin Gebiner, and Khaim Pupko to "Zeyer khosheve fraynd," January 26, 1941, YIVO RG 1400 Bund Archives (Schulman, Algemeyne Entsiklopedye), box 10.

13. Abramovitch's apartment was still used as the address on much of the official correspondence for several years.

14. Weinreich had arrived in New York on March 10, 1940.

15. See the letters from Rozin to Steinberg in CAHJP Aaron Steinberg Papers P159, XXII Letters K.

16. In spite of the general excitement surrounding the continuation of the *Algemeyne entsiklopedye* in America, few reviews of *Yidn beys* appeared in the press. An exception is the favorable review by Yohanan Twersky, in *Tsukunft* 46, no. 2 (November 1941): 124–127.

17. For a brief history of the National Refugee Service, see the "Scope and Content Note" of its archival collection held at YIVO, RG 248, accessed October 31,

2021, https://archives.cjh.org/repositories/7/resources/3595. Also see Sharon Lowenstein, "The National Refugee Service (NRS)," in *Jewish American Volunteer Organizations*, ed. Michael N. Dobkowski (Westport, CT: Greenwood Press, 1986), 364–372.

18. "General Encyclopedia in Yiddish: History," May 15, 1942, YIVO A. Kin Papers RG 554, folder R.

19. Historian Gerhard L. Weinberg estimates that by December 1942, more than 2.8 million Soviet POWs were murdered in this way, of 3.9 million captured. Gerhard L. Weinberg, *A World at Arms: A Global History of World War II* (Cambridge: Cambridge University Press, 1994), 300.

20. Abramovitch, *In tsvey revolutsyes*.

21. Elias Tcherikower, *Yidn in frankraykh: shtudyes un materyaln*, 2 vols. (New York: YIVO, 1942).

22. "Hakdome," *Algemeyne entsiklopedye: Yidn giml* (New York, 1942), unpaginated.

23. Ibid.

24. On Zygielbojm's suicide, see Daniel Blatman, "On a Mission against All Odds: Szmuel Zygielbojm in London (April 1942–May 1943)," *Yad Vashem Studies* 20 (1990): 237–271; and Isabelle Hertz, "'Morituri vos salutanat': Szmuel Zygielbojm's Suicide in May 1943 and the International Socialist Community in London," *Holocaust and Genocide Studies* 14.2 (2000): 242–265.

25. Sh. Niger, "Yidishe literature fun mitn 18-tn y"h biz 1942," in *Algemeyne entsiklopedye: Yidn giml* (New York: American Friends of the Yiddish Encyclopedia, 1941), cols. 65–174; Ben-Adir, "Moderne gezelshaftlekhe un natsyonale shtremungen bay yidn," in ibid., 449–526.

26. Known in Russian as the Sionistko-sotsialisticheskaia Rabochaia Partiia. For a discussion of Shmuel Charney's early work on behalf of modern literary Yiddish, see Trachtenberg, "Shmuel Niger and the Making of Yiddish High Culture," chap. 3 in *Revolutionary Roots*, 82–107. For a full biography, see L[eyb].V[asserman], "Niger, Sh." in *Leksikon fun der nayer yidisher literatur*, ed. Shmuel Niger and Yankev Shatzky (New York: Alveltlekhn yidishn kultur-kongres, 1956–1981), 190–210.

27. Niger, "Yidishe literature fun mitn 18-tn y"h biz 1942," 165–166.

28. Jonathan Frankel, *Jewish Politics and the Russian Revolution of 1905* (Tel Aviv: Tel Aviv University Press, 1982), 8.

29. Ben-Adir, "Moderne gezelshaftlekhe un natsyonale shtremungen bay yidn," in *Algemeyne entsiklopedye: Yidn giml*, col. 526.

30. Jacob Lestschinsky, "Ben-Adir," in *Algemeyne entsiklopedye*, vol. 5 (New York: Dubnov-fond and CYCO, 1944), cols. 508–511.

31. Bernard D. Weinryb, "Review of *Algemeyne entsiklopedye, Yidn* Vols. 1–2," *Jewish Social Studies* 4 (1942): 85–86.

32. Ibid., 86.

33. "General Encyclopedia in Yiddish: History," May 15, 1942, YIVO A. Kin Papers RG 554, folder R.

34. A. Rozin to Aaron Steinberg, April 27, 1942, in CAHJP Aaron Steinberg Papers P159, XXII Letters K.

35. Iulii Brutskus had fled to France following the Nazi rise to power. He was arrested and detained by Vichy authorities following the 1940 invasion and released after the intervention of allies in the United States. Dov Levin, "Brutskus, Iulii," in *YIVO Encyclopedia*, ed. Gershon David Hundert, 250–251.

36. The editors also noted the passing of Petr Garvi, who contributed several entries to volume 5.

37. "Hakdome," *Algemeyne entsiklopedye*, vol. 5, unpaginated.

38. See the discussion of the reporting by the American Jewish press during the Holocaust in Yosef Gorny, *The Jewish Press and the Holocaust, 1939–1945: Palestine, Britain, the United States, and the Soviet Union* (Cambridge: Cambridge University Press, 2011), 80–102 and 143–175.

39. For the historian Koppel S. Pinson, one of the few to review volume 5, the amount of Jewish content was insufficient; he criticized the editors for omitting important Jewish figures as well as demographic information on Jews in geographical entries. See Koppel S. Pinson, review of *Algemeyne entsiklopedye*, vol. 5, in *Jewish Social Studies* 7, no. 1 (January 1945): 76–78.

40. Curiously, there is a comparatively long essay on "bookkeeping," by Mikhl Ivenski, which occupies eight columns plus two pages of tables.

41. In response to a request by Daniel Charney that he emigrate to the United States, Dubnow had replied, "Of course life is more peaceful in America, but we have no right to abandon the old nest." Dubnov-Erlich, 239.

42. Ibid., 237, 243. Also see Kuznitz, "YIVO's 'Old Friend and Teacher,'" 492–494.

43. Dubnov-Erlich, 247.

44. For a discussion of the Strashun Library under the Soviet Union and Nazi Germany, see Rabinowitz, *The Lost Library*, 77–86.

45. Kuznitz, *YIVO and the Making of Modern Jewish Culture*, 181.

46. On Prilutski as head of YIVO, see the discussion in Weiser, *Jewish People, Yiddish Nation*, 254–258.

47. Ibid., 254, and Kuznitz, *YIVO and the Making of Modern Jewish Culture*, 182.

48. Rabinowitz, 82–85.

49. On the destruction of YIVO in Vilna and the efforts to rescue of many of its holdings, see Fishman, *Embers Plucked from the Fire*, and Fishman, *The Book Smugglers*.

50. Fishman, *Embers*, 4–5.

51. Jacob Lestschinsky, *Vuhin geyen mir? Yidishe vanderung a mol un haynt* (New York: Yidish-natsyonaler Arbeter-farband, 1944).

52. Jacob Lestschinsky, *Crisis, Catastrophe and Survival: A Jewish Balance Sheet, 1914–1948* (Institute of Jewish Affairs of the World Jewish Congress: New York, 1948), 74.

53. Ibid., 82, 83.

54. Ibid., 78.

55. Gennady Estraikh, "Jacob Lestschinsky: A Yiddishist Dreamer and Social Scientist," *Science in Context* 20, no. 2 (2007): 233.

56. The literature on the efforts to recover Jewish books and artifacts after the Holocaust is extensive and includes Leff, *The Archive Thief*; Rabinowitz, *The Lost Library*; Fishman, *The Book Smugglers*; Mark Glickman, *Stolen Words: The Nazi Plunder of Jewish Books* (Philadelphia: The Jewish Publication Society, 2016); Bilha Shilo, "'Funem Folk, Farn Folk, Mitn Folk': The Restitution of the YIVO Collection from Offenbach to New York," *MORESHET Journal for the Study of the Holocaust and Antisemitism* 14 (2017): 362–412; Jason B. Lustig, "'A Time to Gather': A History of Jewish Archives in the Twentieth Century," PhD diss. (University of California, Los Angeles, 2017), in particular chap. 6, "Contested Fragments: Framing the Jewish Past and Forging a Jewish Future," 360–427; and Nancy Sinkoff, *From Left to Right: Lucy S. Dawidowicz, the New York Intellectuals, and the Politics of Jewish History* (Detroit: Wayne State University Press, 2020).

57. Baron wrote on the imperative to rescue European cultural artifacts in the inaugural issue of *Commentary* in 1945. See Salo W. Baron, "The Spiritual Reconstruction of European Jewry," *Commentary* (Dec. 1, 1945): 4–12.

58. Rachel Rojanski, "The Final Chapter in the Struggle for Cultural Autonomy: Palestine, Israel and Yiddish Writers in the Diaspora, 1946–1951," *Journal of Modern Jewish Studies* 6, no. 2 (July 2007): 185–204. Also see the discussions on changes among the Yiddish linguists at and around YIVO in Burko, "Saving Yiddish: Yiddish Studies and the Language Sciences in America, 1940–1970." For a related effort by members of the Jewish Labor Bund to reestablish itself as a transnational movement after the Holocaust, see David Slucki, *The International Jewish Labor Bund after 1945: Toward a Global History* (New Brunswick, NJ: Rutgers University Press, 2012).

59. Rojanski, 188.

60. *Algemeyne entsiklopedye: Yidn hey* (New York: Dubnov-fond un Entsiklopedye-komitet, 1957).

61. Kassow, *Who Will Write Our History?* and Garbarini, *Numbered Days*.

62. Jockusch, *Collect and Record*, 4.

63. Smith, *The Yiddish Historians*.

64. Hasia R. Diner, *We Remember with Reverence and Love: American Jews and the Myth of Silence after the Holocaust, 1945–1962* (New York: New York University Press, 2009).

65. Jack Kugelmass and Jonathan Boyarin, eds. and trans., *From a Ruined Garden: The Memorial Books of Polish Jewry* (New York: Schocken Books, 1983).

66. Raphael Abramovitch, ed., *Di farshvundene velt / The Vanished World* (New York: Forward Association, 1947).

67. Kalman Weiser, "Coming to America: Max Weinreich and the Emergence of YIVO's American Center," in *Choosing Yiddish: New Frontiers of Language and Culture*, ed. Lara Rabinovitch et al. (Detroit: Wayne State University Press, 2012), 240.

68. M. Weinreich and N. Feinerman to Adolph Held, October 1, 1940, (TL/RWLA) Jewish Labor Committee Archives, box 39, folder 5, "Rescue Oct 1–15, 1940."

69. Markus Krah, "Partisan Reviews and Commentaries on Eastern European Judaism: Postwar American-Jewish Intellectual Journals and the Reconstruction of the Eastern European Past," in *Reconstructing the Old Country: American Jewry in the Post-Holocaust Decades*, ed. Eliyana R. Adler and Sheila E. Jelen (Detroit: Wayne State University Press), 89. Also see Krah, *American Jewry and the Reinvention of the East European Jewish Past*.

70. A. A. Roback, *The Story of Yiddish Literature* (New York: Yiddish Scientific Institute, American Branch, 1940). For a contemporary review, see Israel Knox, review of A. A. Roback, *The Story of Yiddish Literature*, in *Jewish Social Studies* 3, no. 2 (April 1941), 224–226.

71. Weiser, "Coming to America," 242.

72. Quoted in Krah, *American Jewry and the Re-invention of the East European Jewish Past*, 65.

73. Also see Avraham Novershtern, "From the Folk to the Academics: Study and Research of Yiddish after the Holocaust," in *Encyclopaedia Judaica Yearbook* 1988/89 (Jerusalem: Keter), 14–24; Avraham Novershtern and Cecile Esther Kuznitz, "Yiddish Research after the Holocaust," in *Encyclopaedia Judaica*, 2nd ed., ed. Fred Skolnik, 358–367; and Burko, "Saving Yiddish: Yiddish Studies and the Language Sciences in America, 1940–1970."

74. Lederhendler, "The Eastern European Jewish Past and Its Historians: Cultural Interventions in Postwar America," 25.

75. YIVO A. Kin Papers RG 554, folder R.

76. Preface to *The Jewish People: Past and Present*, vol. 1, ed. Raphael Abramovitch et al. (New York: Jewish Encyclopedic Handbooks / Central Yiddish Culture Organization, 1946), unpaginated.

77. See the correspondence between Abramovitch and Lévi-Strauss, YIVO A. Kin Papers RG 554, folder R.

78. See the correspondence between Scholem and Menes, YIVO A. Kin Papers RG 554, folder G. In a letter dated June 5, 1945, Scholem writes (errors in English-language original):

> But I feel I should tell you that I wouldnt have accepted your offer because I think you were not entitled to inform me only post factum of your publishing my articles from Yiddish Encyclopedia in English translation and in another setting without having first asked for my consent. I hope you will understand my position: I was asked by you to write these articles for Yiddish readers and I might or might not have been willing to do the same for English readers or I might have preferred to do it with my own publisher. There was never a question of your having secured rights on an English or any other translation of these essays. Therefore I was very much surprised to hear from you about the inclusion of these articles in your English handbook and it is only honest to say that I resented this piece of information pretty much. I have read the Yiddish translation of my articles and compared them with the originals and found that with all due respect to the translator there are many places where the Yiddish text does not represent at all what I wanted to say.

79. Ashley Montagu, *Man's Most Dangerous Myth: The Fallacy of Race* (New York: Columbia University Press, 1942).

80. M. F. Ashley Montagu, "Race Theory in the Light of Modern Science," in *The Jewish People: Past and Present*, 1:3.

81. Ibid., 8.

82. See, for example, Stefan Kühl, *The Nazi Connection: Eugenics, American Racism, and German National Socialism* (Oxford: Oxford University Press, 1994) and James Q. Whitman, *Hitler's American Model: The United States and the Making of Nazi Race Law* (Princeton: Princeton University Press, 2017).

83. Louis L. Mann, review of *The Jewish People: Past and Present*, vol. 1, *New York Times Book Review*, November 2, 1947, 28.

84. Excerpts from reviews appearing in *National Jewish Monthly* and *Jewish Frontier* appeared in marketing materials for JPPP. See JDC Archives, Records of the New York office of the American Jewish Joint Distribution Committee, 1945–1954, Jewish Encyclopedic Handbooks, 1947–1948, 1953–1954 Folder; Jewish Encyclopedic Handbooks, 1947–1948, 1953–1954 Folder, "The Jewish People: Past and Present."

85. Theophile J. Meek, review of *The Jewish People: Past and Present*, vol. 1, *Journal of Biblical Literature* 69, no. 4 (December 1950): 401–402.

86. Bentley Glass, review of *The Jewish People: Past and Present*, vol. 1, *Quarterly Review of Biology* 23, no. 1 (March 1948): 96.

87. Ellis Rivkin, review of *The Jewish People: Past and Present*, vol. 1, *Jewish Quarterly Review* 40, no. 1 (July 1949): 121.

88. Ibid., 123–124.

89. Milton Himmelfarb, "Jewish History Freshly Appraised: The First Encyclopedia in the Newer Tradition," review of *The Jewish People: Past and Present*, vol. 1, *Commentary* (January 1, 1947): 479.

90. Ibid., 483, 487

91. Ibid., 481.

92. Louis L. Mann, review of *The Jewish People: Past and Present*, vol. 2, *New York Times Book Review*, May 8, 1949, 29.

93. Carl E. Purinton, review of *The Jewish People: Past and Present*, vol. 2, *Journal of Bible and Religion*, May 8, 1949, 212.

94. Mark M. Krug, review of *The Jewish People: Past and Present*, vol. 2, *Journal of Jewish Education* 21, no. 2 (1950): 69, 71.

95. Review of *The Jewish People: Past and Present*, vol. 3, *Journal of Bible and Religion* 21, no. 1 (January 1953), 58.

96. Orlinsky, review, 82.

97. Edward S. Shapiro, *A Time for Healing: American Jewry since World War II* (Baltimore: The Johns Hopkins University Press, 1992), 92.

98. The Publishers, preface to *The Jewish People: Past and Present*, (New York: Jewish Encyclopedic Handbooks, Inc., 1955), 4: unpaginated.

99. Anita Libman Lebeson, "The History of the Jews in the United States," in *The Jewish People: Past and Present*, vol. 4, 1–55; Lebeson, *Pilgrim People* (New York: Harper Brothers, 1950).

100. Jacob Lestschinsky, "Economic and Social Development of American Jewry," in *The Jewish People: Past and Present*, 4:65.

101. "Income & Expenditure Totals from November 1943 to December 1952," YIVO *Algemeyne Entsiklopedye* Papers, RG 1149, folder 7. Also see Nathan Chanin and Shlama [*sic*] Gilinsky to Julius A. Bell, January 25, 1960, YIVO Algemeyne Entsiklopedye Papers RG 1149, box 7, folder 94, which reports lower numbers, likely reflecting the project's often crude record keeping. For a look at the life of a traveling salesman for the *Algemeyne entsiklopedye* and *JPPP*, see A. M. Orzhitzer, *Fun Vankuver biz Eylat: vanderungen mit der yidisher entsiklopedye, reportazhn, bilder un dertseylungen* (Tel Aviv: Ostrover, 1965).

102. An October 27, 2021, search of the journals in ProQuest reveals 233 citations containing "The Jewish People: Past and Present."

103. See JDC Archives, Records of the New York Office of the American Jewish Joint Distribution Committee, 1945–1954, Jewish Encyclopedic Handbooks, 1947–1948, 1953–1954 Folder, Jewish Encyclopedic Handbooks, 1947–1948,

1953–1954 Folder, Letter from A. Menes and S. Gilinsky to Moses Leavitt, December 16, 1953.

104. Including bank loans provided by Public National Bank and Trust Company and grants awarded by the Atran foundation and the Conference on Material Claims against Germany. See YIVO Algemeyne Entsiklopedye Papers RG 1149, box 8, folder 120. For internal discussions about finances in the late 1940s, see YIVO Algemeyne Entsiklopedye Papers RG 1149, box 1, folder 23.

105. See YIVO Algemeyne Entsiklopedye Papers RG 1149, box 8, folders 193 and 216.

106. Eli Lederhendler, *New York Jews and the Decline of Urban Ethnicity, 1950–1970* (Syracuse: Syracuse University Press, 2001), 63–92.

107. Schwarz, *Survivors and Exiles* 3. The information on the postwar efforts to reinvigorate Yiddish culture draws largely on Schwarz's study. Also see Zachary M. Baker, *Essential Yiddish Books: 1000 Great Works from the Collection of the National Yiddish Book Center* (Amherst, MA: National Yiddish Book Center, 2004); Rebecca Margolis, "Transitions: 1945 and Beyond," chap. 6 in *Jewish Roots, Canadian Soil: Yiddish Cultural Life in Montreal, 1905–1945* (Montreal: McGill-Queen's University Press, 2011), 190–207; Simon Perego, "Commemorating the Holocaust during the First Postwar Decade: Jewish Initiatives and Non-Jewish Actors in France," in *Als der Holocaust noch keinen Namen hatte*, ed. Regina Fritz, Béla Rásky, and Éva Kovács, 223–239; and Ibid., "Yiddish or Not? Holocaust Remembrance, Commemorative Ceremonies, and Questions of Language among Parisian Jews, 1944–1967," *Journal of Modern Jewish Studies* 20, no. 2 (2021): 222–247.

108. Gennady Estraikh, *Yiddish in the Cold War* (Oxford: Legenda, 2008), 9.

109. See the minutes of meetings from 1947, YIVO Algemeyne Entsiklopedye Papers RG 1149, box 1, folder 23.

110. Abramovitch to Steinberg, May 29, 1949. University of Southampton Archives, Aaron Zakharovich Steinberg Papers, MS 262, 2/4. Abramovitch repeatedly beseeched Steinberg to submit essays for the volumes, but none appeared in time for publication. Steinberg is, however, listed as one of the editors of *Yidn daled*.

111. Other plans for *Yidn daled* included sections on the Jewish world outside of Europe, including the Americas, the "land of Israel," aid efforts on behalf of European Jewry, Jewish cultural activity during the time of the catastrophe, and an accounting of the status of Jews at the end of the war. See "Band Yidn D," YIVO Algemeyne Entsiklopedye Papers RG 1149, box 1, folder 23.

112. "Hakdome," *Algemeyne entsiklopedye: Yidn daled* (New York: Dubnovfond and CYCO, 1950), unpaginated.

113. On the postwar reconstruction of Jewish life in Europe see, for example, Anson Rabinbach and Jack Zipes, eds., *Germans and Jews since the Holocaust:*

The Changing Situation in West Germany (New York: Holmes and Meier, 1986); Karen Auerbach, *The House at Ujazdowskie 16: Jewish Families in Warsaw after the Holocaust* (Bloomington: Indiana University Press, 2013); Jay Howard Geller, *Jews in Post-Holocaust Germany, 1945–1953* (Cambridge: Cambridge University Press, 2005); Leonid Smilovitsky, "Jews under Soviet Rule," *Cahiers du monde russe* 49, no. 2–3 (2008): 475–514; and Seán Hand and Steven T. Katz, eds., *Post-Holocaust France and the Jews, 1945–1955* (New York: New York University Press, 2015).

114. *Yidn giml* and volume 5 of the *normale* series, both of which were published in the United States during the war, were composed primarily in Europe before or in the first year of the war.

115. Sarah Abrevaya Stein, "Two New Books Offer a Window into the History of Salonica's Jewish Community," *Forward*, August 25, 2006, accessed October 31, 2021, http://old.forward.com/articles/1431/index.html.

116. Friedman, "Di yidishe entsiklopedye—a kapitl kultur-geshikhte fun undzer dor," 130–133.

117. Jacob Robinson and Philip Friedman, *Guide to Jewish History under Nazi Impact* (New York: YIVO Institute for Jewish Research, 1960).

118. Friedman, "Di yidishe entsiklopedye—a kapitl kultur-geshikhte fun undzer dor," 130.

119. "Income & Expenditure Totals from November 1943 to December 1952," YIVO *Algemeyne Entsiklopedye* Papers, RG 1149, folder 7.

120. See records in YIVO *Algemeyne Entsiklopedye* Papers, RG 1149, folder 7.

121. See records in YIVO *Algemeyne Entsiklopedye* Papers, RG 1149, folder 15.

122. Shloyme Bikl and Leybush Lehrer, eds., *Shmuel Niger-bukh* (New York: YIVO Institute of Jewish Research, 1958).

123. Minutes of Encyclopedia Committee meeting, April 30, 1955, YIVO Algemeyne Entsiklopedye Papers RG 1149, box 1, folder 4.

124. Liebich, 55, 273.

125. Ibid., 273.

126. Ibid., 275.

127. "Guide to the American Labor Conference on International Affairs Records," Tamiment Library and Robert F. Wagner Labor Archives, accessed October 31, 2021, http://dlib.nyu.edu/findingaids/html/tamwag/tam_038/.

128. Howard Brick, *Daniel Bell and the Decline of Intellectual Radicalism: Social Theory and Political Reconciliation in the 1940s* (Madison: The University of Wisconsin Press, 1986), 150–151.

129. Liebich, 299; Raphael R. Abramovitch, *The Soviet Revolution, 1917–1939* (New York: International Universities Press, Inc., 1962).

130. See the advertisement for the book in the *ALA Bulletin* 56, no. 4 (April 1962): 286.

131. Robert V. Daniels, review of *The Soviet Revolution, 1917–1939*, by Raphael R. Abramovitch, *Commentary*, January 1963, accessed October 31, 2021, https://www .commentarymagazine.com/articles/robert-daniels/the-soviet-revolution-1917 -1939-by-raphael-r-abramovich. For critical reviews, see George B. Carson, review of *The Soviet Revolution, 1917–1939*, by Raphael R. Abramovitch, *Journal of Modern History* 35, no. 2 (June, 1963): 210–211.

132. In Yiddish, the group remained *"Algemeyne Entsiklopedye in Yidish."* Pat's surname is occasionally rendered "Patt."

133. Kh[aim]-L[eyb] F[uks], "Pat, Emanuel," *Leksikon fun der nayer yidisher literatur* 7, cols. 75–76.

134. Abraham J. Dubelman, "Latin America," in *American Jewish Year Book* (1951): 213.

135. See Faye Ran, "Leyzer Ran (1912–1955): Linguistic and Literary Prodigy, and Champion of Yiddish and Yiddishkeit," in *Catalog of the Leyzer Ran Collection in the Harvard College Library*, ed. Charles Berlin (Cambridge, MA: Harvard Library, 2017), 3–8.

136. In 1954, Gilinsky came under sustained criticism by Szmul (Samuel) Ambaras, an employee who was responsible for handling the *Entsiklopedye*'s English-language correspondence, over his alleged mismanagement, hostility toward coworkers, and "intrigue." Among the allegations was that Gilinsky funded a vacation to Mexico at the *Entsiklopedye*'s expense and was paying himself a regular salary at a time when no one else was. Following an investigation, Gilinsky was formally cleared of the allegations. Afterward, Ambaras was let go from the organization and began a successful career as a bookseller. See letters in YIVO RG 1400 Bund Archives (Schulman, Algemeyne Entsiklopedye), box 8. Also private correspondence with Robert Ambaras, March 2, 2021. I am grateful to Robert Ambaras for sharing information on this matter.

137. Alec Eliezer Burko writes that Atran was a successful textile manufacturer from Ukraine who had spent time in Berlin in the 1920s and then moved to Paris. With his family he fled France for the United States in 1940 and was highly successful in New York real estate. In 1945, he launched the Atran Foundation, which funded Yiddish cultural projects, including a chair in Yiddish at Columbia University, that was first held by Uriel Weinreich, son of Max Weinreich. See "Saving Yiddish: Yiddish Studies and the Language Sciences in America, 1940–1970," 74–75.

138. Shloyme Gilinsky to Judah J. Shapiro, January 24, 1955, YIVO RG 1400 Bund Archives, box 10, folder 1955–1957. The total number of subscribers was 9,788, 7,500 of whom had subscribed to all nine volumes.

139. Minutes from April 30, 1955, meeting. YIVO Algemeyne Entsiklopedye Papers RG 1149, box 1, folder 4.

140. On the Claims Conference's support to Jewish cultural organizations, see Marilyn Henry, *Confronting the Perpetrators: A History of the Claims Conference* (London: Vallentine Mitchell, 2007), 185–213.

141. See the one-page description "Zekster alef-beys-band fun der entsiklopedye," Leyzer Ran Collection, Notes and clippings: collection 1, Harvard University.

142. Isaac Landman, ed., *The Universal Jewish Encyclopedia: An Authoritative and Popular Presentation of Jews and Judaism since the Earliest Times* (New York: The Universal Jewish Encyclopedia, Inc., 1939–1943); *Ha-entsiqlopedya ha-'ivrit: klalit, yehudit ve-eretsyisr'elit* (Jerusalem—Tel Aviv: Hevra le-hotsa'at entsiqlopedyot, 1949–1981).

143. See Noam Pianko, "Text, Not Territory: Simon Rawidowicz, Global Hebraism, and the Center of Decentered National Life," chap. 3 in *Zionism and the Roads Not Taken* (Bloomington: Indiana University Press, 2010), 61–93.

144. Simon Rawidowicz, ed., *Sefer Shimon Dubnov: Maamarim, Igrot* (London: Ararat Publishing Society, 1954).

145. See David N. Myers, *Between Jew and Arab: The Lost Voice of Simon Rawidowicz* (Waltham, MA: Brandeis University Press, 2008).

146. Simon Rawidowicz papers, file "Yiddish Encyclopedia." Also see YIVO *Algemeyne Entsiklopedye* Papers, RG 1149, folder 48; and the letters of Simon Rawidowicz to Abraham Ravid, November 7, 1955, and January 12, 1956, as published in Benjamin Ravid, "In Search of Lost Times and Places: Simon Rawidowicz Reflects on His Formative Years in Grajewo and Białystok," *Polin Studies in Polish Jewry* 29 (2017): 394–395.

147. Benjamin C. I. Ravid, "Introduction: The Life and Writings of Simon Rawidowicz," in *State of Israel, Diaspora and Jewish Continuity: Essays on the "Ever-Dying People,"* by Simon Rawidowicz, repr. (Hanover, NH: Brandeis University Press, 1986), 37–38.

148. See Salo W. Baron to Simon Rawidowicz, "February 4, 1957," Simon Rawidowicz papers, file "Yiddish Encyclopedia." Among other members of the board were Philip Friedman, Jacob Lestschinsky, the illustrious rabbi and civil rights leader Abraham Joshua Heschel, former JLC leader and head of the National Jewish Community Relations Advisory Council Isaiah Minkoff, and Aaron Steinberg.

149. The English titles are slightly revised for the Yiddish translations.

150. Morton Weinfeld, "Louis Rosenberg and the Origins of the Socio-Demographic Study of Jews in Canada," *Jewish Population Studies (Papers in Jewish Demography)*, Avraham Harman Institute of Contemporary Jewry, 1993: 39–53.

151. Unsurprisingly, the entry does not engage with what were then widely viewed as the less-honorable economic and social building elements of the Jewish

community of Buenos Aires, some of whom were deeply engaged with the city's sex trade. See Mir Yarfitz, *Impure Migration: Jews and Sex Work in Golden Age Argentina* (New Brunswick, NJ: Rutgers University Press, 2019).

152. It is not possible to confirm the number killed, and estimates at the time ranged from a few dozen to as many as 1,500. See Victor A. Mirelman, "The Semana Trágica of 1919 and the Jews in Argentina," *Jewish Social Studies* 37, no. 1 (1975): 61–73.

153. In 1974, Leyzer Ran would go on to publish the work that would secure his reputation as the most well-regarded chronicler of Vilna's Jewish past. See Leyzer Ran, *Yerusholaim-delite: ilustrirt un dokumentirt*, 3 vols. (New York: Vilner Albom-komitet, 1974).

154. Shloyme Gilinsky to Philip Friedman, August 6, 1957. YIVO Philip Friedman Papers RG 1258, folder 692.

155. On the title page, the date is given as 1963, but on the copyright page, it is listed as 1964, reflecting when the volume actually appeared in print.

156. YIVO *Algemeyne Entsiklopedye* Papers, RG 1149, folders 21 and 22. Also see YIVO Philip Friedman Papers RG 1258, folder 692.

157. On Friedman, see Stauber, "Laying the Foundations for Holocaust Research: The Impact of Philip Friedman"; Jockusch, *Collect and Record!*; Aleksiun, "Philip Friedman and the Emergence of Holocaust Scholarship: A Reappraisal"; Ibid., "An Invisible Web"; and Smith, *The Yiddish Historians*.

158. In the 1950s, Shapiro was a leader with the Conference on Material Claims against Germany and the B'nai B'rith Hillel Foundations. The title of his 1955 doctoral dissertation at Harvard is "A Report of an Experience in the Field of Educational Reconstruction in Europe After World War II (1948–1954)." Tenenbaum was the author of *Race and Reich: The Story of an Epoch* (New York: Twayne Publisher, 1956), one of the first attempts to write a study of Nazi racial attitudes and their implementation in the Holocaust. At one time a member of the executive committee of the Jewish Historical Institute in Warsaw, Isaiah Trunk in the late 1950s was an archivist at YIVO and wrote widely on the destruction of Jewish communities in the Holocaust.

159. See the discussion in Diner, *We Remember with Reverence and Love*. Also see David Cesarani and Eric J. Sundquist, eds., *After the Holocaust: Challenging the Myth of Silence* (New York: Routledge, 2011).

160. Lawrence Douglas, *The Memory of Judgment: Making Law and History in the Trials of the Holocaust* (New Haven, CT: Yale University Press, 2005).

161. These included, among others, the documentation effort by the Jewish Historical Institute in Warsaw, David Boder's interviews with survivors in displaced persons camps, and Ben Stonehill's recordings of Jewish folk songs among survivors who had been resettled in the United States. On the Jewish Historical Institute, see Jockusch, *Collect and Record!* and Annette Wieviorka, *The Era of the*

Witness (Ithaca, NY: Cornell University Press, 2006). On Boder, see David P. Boder, *I Did Not Interview the Dead* (Urbana: University of Illinois Press, 1949). On Stonehill, see *Stonehill Jewish Song Archive*, curated by Miriam Isaacs, accessed October 31, 2021, https://stonehilljewishsongs.wordpress.com.

162. For the complicated publication history of Anne Frank's diary, see Jeffrey Shandler, "From Diary to Book: Text, Object, Structure," in *Anne Frank Unbound: Media, Imagination, Memory,* ed. Barbara Kirshenblatt-Gimblett and Jeffrey Shandler (Bloomington: Indiana University Press, 2012), 25–58.

163. See Rachel Deblinger, "'In a World Still Trembling': American Jewish Philanthropy and the Shaping of Holocaust Survivor Narratives in Postwar America, 1945–1953," PhD diss. (University of California, Los Angeles, 2014).

164. Along with the "Yiddish historians," whom Mark L. Smith has discussed in his study, scholars in Israel as well began researching the Holocaust, with the first conference held in Palestine at the Hebrew University in 1947, one year before the state's founding. On debates within early Israeli historical approaches to the Holocaust, see Roni Stauber, "Confronting the Jewish Response during the Holocaust: Yad Vashem—A Commemorative and a Research institute in the 1950s," *Modern Judaism* 20 (2000): 277–298; and Boaz Cohen, "Setting the Agenda of Holocaust Research: Discord at Yad Vashem in the 1950s," in *Holocaust Historiography in Context: Emergence, Challenges, Polemics and Achievements,* ed. David Bankier and Dan Michman (Jerusalem: Yad Vashem, and New York: Berghahn Books, 2008), 255–292.

165. Smith, xvi. Also see chap. 2, "Holocaust History as Jewish History."

166. Ibid., xvii. Also see chap. 5, "The Search for Answers."

167. On this cohort of scholars, see Doris L. Bergen, "Out of the Limelight or In: Raul Hilberg, Gerhard Weinberg, Henry Friedlander, and the Historical Study of the Holocaust," in *The Second Generation: Émigrés from Nazi Germany as Historians,* ed. Andreas W. Daum, Hartmut Lehmann, and James J. Sheehan (New York: Berghahn: 2016), 229–243. Also see Lawrence Baron, "The Holocaust and American Public Memory, 1945–1960," *Holocaust and Genocide Studies* 17, no. 1 (Spring 2003): 62–88. Other widely read works included some of the first attempts at broad overviews of the genocide, such as Gerald Reitlinger's *The Final Solution* (1953), Leon Poliakov's *Harvest of Hate* (1954), and Joseph Tenenbaum's *Race and Reich* (1956).

168. Raul Hilberg, *The Destruction of the European Jews* (Chicago: Quadrangle Books, 1961).

169. Quoted in Nathaniel Popper, "A Conscious Pariah," *The Nation,* April 19, 2010, accessed October 31, 2021, https://www.thenation.com/article/archive/conscious-pariah.

170. Roni Stauber, "Laying the Foundations for Holocaust Research," 36–39.

171. Jewish Encyclopedic Handbooks, Inc. "Memorandum," January 1960, Tamiment Library and Robert F. Wagner Labor Archives, Isaiah Minkoff Papers, box 5, folder 23. Punctuation in the English original.

172. Gringauz's presence among the manuscript readers is likewise notable, given that he was a strong early skeptic of Holocaust memoirs and testimonies, having once declared that "most of the memoirs and reports are full of preposterous verbosity, graphomanic exaggeration, dramatic effects, overestimated self-inflation, dilettante philosophizing, would-be lyricism, unchecked rumors, bias, partisan attacks and apologies," a critique that has in more recent years been seized upon and used by Holocaust deniers. However, Gringauz did not summarily dismiss these materials as without value for historians but rather called upon scholars to establish clear methodological strategies for contending with them. See Samuel Gringauz, "Some Methodological Problems in the Study of the Ghetto," *Jewish Social Studies* 12, no. 1 (January 1950): 65.

173. An English-language version of this map was reproduced on the inside covers of Yuri Suhl, ed., *They Fought Back: The Story of the Jewish Resistance in Nazi Europe* (New York: Crown Publishers, 1967). On the slander of Jewish passivity during the Holocaust, see Tom Segev, *The Seventh Million: The Israelis and the Holocaust*, trans. Haim Watzman (New York: Henry Holt, 2000); and Yael S. Feldman, "'Not as Sheep Led to Slaughter'? On Trauma, Selective Memory, and the Making of Historical Consciousness," *Jewish Social Studies: History, Culture, Society*, n.s., 19, no. 3 (Spring/Summer 2013): 139–169.

174. See *Algemeyne entsiklopedye: Yidn vov*, 244. For a discussion of the Sonderkommando photographs, see Georges Didi-Huberman, *Images in Spite of All: Four Photographs from Auschwitz*, trans. Shane B. Lillis (Chicago: University of Chicago Press, 2008).

175. William Glicksman, review of *Algemeyne entsiklopedye: Yidn vov*, *YIVO Bleter* 43 (1966): 323–327.

176. "Barikht fun di finantsn," YIVO *Algemeyne Entsiklopedye* Papers, RG 1149, folder 7.

177. Iser, Goldberg, "Hakdome," *Algemeyne entsiklopedye: Yidn zayen* (New York: Dubnov-fond un entsiklopedye-komitet, Jewish Encyclopedic Handbooks Inc., 1966) unpaginated.

Conclusion

1. CYCO has since relocated to New York's Long Island City.

2. Burko, "Saving Yiddish: Yiddish Studies and the Language Sciences in America, 1940–1970."

3. Judah Achilles Joffe and Yudel Mark, eds., *Groyser verterbukh fun der yidisher shprakh*, 4 vols. (New York: Komitet farn groysn verterbukh fun der yidisher shprakh, 1961–1980); Max Weinreich, *Geshikhte fun der yidisher shprakh*, vols. 1–4 (New York: YIVO, 1973).

4. See Novershtern and Kuznitz, "Yiddish Research after the Holocaust," and Cecile E. Kuznitz, "Yiddish Studies," in *The Oxford Handbook of Jewish Studies*, ed. Martin Goodman (Oxford: Oxford University Press, 2002), 541–571.

5. Jeffrey Shandler, *Adventures in Yiddishland: Postvernacular Language & Culture* (Berkeley: University of California Press, 2006), 4–5.

6. Ilan Stavans, "O, R*O*S*T*E*N, My R*O*S*T*E*N!" in *How Yiddish Changed America and How America Changed Yiddish*, ed. Ilan Stavans and Josh Lambert (Restless Books: Brooklyn, 2020), 119. Also see Burko, 138–141. I am grateful to Sunny Yudkoff, whose 2021 presentation, "*The Joys of Yiddish*: A Reception History," to the North Carolina Jewish Studies Seminar has shaped my understanding of Rosten's *Joys* and its reception.

7. See, for example, Endel Markowitz, *The Encyclopedia Yiddishanica: A Compendium of Jewish Memorabilia: An Anthology of Jewish History, Culture, Religion, Language, Idioms, Colloquialisms and Teachings* (Fredericksburg, VA: Haymark Publications, 1980; Herman Galvin and Stan Tamarkin, *The Yiddish Dictionary Sourcebook: A Transliterated Guide to the Yiddish Language* (Hoboken: Ktav Publishing House Inc., 1986); Lita Epstein, *If You Can't Say Anything Nice, Say It in Yiddish: The Book of Yiddish Curses and Insults* (New York: Fall River Press, 2006); and Stephanie Butnick, Liel Leibovitz, and Mark Oppenheimer, *The Newish Jewish Encyclopedia: From Abraham to Zabar's and Everything in Between* (New York: Artisan, a Division of Workman Publishing, 2019).

8. Jeffrey Shandler, *Yiddish: Biography of a Language* (Oxford: Oxford University Press, 2020), 175.

9. Gershon David Hundert, preface to *The YIVO Encyclopedia of Jews in Eastern Europe*, xi–xii.

10. Ibid., ix.

11. The *YIVO Encyclopedia* is available online at http://yivoencyclopedia.org. A keyword search of "Algemeyne entsiklopedye" produces eight results. The entries that mention the *Algemeyne entsiklopedye* directly include "Ben-Adir," "Einhorn, Dovid," "Tsherikover, Elye," and "Steinberg Brothers." No mention of the *Algemeyne entsiklopedye* appears in the entry dedicated to Abramovitch.

BIBLIOGRAPHY

Chronology of the *Algemeyne entsiklopedye* and *The Jewish People: Past and Present*

Algemeyne entsiklopedye: Probeheft. Berlin: Dubnov-fond, 1932.
    2nd ed., Berlin: Dubnov-fond, 1933.
Algemeyne entsiklopedye. Vol. 1. Paris: Dubnov-fond, 1934.
    Reprint, New York: Central Yiddish Culture Organization, 1948.
Algemeyne entsiklopedye. Vol. 2. Paris: Dubnov-fond, 1935.
    Reprint, New York: Central Yiddish Culture Organization, 1948.
Algemeyne entsiklopedye. Vol. 3. Paris: Dubnov-fond, 1936.
    Reprint, New York: Central Yiddish Culture Organization, 1948.
Algemeyne entsiklopedye. Vol. 4. Paris: Dubnov-fond, 1937.
    Reprint, New York: Central Yiddish Culture Organization, 1948.
Algemeyne entsiklopedye: Yidn alef. Paris: Dubnov-fond, 1939.
    Reprint, New York: Central Yiddish Culture Organization and S. Dubnov
        Fund, 1941.
    Reprint, New York: Central Yiddish Culture Organization, 1948.
Algemeyne entsiklopedye: Yidn beys. Paris: Dubnov-fond, 1940.
    Reprint, New York: Central Yiddish Culture Organization, 1940.
    Reprint, New York: Central Yiddish Culture Organization, 1948.
Algemeyne entsiklopedye: Yidn giml. New York: Dubnov-fond un TsIKO,
    1942.
    Reprint, New York: Central Yiddish Culture Organization, 1948.
Algemeyne entsiklopedye. Vol. 5. New York: Dubnov- und TsIKO, 1944.

Reprint, New York: Central Yiddish Culture Organization, 1948.

Algemeyne entsiklopedye: Yidn daled. New York: Dubnov-fond un TsIKO, 1950.

Algemeyne entsiklopedye: Yidn hey. New York: Dubnov-fond un Entsiklopedye-komitet, 1957.

Algemeyne entsiklopedye: Yidn vov. New York: Dubnov-fond un Entsiklopedye-komitet, 1964.

Algemeyne entsiklopedye: Yidn zayen. New York: Dubnov-fond un Entsiklopedye-komitet, 1966.

The Jewish People: Past and Present. Vol. 1. New York: Jewish Encyclopedic Handbooks, 1946.

Reprint, New York: Jewish Encyclopedic Handbooks, 1955.

The Jewish People: Past and Present. Vol. 2. New York: Jewish Encyclopedic Handbooks and Central Yiddish Culture Organization, 1948.

Reprint, New York: Jewish Encyclopedic Handbooks, 1955.

The Jewish People: Past and Present. Vol. 3. New York: Jewish Encyclopedic Handbooks and Central Yiddish Culture Organization, 1952.

Reprint, New York: Jewish Encyclopedic Handbooks, 1955.

The Jewish People: Past and Present. Vol. 4. New York: Jewish Encyclopedic Handbooks, 1955.

Archival Sources

Central Archives of the History of the Jewish People, Jerusalem
    Simon Dubnow Papers
    P159: Aaron Steinberg Papers
Harvard University, Cambridge, Massachusetts
    MS Am 2518: Abraham Aaron Roback Papers
    Leyzer Ran Collection
International Institute of Social History, Amsterdam
    Rafail R. Abramovič Papers
    Alexander Berkman Papers
    Eduard Bernstein Papers
Simon Rawidowicz Archive, Newton, Massachusetts, USA
Robert F. Wagner Labor Archives, Tamiment Library, New York City
    Holocaust Era Records of the Jewish Labor Committee, Series 1, 1934–1947
    Isaiah M. Minkoff Papers, 1930–1984
University of Cape Town, Cape Town
    BC1155: Sholem Schwartzbard Papers
University of Southampton, Southampton, England

MS 262: Aaron Zakharovich Steinberg Papers
YIVO Institute for Jewish Research, New York City
   RG 1.1 YIVO (Vilna): Administration, Records, 1925–1941
   RG 82: Elias Tcherikower Papers
   RG 85: Sholem Schwartzbard Papers
   RG 87: Simon Dubnow Papers
   RG 204: David Pinski Papers
   RG 208: Chaim Zhitlowsky Papers
   RG 227: Alexander Mukdoni Papers
   RG 339: Jacob Lestschinsky Papers
   RG 356: Jacob Shatzky Papers
   RG 360: Shmuel Niger Papers
   RG 394: Ben-Adir Papers
   RG 554: Abraham Kin Papers
   RG 584: Max Weinreich Papers
   RG 1139: Abraham Cahan Papers
   RG 1149: *Algemeyne Entsiklopedye*
   RG 1258: Philip Friedman Papers
   RG 1400: Bund Archives (Schulman, *Algemeyne Entsiklopedye*)
   RG 1456: Raphael Abramovitch Papers

Theses and Unpublished Manuscripts

Burko, Alec Eliezer. "Saving Yiddish: Yiddish Studies and the Language Sciences in America, 1940–1970." PhD diss., Jewish Theological Seminary, 2019.

Deblinger, Rachel. "'In a World Still Trembling': American Jewish Philanthropy and the Shaping of Holocaust Survivor Narratives in Postwar America, 1945–1953." PhD diss., University of California, Los Angeles, 2014.

Karlip, Joshua Michael. "The Center That Could Not Hold: *Afn Sheydveg* and the Crisis of Diaspora Nationalism." PhD diss., Jewish Theological Seminary, 2006.

Lustig, Jason B. "'A Time to Gather': A History of Jewish Archives in the Twentieth Century." PhD diss., University of California, Los Angeles, 2017.

Melfi, Francesco. "A Rhetoric of Image and Word: The Magazine Milgroym/ Rimon, 1922–1924 and the Jewish Search for Inclusivity." PhD diss., Jewish Theological Seminary, 1996.

Underwood, Nicholas Lee. "Staging a New Community: Immigrant Yiddish Culture and Diaspora Nationalism in Interwar Paris, 1919–1940." PhD diss., University of Colorado, 2016.

Published Sources

A. B. "Di yidishe amerike far der yidisher entsiklopedye." *Literarishe bleter* 26 (1931): 499–500.

Abramovitch, Raphael. "A briv tsum redaktor fun 'Forverts' vegn der entsiklopedye af yidish." *Forverts,* February 3, 1935.

———, ed. *Di farshvundene velt / The Vanished World.* New York: Forward Association, 1947.

———. *In tsvey revolutsyes: di geshikhte fun a dor.* 2 vols. New York: Arbeter-ring, 1944.

———. *The Soviet Revolution, 1917–1939.* New York: International Universities Press Inc., 1962.

Abramovitch, Raphael, and Avrom Menes. *Leyenbukh tsu der geshikhte fun yisroel.* Vol. 1. Berlin: Wostok, 1923.

Adelman, Jeremy. *Worldly Philosopher: The Odyssey of Albert O. Hirschman.* Princeton, NJ: Princeton University Press, 2013.

Adler, Friedrich, R. Abramovitch, Léon Blum, and Émile Vandervelde, eds. *The Moscow Trial and the Labour and Socialist International.* London: The Labour Party, 1931.

Aleksiun, Natalia. "An Invisible Web: Philip Friedman and the Network of Holocaust Research." In *Als der Holocaust noch keinen Namen hatte: zur frühen Aufarbeitung des NS Massenmordes an den Juden / Before the Holocaust Had Its Name: Early Confrontations of the Nazi Mass Murder of the Jews,* edited by Regina Fritz, Béla Rásky, and Éva Kovács, 149–165. Vienna: New Academic Press, 2016.

———. "Philip Friedman and the Emergence of Holocaust Scholarship: A Reappraisal." In *Simon Dubnow Institute Yearbook* 11 (2012): 333–46.

Alquit, Boris. "Refleksiyes: notitsn af der zayt fun umshtrerblekhkayt. *Inzikh* 21 (February 1936): 108–112.

Alroey, Gur. *Zionism without Zion: The Jewish Territorial Organization and Its Conflict with the Zionist Organization.* Detroit: Wayne State University Press, 2016.

Alt, Arthur Tilo. "The Berlin *Milgroym* Group and Modernism." *Yiddish* 6, no. 1 (1985): 33–43.

———. "A Survey of Literary Contributions to the Post-World War I Yiddish Journals of Berlin." *Yiddish* 7, no. 1 (1987): 42–52.

———. "Yiddish and Berlin's *Scheunenviertel." Shofar* 9, no. 2 (Winter 1991): 29–43.

Alter, Robert. *The Invention of Hebrew Prose: Modern Fiction and the Language Revolution.* Seattle: University of Washington Press, 1988.

Anderson, Benedict. *Imagined Communities: Reflections on the Origins and Spread of Nationalism*. Rev. ed. London: Verso, 1991.

Ariel, Yaakov Shalom. "A Proud Announcement: *The Jewish Encyclopedia* and the Coming of Age of Jewish Scholarship in America." In *Simon Dubnow Institute Yearbook* 9 (2010): 381–404.

Arsen'ev, K. K., ed. *Novyi entsiklopedicheskii slovar'*. St. Petersburg: Brockhaus and Efron, 1911–1916.

Appiah, Kwame Anthony and Henry Louis Gates Jr., eds. *Africana: The Encyclopedia of the African and African American Experience*. 2nd ed. Oxford: Oxford University Press, 2005.

Aschheim, Steven E. *Brothers and Strangers: The East European Jew in German and German Consciousness, 1800–1923*. Madison: University of Wisconsin Press, 1982.

———. "The Double Exile: Weimar Culture and the East European Jews, 1918–1923." In *Towards the Holocaust: The Social and Economic Collapse of the Weimar Republic*, edited by Michael N. Dobkowski and Isidor Wallimann, 227–241. Westport, CT: Greenwood Press, 1983.

Auerbach, Karen. *The House at Ujazdowskie 16: Jewish Families in Warsaw after the Holocaust*. Bloomington: Indiana University Press, 2013.

Baker, Zachary M. *Essential Yiddish Books: 1000 Great Works from the Collection of the National Yiddish Book Center*. Amherst, MA: National Yiddish Book Center, 2004.

Baldwin, Neil. *Henry Ford and the Jews: The Mass Production of Hate*. New York: Public Affairs, 2001.

Band, Arnold J. "From Diaspora to Homeland: The Transfer of the Hebrew Literary Center to Eretz Yisrael." In *Studies in Modern Jewish Literature*, 143–156. Philadelphia: Jewish Publication Society, 2003.

Baron, Lawrence. "The Holocaust and American Public Memory, 1945–1960." *Holocaust and Genocide Studies* 17, no. 1 (Spring 2003): 62–88.

Baron, Salo W. "The Spiritual Reconstruction of European Jewry." *Commentary*, December 1, 1945, 4–12.

Bassok, Ido. "Mapping Reading Culture in Interwar Poland—Secular Literature as a New Marker of Ethnic Belonging among Jewish Youth." In *Simon Dubnow Institute Yearbook* 9 (2010): 15–36.

Baumgarten, Jean, and Alan Astro. "Yiddish in France: A Conversation with Rachel Ertel." *Shofar: An Interdisciplinary Journal of Jewish Studies* 14, no. 3 (Spring 1996): 125–137.

Bechtel, Delphine. "Babylon or Jerusalem: Berlin as Center of Jewish Modernism in the 1920s." In *Insiders and Outsiders: Jewish and Gentile Culture in*

Germany and Austria, edited by Dagmar C. G. Lorenz and Gabriele Wein-
berger, 116–23. Detroit: Wayne State University Press, 1994.

———. "Cultural Transfers between 'Ostjuden' and 'Westjuden': German-
Jewish Intellectuals and Yiddish Culture 1897–1930. In *Leo Baeck Institute
Year Book* 42 (1997): 67–83.

———. "1922, *Milgroym*, a Yiddish Magazine of Arts and Letters, Is Founded in
Berlin by Mark Wischnitzer." In *Yale Companion to Jewish Writing and
Thought in German Culture 1096–1996*, edited by Sander L. Gilman and Jack
Zipes, 420–426. New Haven, CT: Yale University Press, 1997.

Belgum, Kirsten. "Translated Knowledge in the Early Nineteenth Century:
Jewish and Judaism in Brockhaus' *Conversations-Lexikon* and the *Encyclopaedia Americana*." In *Simon Dubnow Institute Yearbook* 9 (2010): 303–322.

Bergen, Doris L. "Out of the Limelight or In: Raul Hilberg, Gerhard Weinberg,
Henry Friedlander, and the Historical Study of the Holocaust." In *The Second
Generation: Émigrés from Nazi Germany as Historians*, edited by Andreas W.
Daum, Hartmut Lehmann, and James J. Sheehan, 229–243. New York:
Berghahn: 2016.

Bikl, Shloyme, and Leybush Lehrer, eds. *Shmuel Niger-bukh*. New York: YIVO
Institute of Jewish Research, 1958.

Birnbaum, Pierre. *The Anti-Semitic Moment: A Tour of France in 1898*. Translated
by Jane Marie Todd. New York: Hill and Wang, 2003.

Black, Edwin. *War against the Weak: Eugenics and America's Plan to Create a
Master Race*. New York: Thunder's Mouth Press, 2003.

Blair, Ann M. *Too Much to Know: Managing Scholarly Information before the
Modern Age*. New Haven, CT: Yale University Press, 2010.

Blatman, Daniel. "On a Mission against All Odds: Szmuel Zygielbojm in London
(April 1942–May 1943)." *Yad Vashem Studies* 20 (1990): 237–271.

Blau, Amy. "Max Weinreich in Weimar Germany." In *Yiddish in Weimar Berlin:
At the Crossroads of Diaspora Politics and Culture*, edited by Gennady Estraikh
and Mikhail Krutikov, 163–178. Oxford: Legenda, 2010.

Boder, David P. *I Did Not Interview the Dead*. Urbana: University of Illinois Press,
1949.

Boyarin, Jonathan. *Polish Jews in Paris: The Ethnography of Memory*. Bloomington: Indiana University Press, 1991.

Brandt, Willy, and Leo Lania. *My Road to Berlin*. London: Peter Davies, 1960.

Brenner, David A. "'Making Jargon Respectable': Leo Winz, Ost und West and
the Reception of Yiddish Theatre in Pre-Hitler Germany." In *Leo Baeck
Institute Year Book* 42 (1997): 51–66.

Brenner, Michael. *The Renaissance of Jewish Culture in Weimar Germany*. New
Haven, CT: Yale University Press, 1996.

Bromberg, Eli. "We Need to Talk about Shmuel Charney." *In geveb*, October 2019. Accessed October 31, 2021. https://ingeveb.org/articles/we-need-to-talk-about-shmuel-charney.

Breuer, Mordechai, and Michael Graetz. *Tradition and Enlightenment 1600–1780.* Vol. 1 of *German-Jewish History in Modern Times,* edited by Michael A. Meyer and assistant-edited by Michael Brenner. New York: Columbia University Press, 1996.

Brick, Howard. *Daniel Bell and the Decline of Intellectual Radicalism: Social Theory and Political Reconciliation in the 1940s.* Madison: University of Wisconsin Press, 1986.

Brinkmann, Tobias. "From Hinterberlin to Berlin: Jewish Migrants from Eastern Europe in Berlin before and after 1918." *Journal of Modern Jewish Studies* 7, no. 3 (November 2008): 339–355.

Brisman, Shimeon. *A History and Guide to Judaic Encyclopedias and Lexicons.* Cincinnati: Hebrew Union College, 1987.

Brodkin, Karen. *How Jews Became White Folks and What That Says about Race in America.* New Brunswick, NJ: Rutgers University Press, 1998.

Broido, Vera. *Lenin and the Mensheviks: The Persecution of Socialists under Bolshevism.* Aldershot, England: Gower Publishing Company, 1987.

Brown, Nancy. "No Longer a Haven: Varian Fry and the Refugees of France." In *The Memory of the Holocaust in the 21st Century: Yad Vashem Second International Conference on the Holocaust and Higher Education.* Jerusalem: Yad Vashem International Task Force on Holocaust Education, Remembrance and Research, 1999.

Brym, Robert J. *The Jewish Intelligentsia and Russian Marxism: A Sociological Study of Intellectual Radicalism and Ideological Divergence.* New York: Schocken Books, 1978.

Budnitskii, Oleg. *Russian Jews between the Reds and the Whites, 1917–1920.* Translated by Timothy J. Portice. Philadelphia: University of Pennsylvania Press, 2012.

Butnick, Stephanie, Liel Leibovitz, and Mark Oppenheimer. *The Newish Jewish Encyclopedia: From Abraham to Zabar's and Everything in Between.* New York: Artisan, a division of Workman Publishing, 2019.

Caron, Vicky. "The Politics of Frustration: French Jewry and the Refugee Crisis in the 1930s." *Journal of Modern History* 65, no. 2 (June 1993): 311–356.

———. "Prelude to Vichy: France and the Jewish Refugees in the Era of Appeasement." *Journal of Contemporary History* 20, no. 1 (January 1985): 157–176.

———. *Uneasy Asylum: France and the Jewish Refugee Crisis, 1933–1942.* Stanford, CA: Stanford University Press, 1999.

Carr, Jessica L. *The Hebrew Orient: Palestine in Jewish American Visual Culture, 1901–1938.* Albany: State University Press of New York, 2020.

Carson, George B. Review of *The Soviet Revolution, 1917–1939,* by Raphael R. Abramovitch. *Journal of Modern History* 35, no. 2 (June 1963): 210–211.

Cassel, David, and Moritz Steinschneider. *Plan der Real-Encyclopädie des Judenthums, zunächst für die Mitarbeiter.* Krotoschin: B. L. Monasch & Sohn, 1844.

Cesarani, David, and Eric J. Sundquist, eds. *After the Holocaust: Challenging the Myth of Silence.* New York: Routledge, 2011.

Charney, Daniel. "Der onheyb iz gemakht (a briv fun Berlin)." *Yidish: Vokhnshrift fun der yidisher kultur-gezelshaft,* May 27, 1932, 13.

———. "Dos yidishe Berlin." *Literarishe bleter* 20 (1932): 312–3.

———. "In der laboratorye fun der yidisher entsiklopedye." *Literarishe bleter* 29 (1934): 454–56.

———. "Vifil in di oyses lign." *Literarishe bleter* 11 (1935): 171.

Cohen, Boaz. "Setting the Agenda of Holocaust Research: Discord at Yad Vashem in the 1950s." In *Holocaust Historiography in Context: Emergence, Challenges, Polemics and Achievements,* edited by David Bankier and Dan Michman, 255–292. Jerusalem: Yad Vashem and New York: Berghahn Books, 2008.

Cohen, Richard I. *The Burden of Conscience: French Jewish Leadership during the Holocaust.* Bloomington: Indiana University Press, 1987.

Collison, Robert. *Encyclopaedias: Their History throughout the Ages.* New York and London: Hafner Publishing Company, 1964.

Collomp, Catherine. "The Jewish Labor Committee, American Labor, and the Rescue of European Socialists, 1934–1941." *International Labor and Working-Class History* 68 (Fall 2005): 112–133.

———. *Rescue, Relief, and Resistance: The Jewish Labor Committee's Anti-Nazi Operations, 1934–1945.* Translated by Susan Emanuel. Detroit: Wayne State University Press, 2021.

———. *Résister au nazisme. Le Jewish Labor Committee New York, 1934–1945.* Paris: CNRS Éditions, 2016.

Daniels, Robert V. Review of *The Soviet Revolution, 1917–1939,* by Raphael R. Abramovitch. *Commentary,* January 1963. Accessed October 31, 2021. https://www.commentarymagazine.com/articles/robert-daniels/the-soviet-revolution-1917-1939-by-raphael-r-abramovich.

Darnton, Robert. *The Great Cat Massacre and Other Episodes in French Cultural History.* New York: Vintage, 1984.

Deutsch, Nathaniel. "When Culture Became the New Torah: Late Imperial Russia and the Discovery of Jewish Culture." *Jewish Quarterly Review* 102, no. 3 (Summer 2012): 455–473.

Diamond, Hanna. *Fleeing Hitler: France 1940*. Oxford: Oxford University Press, 2007.

Diderot, Denis. "Encyclopédie." Reprinted in *The Portable Enlightenment Reader*, edited by Isaac Kramnick, 17–18. New York: Penguin Books, 1995.

Didi-Huberman, Georges. *Images in Spite of All: Four Photographs from Auschwitz*. Translated by Shane B. Lillis. Chicago: University of Chicago Press, 2008.

Diner, Hasia R. *The Jews of the United States*. Berkeley: University of California Press, 2004.

———. *We Remember with Reverence and Love: American Jews and the Myth of Silence after the Holocaust, 1945–1962*. New York: New York University Press, 2009.

Dinnerstein, Leonard. *Antisemitism in America*. New York: Oxford University Press, 1994.

Dizhur, B. "Az men lebt, derlebt men!" *Literarishe bleter* 11 (1935): 168–9.

Dizhur, E[lyohu]. "Der vikhtiker uftu fun dem Dubnov-fond (arum der algemeyner entsiklopedye in yidish)." *Parizer haynt*, May 18, 1932, 2.

Doig, Kathleen Hardesty. "Encircling Encyclopedias." *Eighteenth-Century Studies* 36, no. 3 (Spring 2003): 441–444.

Dohrn, Verena. "Diplomacy in the Diaspora. The Jewish Telegraphic Agency in Berlin, 1922–1933." In *Leo Baeck Institute Year Book* 54 (2009): 219–241.

Dohrn, Verena and Anne-Christin Saß, "Einführung." In *Transit und Transformation: Osteuropäisch-jüdische Migranten in Berlin 1981–1939*, edited by Verena Dohrn and Gertrud Pickhan, 9–22. Göttingen: Wallstein Verlag, 2010.

Dohrn, Verena and Gertrud Pickhan, eds. *Transit und Transformation. Osteuropäische Migranten in Berlin 1918–1939*. Göttingen: Wallstein Verlag, 2010.

Dorf, Khaim. "Bleterndik di entsiklopedye." *Literarishe bleter* 11 (1935): 172–3.

Douglas, Lawrence. *The Memory of Judgment: Making Law and History in the Trials of the Holocaust*. New Haven, CT: Yale University Press, 2005.

Dubelman, Abraham J. "Latin America." In *American Jewish Year Book* 52 (1951): 201–13.

Du Bois, W. E. B. and Guy B. Johnson. *Encyclopedia of the Negro: Preparatory Volume with Reference Lists and Reports*. New York: Phelps-Stokes Fund, 1945.

Dubnov-Erlich, Sophie. *The Life and Work of S. M. Dubnov: Diaspora Nationalism and Jewish History*. Edited by Jeffrey Shandler. Translated by Judith Vowles. Bloomington: Indiana University Press, 1991.

"The Dubnov Yiddish Encyclopaedia." Daily news bulletin. *Jewish Telegraphic Agency*, February 20, 1931.

Dubnow, Simon. *Buch des Lebens: Erinnerungen und Gedanken Materialien zur Geschichte meiner Zeit*. Band 3, 1922–1933. Translated by Vera Bischitzky. Göttingen: Vandenhoeck & Ruprecht, 2005.

————. *Dos bukh fun mayn lebn.* Translated by Y. Birnboym. Buenos Aires: Alveltlekher yidisher kultur-kongres, 1963.

————. *Fun "zhargon" tsu yidish un andere artiklen: literarishe zikhroynes.* Vilna: B. Kletskin, 1929.

————. *Di nayste geshikhte fun yidishn folk fun di alte tsaytn biz tsu hayntiker tsayt.* Translated by Nokhem Shtif and Khaim-Shloyme Kazhdan. Warsaw: Kultur-lige, 1931.

————. *Weltgeschichte des jüdischen Volkes.* Translated by Aaron Steinberg. Berlin: Jüdischer Verlag 1925–1929.

Elbogen, Ismar, Josef Meisl, and Mark Wischnitzer, eds. *Festschrift zu Simon Dubnows siebzigstem Geburtstag.* Berlin: Jüdischer Verlag, 1930.

Engel David. *Historians of the Jews and the Holocaust.* Stanford: Stanford University Press, 2009.

————. "Poland since 1939." In *The YIVO Encyclopedia of Jews in Eastern Europe*, edited by Gershon David Hundert, 1404–1405. New Haven, CT: Yale University Press, 2008:

Engelhardt, Arndt. *Arsenale Jüdischen Wissens: Zur Entstehungsgeschichte der* Encyclopaedia Judaica. Göttingen: Vandenhoeck and Ruprecht, 2013.

————. "Divergierende Perspektiven. Zur Rezeption der deutsch-jüdischen Enzyklopädien in der Weimarer Republik." *Trumah* 17 (2007): 39–53.

————. "The *Encyclopaedia Judaica* (1928–1934): A Cultural Arsenal of Knowledge at an Existential Junction." Translated by William Templer. *Simon Dubnow Institute Yearbook* 9 (2010): 427–457.

————. "Die *Encyclopaedia Judaica*: Verhandlung von Deutungshoheit und kollektiver Zugehörigkeit in jüdischen Enzyklopädien der Zwischenkriegszeit." In *Allgemeinwissen und Gesellschaft: Akten des Internationalen Kongresses über Wissenstransfer und Enzyklopädische Ordnungssysteme, vom 18. bis 21. September 2003 in Prangins*, edited by Paul Michel, Madeleine Herren and Martin Rüesch, 255–246. Aachen: Shaker Verlag, 2007.

————. "Moritz Steinschneider's Notion of Encyclopedias." In *Studies on Steinschneider: Moritz Steinschneider and the Emergence of the Science of Judaism in Nineteenth Century Germany*, edited by Reimund Leicht and Gad Freudenthal, 109–153. Leiden, Boston: Brill, 2012.

————. "Palimpsests and Questions of Canonisation: The German-Jewish Encyclopedias in the Weimar Era." *Journal of Modern Jewish Studies* 5, no. 3 (2006): 301–321.

Engelhardt, Arndt, and Ines Prodhöl. Introduction to *Simon Dubnow Institute Yearbook* 9 (2010): 233–245.

Epstein, Lita. *If You Can't Say Anything Nice, Say It in Yiddish: The Book of Yiddish Curses and Insults*. New York: Fall River Press, 2006.

Ershter alveltlekher yidisher kultur-kongres: Pariz 17–21 Sept. 1937, Stenografisher barikht. Paris: Tsentral-farlag fun alveltlekhn yidishn kultur-farband, 1937.

Erskine, Hazel Gaudet. "The Polls: Religious Prejudice, Part 2: Anti-Semitism." *The Public Opinion Quarterly* 29, no. 4 (Winter 1965–1966): 649–664.

Estraikh, Gennady. "The Berlin Bureau of the *Forverts*." In *Yiddish in Weimar Berlin: At the Crossroads of Diaspora Politics and Culture*, edited by Gennady Estraikh and Mikhail Krutikov, 141–162. Oxford: Legenda, 2010.

———. "Charney, Daniel." In *The YIVO Encyclopedia of Jews in Eastern Europe*, edited by Gershon David Hundert, 1913–1914. New Haven, CT: Yale University Press, 2008.

———. "Jacob Lestschinsky: A Yiddishist Dreamer and Social Scientist." *Science in Context* 20, no. 2 (June 2007): 215–237.

———. "A Quest for Yiddishland: The 1937 World Yiddish Cultural Congress." *QUEST Issues in Contemporary Jewish History* 17 (September 2020): 96–117.

———. *Transatlantic Russian Jewishness: Ideological Voyages of the Yiddish Daily Forverts in the First Half of the Twentieth Century*. Boston: Academic Studies Press, 2020.

———. "Vilna on the Spree: Yiddish in Weimar Berlin." *Aschkenaz—Zeitschrift für Geschichte und Kultur der Juden* 16 (2006): 103–127.

———. "Weimar Berlin—An International Press Centre." In *Transit und Transformation: Osteuropäisch-jüdische Migranten in Berlin 1981–1939*, edited by Verena Dohrn and Gertrud Pickhan, 77–92. Göttingen: Wallstein Verlag, 2010.

———. *Yiddish in the Cold War*. Oxford: Legenda, 2008.

Evans, Richard J. *The Third Reich at War*. New York: Penguin Press, 2008.

Fainholtz, Tzafrir. "The Jewish Farmer, the Village and the World Fair: Politics, Propaganda, and the 'Israel in Palestine' Pavilion at the Paris International Exhibition of 1937." *MODSCAPES 2018*. Accessed October 31, 2021. https://www.shsconferences.org/articles/shsconf/pdf/2019/04/shsconf_modscapes2018_10004.pdf.

Feldman, Yael S. "'Not as Sheep Led to Slaughter'? On Trauma, Selective Memory, and the Making of Historical Consciousness." *Jewish Social Studies: History, Culture, Society*, n.s., 19, no. 3 (Spring/Summer 2013): 139–169.

Fink, Carole. *Defending the Rights of Others: The Great Powers, the Jews, and International Minority Protection, 1878–1938*. Cambridge: Cambridge University Press, 2006.

Finkelstein, Louis, ed. *The Jews: Their History, Culture, and Religion*. New York: Harper, 1949.

Fishman, David E. *The Book Smugglers: Partisans, Poets, and the Race to Save Jewish Treasures from the Nazis*. Lebanon, NH: ForeEdge, University Press of New England, 2017.

————. *Embers Plucked from the Fire: The Rescue of Jewish Cultural Treasures in Vilna*. New York: YIVO Institute for Jewish Research, 1996.

————. *The Rise of Modern Yiddish Culture*. Pittsburgh: University of Pittsburgh Press, 2005.

Foucault, Michel. *The Order of Things: An Archaeology of the Human Sciences*. New York: Pantheon Books, 1970.

Fraiman, Sarah. "The Transformation of Jewish Consciousness in Nazi Germany as Reflected in the German Jewish Journal *Der Morgen*, 1925–1938." *Modern Judaism* 20 (2000): 41–59.

Frankel, Jonathan. *Jewish Politics and the Russian Revolution of 1905*. Tel Aviv: Tel Aviv University Press, 1982.

————. *Prophecy and Politics: Socialism, Nationalism, and the Russian Jews, 1862–1917*. Cambridge: Cambridge University Press, 1981.

Freidenreich, Fradle Pomerantz. *Passionate Pioneers: The Story of Yiddish Secular Education in North America, 1910–1960*. Teaneck, NJ: Holmes & Meier Publishers, 2010.

Friedman, Philip. *Roads to Extinction: Essays on the Holocaust*. Edited by Ada June Friedman. New York and Philadelphia: Jewish Publication Society of America, 1980.

————. "Di yidishe entsiklopedye—a kapitl kultur-geshikhte fun undzer dor." *Tsukunft* 56, no. 3 (March 1951): 130–133.

Fuks, Leo, and Renate Fuks. "Yiddish Publishing Activities in the Weimar Republic, 1920–1933." In *Leo Baeck Institute Year Book* 30 (1988): 417–434.

Galvin, Herman, and Stan Tamarkin. *The Yiddish Dictionary Sourcebook: A Transliterated Guide to the Yiddish Language*. Hoboken: Ktav Publishing House Inc., 1986.

Garbarini, Alexandra. *Numbered Days: Diaries and the Holocaust*. New Haven, CT: Yale University Press, 2006.

Gassenschmidt, Christoph. *Jewish Liberal Politics in Tsarist Russia, 1900–1914: The Modernization of Russian Jewry*. New York: New York University Press, 1995.

Gaymon, Alva E. "Portugal Holding Delicate Position." *New York Times*, July 28, 1940.

Geller, Jay Howard. *Jews in Post-Holocaust Germany, 1945–1953*. Cambridge: Cambridge University Press, 2005.

Gergel, Nokhem. "Tsvey institutn." *Literarishe bleter* 24 (1930): 442–443.

Gilbert, Martin. *Atlas of the Holocaust*. London: Michael Joseph Limited, 1982.

Glass, Bentley. Review of *The Jewish People: Past and Present*, vol. 1, edited by R. Abramovitch, Ben-Adir, J. D. Brutzkus, A. Kin, Jacob Lestschinsky, A. Menes, A. Steinberg, and E. M. Tcherikower. *Quarterly Review of Biology* 23, no. 1 (March, 1948): 96.

Glickman, Mark. *Stolen Words: The Nazi Plunder of Jewish Books*. Philadelphia: The Jewish Publication Society, 2016.

Glicksman, William. Review of *Algemeyne entsiklopedye: Yidn vov*, edited by Nathan Chanin and Iser Goldberg. *YIVO Bleter* 43 (1966): 323–327.

Goldberg, Iser. "What Is a Jew?" *Canadian Jewish Chronicle*, November 16, 1951, 5.

Goldstein, Eric L. *The Price of Whiteness: Jews, Race, and American Identity*. Princeton: Princeton University Press, 2006.

Gorelik, Shmarye, A. Vayter, and Shmuel Niger. "Tsu di lezer." *Di literarishe monatsshriftn: fraye bine far literature un kunst* 1 (February 1908): 7–8.

Gorny, Yosef. *The Jewish Press and the Holocaust, 1939–1945: Palestine, Britain, the United States, and the Soviet Union*. Cambridge: Cambridge University Press, 2011.

Gray, Christopher. "Streetscapes/The Jewish Daily Forward Building, 175 East Broadway; A Capitalist Venture with a Socialist Base." *New York Times*, July 19, 1988.

Green, Nancy. *The Pletzl of Paris: Jewish Immigrant Workers in the Belle Epoque*. New York: Holmes and Meier, 1986.

Gringauz, Samuel. "Some Methodological Problems in the Study of the Ghetto." *Jewish Social Studies* 12, no. 1 (January 1950): 65–72.

Gruner, Wolf. *The Holocaust in Bohemia and Moravia: Czech Initiatives, German Policies, Jewish Responses*. New York: Berghahn Books, 2019.

Hand, Seán, and Steven T. Katz, eds. *Post-Holocaust France and the Jews, 1945–1955*. New York: New York University Press, 2015.

Harkavy, Alexander. *Yidish-english-hebreisher verterbukh*. New York: Alexander Harkavy, 1925.

Harshav, Benjamin. *Language in Time of Revolution*. Berkeley: University of California Press, 1993.

Hasak-Lowy, Todd. *Here and Now: History, Nationalism, and Realism in Modern Hebrew Fiction*. Syracuse: Syracuse University Press, 2008.

Henry, Marilyn. *Confronting the Perpetrators: A History of the Claims Conference*. London: Vallentine Mitchell, 2007.

Herren, Madeleine. "General Knowledge and Civil Society: An Accurate and Popular View of the Present Improved State of Human Knowledge." In *Allgemeinwissen und Gesellschaft: Akten des Internationalen Kongresses über Wissenstransfer und Enzyklopädische Ordnungssysteme, vom 18. bis 21.*

September 2003 in Prangins, edited by Paul Michel, Madeleine Herren, and Martin Rüesch, 489–511. Aachen: Shaker Verlag, 2007.

Hertz, Isabelle. "Morituri vos salutanat": Szmuel Zygielbojm's Suicide in May 1943 and the International Socialist Community in London." *Holocaust and Genocide Studies* 14, no. 2 (2000): 242–265.

Hilberg, Raul. *The Destruction of the European Jews.* Chicago: Quadrangle Books, 1961.

Himmelfarb, Milton. "Jewish History Freshly Appraised: The First Encyclopedia in the Newer Tradition." Review of *The Jewish People: Past and Present*, vol. 1, edited by R. Abramovitch, Ben-Adir, J. D. Brutzkus, A. Kin, Jacob Lestschinsky, A. Menes, A. Steinberg, and E. M. Tcherikower. *Commentary* (January 1, 1947): 479–487.

Hoffman, Matthew. "From Czernowitz to Paris: The International Yiddish Culture Congress of 1937." In *Czernowitz at 100: The First Yiddish Language Conference in Historical Perspective*, edited by Kalman Weiser and Joshua A. Fogel, 151–164. Lanham, Maryland: Lexington Books, 2010.

Hoffman, Stephanie, and Ezra Mendelsohn, eds. *The Revolution of 1905 and Russia's Jews.* Philadelphia: University of Pennsylvania Press, 2008.

Holocaust Encyclopedia, s.v. "German Invasion of Poland: Jewish Refugees, 1939." Washington, DC: United States Holocaust Memorial Museum. Accessed October 31, 2021. https://encyclopedia.ushmm.org/content/en/article/german-invasion-of-poland-jewish-refugees-1939.

Hundert, Gershon David. "The Impact of Knowledge: The YIVO Encyclopedia of Jews in Eastern Europe." *Osteuropa* (2008): 75–87.

———, ed. *The YIVO Encyclopedia of Jews in Eastern Europe.* New Haven: Yale University Press, 2008.

Hyman, Paula. *From Dreyfus to Vichy: The Remaking of French Jewry, 1906–1939.* New York: Columbia University Press, 1979.

———. *The Jews of Modern France.* Berkeley: University of California Press, 1998.

Ignatiev, Noel. *How the Irish Became White.* New York: Routledge, 2009.

Isaacs, Miriam. *Stonehill Jewish Song Archive.* Accessed October 31, 2021. https://stonehilljewishsongs.wordpress.com.

Ivanov, Alexander. "Facing East: The World ORT Union and the Jewish Refugee Problem in Europe, 1933–38." *East European Jewish Affairs* 39, no. 3 (2009): 369–388.

Ivanovitsh, S. "A groyser kultur-uftu." *Literarishe bleter* 11 (1935): 165–6.

Jacobs, Joseph. *The Jewish Encyclopedia: A Guide to Its Contents, an Aid to Its Use.* New York and London: Funk & Wagnalls, 1906.

Jockusch, Laura. *Collect and Record!: Jewish Holocaust Documentation in Early Postwar Europe.* New York: Oxford University Press, 2012.

Joffe, Judah Achilles, and Yudel Mark, eds. *Groyser verterbukh fun der yidisher shprakh.* 4 vols. New York: Komitet farn groysn verterbukh fun der yidisher shprakh, 1961–1980.

Kadar, Naomi Prawer. *Raising Secular Jews: Yiddish Schools and Their Periodicals for American Children, 1917–1950.* Waltham, MA: Brandeis University Press, 2016.

Kaplan, Edward K., and Samuel H. Dresner. "Heschel in Vilna." *Judaism* 43, no. 3 (1998): 278–295.

Kaplan, Marion. *Hitler's Jewish Refugees: Hope and Anxiety in Portugal.* New Haven: Yale University Press, 2020.

Karlip, Joshua M. "At the Crossroads between War and Genocide: A Reassessment of Jewish Ideology in 1940." *Jewish Social Studies* 11, no. 2 (Winter 2005): 170–201.

———. *The Tragedy of a Generation: The Rise and Fall of Jewish Nationalism in Eastern Europe.* Cambridge, MA: Harvard University Press, 2013.

Kassow, Samuel. *Who Will Write Our History?: Emanuel Ringelblum, the Warsaw Ghetto, and the Oyneg Shabes Archive.* Bloomington: Indiana University Press, 2007.

Katsenelson, Yehude-Leyb, Baron David Günzburg, Simon Dubnow, and Albert Harkavy, eds. *Evreiskaia entsiklopediia.* St. Petersburg: Brokhaus-Efron, 1906–1913.

Kautsky, Karl. *Das Erfurter Programm in seinem grundsätzlichen Theil.* Stuttgart: J. H. W. Dietz, 1892.

Khinoy, Mark. "What Happened to Abramovich?: Leafing through Volume 'A' of the New Soviet Encyclopedia." *Commentary* 11, no. 6 (June 1951): 591–592.

Klatzkin, Jacob, Nahum Goldmann, and Ismar Elbogen, eds. *Encyclopaedia Judaica.* Berlin: Eshkol, 1928–1934.

Klinov, Yeshayahu. "Shekheyonu." *Haynt,* May 2, 1932, 7.

Knox, Israel. Review of *The Story of Yiddish Literature,* by A. A. Roback. *Jewish Social Studies* 3, no. 2 (April 1941): 224–226.

Koralnik, Avrom. "Vegn a yidisher entsiklopedye." *Der Tog,* May 16, 1931.

Krah, Markus. *American Jewry and the Re-invention of the East European Jewish Past.* Berlin: De Gruyter Oldenbourg, 2018.

———. "Partisan Reviews and Commentaries on Eastern European Judaism: Postwar American-Jewish Intellectual Journals and the Reconstruction of the Eastern European Past." In *Reconstructing the Old Country: American Jewry in the Post-Holocaust Decades,* edited by Eliyana R. Adler and Sheila E. Jelen, 87–110. Detroit: Wayne State University Press, 2017.

Kramnick, Isaac, ed. *The Portable Enlightenment Reader.* New York: Penguin Books, 1995.

Krivitsky, Walter G. *In Stalin's Secret Service: An Expose of Russia's Secret Policies by the Former Chief of the Soviet Intelligence in Western Europe.* New York: Harper and Brothers, 1939.

Krug, Mark M. Review of *The Jewish People: Past and Present,* vol. 2, edited by R. Abramovitch, Ben-Adir, J. D. Brutzkus, A. Kin, Jacob Lestschinsky, A. Menes, A. Steinberg, E. M. Tcherikower, and Mark Wischnitzer. "Comments on Books and Writings," *Journal of Jewish Education* 21, no. 2 (1950): 69–72.

Kugelmass, Jack, and Jonathan Boyarin, eds. and trans. *From a Ruined Garden: The Memorial Books of Polish Jewry.* New York: Schocken Books, 1983.

Kühl, Stefan. *The Nazi Connection: Eugenics, American Racism, and German National Socialism.* Oxford: Oxford University Press, 1994.

Kühn-Ludewig. Maria. *Jiddische Bücher aus Berlin (1918–1936): Titel, Personen, Verlage.* Nümbrecht, Germany: Kirsch-Verlag, 2006.

Kuznitz, Cecile. "Yiddish Studies." In *The Oxford Handbook of Jewish Studies,* edited by Martin Goodman, 541–571. Oxford: Oxford University Press, 2002.

———. *YIVO and the Making of Modern Jewish Culture: Scholarship for the Yiddish Nation.* Cambridge, Cambridge University Press, 2014.

———. "YIVO's 'Old Friend and Teacher': Simon Dubnow and His Relationship to the Yiddish Scientific Institute." In *Simon Dubnow Institute Yearbook* 15 (2016): 477–507.

Landman, Isaac, ed. *The Universal Jewish Encyclopedia: An Authoritative and Popular Presentation of Jews and Judaism since the Earliest Times.* New York: The Universal Jewish Encyclopedia, Inc., 1939–1943.

Lebeson, Anita Libman. *Pilgrim People.* New York: Harper Brothers, 1950.

Lederhendler, Eli. "The Eastern European Jewish Past and Its Historians." In *Reconstructing the Old Country: American Jewry in the Post-Holocaust Decades,* edited by Eliyana R. Adler and Sheila E. Jelen, 23–43. Detroit: Wayne State University Press, 2017.

———. *New York Jews and the Decline of Urban Ethnicity, 1950–1970.* Syracuse: Syracuse University Press, 2001.

Leff, Lisa Moses. *The Archive Thief: The Man Who Salvaged French Jewish History in the Wake of the Holocaust.* Oxford: Oxford University Press, 2015.

Lestschinsky, Jacob. *Crisis, Catastrophe and Survival: A Jewish Balance Sheet, 1914–1948.* New York: Institute of Jewish Affairs of the World Jewish Congress, 1948.

———. "Shimen Dubnov un der yidisher gezelshaftlekher gedank." *Tsukunft* 36, no. 2 (February 1931): 123–129

———. *Vuhin geyen mir? Yidishe vanderung a mol un haynt.* New York: Yidish-natsyonaler arbeter-farband, 1944.

———. "Di yidishe entsiklopedye." *Bikher velt* 2–3 (1919): 10–14.

Levin, Dov. "Brutskus, Iulii." In *The YIVO Encyclopedia of Jews in Eastern Europe,* edited by Gershon David Hundert, 250–251. New Haven, CT: Yale University Press, 2008.

Levine, Glenn S. "Yiddish Publishing in Berlin and the Crisis in Eastern European Jewish Culture 1919–1924." In *Leo Baeck Institute Year Book* 42 (1997): 85–108.

Liebich, André. *From the Other Shore: Russian Social Democracy after 1921.* Cambridge, MA: Harvard University Press, 1997.

Lienhard, John H. "Diderot's Encyclopedia." *Engines of Our Ingenuity,* no. 122. Accessed October 31, 2021. http://www.uh.edu/engines/epi122.htm.

Lowenstein, Sharon. "The National Refugee Service (NRS)." In *Jewish American Volunteer Organizations,* edited by Michael N. Dobkowski, 364–372. Westport, CT: Greenwood Press, 1986.

Malkin, Dov-Ber. "Unzer taynes tsu der ershter yidisher entsiklopedye." *Vokhnshrift* 10 (March 27, 1931): 146–148.

Mann, Louis L. Review of *The Jewish People: Past and Present,* vol. 1, edited by R. Abramovitch, Ben-Adir, J. D. Brutzkus, A. Kin, Jacob Lestschinsky, A. Menes, A. Steinberg, and E. M. Tcherikower. *New York Times Book Review,* November 2, 1947, 28.

———. Review of *The Jewish People: Past and Present,* vol. 2, edited by R. Abramovitch, Ben-Adir, J. D. Brutzkus, A. Kin, Jacob Lestschinsky, A. Menes, A. Steinberg, E. M. Tcherikower, and Mark Wischnitzer. *New York Times Book Review,* May 8, 1949, 29.

Margolis, Rebecca. *Jewish Roots, Canadian Soil: Yiddish Cultural Life in Montreal, 1905–1945.* Montreal: McGill-Queen's University Press, 2011.

Markowitz, Endel. *The Encyclopedia Yiddishanica: A Compendium of Jewish Memorabilia: An Anthology of Jewish History, Culture, Religion, Language, Idioms, Colloquialisms and Teachings.* Fredericksburg, VA: Haymark Publications, 1981.

Marten-Finnis, Susanne, and Igor Dukhan. "Dream and Experiment, Time and Style in 1920s Berlin Émigré Magazines: *Zhar Ptitsa* and *Milgroym. East European Jewish Affairs* 35, no. 2 (December 2005): 225–44.

Mattar, Philip, ed. *The Encyclopedia of the Palestinians.* Rev. ed. New York: Facts on File, 2005.

Meek, Theophile J. Review of *The Jewish People: Past and Present,* vol. 1, edited by R. Abramovitch, Ben-Adir, J. D. Brutzkus, A. Kin, Jacob Lestschinsky, A. Menes, A. Steinberg, and E. M. Tcherikower. *Journal of Biblical Literature* 69, no. 4 (December 1950): 401–402.

Meisel, Nakhmen. "Afn frishn keyver fun Nokhem Gergel." *Literarishe bleter*
   48 (1931): 889–90.

———. "Forgeyer fun der algemeyner entsiklopedye in yidish." *Literarishe bleter*
   10 (1935): 170–171.

———. "Fun troym tsu virklekhkayt: a baratung vegn a yidisher entsiklopedye,
   Berlin 14–15 februar." *Literarishe bleter* 9 (1931): 157–160.

———. *Geven a mol a lebn: dos yidishe kultur-lebn in Poyln tsvishn beyde velt-
   milkhomes*. Buenos Aires: Tsentral-farband fun poylishe yidn in Argentine,
   1951.

———. "A groyse yidishe entsiklopedye." *Literarishe bleter* 13 (1930): 242–244.

———. "Mir hobn keyn mazl nisht tsu a yidisher entsiklopedye." *Yidishe kultur*
   5 (May 1954): 5–11.

———. "Afn frishn keyver fun Nokhum Gergel." *Literarishe bleter* 48 (1931):
   889–890.

Melzer, Emanuel. *No Way Out: The Politics of Polish Jewry 1935–1939*. Cincinnati:
   Hebrew Union College Press, 1997.

Mendelsohn, Ezra. "Jewish Politics in Interwar Poland: An Overview." In *The
   Jews of Poland between Two World Wars*, edited by Yisrael Gutman, Ezra
   Mendelsohn, Jehuda Reinharz, and Chone Shmeruk, 9–19. Hanover, NH:
   Brandeis University Press, 1989.

———. *The Jews of East Central Europe between the World Wars*. Bloomington:
   Indiana University Press, 1983.

Mendes-Flohr, Paul. *Divided Passions: Jewish Intellectuals and the Experience of
   Modernity*. Detroit: Wayne State University Press, 1991.

Mendes-Flohr, Paul, and Jehuda Reinharz, eds. *The Jew in the Modern World:
   A Documentary History*. 3rd ed. Oxford: Oxford University Press, 2011.

Michels, Tony. "Exporting Yiddish Socialism: New York's Role in the Russian
   Jewish Workers' Movement." *Jewish Social Studies* 16, no. 1 (Fall 2009): 1–26.

Mirelman, Victor A. "The Semana Trágica of 1919 and the Jews in Argentina."
   Jewish Social Studies 37, no. 1 (1975): 61–73.

Miron, Guy. *The Waning of Emancipation: Jewish History, Memory, and the Rise of
   Fascism in Germany, France, and Hungary*. Detroit: Wayne State University
   Press, 2011.

Montagu, Ashley. *Man's Most Dangerous Myth: The Fallacy of Race*. New York:
   Columbia University Press, 1942.

Mowrer, Lillian. "Fiesta in Lisbon." *New Yorker*, July 20, 1940: 36–42.

Mukdoni, Alexander. "An algemeyne entsiklopedye in yidish." *Tsukunft* 40, no. 5
   (May 1935): 298–302.

———. "A velt mit visn vegn yidn." *Der Tog*, July 21, 1939.

Muhanna, Elias. *The World in a Box: Al-Nuwayri and the Islamic Encyclopedic Tradition*. Princeton: Princeton University Press, 2018.

Myers, David N. *Between Jew and Arab: The Lost Voice of Simon Rawidowicz*. Hanover, NH: Brandeis University Press, 2008.

———. "'Distant Relatives Happening onto the Same Inn': The Meeting of East and West as Literary Theme and Cultural Ideal." *Jewish Social Studies* 1, no. 2 (Winter 1995): 75–100.

Nathans, Benjamin. "On Russian-Jewish Historiography." in *Historiography of Imperial Russia: The Profession and Writing of History in a Multinational State*, edited by Thomas Sanders, 397–432. Armonk, New York: M. E. Sharpe, 1997.

Niger, Shmuel, and Yankev Shatzky, eds. *Leksikon fun der nayer yidisher literatur*. 8 vols. New York: Alveltlekher yidisher kultur-kongres, 1956–1981.

Niewyk, Donald L. *The Jews in Weimar Germany*. Baton Rouge: Louisiana State University Press, 1980.

Norich, Anita. *Discovering Exile: Yiddish and Jewish American Culture during the Holocaust*. Stanford: Stanford University Press, 2007.

Novershtern, Avraham. "From the Folk to the Academics: Study and Research of Yiddish after the Holocaust." In *Encyclopedia Judaica Yearbook 1988/89*, 14–24. Jerusalem: Keter.

Novershtern, Avraham and Cecile Esther Kuznitz. "Yiddish Research after the Holocaust." In *Encyclopaedia Judaica*, 2nd ed. Detroit: Thomson Gale, 2007.

Orbach, Alexander. "The Jewish People's Group and Jewish Politics in Tsarist Russia, 1906–1914." *Modern Judaism* 10, no. 1 (February 1990): 1–15.

———. *New Voices of Russian Jewry: A Study of the Russian-Jewish Press of Odessa in the Era of the Great Reforms, 1860–1871*. Leiden: Brill Academic Publishers, 1980.

Orlinsky, Harry M. Review of *The Jewish People: Past and Present*, vol. 3, edited by Raphael Abramovitch, Abraham Kin, Jacob Lestschinsky, Abraham Menes, Samuel Niger, Aaron Steinberg, and Mark Wischnitzer. *Journal of Biblical Literature* 75, no. 1 (March 1956): 80–82.

Orzhitzer, A. M. *Fun Vankuver biz Eylat: vanderungen mit der yidisher entsiklopedye, reportazhn, bilder un dertseylungen*. Tel Aviv: Ostrover, 1965.

Pankhurst, Richard. "Jewish Settlement in Ethiopia: Plans for Mass Jewish Settlement in Ethiopia (1936–1943)." Accessed October 31, 2021. https://tezetaethiopia.wordpress.com/2005/04/20/plans-for-mass-jewish-settlement-in-ethiopia-1936-1943br-smallby-richarch-pankhurst.

Perego, Simon. "Commemorating the Holocaust during the First Postwar Decade: Jewish Initiatives and Non-Jewish Actors in France." In *Als der Holocaust noch keinen Namen hatte: zur frühen Aufarbeitung des NS-Massenmordes*

an den Juden / Before the Holocaust Had Its Name: Early Confrontations of the
Nazi Mass Murder of the Jews, edited by Regina Fritz, Eva Kovacs, and Béla
Rásky, 223–239. Vienna: New Academic Press, 2016.

———. "Yiddish or Not? Holocaust Remembrance, Commemorative Ceremonies, and Questions of Language among Parisian Jews, 1944–1967." Journal of
Modern Jewish Studies 20, no. 2 (2021): 222–247.

Perlhefter, Beer and Bella. Be'er Sheva: An Edition of a Seventeenth Century
Yiddish Encyclopedia. Edited by Nathanael Riemer and Sigrid Senkbeil.
Wiesbaden: Harrassowitz Verlag, 2011.

Pianko, Noam. Zionism and the Roads Not Taken. Bloomington: Indiana University Press, 2010.

Pinsker, Shachar M. Literary Passports: The Making of Modernist Hebrew Fiction
in Europe. Stanford: Stanford University Press, 2011.

———. A Rich Brew: How Cafés Created Modern Jewish Culture. New York: New
York University Press, 2018.

Pinson, Koppel S. Review of Algemeyne entsiklopedye, vol. 5, edited by R.
Abramovitch, Ben-Adir, E. Tcherikower, Jacob Lestschinsky, A. Menes, and
A. Kin. Jewish Social Studies 7, no. 1 (January 1945): 76–78.

Poliakov, Léon. Harvest of Hate: The Nazi Program for the Destruction of the Jews
of Europe. Syracuse: Syracuse University Press, 1954.

Popper, Nathaniel. "A Conscious Pariah." The Nation, April 19, 2010. Accessed
October 31, 2021. https://www.thenation.com/article/archive/conscious
-pariah.

Prezidium fun Dubnov-fond. "Vegn 'der entsiklopedye in yidish.'" Literarishe
bleter 39 (1933): 624–625.

Prilutski, Noyekh. "An algemeyne entsiklopedye af yidish!" Moment 10
(December 1935).

Purinton, Carl E. Review of The Jewish People: Past and Present, vol. 2, edited by
R. Abramovitch, Ben-Adir, J. D. Brutzkus, A. Kin, Jacob Lestschinsky,
A. Menes, A. Steinberg, E. M. Tcherikower, and Mark Wischnitzer. Journal of
Bible and Religion 17, no. 3 (July, 1949): 211–212.

Rabinbach, Anson, and Jack Zipes, eds. Germans and Jews since the Holocaust:
The Changing Situation in West Germany. New York: Holmes and Meier,
1986.

Rabinovitch, Simon. "The Dawn of a New Diaspora: Simon Dubnov's Autonomism, from St. Petersburg to Berlin." In Leo Baeck Institute Year Book 50
(2005): 267–288.

———, ed. Jews and Diaspora Nationalism: Writings on Jewish Peoplehood in
Europe and the United States. Waltham, MA: Brandeis University Press, 2012.

Rabinowitz, Dan. *The Lost Library: The Legacy of Vilna's Strashun Library in the Aftermath of the Holocaust.* Hanover, NH: Brandeis University Press, 2019.

Raeff, Marc. *Russia Abroad: A Cultural History of Russian Emigration, 1919–1939.* New York: Oxford University Press, 1990.

Ran, Faye. "Leyzer Ran (1912–1955): Linguistic and Literary Prodigy, and Champion of Yiddish and Yiddishkeit." In *Catalog of the Leyzer Ran Collection in the Harvard College Library,* edited by Charles Berlin, 3–8. Cambridge, MA: Harvard University Library, 2017.

Ran, Leyzer. *Yerusholaim-delite: ilustrirt un dokumentirt.* New York: Vilner Albom Komitet, 1974.

Ravid, Benjamin. "In Search of Lost Times and Places: Simon Rawidowicz Reflects on His Formative Years in Grajewo and Białystok." *Polin Studies in Polish Jewry* 29 (2017): 394–395.

Rawidowicz, Simon, ed. *Sefer Shimon Dubnov: Maamarim, Igrot.* London: Ararat Publishing Society, 1954.

———. *State of Israel, Diaspora and Jewish Continuity: Essays on the "Ever-Dying People."* Edited by Benjamin C. I. Ravid. Reprint. Hanover, NH: Brandeis University Press, 1986.

Reisen, Zalmen. "Af der konferents vegn der yidisher entsiklopedye." *Der Tog,* February 12, 1932.

———, ed. *Leksikon fun der yidisher literatur, prese un filologye.* 4 vols. Vilna: Kletskin, 1926.

———. "Yidishe entsiklopedye un yidishkayt-entsiklopedye." *Literarishe bleter* 10 (1935): 166–8.

Ritterband, Paul. "Counting the Jews of New York, 1900–1991: An Essay in Substance and Method." In *Papers in Jewish Demography,* 199–228, edited by Sergio Della Pergola and Judith Even. Jerusalem: Avraham Harman Institute of Contemporary Jewry, 1997.

Rivkin, Ellis. Review of *The Jewish People: Past and Present,* vol. 1, edited by R. Abramovitch, Ben-Adir, J. D. Brutzkus, A. Kin, Jacob Lestschinsky, A. Menes, A. Steinberg, and E. M. Tcherikower. *Jewish Quarterly Review* 40, no. 1 (July 1949): 121–124.

Roback, A. A. "Di algemeyne entsiklopedye in yidish." *Yidishe kultur* 11 (November 1948): 6–12.

———. "Di algemeyne entsiklopedye in yidish." *Yidishe kultur* 12 (December 1948): 15–19.

———. "A bisl mer vaytzikhtikayt." *Literarishe bleter* 37 (1931): 709–11.

———. "Di shlepe tsu der yidisher entsiklopedye." *Yidishe kultur* 3 (March 1949): 32–36.

———. "Di shprakh un hazbore fun der algemeyne entsiklopedye." *Yidishe kultur* 1 (January 1949): 35–38.

———. *The Story of Yiddish Literature.* New York: Yiddish Scientific Institute, American Branch, 1940.

Robinson, Jacob and Philip Friedman. *Guide to Jewish History under Nazi Impact.* New York: YIVO Institute for Jewish Research, 1960.

Roediger, David R. *Working toward Whiteness: How America's Immigrants Became White.* New York: Basic Books, 2005.

Rojanski, Rachel. "The Final Chapter in the Struggle for Cultural Autonomy: Palestine, Israel and Yiddish Writers in the Diaspora, 1946–1951." *Journal of Modern Jewish Studies* 6, no. 2 (July 2007): 185–204.

Rozin, A. [Ben-Adir]. "A bisl 'makhoyre-haparged' fun der entsiklopedye." *Literarishe bleter* 11 (1935): 164–165.

———. *Farn geshikhtlekhn yom-hadin, dos yidishe folk tsvishn toykhekhe un geule.* Paris: 1940.

Rubin, Adam. "Jewish Nationalism and the Encyclopaedic Imagination: The Failure (and Success) of Ahad Ha'am's *Otsar Hayahadut.*" *Journal of Modern Jewish Studies* 3, no. 3 (November 2004): 247–262.

Rubin, Israel. "Bay di tishlekh fun romanishn kafe." *Literarishe bleter* 3 (1930): 53–54 and 7 (1930): 127–128.

Salant, Yankl. "Frayland-lige." In *The YIVO Encyclopedia of Jews in Eastern Europe* edited by Gershon David Hundert. New Haven: Yale University Press, 2008.

Saß, Anne-Christin. "Reports from the 'Republic Lear': David Eynhorn in Weimar Berlin 1920–24." In *Yiddish in Weimar Berlin: At the Crossroads of Diaspora Politics and Culture,* edited by Gennady Estraikh and Mikhail Krutikov, 179–194. Oxford: Legenda Press, 2010.

Schachter, Allison. *Diasporic Modernisms: Hebrew and Yiddish Literature in the Twentieth Century.* Oxford: Oxford University Press, 2012.

Schechter, Ronald. *Obstinate Hebrews, Representations of Jews in France, 1715–1815.* Berkeley: University of California Press, 2003.

Schütz, Chana C. "Lesser Ury and the Jewish Renaissance." *Jewish Studies Quarterly* 10 (2003): 360–376.

———. "Lesser Ury: Images from the Bible." In *Lesser Ury—Images from the Bible,* 13–25. Boca Raton: Boca Raton Museum of Art, 2003. Exhibition catalog.

Schwartz, Shuly Rubin. *The Emergence of Jewish Scholarship in America: The Publication of the* Jewish Encyclopedia. Cincinnati: Hebrew Union College Press, 1991.

Schwarz, Jan. *Survivors and Exiles: Yiddish Culture after the Holocaust.* Detroit: Wayne State University Press, 2015.

Segev, Tom. *The Seventh Million: The Israelis and the Holocaust*. Translated by
    Haim Watzman. New York: Henry Holt, 2000.
Shalit, Moyshe. "Biografishe leksikonen." *Bikhervelt* 4 (1928): 23–31, and 5 (1928):
    9–17.
————. "Di *Encyklopaedia Judaica*." *Yidishe velt* 6 (September 1928): 457–470.
————. "Entsiklopedyes." *Bikhervelt* 1 (April 1928): 37–46.
————. "Vegn an entsiklopedye af yidish." *Literarishe bleter* 3 (1931): 37–40.
————. "Di yidishe entsiklopedye—a fakt." *Literarishe bleter* 11 (1935): 161–3.
Shandler, Jeffrey. *Adventures in Yiddishland: Postvernacular Language & Culture*.
    Berkeley: University of California Press, 2006.
————. "From Diary to Book: Text, Object, Structure." In *Anne Frank Un-
    bound: Media, Imagination, Memory*, edited by Barbara Kirshenblatt-
    Gimblett and Jeffrey Shandler, 25–58. Bloomington: Indiana University
    Press, 2012.
————. "Keepers of Accounts: The Practice of Inventory in Modern Jewish
    Life." The Jean & Samuel Frankel Center for Judaic Studies David W. Belin
    Lecture in American Jewish Affairs, University of Michigan. Ann Arbor,
    Michigan, 2010.
————. *Yiddish: Biography of a Language*. Oxford: Oxford University Press,
    2020.
Shapiro, Edward S. *A Time for Healing: American Jewry since World War II*.
    Baltimore: Johns Hopkins University Press, 1992.
————, ed. *Yiddish in America: Essays on Yiddish Culture in the Golden Land*.
    Scranton, Pennsylvania: University of Scranton Press, 2008.
Shapiro, Henry D. Review of *The Emergence of Jewish Scholarship in America: The
    Publication of the Jewish Encyclopedia*, by Shuly Rubin Schwartz. *AJS Review*
    19, no. 1 (1994): 112–114.
Shapiro, Leon. *The History of ORT: A Jewish Movement for Social Change*. New
    York: Schocken Books, 1980.
Shapiro, Menakhem. "A por bamerkungen vegn der algemeyner entsiklopedye in
    yidish." *Haynt*, April 3, 1936, 7.
Shilo, Bilha. "'Funem Folk, Farn Folk, Mitn Folk': The Restitution of the YIVO
    Collection from Offenbach to New York." *Moreshet* 14 (2017): 362–412.
Shinar, Mordechai. "S.J. Yatzkan and the Jewish Journalism in France." *Our
    Press: World Federation of Jewish Journalists* 3 (1989): 30–35.
Shmeruk, Chone. "Hebrew-Yiddish-Polish: A Trilingual Jewish Culture." In *The
    Jews of Poland between Two World Wars*, edited by Yisrael Gutman, Ezra
    Mendelsohn, Jehuda Reinharz, and Chone Shmeruk, 285–311. Hanover, NH:
    Brandeis University Press, 1989.

Shneer, David. *Yiddish and the Creation of Soviet Jewish Culture, 1918–1930.*
Cambridge: Cambridge University Press, 2004.

Shternshis, Anna. *Soviet and Kosher: Jewish Popular Culture in the Soviet Union,
1923–1939.* Bloomington: Indiana University Press, 2006.

Shtif, Nokhem. "Oytobiografye." *YIVO Bleter* 5 (1933): 195–225.

———. "Vegn a yidishn akademishn institut." In *Di organizatsye fun der yidisher
visnshaft,* 3–33. Vilna: Tsentraler Bildungs-komitet and Vilbig, 1925.

Sinanoglou, Penny. *Partitioning Palestine: British Policymaking at the End of
Empire.* Chicago: University of Chicago Press, 2019.

Singer, Isidore, ed. *The Jewish Encyclopedia.* New York: Funk and Wagnalls,
1901–1906.

Sinkoff, Nancy. *From Left to Right: Lucy S. Dawidowicz, the New York Intellectuals,
and the Politics of Jewish History.* Detroit: Wayne State University Press, 2020.

———. "Lucy S. Dawidowicz and the Restitution of Jewish Cultural Property."
American Jewish History 100, no. 1 (2016): 117–147.

Slucki, David. *The International Jewish Labor Bund after 1945: Toward a Global
History.* New Brunswick, NJ: Rutgers University Press, 2012.

Slutski, B. "A burzhuaze, klerikal-natsyonalistishe entsiklopedye unter der maske
fun veltlekhkayt, umparteyishkayt un 'sotsyal-gezonenkayt.'" *Visnshaft un
Revolutsye* 2, no. 6 (1935): 163–194.

Smilovitsky, Leonid. "Jews under Soviet Rule." *Cahiers du monde russe* 49,
nos. 2–3 (2008): 475–514.

Smith, Mark L. *The Yiddish Historians and the Struggle for a Jewish History of the
Holocaust.* Detroit: Wayne State University Press, 2019.

Soltes, Mordechai. "The Yiddish Press: An Americanizing Agency." In *American
Jewish Year Book* 26 (1924–25): 165–372.

Sorkin, David. *Moses Mendelssohn and the Religious Enlightenment.* Berkeley:
University of California Press, 1996.

Stauber, Roni. "Confronting the Jewish Response during the Holocaust: Yad
Vashem—A Commemorative and a Research Institute in the 1950s." *Modern
Judaism* 20 (2000): 277–298.

———. "Laying the Foundations for Holocaust Research: The Impact of Philip
Friedman." *Search and Research Lectures and Papers,* vol. 15. Jerusalem: Yad
Vashem International Institute for Holocaust Research, 2009.

Stavans, Ilan. "O, R*O*S*T*E*N, My R*O*S*T*E*N!" In *How Yiddish Changed
America and How America Changed Yiddish,* edited by Ilan Stavans and Josh
Lambert, 114–125. Restless Books: Brooklyn, 2020.

Stein, Sarah Abrevaya. *Making Jews Modern: The Yiddish and Ladino Press in the
Russian and Ottoman Empires.* Bloomington: Indiana University Press, 2003.

———. "Two New Books Offer a Window into the History of Salonica's Jewish Community." *Forward*, August 25, 2006. Accessed October 31, 2021. http://old .forward.com/articles/1431/index.html.

Stiftung Jüdisches Museum Berlin. *Berlin Transit: Jüdische Migranten aus Osteuropea in den 1920er Jahren*. Göttingen: Wallstein Verlag, 2012.

Suhl, Yuri, ed. *They Fought Back: The Story of the Jewish Resistance in Nazi Europe*. New York: Crown Publishers, 1967.

Svet, Herman. "Di algemeyne entsiklopedye in der yidisher shprakh vert a fakt." *Moment*, December 22, 1933.

———. "Der ershter aroysfor fun der Dubnov-entsiklopedye." *Moment*, May 13, 1932.

——— [Gershon Swet]. "With the Wurmbrands in Pre-Hitler Berlin." In *Michael Wurmbrand: The Man and His Work*, edited by Kurt R. Grossman, 17–21. New York: Philosophical Library, 1956.

Szajkowski, Zosa. "150 yor yidishe prese in Frankraykh—biblyografye fun der yidisher prese in Frankraykh un in di kolonyes." In *Yidn in Frankraykh: shtudyes un materyaln*, edited by Elias Tcherikower, 236–308. New York: YIVO, 1942.

Taylor, Melissa Jane. "American Consuls and the Politics of Rescue in Marseille, 1936–1941." *Holocaust and Genocide Studies* 30, no. 2 (Fall 2016): 247–275.

Tcherikower, Elias. "Di ranglenishn fun yidish in Daytshland." *Literarishe bleter* 20 (1932): 309–311.

———. *Yidn in Frankraykh: shtudyes un materyaln*. 2 vols. New York: YIVO, 1942.

Tenenbaum, Joseph. *Race and Reich: The Story of an Epoch*. New York: Twayne Publishers, 1956.

Thompson, Dorothy. "Refugees: A World Problem." *Foreign Affairs* 16, no. 3 (April 1938): 375–387.

Tobias, Henry. "The Bund and the First Congress of the RSDWP: An Addendum." *Russian Review* 24, no. 4. (October 1965): 393–406.

Trachtenberg, Barry. "From Edification to Commemoration: *Di Algemeyne Entsiklopedye*, the Holocaust, and the Collapse of Eastern European Jewish Life." *Journal of Modern Jewish Studies* 5, no. 3 (November 2006): 285–300.

———. *The Revolutionary Roots of Modern Yiddish, 1903–1917*. Syracuse: Syracuse University Press, 2008.

Di tsentral farvaltung fun yidishn visnshaftlekhn institut. "Aroyslozndik di YIVO-bleter." *YIVO Bleter* 1, no. 1 (January 1931): 1–3.

Twersky, Yohanan. Review of *Algemeyne entsiklopedye: Yidn beys*, edited by R. Abramovitch, A. Ben-Adir, E. Tcherikower, A. Menes, A. Kin, and A. Steinberg. *Tsukunft* 46, no. 2 (November 1941): 124–127.

Underwood, Nick. "Exposing Yiddish Paris: The Modern Jewish Culture Pavilion at the 1937 World's Fair." *East European Jewish Affairs* 46, no. 2 (2016): 160–175.

———. *Yiddish Paris: Staging Nation and Community in Interwar France.* Bloomington: Indiana University Press, 2022.

Valencia, Heather. "A Yiddish Poet Engages with German Society: A. N. Stencl's Weimar Period." In *Yiddish in Weimar Berlin: At the Crossroads of Diaspora Politics and Culture,* edited by Gennady Estraikh and Mikhail Krutikov, 54–72. Oxford: Legenda, 2010.

Varshavyak, Y. "An algemeyne entsiklopedye af hebreish." *Moment,* September 13, 1935.

Veidlinger, Jeffrey. "'Emancipation: See Anti-Semitism'—The *Evreiskaia entsiklopediia* and Jewish Public Culture." *Simon Dubnow Institute Yearbook* 9 (2010): 405–426.

———. "From Ashkenaz to Zionism: Putting Eastern European Jewish Life in (Alphabetical) Order." Review essay of *YIVO Encyclopedia of Jews in Eastern Europe. AJS Review* 33:2 (November 2009), 379–389.

———. *Jewish Public Culture in the Late Russian Empire.* Bloomington: Indiana University Press, 2009.

Volodarksy, Boris. *Stalin's Agent: The Life and Death of Alexander Orlov.* Oxford: Oxford University Press, 2015.

Warren, Donald. *Radio Priest: Charles Coughlin, The Father of Hate Radio.* New York: Free Press, 1996.

Web, Marek. "Dubnov and Jewish Archives: An Introduction to His Papers at the YIVO Institute." In *A Missionary for History: Essays in Honor of Simon Dubnov,* edited by Kristi Groberg and Avraham Greenbaum, 87–92. Minneapolis: University of Minnesota Press, 1998.

Weber, Ronald. *The Lisbon Route: Entry and Escape in Nazi Europe.* Lanham, Maryland: Ivan R. Dee, 2011.

Weinberg, David H. *A Community on Trial: The Jews of Paris in the 1930s.* Chicago: University of Chicago Press, 1977.

Weinberg, Gerhard L. *A World at Arms: A Global History of World War II.* Cambridge: Cambridge University Press, 1994.

Weinfeld, Morton. "Louis Rosenberg and the Origins of the Socio-Demographic Study of Jews in Canada." *Jewish Population Studies (Papers in Jewish Demography).* Avraham Harman Institute of Contemporary Jewry, 1993: 39–53.

Weinreich, Max. *Geshikhte fun der yidisher shprakh.* 4 vols. New York: YIVO, 1973.

Weinreich, Uriel. *Modern English-Yiddish, Yiddish-English Dictionary.* New York: YIVO Institute for Jewish Research and McGraw-Hill, 1968.

Weiser, Kalman. "The Capital of 'Yiddishland'?" In *Warsaw. The Jewish Metropolis: Essays in Honor of the 75th Birthday of Professor Antony Polonsky*, edited by Glenn Dynner and François Guesnet, 298–322. Leiden and Boston: Brill, 2015.

———. "Coming to America: Max Weinreich and the Emergence of YIVO's American Center." In *Choosing Yiddish: New Frontiers of Language and Culture*, edited by Lara Rabinovitch, Shiri Goren, and Hannah S. Pressman, 233–252. Detroit: Wayne State University Press: 2012.

———. "Folkists." In *The YIVO Encyclopedia of Jews in Eastern Europe*, edited by Gershon David Hundert, 520–521. New Haven: Yale University Press, 2008.

———. *Jewish People, Yiddish Nation: Noah Prylucki and the Folkists in Poland.* Toronto: University of Toronto Press, 2011.

Wenren, Jun. *Ancient Chinese Encyclopedia of Technology: Translation and Annotation of Kaogong Ji, the Artificers' Record.* New York: Taylor & Francis, 2012.

Werth, Léon. *33 Days.* Translated by Austin Denis Johnston. Brooklyn: Melville House Publishing: 2015.

Wertheimer, Jack. *Unwelcome Strangers: East European Jews in Imperial Germany.* New York: Oxford University Press, 1987.

Whitman, James Q. *Hitler's American Model: The United States and the Making of Nazi Race Law.* Princeton: Princeton University Press, 2017.

Wiener, Theodore. "Encyclopedias." In *Encyclopaedia Judaica*, 2nd ed., 399–402. Detroit: Thomson Gale, 2007.

Wieviorka, Annette. *The Era of the Witness.* Translated by Jared Stark. Ithaca, NY: Cornell University Press, 2006.

Wischnitzer, Mark. "Shimen Dubnov, der organizator fun der yidisher geshikhts-visnshaft in Rusland." *Tsukunft* 36, no. 1 (January 1931): 57–61.

Weinryb, Bernard D. Review of *Algemeyne entsiklopedye, Yidn* vols. 1–2, edited by Raphael Abramovitch et al. *Jewish Social Studies* 4 (1942): 85–86.

Yarfitz, Mir. *Impure Migration: Jews and Sex Work in Golden Age Argentina.* New Brunswick, NJ: Rutgers University Press, 2019.

Yashunsky, Yosef. "Farnem un kharakter fun der yidisher entsiklopedye." *YIVO Bleter* 3 (1932): 121–39.

———. "Pruvn fun yidishe entsiklopedyes." *Bikhervelt* 2 (1922): 127–132.

———. "Tsu der diskusye vegn an algemeyner entsiklopedye af yidish," *YIVO Bleter* 2 (December 1931): 289–307.

———. "A yidishkayt-entsiklopedye." *Literarishe bleter* 12 (1933): 182–3.

Yeo, Richard. *Encyclopaedic Visions: Scientific Dictionaries and Enlightenment Culture.* Cambridge: Cambridge University Press, 2001.

Yidisher Visnshaftlekher Institut. *Barikht fun der konferents fun dem yidishn visnshaftlekhn institut: opgehaltn in Vilne fun 24tn bizn 27tn oktober 1929*. Vilna: YIVO, 1930.

Yulski, H. "Di entsiklopedye af yidish." *Vokhnshrift far literatur, kunst un kultur* 7 (March 6, 1931): 102–103.

Zaagsma, Gerben. "The Local and the International—Jewish Communists in Paris between the Wars." In *Simon Dubnow Institute Yearbook* 8 (2009): 345–363.

———. *Jewish Volunteers, the International Brigades and the Spanish Civil War.* London: Bloomsbury, 2017.

———. "*La Naïe Presse* pendant les années 30," *Presse Nouvelle Magazine* 24/228 (2005): 4–5.

———. "Transnational Networks of Jewish Migrant Radicals: The Case of Berlin." In *Transit und Transformation: Osteuropäisch-jüdische Migranten in Berlin 1981–1939*, edited by Verena Dohrn and Gertrud Pickhan, 218–233. Göttingen: Wallstein Verlag, 2010.

Zeitlin, Hillel, and Shoyl Stupnitski, *Ersht yidish entsiklopedish verterbukh*. Warsaw: Verlag Hantbikher, 1917.

Zeltser, Arkadi. "Abramovich, Rafail." In *The YIVO Encyclopedia of Jews in Eastern Europe*, edited by Gershon David Hundert, translated by Yisrael Cohen, 1–2. New Haven: Yale University Press, 2008.

———. "Soviet Yiddish-Language Schools." In *The YIVO Encyclopedia of Jews in Eastern Europe*, edited by Gershon David Hundert, translated by Yisrael Cohen, 1790–1791. New Haven: Yale University Press, 2008.

Zhitlowski, Chaim. "A groyser kultur-uftu." *Der Tog*, May 24, 1931.

———. "Zoln mir do boyen undzer kultur in english?" *Der Tog*, May 9, 1931.

Zilberfarb, Moyshe, Yoysef Khmurner and Khaim-Shloyme Kazhdan. Untitled editorial. *Bikhervelt* 1 (April 1928): 1–2.

Zimmerman, Joshua D. "TSYSHO." In *The YIVO Encyclopedia of Jews in Eastern Europe*, edited by Gershon David Hundert, 1919–1920. New Haven: Yale University Press, 2008.

INDEX

Page numbers in italics refers to figures.